Praise for Hammer and Tickle

'An excellent anthology of anecdotes knowledgeably linked into the history of the Soviet period . . . very enjoyable to read'
Daily Telegraph

'Wonderful . . . this isn't just a joke book. Instead, Lewis embarks on a deeply scholarly examination and analysis of the communist joke . . . an excellent job' *New Statesman*

'Explores the wealth of subversive humour during the long, bleak decades of communism' *Irish Independent*

'[An] entertaining and thoughtful study' *Evening Standard*

'Ben Lewis's grimly entertaining study is no mere joke compendium' *Scotsman*

'A fascinating attempt to get to grips with communism's rise and fall in Europe through its funny bone . . . their cultural significance shouldn't be underestimated' *Metro*

Ben Lewis's documentary film *Hammer and Tickle: The Communist Joke Book* was broadcast on BBC4, and on a score of other TV channels across the world, in 2006. His article on Communist jokes for *Prospect* magazine received the greatest number of hits on their website of any article that year. Ben Lewis has won numerous international awards for his documentaries. He is also a television presenter and writer, who contributes regularly to *Prospect*, the *Evening Standard* and the *Sunday Telegraph*.

HAMMER & TICKLE

The History of
Communism Told Through
Communist Jokes

BEN LEWIS

PHOENIX

A PHOENIX PAPERBACK

First published in Great Britain in 2008
by Weidenfeld & Nicolson
This paperback edition published in 2009
by Phoenix,
an imprint of Orion Books Ltd,
Orion House, 5 Upper St Martin's Lane,
London WC2H 9EA

An Hachette UK company

7 9 10 8 6

A CIP catalogue record for this book
is available from the British Library.

ISBN 978-0-7538-2582-2

Printed and bound by Clays Ltd, Elcograf S.p.A.

The Orion Publishing Group's policy is to use papers that
are natural, renewable and recyclable products and
made from wood grown in sustainable forests. The logging
and manufacturing processes are expected to conform to
the environmental regulations of the country of origin.

www.orionbooks.co.uk

For Nick and Dad, und für K.

CONTENTS

CONTENTS

The higher the slavery, the more exquisite the buffoonery.

Anthony Ashley Cooper, Third Earl of Shaftesbury,
Sensus Communis, 1711

It's the law of Faust: the worse the times, the better the jokes.

Ernst Röhl, interview with the author

The final phase of a historic political system is *comedy*.

(*Die letzte Phase einer weltgeschichtlichen Gestalt ist ihre* Komödie).

Karl Marx, Introduction to *A Contribution to the Critique of Hegel's Philosophy of Right* in *Deutsch-Französische Jahrbücher*, February 1844

The truth is forbidden, it is expelled;
All the doors and the windows are closed to it now.
And yet, I believe in the people's instinct for the truth,
I still believe in common sense.

An *anekdot* goes amongst the people
Its way to the soul is through eyes and ears.
Perhaps, this *anekdot* won't reach our grandsons,
But at least our contemporaries will speak their heart in it.

Great men, decorated with crowns or with wreaths,
May be flattered most cleverly and skilfully.
But the people crack a good joke about them –
And perish all the praise, be it written or verbal.

The historians, digging through the archives,
May curse or glorify these people tomorrow.
But our trial by anger or laughter,
Is by far fairer than latterday judgements.

From 'Impatience', Lazar Shereshevsky,
Gulag survivor and poet, 1955

ACKNOWLEDGEMENTS

The first person I want to thank is Nick Fraser, commissioning editor for the Storyville documentary strand at the BBC. This project began life as a feature-length documentary and it would never have come to anything without Nick's passionate support. From the beginning he showed confidence where others showed doubt. Thanks to him and my French producer Christine Camdessus, we were able to raise finance from the BBC, Arte and broadcasters all over the world. I would also like to thank many hugely supportive European commissioning editors, who comprise an unsung intellectual elite – Martin Pieper from ZDF, Mette Hoffman Meyer from TV2, Hans Robert Eisenhauer from Arte, Ikke Vehkalahti from Finnish YLE, Nathalie Windhorst from VPRO in Holland, as well as my brilliant line producer and business partner Fiona O'Doherty, my composer Daniel Pemberton, my Canadian co-producers Leah Mallen and Trish Dolmen from Screen Siren, the European Union Media Fund, Michael Burns formerly of the Documentary Channel in Canada, the documentary pitching forum at the Amsterdam Documentary Festival, IDFA, where I first unveiled this eccentric idea, Leena Pasanen now at EDN, Seth Benedict Graham at SSEES, who wrote an inspiring PhD thesis on the 'Russo-Soviet Anekdot', and Richard Klein, an early supporter of my films at BBC2, Roly Keating, Antoine Monot at the Zurich Film Festival, Catherine 'Mastermind' Story, and lastly Thor Halvorssen and Rob Pfaltzgraff from MPI, an American Libertarian film fund, whose dubious politics are far removed from mine, but who very generously contributed finance to the finished film to cover our overspend.

A team of smart and dedicated people across Europe helped me research the material in this book: Kriszta Fenyo in Hungary, Alexandra Solomon in Romania, Maria Oleneva in Russia, Pavel Stroilov and Dimitri Collingridge in London, Magda 'Gorfi' Gorfinska and Pia Turunen-Rusinek in Poland, Luca Chiari in Paris, and Juergen Nowak, former editor of *Eulenspiegel*, Jana Cisar, Anna-Claire Schroeder, Elvira Geppert and my DP Frank-Peter Lehmann in Germany. At St Peter's College, Oxford, Timothy Johnston, Junior Research Fellow in Modern European History, read my final draft and discussed its historical content.

I owe a debt of imagination and intellect to my unofficial mentor at Cambridge University, Dalibor Vesely, a brilliant émigré Czech professor of architecture, who introduced me to phenomenology and taught me European modes of thought.

Then there are my more recently acquired friends from the world of letters who believed in me and this book. My literary agent Claire Patterson from Janklow Nesbitt told me I was a writer before I was one. Alex Linklater, as deputy editor of *Prospect*, gave me my first significant job in journalism writing a column about contemporary art, and later took the trouble to read through this manuscript and point out a myriad of incoherent thoughts. Finally I would like to thank my editor, Alan Samson, whose comments on my first draft, in equal measure enthusiastic and critical, were as crisp and invigorating as a frozen shot of bison-grass vodka.

FOREWORD

I have not taken many liberties with this book, but any book about jokes and Communism that reaches across countries and eras must take some. First I have chosen to use the Western term for the political system of the Soviet Union and Bloc, Communism, rather than the word they used themselves in this period, Socialism. Socialism is, I agree, a nicer word, but carries the second meaning of an ideology that is still extant in Europe. Second, I have given the term 'Communist jokes' to what could more precisely be described as anti-Communist or anti-Soviet jokes – this is because I think the looser term better captures the sense of shared culture. The jokes in this book are historically documented, but, since everyone tells jokes in their own way, I have permitted myself to rewrite many of them in my own style. There are a significant number of Communist jokes which rely on puns that cannot be translated into English from their various original languages and, since a joke loses most of its wit when it requires explanation, I have decided to omit these.

The jokes in this book come from European Communist societies and Russia. For whatever reason the same phenomenon didn't exist in the same way in South East Asia or China. I've made little mention of the Communist jokes of Yugoslavia, because they were identical to those told in the rest of Communist Europe. I've also left out Cuban Communist jokes because for the most part they weren't produced by Cubans living in Cuba. This is not an all-encompassing compilation of all Communist jokes. I have used the jokes to illustrate my story and argument, and many, even some of the best, have been left out – like the one about the old Jew on his deathbed who asks the rabbi, as his dying wish, to be made a member of the Communist Party, because 'It's better that one of them dies, than one of us.' I hope the reader will pardon these gaps, simplifications and short cuts in my text.

INTRODUCTION

Remembrance of Jokes Past

Fig. 1. Carpet wall-hanging with Marx, Engels and Lenin, industrially
produced by Halbmond, Ölnitz, Saxony, probably 1980s,
Stasi Museum, Berlin

Did you hear about the political system that was laughed out of existence?

Many people who'd lived in the Soviet Bloc told me that humour had brought down Communism, but few could explain how. As I travelled round central and eastern Europe in search of the artefacts of a funny past, this grand claim hovered in my mind like the first line of a joke, and my journey became the quest for the punchline.

I learned many punchlines over many years. *What would happen if Communism triumphed in Saudi Arabia? Is it possible to wrap an elephant in newspaper? What has forty legs and four teeth? Is*

Marxism–Leninism a science? What is the prize for the best political joke? Why is Hungary the largest country in the world? How do you quadruple the value of a Trabant? Are the Russians our brothers or our friends? And why, despite all the shortages, was East German toilet paper always two-ply? The answers to these questions cannot be found in other history books, but they lie between the pages of this one, because they are questions raised and answered by Communist jokes, the strange, enticing, magical and unexpected cultural legacy of seventy-two years of Marxism–Leninism.

I first fell in love with the Communist joke on Bulevard Dimitri Cantemir, one of the epic avenues of monolithic apartment blocks of unclad concrete that were built in Bucharest in the seventies. I was talking to Doina Doru, a beautiful blonde woman in her fifties, who had worked as a proof-reader for one of the state newspapers when Ceauşescu ruled Communist Romania.

A colleague introduced me to Doina. I was in the city making a television programme about Ceauşescu's propaganda. I had spent weeks in the film archive surrounded by piles of rusting 35 mm film canisters, looking through footage of the shows the regime staged to celebrate its own importance. I watched hundreds of factory workers, filling the stands around a stadium, holding up coloured cards, which would form a gigantic jigsaw revealing one minute a tractor ploughing a field and the next a picture of the dictator's wife in a lab coat. Scores of dancers performed 'construction' and 'battle' routines in the arena with toy rifles and uniforms made of paper. Then the dancers would withdraw and hundreds of choreographed children would swarm on and take up positions so that their thin bodies spelt the words 'Long Live Ceauşescu'. On some days, I would traipse round Bucharest meeting former artists and poets who'd eulogised the incompetent Romanian despot in their work, and try to persuade them – usually unsuccessfully – to go on camera. 'We used to tell a lot of jokes,' my Romanian friends would say to me; 'Doina remembers them all.' And after all the propaganda reels, the jokes seemed like the perfect antidote, so I went to see her.

Doina sat in her tiny flat and tried to evoke what Romania had been like in the eighties for me, someone who had been growing up in a detached red-brick house in Hampstead Garden Suburb at the time. She recited the familiar list of the shortages in Communist economies in their death throes: no meat, no make-up, no toilet paper, no tampons, no heating. My mind dulled as I heard these familiar historical facts, which I had read so often in books. Then she said: 'We used to have this joke back then: What is colder in Romania than the cold water? The hot water.'

That was funny. We both laughed a particular laugh – the chuckle at unhappy truth which lies at the source of all 'gallows humour'. Doina's hot water is still my favourite Communist joke – as simple, beautiful and true as a Japanese haiku. 'We had so many jokes back then,' she continued; 'I think they were tiny masterpieces, some of them.'

Doina told me many that afternoon. Did I know this one? she asked me, and I must hear that one! ... 'I've just remembered ...'

'There was another joke that was almost true – true to life. Ceauşescu is very angry because he is not hearing any jokes about him. So he orders a huge mass meeting, and announces, 'From now on you are going to work without pay.' And nobody says anything. 'Okay,' he continues, 'and from now on you are all going to work for me.' Nobody says anything. 'Tomorrow everybody is condemned to death by hanging,' he adds. Nobody says anything. 'Hey,' he says, 'are you crazy? Don't you people have anything to say? Aren't you going to protest?' There's one tiny guy who says, 'Mr President, I have a question: do we bring our own rope or is the trade union going to give it to us?' So that was the situation. He was hanging us and we were asking if we should supply our own rope. The situation was so desperate that this kind of joke was reflecting our reality. They were always like this.'

She sat in a cheap wicker armchair. If she had been born on the other side of the Iron Curtain, her alert and articulate mind would have made her the editor of a topical magazine, but those job opportunities had never existed in late twentieth-century Romania.

'Why, went another Romanian Communist joke, did Ceauşescu hold a mass rally on the first of May? To see how many people had survived the winter.

'Do you know when the foundations of the Romanian economy were laid? As far back as biblical times – Jesus was put on the cross, they asked him to stretch out each hand and knocked a nail in. Then they said, "Please cross your legs. We only have one nail left."

'What is the difference between Romanian radio and Romanian

newspapers? You can wrap a fish in the newspaper.'

Sometimes I giggled and sometimes I groaned. At this historical distance not all of the jokes were funny, but I found I liked the ones that weren't as much as the ones that were. Later, lying down in my pastel-coloured post-Communist hotel bedroom, I realised why: it was the same melancholic – almost Proustian – sense of pleasure I got entering a bar or nightclub in the morning. The dusty smell of stale cigarettes and ammonia hangs in the air and makes me think wistfully of another party I missed. The jokes that didn't make me laugh reminded me of the words of the famous novelist L. P. Hartley in *The Go-Between*: 'The past is a foreign country. They do things differently there.' I should tell you now that my book is about why people laughed, not what makes people laugh. It is a history of humour, more than a humorous history.

What mattered most wasn't the jokes themselves; it was how the people who told them felt about them. Millions of former citizens of Communist states considered the jokes an act of rebellion. Doina insisted that joke-telling was 'dangerous – you could go to prison for it'. And she even felt she had had a close call herself, participating in the riskiest of subversive activities.

As a proof-reader, her most challenging task had been to check that the names of Nicolae Ceauşescu and his wife Elena were spelt correctly each one of the thirty-odd times they were mentioned in the daily *gazeta* (forty times, during Party conferences, she remembered). This was no small matter. It was Ceauşescu's misfortune that his first name could, with minor alteration – to 'Nicholai' – mean small penis in Romanian. 'You could go to jail for making that mistake.

'It happened to me,' she said emphatically, looking at me with her disconcertingly youthful blue eyes. But when I asked her for the exact details, it turned out to be another, lesser mistake with a less awful fate. 'You also had to be very careful about the word "comrade". If you missed out one letter of the Romanian word for comrade, you had a word that meant "wicked convict". So one morning when I went to work my editor told me that I had to go to "the comrade in room such-and-such", which was how he referred to the Securitate officer. I said, "My goodness what did I do?" And he said, "Look on the front page: you misspelt the word 'comrade'." I was questioned for several hours about the mistake. They asked me if I supported the

4

Party, and then they interrogated all my colleagues – Did I ever say anything critical about the government or Ceauşescu? My only defence was, you know, I signed off the proof of this newspaper. If I wanted to undermine something or to fight against our illustrious President I wouldn't have been so stupid as to sign it. But it took me more than four or five hours to convince them.'

Doina's story was not as horrifying as I had hoped, but the disappointment did not deter me. The culture of jokes she described cast an instant unshakeable spell. Almost twenty years after the fall of Communism, the nostalgia of the dispossessed and the gloating of the victors had made it difficult to get an objective sense of what it had been like to live then. I spoke a smattering of Romanian – enough at least to understand the taxi-driver who said, 'Ceauşescu – Patriot,' as he threw his eighties-model Dacia over the potholes of Bucharest's main roads. Romania was full of poor people like him, on whom the trickle-down effect of Capitalism had not yet trickled down. They looked back at the old times with unappealing fondness. But I was equally unsatisfied by the smug line taken in the new right-wing histories of post-war Europe, which I had piled on my desk at home, in which the terrible litany of Communist crimes – its Gulags, purges and economic disasters – were recited as if Capitalism did not have its own counterparts (starting with the Belgians in the Congo, continuing with McCarthyism, South America's military dictatorships and the economic shock medicine of the IMF). The jokes seemed to offer a third way. They came, anonymously and contemporaneously, from the mouths of ordinary people. At this time, they appeared to me untainted by the agendas of historians, the propaganda of state agencies, or the vagaries of personal memories.

'Sociologically speaking,' Doina said, assuming a momentary intellectual air, 'these jokes were a state of mind and they represented a reaction of a segment of the population to something. So I think they did change something. They changed something in people. The jokes gave them courage. It was a way of standing up – of saying no, we don't like this, we don't agree to this …'

Outside the window one of Bucharest's decrepit trams clanked by, so noisy that it drowned out Doina's words.

Although I never married a Communist, I often woke up next to one. She had the most beautiful hair in central Europe – thick, curly, inky black. She wasn't turned on by my fascination with Communist humour, but I found her antiquated political sympathies highly alluring.

Ariane grew up in a boring town way down at the bottom of East Germany. In those days it had a population of a quarter of a million. Since the fall of the Wall, it's shrunk to a hundred thousand. They built a new railway line from Leipzig to Munich, she told me, which bypassed her place of birth – 'They just decided we were no longer on the map.'

This small detail in the transport policy of the united Germany became a potent symbol to her of the way the West German state had ruthlessly eradicated the DDR. The slow dismantling of the East German parliament building in Berlin, with its cheapo copper-coloured reflective glass and asbestos-ridden core, was more evidence of the same. She said: 'They have drawn it out as long as possible to rub our noses in it.'

I had always wanted to be a Communist – all the coolest people at school were – but I had never been persuaded by their arguments. In the morning breaks I would sit in the common room, aged fifteen, and read the newspapers, homing in on the left-wing columnists, who explained why Pershing missiles should not be deployed in Europe. My best friend went on CND marches; I wanted to go too, but I thought democracy was worth defending with violence. Perhaps that was because I was Jewish, or because my parents voted for Maggie. On the weekends, while shopping for fashionable psycho-billy T-shirts in Camden market, I would pop into the alternative book shop and buy *Class War*, an anarchist magazine, which urged the workers to seize power and kill the rich. Unlike many of my peers, I felt that my comfortable background and expensive education prevented me from supporting this cause. But I did, decades later, move closer to Communism in one way.

There were so many arguments. 'Don't you ever question democracy?' Ariane asked me. 'Why question only Communism?'

'If you question Communism, you end up with democracy,' I replied. 'If you question democracy, you end up with' – deliberate ironic pause from me – 'more democracy.'

Sometimes I texted her on my mobile phone with the latest jokes I'd read:

Why did elections in East Germany always last two days?
So every citizen could decide for himself or herself whether they wanted to vote on Friday or Saturday.

Before the great October Revolution, how did the poor oppressed Russian people endure their terrible fate under the Tsar?
They just thought what things would be like afterwards, and then they could bear it for a while longer.

She generously accompanied me to the major DDR tourist attractions, like the old headquarters of the East German political police, the Stasi. She had never been a fan of the grey state itself, and had joined the protests in 1989; but she resented the way the country she grew up in had been dismissed. 'This is the history of the victors,' she told me.

On some afternoons she led me back into her past, through the inner courtyards and stairwells of the apartment blocks where she used to live as a squatter in Berlin in the nineties – they were covered in luminous graffiti and cartoons. Ariane had made an effortless transition from teenage Communist punk to anti-Capitalist. After the Wall fell, she had moved into one of the scores of empty buildings in East Berlin. At this time, hundreds of young East Germans occupied these crumbling blocks, whose masonry was often still peppered with the bullet holes from the closing moments of the Third Reich. The most famous was Tacheles, an enormous former department store, four storeys high. Its staircases remained intact, but at the rear it was completely open, so that it resembled a series of caves cut into a cliff face. When you looked up, you could see people living there. Nineteen-ninety was a halcyon year; but in November, the West German police arrived with batons and water cannon and emptied the main street in the 'Battle of Mainzer Strasse'.

'The West German police used a level of violence that I had never seen in East Germany,' she said.

Now, fifteen years on, Ariane was a successful 'emerging' artist, with galleries in Berlin, Cologne and London. She'd been in group shows in the Pompidou and Tate and was working on her first solo show in New York. Ariane was surfing the contemporary art boom of the early twenty-first century, with her own – highly marketable, rather expensive – brand of Communist nostalgia. She made large collages based on old propaganda images, which she overpainted with abstract modernist stylings. She watched Communism fading into the distance through a haze of paint, a set of awkward poses and impossible dreams.

'Why are you still a Communist, after all your country suffered at the hands of Stalin?' I asked.

'What else is there to be nowadays,' she replied.

But with her it was more than a fashion statement. She had used the proceeds of one of her shows to renovate an old sixties, Soviet-era neon, perched on top of a building in an East German town. An arabesque of multicoloured light traced the outline of a female athlete throwing a ball. It made me think of the damaging performance-enhancing drugs that Communist Olympic trainers fed to child athletes, but Ariane's gesture was so tender that I'd never brought this up. Her love for Communism reminded me of the old joke:

A schoolgirl is asked by her teacher to write an essay for her homework, entitled: 'Why I love the Soviet Union'. The girl goes home and asks her father, 'Daddy, why do you love the Soviet Union?'

'I don't love it, I hate it,' her father replies.

The little girl goes to her mother and then her brother and she gets the same answer from both.

Then she goes upstairs and does her homework. She writes: 'I love the Soviet Union because nobody else does ...'

Ariane and I were proof that opposites attract: she with her images, I with my words; she with her state propaganda, I with my underground jokes. Something, I knew, would have to give. But what? I calculated there were three options. Number one: our relationship would be destroyed by the jokes. Number two: her politics would not survive the jokes. Number three: my interest in the jokes would not survive our relationship.

Today there are few certifiably Communist regimes left in the world. The Chinese say they are Communist, but they are, in reality, an autocratic Capitalist society with strong central direction. North Korea and Cuba are the only states that still play by the economic and political rules of Marx and Lenin. Yet once upon a time Communism looked like a serious competitor with Capitalism, and one that might actually eventually triumph over it. By the early 1980s almost one-third of the world's population lived in Communist states.

Communism had many ancient precedents. If you define it as the common ownership of property, it started life in monastic communities and was imagined by Sir Thomas More in his *Utopia*. But it was first articulated as a political ideology by Karl Marx and Friedrich Engels in *The Communist Manifesto* published in 1848, itself a year of revolution. Marx and Engels were horrified by the appalling living conditions, the 'naked, shameless, direct, brutal exploitation' and lack of political freedom of the new urban proletariat – 'the slaves of the bourgeois class' – which had been generated by accelerating industrialisation in Europe. Directed against these phenomena, their Communism was a socio-political system, a revolutionary strategy and a prophecy, all at once.

They imagined a new society in which all property was publicly owned, class divisions had disappeared, government ceased to exist, there were no longer any wars, religion was 'abolished' and there was free education for all. Individuals would be free to pursue whatever kind of work activities they wanted and wealth would be distributed 'from each according to his ability, to each according to his needs'. The way to realise this new society was revolution: the working classes, represented by the Communist Party, were to seize power – 'Let the ruling classes tremble at Communist revolution. The workers have nothing to lose but their chains.'

For a time the new rulers were to bypass democracy with 'the forcible overthrow of all existing social conditions', abolishing private property and appropriating and then managing businesses, farms and factories in a 'dictatorship of the proletariat', in which they also established 'industrial armies, especially for agriculture'. This transitional phase was renamed 'Socialism' by Lenin, who followed Marx arguably with considerable fidelity. (Fig. 1) Even Lenin's great innovation – to assert that Russia could bypass a bourgeois phase and leap from feudalism to Communism – had been considered by Marx. After an unspecified period Marx and Engels imagined that the socialist state would develop into the Utopia of Communism – an end-phase that Soviet leaders often claimed was approaching, but never claimed had been reached.

All this historical development, Marx and Engels surmised, was inevitable, since the development from 'feudal' government by the upper class of the monarchy and aristocracy was giving way in the nineteenth century to government by the middle class, and the logical next step was the final one, down the social ladder, to the working class.

In 1917 this theory was put into practice in Russia by Lenin and his political party, the Bolsheviks. For the next seventy-two years they would try to realise Marx and Engels' vision in a state they named the Soviet Union. Shortly after 1945, when the Soviets had occupied most of central and eastern Europe, many new countries were compelled to join this doomed project – the Baltic states, Poland, Czechoslovakia, Romania, Bulgaria, Yugoslavia, Hungary, Albania, half of Germany and, further afield, half of Korea, then China, Cuba and half of Vietnam.

Communism was a theory for a rational Utopia enforced by some of the greatest historical figures of the twentieth century, imposed on people on a large and small scale. It produced the big ideological struggle of the twentieth century. There are tens of thousands of books on the subject. Yet little serious historical consideration has been given to one of its most distinctive products: jokes.

In certain cultures specific cultural forms rise to prominence and become the defining way they express their ideas and values. The Greeks had their myths, the Elizabethans had their plays. In the postwar period, pop music defined Western culture in Britain and America. The Communists had political jokes. Of course there was every other kind of imaginative activity under Communism – films, rock, punk and classical music, plays and novels; everything except hip hop. And of course the Communists told the usual gamut of jokes – including ones about sex, stupid people and racial minorities. Yet political jokes were the dominant form.

Communism is the only political system to have created its own international brand of comedy. It was a brand defined as much by the loyalty and enthusiasm of its consumers as by the constant supply of alluring new products and carefully constructed rebellious images developed by its (mostly anonymous) creative team.

'Anecdotes were our way of speaking the truth,' Gulag survivor Simon Vilensky told me. 'I met people in the camps arrested for just listening to anecdotes.'

'You can tell the whole history of Communism in jokes,' said another Gulag prisoner, Lazar Shereshevsky.

'Every day there was a new joke. No one knew where they came from or who invented them, but everyone told them,' explained Ernst Röhl, whose sense of humour earned him half a year in solitary confinement in 1961.

Jokes were not confined to opponents of the regime. The apparatchiks loved them too. Guenter Schabowski, the East German newspaper editor and Politburo member, told me: 'At the paper *Neues Deutschland* we told each other jokes in the canteen. We weren't blind to the failings of the system, but we convinced ourselves that this was only because it was early days and the class enemy was perpetrating sabotage wherever he could. One day, we thought, all problems would be solved and there wouldn't be any more jokes because there wouldn't be anything left to joke about.'

The dissident Vladimir Bukovsky, who was imprisoned in Soviet psychiatric clinics in the sixties, wrote:

One day someone ought to erect a monument to the political joke. This astonishing form of creation is especially popular in the socialist countries where people are deprived of information and a free press, and public opinion, banned and suppressed, finds expression in this form. Packed to the hilt with information, a Soviet joke is worth volumes of philosophical essays. The simplification of the joke exposes the absurdity of all propaganda tricks. The jokes have survived the hardest times, stood their ground, multiplied into families of jokes and in them you can study the entire history of the Soviet regime ... In the jokes you can find the thing that has left no trace in the printed sources: the people's opinion of events.

There are a handful of reasons why Communist *political* jokes were special. They had a unique homogeneity: the monopoly of state power meant that any joke about any aspect of politics, the economy or media was a joke about Communism. The Soviet state gave the jokes more unity by banning them. They criminalised all political jokes as 'anti-Soviet propaganda' and they attempted to replace them – unsuccessfully, most people claimed – with their own brand of dull official humour, which they disseminated in satirical magazines. After the Second World War, Communist jokes crossed borders and were told in each Soviet Bloc state, showing once again how shared this culture was. As the historian of everyday life in East Germany Stefan Wolle writes: 'The political joke was one of the defining phenomena of the East German state, specific to and inseparable from the system. The collections published in books are valuable but they are merely a pale ghost of the thriving culture of joke-telling, which has now been lost for ever.'

Along with homogeneity, Communist jokes had other qualities, such as ubiquity, longevity and variety. The jokes encompassed an unusually broad range. They covered every aspect of daily life – the queues, the personality cults of the leaders, the propaganda of the media, the theories of Marx. They described the characters of each Soviet leader from Stalin through Khrushchev and Brezhnev to Gorbachev. They covered many major political events – including the Great Terror and Gulag, Sputnik, the invasion of Czechoslovakia, and the anniversaries of the Revolution and Lenin's birth.

Many jokes were recycled to apply to situations decades apart, indicating the continuity of the experience of Communism. At the same time, new jokes were constantly emerging. One explanation for the sheer quantity of jokes is the utopian ambition and prophetic nature of Communism (Fig. 2), which meant that jokers were constantly able to point out the 'disconnect' – to use the parlance of our times – between what should be, and what was, happening. The jokes changed their tone and content according to each era of Soviet history – from the novelty of post-Revolutionary Russia, to Stalin's bureaucracy of repression, to the economic failures of Khrushchev, the apathy of the era of stagnation, and then the growing sense of irresistible change in the eighties.

Nowadays, looking back, all former Soviet citizens tell the same mythical tale about the jokes: Once upon a time, in a land far, far away, people lived under a very different political system, now lost in the mists of time. It was called Communism. The Communists said there would be more of everything under Communism, and they were right. The party conferences were larger, the queues were longer, there were ten times as many secret policemen; and there wasn't just one Germany, there were two.

But there was one thing there was more of than anything else under Communism, and that was jokes.

At night, after work, when they sat around the kitchen table with their friends, when they had parties, when they met in a bar, people whiled away the hours telling Communist jokes. In the world of Communism there was a joke for every aspect of the people's lives and every event.

The rulers of Communism were wicked and they hated many things – the bourgeois, the liberals, imperialists, free elections, wealthy farmers and Capitalists, but there was one thing they hated more than anything else and that was Communist jokes. Whenever they heard someone telling a joke they threw them in prison. But the people were very brave and refused to stop telling them. Many years passed in laughter and suffering. Slowly but surely the jokes eroded the strength of the leaders of Communism. Then, one day, people had enough of joke-telling and they rose up against their cruel rulers. The leaders quickly admitted the jokers had been right all along and Communism ended.

But sadly the joke-telling ended too. Life wasn't as funny as it used to be, and people didn't live quite as happily ever after as they do in other fairy tales.

They dropped through my letter box at an average of two a day for a couple of months. I enjoyed the meticulous ways many of them had been wrapped – not just in a cardboard envelope or Jiffy bag, but often also in tightly folded sheets of grey tissue paper, like clothes bought from a designer shop.

Although Communism was famously backward and the parcels were charmingly handmade, I was making use of the latest technology. On the internet thousands of second-hand-book shops from North America, Germany and the EU, Australia and New Zealand had uploaded details of their stock to a communal website. I typed in keywords: 'Communism + joke' in all kinds of languages, the names of eastern European countries and the term 'humour', and the titles of the satirical magazines published in the Soviet

Fig. 2. Wood inlay scene depicting the construction of Socialism in the DDR, inlaid precious imported wood, Maria Wild, Intaglio Master, Leipzig, *circa* 1970s, Stasi Museum, Berlin 1875

Bloc. I ordered everything I could. *The Political Joke in East Germany* by Clement de Wroblewsky (Hamburg, 1986) arrived from a book shop in Eicklingen, in the German province of Lower Saxony. *Hammer and Tickle: Clandestine Laughter in the Soviet Union* (The Golem Press, 1980) – whose title I have borrowed for my book – was sent to me from Tulsa, Oklahoma. And *Look, Comrade: the People Are Laughing – Underground Wit, Satire and Humour from Behind the Iron Curtain* (Toronto, 1973) was dispatched by a bookseller in Derbyshire, England. Soon I had an international collection of books on Communist humour such as would have been impossible to assemble any earlier in human history, and which was also more exhaustive than anything in the world's copyright libraries.

All these books presented the Communist jokes as the patrimony of central and eastern Europe and of Russia. The Chinese have a great sense of humour but neither they nor the Vietnamese and Cambodians appear to have expressed their experiences of Communism this way. The Cubans told many jokes about Castro, but these weren't Communist jokes in the same way as the European ones were – that is, clearly invented by people living inside the system. Many European Communist jokes were adapted into Cuban ones, and the new ones were invented as much by Cuban exiles and right-wing Americans as they were by Cubans. For this reason, it's very difficult to study them as genuine expressions of Communist citizens.

The most famous of all the joke collections was *1001 Jokes* by the Slovak writer Jan Kalina, published in 1969 in Bratislava. Kalina had actually delivered his manuscript three years earlier, as the political liberalisation that culminated in the Prague Spring gathered pace. Typically, there wasn't enough paper to print the book on at the time, even though the printer had no other work to do. Consequently it only came out after Soviet tanks had invaded and brought the 'experiment in democratic Communism' to an end. The edition of 25,000 was sold out in two weeks.

For several years Kalina was permitted to continue his life. It was only when he discovered a listening device in his flat and began to make loud jokes about it, finally photographing it and sending the prints to the President, that the state arrested him. In the course of his trial, on 23 October 1972, the prosecution asked, 'What did you show the writer P.B. in your flat on the sixteenth of July 1970?' Kalina replied with the well-known joke:

You remember the police investigator who asks the accused: 'What were you doing five years ago on 23 October at 17.15?' The accused replies promptly: 'I remember exactly. I had one eye on my clock and the other on my calendar.'

Among the evidence of disruption presented by the state were testimonies from the printer's employees that the typesetters laughed so much when they set the book that people from other desks got up and went over to see what was so funny. The prosecution also maintained that the listening device, which Kalina had found under his floorboards, had been planted by Western secret agents.

'I never told that joke!' Kalina responded.

The case lasted three days and he was sentenced to two years 'for collecting and disseminating inflammatory audio recordings and texts with content hostile to the state ... and for preparing to publish a humorous–satirical book which crudely insulted the state and society of the Czechoslovak Republic and its solidarity with the Soviet Union'. Following his release he moved to Germany. In 1980 the story of his joke book and trial became the subject of a British television drama, *Tiny Revolutions*.

In total, I acquired around forty compilations of Communist jokes, mostly from small, long-defunct publishing houses, spanning the sixties to the present day. Among the earliest was *Humour Behind the Iron Curtain*, written in German by one Mishka Kukin, which was a pseudonym of Simon Wiesenthal. I imagined the Nazi-hunter putting together his jokes on a card file on aeroplanes as he flew missions to capture Nazis. The jokes from the other side of the political spectrum would have provided some much-appreciated light relief from his day job, while still relating thematically to his battle against a cruel dictatorship. In the seventies, sociologists found the jokes diverting too, a wonderful subject for an end-of-term lecture, which they could also publish in books. Émigrés in Germany and North America formed another, third subgroup of authors: no sooner had they escaped from the Soviet Bloc than they began writing down all the jokes they remembered.

In the introductions to these books the authors would often recall the culture of joke-telling, as Alex Beam, Leningrad correspondent for McGraw Hill's World News describes in the city in which he was posted:

Jokes, or *anekdoty*, are the home-made glue that binds together all Soviet citizens in their dislike for the empty falsehoods of the government's long-playing propaganda machine. In company, the first few jokes emerge after several rounds of drinking, like little secrets. By the time tea is served, the jokes start to flow, and flow, and flow. During one drunken evening, I remember our Armenian host had guided us through several broad categories of jokes: Stalin jokes, Brezhnev jokes, emigration jokes and jokes about Georgians (a local treat). At three in the morning, he rose, swaying, to announce a new round of *anekdoty*: 'And now ... jokes about camels!'

Perhaps I was reading through these yellowed paperbacks in a spirit of excessive seriousness, but I quickly observed major shortcomings in the existing literature on Communist jokes.

One obvious vice of the joke books was their nationalism. They all contained roughly the same jokes, yet each author claimed that most of the jokes originated in their own country. If I read a book by a Czech, it would say that the Czechs, with their long tradition of humour typified by *The Good Soldier Schwejk*, made the best Communist jokes. If an American sociologist had visited Romania, then she would state that it was there that the best jokes were told. If I was reading a Russian book, I learned that it was the Russians with their culture of the witty story, the *anekdot*, who made the most significant contribution to the corpus of Communist jokes. The only country where joke-book authors did not make this kind of boast was East Germany, and there was an obvious explanation for that: they knew no one would believe them. The claims of origin extended beyond nations to cities and religions. There was *Political Jokes of Leningrad* (1977) and *The Book of Soviet Jewish Jokes*, which reversioned the gags so that they all became Jewish, which, given the large number of hilarious bona fide Jewish Communist jokes, seemed a little greedy.

There was one advantage to all these competing claims and over-laps: they revealed the limited number of Communist jokes passed around the Soviet Bloc. There were a total of around a thousand to fifteen hundred, a relatively small number, perhaps, given the fame they have achieved.

Dating is another issue the joke books tended to gloss over. The first ever book of Communist jokes, *The Kremlin and the People* by émigré Yevgeny Andreevich, was printed in Munich in 1951. The author outlined, for the first time in print, the myth of the Communist joke, which has remained mostly uncontested:

> A political joke is often the only weapon available to those who live under a totalitarian regime ... Their content is practically always anti-Soviet, an excellent indication of the real frame of mind of people under Stalin ... For disseminating these jokes innumerable people have been arrested and sent to camps by the secret police. The usual sentence for joke-tellers has been five years.

Andreevich's small book is highly useful, because all the jokes in it can, of course, be verified as belonging to the era of Lenin and Stalin. But within that time-frame, 1917-51, it's difficult to know what got invented when, except by roughly ascribing the topic to events – collectivisation jokes to 1929 – 31, Terror jokes to the 1930s, and so on. Occasionally greater precision is possible when the jokes are mentioned in memoirs of the time, like those of the writer Mikhail Bulgakov.

Several Western joke-compilers have taken their dates from *The Soviet Union Through the Prism of the Political Anecdote* written by two Russian émigrés, Dora Shturman and Sergey Tictin. This book was printed up in Jerusalem in 1985 by a Cold War publishing house bankrolled by the Americans, and claims to date hundreds of Communist jokes to the decade, from the twenties to the eighties. But the data on which the chronology is based is laughable: it's when the authors or their friends remember hearing them. Furthermore, in their introduction the pair admit that no joke in their collection was heard or written down by them before 1956.

When the jokes began to pall, I turned for some light relief to the small number of sociological texts on the subject, mostly written by Germans. The first of these appears to have been an article published in an obscure periodical in 1972, Joerg K. Hoensch's 'On the Phenomenology and Sociology of the Political Joke in East Europe'. I made my way slowly through another academic paperback called *The Culture of Joking in East Germany: A Contribution to Linguistics [Sprachkritik]*, written by a husband-and-wife team, he a university lecturer in German philology, she a highly qualified pharmacist. Perhaps I missed the subtlety of the concepts in a foreign language, but, despite the pleasurable crunchiness of the German terminology, I was left with the sensation of having chewed a lot but eaten little:

'In every instance, the joke corrects an official appearance [*Schein*] insofar as it counters with an alternative presence [*Sein*]. The appearance is constructed through the buttress of an exaggerated language; the opposing construction of the presence makes use of the de-ideologised language of everyday speech.' Which means that Communist jokes presented a hidden truth.

Yet I wasn't outraged by the pretentiously expressed platitude, which is par for the course in the human sciences. Instead, the more I read, the more alarmed I became by one giant lacuna: neither the compilers of the joke books nor the authors of sociological texts had made any attempt to define the Communist sense of humour. Of course there were obvious differences in subject matter, the product of a new political situation. There were new jokes about the Gulag and long queues for food, because neither the Gulag nor long queues had existed in this way before; but were these new *kinds* of jokes? Were Communist jokes simply the application of pre-existing kinds of humour to a new social order, or did something new arise?

No one dared say. There were too many pitfalls. It was difficult to differentiate *what* was being joked about from *how* it was being joked about. There was such a diversity of jokes that it seemed impossible to find an over-arching commonality. And there was too much continuity between our sense of humour in ancient times and now. But if Communist jokes were such an important cultural phenomenon, then, it seemed to me, there had to be qualities which made Communist *joking* different.

This was a question that I would be prepared to leave my sofa and books to answer. It would require a journey of investigation across central and eastern Europe and Russia, but that would only be half of my mission.

Until now, there has been broad agreement about the first part of the urban myth of Communist jokes. The consensus has been that the jokes constitute a 'body' of literary creation directed against Communism and that the state fought a war with the joke-tellers. But beyond that, thinking on Communist humour has divided into two different schools, minimalist and maximalist, each supported by joke-collectors, novelists, theorists and historians.

The minimalists argue that the jokes were a way of countering propaganda and preserving a sense of truth. They find their intellectual roots in Freud's *Jokes and their Relation to the Unconscious* (1905), in which he argued that jokes unmask hidden truths and thereby offer a moment of 'release' for the mind. Freud saw the implications of this theory in the political sphere, where 'tendentious jokes are especially favoured against persons in exalted positions who claim to exercise authority, a liberation from its pressure'. But jokes, Freud and the minimalists say, can do nothing more than offer a moment of personal gratification.

There is invariably some reference to jokes in the great Russian literature of the period. In Vasily Grossman's novel *Life and Fate* one of the characters reflects:

He remembered looking at his assistant's face after making a thoughtless joke about Stalin's having formulated the laws of gravity long before Newton. Why, why, why all these jokes? It was mad to make such jokes – like banging a flask of nitroglycerine with a hammer. What power and clarity lies in the word! In the unfettered, carefree word! The word that is still spoken in spite of all one's fears.

Few history books on Communism do not contain a couple of sentences about the importance of jokes, yet they all tend to follow the minimalist line. The Russian historian of Soviet first secretaries, Dimitri Volkoganov, slips them into his grand narrative in a paragraph about opposition:

There were always tiny islands of free-thinking, dignity and his-torical perspective. Sometimes this was expressed in absurd ways, for instance in political jokes, which proliferated in the worst of times and which it was dangerous to repeat ... Such small weak protests ... had no effect on the supremacy of the system for seventy years, but at least they underlined the fact that, if conscience survives, there is a chance.

So much for the minimal position.

The maximalists go much further, and argue that jokes played a part in the destruction of Communism.

The reluctant guru of this school is George Orwell. In 1945 he wrote an article about English humour that contained the legendary line: 'Every joke is a tiny revolution.' The quotation has always been used out of context. Orwell was not claiming that jokes could bring down a totalitarian system, such as the ones he described in his anti-Communist novels *Animal Farm* and *1984*. His line comes from a newspaper column, in which he argued that contemporary British humour lacked teeth; but it has become nevertheless part of the catechism.

A thing is funny when – in some way that is not actually offensive or frightening – it upsets the established order. Every joke is a tiny revolution. If you had to define humour in a single phrase, you might define it as dignity sitting on a tintack. Whatever destroys dignity and brings down the mighty from their seats, preferably with a bump, is funny. And the bigger the fall, the bigger the joke. It would be better fun to throw a custard pie at a bishop than at a curate. With this general principle in mind, one can, I think, begin to see what has been wrong with English comic writing during the present century.

Yet, whatever his ostensible subject, there was a good reason for the assumption that Orwell was thinking of Communist jokes when he wrote the paragraph above. He was a keen student of Communist humour. He acknowledged that a Soviet satirical novel from the 1920s, Yevgeny Zamyatin's *We*, was the inspiration for *1984*, and a handful of the aphorisms in *Animal Farm* echo jokes. 'Four legs good, Two legs better,' for example, has hints of the following:

A Communist official announces at a meeting, 'Two times two is six.' His words are drowned out by applause.
But then someone from the back shouts out, 'That's wrong, two times two is four.' That man is immediately arrested and disappears for twenty years.
Having returned from Siberia, he once again finds himself at a meeting, where he recognises the same Communist official on the podium, announcing to loud applause, 'Two times two is five.'
The ex-prisoner can't keep silent: 'No, two times two is four.'
After the meeting the official comes over to him, embraces him and whispers, 'Surely you don't want two times two to be six again?'

Milan Kundera was another famous writer who sprayed the perfume of political agency on the jokes. He called his first novel, published just before the Soviet invasion of Czechoslovakia in 1968, *The Joke*. A young Czech student is arrested after sending his girlfriend a postcard with the line: 'Optimism is the opium of the people', a

20

cynical adaptation of Marx's famous 'Religion is the opium of the people.' For this he receives the entirely plausible penalties of expulsion from university and forced labour in a coal mine. A friend tells the protagonist: 'No great movement designed to change the world can bear sarcasm or mockery, because they are a rust that corrodes everything it touches.'

Folklorist Alan Dundes gave this argument one of its most succint formulations in his compilation of Communist jokes, *First Prize: Fifteen Years*. The jokes, he said, were 'veritable fictional bullets firing a constant barrage at a repressive system and its leadership'.

What was the meaning of the cultural artefacts of the jokes? Were they acts of revolution as Orwell suggested? Or an impotent though pleasurable grumble, which sometimes signalled a patient belief in Communism? I was drawn to the lofty claims of the maximalists, but their theory had one fundamental weakness: they had no evidence which showed how the jokes actually brought down the system. Did it exist?

I was an ingénue, saturated in obsolete Cold War clichés. Over the coming months, I would slowly discover that the arguments of minimalists and maximalists alike were simplistic and flawed. If I'd known what a minefield the study of Communist jokes would be, I would have stayed at home. But I didn't. Like any number of other major research projects, the starting motor was the optimism of ignorance.

It was a Holy Grail worthy of Monty Python. I resolved to set out on a personal journey across the countries of the former Soviet Bloc. On the way I would attempt to define the distinctive humorous properties of the Communist joke, but my ultimate goal would be loftier, and riskier. With no regard for the financial, physical or emotional cost, I vowed not to stop until I had found the proof that tied the telling of the jokes to the tumbling of the system.

Fig. 3. Carpet wall-hanging in red 'shag-pile', depicting the handshake symbol of the DDR, unique product, *circa* 1970s, Stasi Museum, Berlin.

ONE

Laughter under Lenin

I walked through long grass and weeds. I was looking up, and kept stumbling over pieces of rusting ironwork and the broken cogs of large machines. My eyes swept across the façade of the ruined factory on the outskirts of Moscow. There was hardly a fragment of glass left in the chequerboard of windows. I pushed to one side a long sliding iron door, which emitted the rasping high-pitched squeak of unoiled rollers, and I stepped inside. High up on an interior wall I found what I was looking for: the faded text of one of Lenin's most famous slogans, his best-remembered pledge to modernise Russia.

Communism = Soviet Power plus Electrification

I inhaled deeply. For scholars in my field I was at an important archaeological site, which hosted the earliest extant source material for a Communist joke.

Lenin's line, coined shortly after the Revolution, betrays the naïvety of the 'science' of Marxism. The reorganisation of society according to the logic of a theory with quotas set by a benign centralised state for industrial and agricultural production, as well as for deportations and executions, would, they believed, create a utopian society of equals. The Communists had some early successes. They swiftly reduced illiteracy and within ten years they had built an electricity network that reached across the Soviet Union. But Lenin's equation also carried with it the mathematical implication of its own failure. Jokers of the twenties performed simple algebra on the formula and came up with other variants, such as:

Electrification = Communism minus Soviet Power

In the end Communism proved incapable of bringing Russia modernity on the scale that it promised. As I stood in the industrial ruin, craning my neck upwards, contemplating this gigantic failure of human effort, I was overcome with a sense of the sublime. I felt like an eighteenth-century Englishman on the Grand Tour, beholding for the first time in his life the panorama of the Roman Forum with its crumbling Ionic columns and cracked pediments, or, having climbed a steep Swiss Alp, looking across the expanse of a glacier under a darkening tempestuous sky. The scene was both picturesque and fearsome – an image of hubris and of a heroic struggle.

Then I woke up. It was a dream about a world I would never see. That old slogan had long been washed off the walls of Soviet factories, which had themselves long been torn down. I thought about what the dream meant with its Piranesian sense of scale: Lenin's maths, and the fun had with it, tell us that Communist jokes were a David and Goliath struggle: small pebbles of wit slung against the hectoring Soviet giant.

In the beginning there was no Communism and no Communist jokes. Then came the Russian Revolution.

On 23 February 1917 disgruntled workers marched against a shortage of bread. The march became a general strike, then a riot. The police opened fire. Garrisons of soldiers mutinied and joined the revolution, and a week later, 1 March, the Tsar abdicated. At the parliament, construction and factory workers, trade unionists and soldiers quickly set up an impromptu council, the *Soviet*, in the left-hand side of the building. Among the political parties represented there: Lenin's Bolsheviks. At first an alliance of liberally minded noblemen formed a provisional government and ran Russia, but they made the mistake of not ending their country's highly unpopular involvement in the First World War. Six months later Lenin seized power in what was largely a military coup.

In the Russian Revolution two tectonic plates crashed against each other: the past and future. On one side was anachronistic but implacable reactionism. The Tsar still believed in absolute monarchy and divine rule. Serfdom had only been abolished in 1861; a third of peasant farms didn't own a horse and most still used wooden ploughs, a technology that dated back to the Roman Empire. Ranged against this primitive life form was pitiless modernity. Russia was not industrialised, but it was experiencing the industrialised mass murder of the First World War. It lost more soldiers than any other participating nation: 1.7 million. More important for the Revolution was the impact the trenches had on the minds of those who survived: its reluctant army, where mutinies were commonplace after 1916, had become brutalised and radicalised. Hence the violent solution to Russia's problems that was Leninism.

Compared to subsequent periods, there are relatively few Communist jokes from the first decade of the Revolution, but this is my favourite:

An old peasant woman is visiting Moscow zoo, when she sets eyes on a camel for the first time. 'Oh my God,' she says, 'look what the Bolsheviks have done to that horse.'

This is the Communist joke at its peerless best – a minimum of means with a maximum of meanings. It describes the amazement of ordinary Russians at the new world created by the Communists, as well as their bafflement at its ideas and ambitions. The notion of a horse becoming a camel alludes to the economic transformation promised by the Bolsheviks and suggests, prophetically, the pointlessness of many of the big industrial projects. The animal metaphor gives the joke the weight of an Aesopian fable.

A score of other jokes chart in less skilful fashion how Lenin turned the social order upside down. Banks were nationalised and the deposit boxes of the wealthy emptied by Bolshevik agents. Private trade of any significant size was banned and businessmen branded as 'speculators'. The result was an instant shortage of basic commodities, like sugar.

Two policemen stop a passer-by and demand his papers. He has only the report of his urine analysis.

1st Policeman: Analysis – albumen, negative; sugar negative.

2nd Policeman: No sugar. Means he is not a speculator. Proceed, citizen.

In December 1917 Lenin called publicly for 'a war to the death against the rich'. Well-to-do families were forced to share their mansions with poor families – often the former were moved into the servants' quarters while the new inhabitants got the best rooms. In the streets penniless aristocrats swept the pavements or sold matches to survive. In the countryside peasants took land away from the landowners or set their own rents. Local soviets were encouraged to invent taxes on the rich.

The Cheka, Lenin's growing political police force, took hostages until the tax was paid, often executing a few to speed things along. As one of this organisation's founders put it, 'The Cheka is not an investigating commission, a court or a tribunal. It is a fighting organ on the internal front of civil war ... It does not judge, it strikes. It does not pardon it destroys ...'

After the October Revolution, God sends three observers to Russia: St Luke, St George and St Peter. They send him three telegrams.
'I've fallen into the hands of the Cheka – St Luke.'
'I've fallen into the hands of the Cheka – St George.'
'All's well. Doing fine. Cheka Superintendent Petrov.'

The flimsy Tsarist legal system disappeared; in its place came the Bolsheviks' people's courts, where laws and punishments were invented *ad hoc* by village crowds and soviet officials. The land and property of the Church were confiscated. In a secret order Lenin wrote, 'The more members of the reactionary bourgeoisie and clergy we shoot, the better.'

When peasants saw the new silver coins that the government used to pay for agricultural produce in 1922, they crossed themselves.
'Why are you crossing yourselves?' asks the village priest. 'The money is Soviet.'
'Yes, but the silver is the Church's.'

Deprived of the incentives of the market, the Soviet economy collapsed. Its nationalised businesses were supervised by a bureaucracy that quadrupled in size between 1917 and 1921 to 2.4 million employees,

An inspector is at a factory conducting an inspection. He addresses one worker: 'What do you do here?'
'Nothing.'
'And what do you do here?' he asks another.
'Nothing.'
He writes in his report: 'The second worker may be released for unnecessary duplication.'

Revolution followed world war, and civil war followed Revolution. At the same time as the 'Red' Bolsheviks were re-engineering Russian society, moderate left-wing and tsarist 'White' forces formed an alliance against them and fought a war of massacres, famines, reprisals and torture. The civil war gave rise to 'war Communism', a kind of state of emergency in which the Bolsheviks used military force to seize grain from the peasants. That created another war, this time with the peasants. Trains full of Red Army troops, with Trotsky himself at the helm, left Moscow station on missions to obtain grain from the hinterland.

Liski station calls Moscow: 'Chairman of the Revolutionary Military Committee Trotsky calling.'

'This is Chairman of the Soviet People's Committee Lenin.'

'Comrade Lenin, immediately dispatch two tankers of grain alcohol to Liski station.'

'What for, Comrade Trotsky?'

'The peasants have sobered up,' Trotsky replies. 'They want to know why the Tsar was deposed.'

In 1921 'war Communism' was replaced by the New Economic Policy, which re-allowed some private enterprise in Soviet Russia and spelt a temporary end to the famines and shortages. Under the New Economic Policy the first Soviet vodka was produced which was 2% more proof than the tsarist vodka – 42% instead of 40%. The joke was, 'Did we really need a revolution for just two per cent?' Soviet industrial and agricultural output crawled back to the level it had been at before 1917.

A Party worker is trying to explain what Communism will be like: 'There will be plenty of everything – food, clothing, all kinds of merchandise. You will be able to travel abroad.'

'Oh,' says an old woman, 'just like under the Tsar.'

The jokes mocked the new ideology. They exposed the unintentional 'truths' contained in the new political catechism, the redefinition of norms to conceal failures, and the dream that Communism would spread like wildfire across Europe (Fig. 4).

Lenin is working late at night. Around 3 a.m. he takes a nap and tells the young Red Army guard to wake him at seven.

The soldier spends all night worrying how to address him. Should he say, 'It's time to get up, Mr Lenin'? Too formal; or 'Wakey wakey Comrade Lenin'? Too familiar.

Eventually 7 a.m. arrives and the soldier starts singing the Internationale – which begins: 'Arise, ye wretched of the earth.'

Word has it in Moscow that the People's Commissar has ordered that, due to the fuel shortage, all thermometers are to be set four degrees higher.

A Jew talking to his friend: 'My son Moses and I are doing very fine. Moisha works in the Comintern as a black African Communist, while I sit in the Kremlin, at the top of Ivan the Great Bell Tower, waiting to ring the bell for the World Revolution.'
'Well, it must be a rather dull job to wait for the World Revolution,' his friend says.
'Oh yes, but it is a job for life.'

Some Communist jokes had precursors in nineteenth-century political wit.

A new lodger moves into his room. The walls are bare but there is one nail and the ubiquitous framed pictures of Lenin and Trotsky. 'I

Fig. 4. Lenin at the World Conference (D. Moor, *Krokodil*, 1922). This is an example of one of the many cartoons in which Lenin is depicted terrifying Western politicians. The Bolsheviks thought World Revolution would swiftly follow their own – they were wrong.

don't know which one of them to hang and which to put with his face against the wall.'

Disillusionment with political leaders and their promises was not exclusive to Communism – this one had been told hundreds of times over with Talleyrand, Metternich, Napoleon and any number of other famous men's names substituted for the architects of the Russian Revolution. Most compilers of books of Communist jokes concede that a handful came from the nineteenth century, but later I would discover that they had suppressed the full scale of the plagiarism. For the moment, I knew only that there was a long tradition on which Communist jokers could draw.

The Russians use a special word for jokes: *anekdoty*.

The Communist *anekdot* has a noble lineage that can be traced back to the sixteenth century. At that time it meant a story about an important person that contained wisdom delivered with wit, such as the ones published in 1788 in *Anecdotes about Emperor Peter the Great, Heard from Various Individuals and Collected by Iakov Shtelin*:

After his victory against the Swedes at the Battle of Poltava, Peter the Great invited some captured officers to his table. He proposed a toast: 'I drink to the health of my military teachers!'

The Swedish Field Marshal Reinschild asked Peter whom he favoured to call by such a name.

'You, sirs,' was Peter's reply.

'In that case, Your Majesty has shown his teachers terrible ingratitude on the battlefield.'

The ruler was so pleased by Reinschild's retort that he immediately ordered that the Field Marshal's sabre be returned to him.

In 1840, the *Dictionary of Russian Synonyms* defined the *anekdot* as a story which 'illuminates the secrets of politics and literature or lays bare the hidden springs of events'.

By the mid-nineteenth century the meaning of *anekdot* had widened to include humorous folk tales – which today sound miserably unfunny – told by peasants. Like the older *anekdoty*, they still carried the sense of a hidden truth revealed, even if it was only the stupidity of the peasant himself.

One winter's day a carriage was travelling on the ice of the Volga River. One of the horses suddenly reared up and tore off towards the bank; the driver jumped down and ran after it, and was about to give it a swat with the whip when the horse fell through the ice, dragging the entire load with it.

'You should thank God you went off under that ice,' shouted the peasant at his disappearing steed, 'otherwise I'd have thrashed you good!'

A young peasant was leaving on a hunting trip and his wife was seeing him off. After walking a mile she started to cry.

'Don't cry, wife, I'll come home soon.'

'You think that's why I'm crying? My feet are frozen!'

As the new century dawned, Russia's cities filled with millions of migrants. Small cabaret theatres opened up with programmes of songs and stand-up comedy. A few of the new comedians were so popular that their sketches were transcribed, so we know that anti-Semitic *anekdoty* were very popular, such as this one from a sketch by A. V. Stepanov from around 1905–10 and performed at the Petersburg Theatre.

A stagecoach full of passengers is travelling from Zhitomir to Kiev when a band of robbers attacks. Their leader commands, 'Halt. Nobody move. Hands up!' All the passengers obediently climb out of the stagecoach and put their hands up. One of them turns to the bandits' leader and says, 'Mr Chief, you're gonna take everything from us in a couple of minutes. Let me go into my pocket with one hand for a moment. I have to give something to the guy standing next to me.'

'Hurry it up!' He points the barrel of his revolver at the traveller.

The passenger goes into his back pocket, takes out one hundred roubles and, turning to his neighbour, says, 'Solomon! Didn't I owe you a hundred roubles? Here, take it. And keep in mind that we're even now.'

By the beginning of the twentieth century there was also a corpus of political *anekdoty*, many about the Tsar, which are the true precursors of the Communist joke.

One day Jacob, a Russian Jew, slipped on the wet river bank and

*fell into the water. Unfortunately, he could not swim and was in
serious danger of drowning.*

*Two Tsarist policemen heard cries for help and rushed over. But
when they saw that it was a Jew, they laughed and just stood there
watching him drown.*

'Help, I can't swim,' shouted Jacob.

'Then you will just have to drown,' they replied.

*Suddenly Jacob shouted out with his last breath: 'Down with the
Tsar!'*

*The policemen immediately rushed into the river, pulled him out,
and arrested him for troublemaking.*

*A man was reported to have said: 'That Nicholas is a moron!' He
was arrested by the policeman for insulting Tsar Nicolas II.*

*'No, sir,' said the man, 'I did not mean our respected Emperor, but
another Nicholas!'*

*'Don't try to trick me,' replied the policeman. 'If you say "moron",
you obviously refer to our Tsar.'*

These jokes about Russia's last Tsar later became jokes about Stalin.

Under Communism the three kinds of *anekdot* – popular joke,
political joke and story containing political wisdom – would fuse into
something new. The environment of the Soviet Union – accelerating
urbanisation, the creation of new communities of workers from
armies of strangers, the mass market for light entertainment and the
distinctive political agenda of Communism would prove an unprecedentedly fertile ground for the invention and dissemination of
anekdoty.

But not quite yet. Compared to later periods, there were, in fact,
relatively few Communist jokes before the 1930s. This could be
explained by the novelty of the system. Russians, one may imagine,
were still learning what was funny about their new state. But there is
also another better explanation: in this era humour was not yet
effectively censored, and it flourished in print. The 1920s consequently
became known as the golden age of Soviet satire.

Ariane and I sat together on the sofa like mirror images of each
other. She adored the paraphernalia and rituals of Communism,
yet I was working on the very thing that diminished them. Open
in my hands was a small French paperback of jokes, entitled:

Communism – Does it Dissolve in Alcohol? Ariane was bent over the coffee table, flicking through issues of *Soviet Life*, a monthly Soviet propaganda magazine, now defunct, which had been expensively produced for foreign consumption. The paper was shiny, the typography jet black, and it was full of colour photographs, which glowed evocatively with the lurid ektachrome palette of old printing technology. Ariane was looking for images to use – art critics would say 'appropriate' – for her own work. She would cut out the ones she liked and take them to a decent printer's, where they made dramatically enlarged photocopies for her. These she then trimmed with a Stanley knife and glued onto mounts in enormous collages, finally adding some paint.

Soviet Life had been launched in 1956, a product of Khrushchev's 'thaw', which encouraged increased cultural contacts with the West. By Soviet standards, it was a lavish publication, designed to show how well 'the era of Communist construction' was going. It carried articles with titles like 'Knowledge × (Talent + Passion) = Science' and 'Uzbekistan: 60 Years of Progress', 'Free Health Care' and 'The Bolshoi Ballet visits Siberia'. It painted the Soviet Union as a panoply of colourful ethnic history, contemporary cultural sophistication, technological progress and generous state handouts. But Communism, of course, is not the only political system capable of mendacious idealisations of itself. The magazine was the outcome of a deal between the superpowers: the Russians were allowed to send thirty thousand copies of their shameless puff *Soviet Life* to the West every month, and in return the Americans could do the same with their equally brazen magazine, *Ameryka*.

I looked over at Ariane. She was at work with her scissors, cutting out a romantic black-and-white photograph of young Leningrad citizens standing on an embankment on the River Neva, watching the sun dip behind the city's spires. They were in silhouette, but you could still see the outline of the worker's dungarees, the baby in the pram and the elderly couple.

I'd also found something in the book I was reading: a topical joke. It was about the Soviet newspaper *Pravda*, but it was easy to adapt.

'A man buys a copy of *Soviet Life*,' I told Ariane, 'and when he gets his change he notices the newsagent has given him too much. He draws the attention of the newsagent to the price printed on the cover and offers the money back. The newsagent shakes his head. 'Well, if you want to believe everything you read in that magazine ...'

She shook her head. The magazines she had collected were in such good condition that they had either never been sold or never been opened. Not that she'd noticed – it wasn't her kind of incidental detail.

Yet, in truth, Ariane was producing work that was conceptually way ahead of mine. I was still fighting the clichéd Cold War battle of the West, in which I searched for fresh evidence about – or found a new angle on – how awful Soviet life was. Ariane had moved beyond hostility to forgiveness. She was looking back with affection on this episode in history, which she saw, like many of her fashionable peers on the contemporary art scene, as a lost world of innocence. Her work contained the tension of ambivalence and contradiction. The faithful way she presented the imagery of Soviet propaganda in her work was both ironic and sincere. The irony flowed from the transparent banality and dishonesty of the pictures; the state lied as badly as a child. On the other hand, a pool of sincerity coagulated in the regime's defiant conviction that it could organise Utopia. Today we are too cynical to try to solve so many problems with just one big idea.

Ariane's work made me think: might the jokes also contain the same ambiguous layers as their counterpart, the propaganda?

I lay on my back on my sofa in my north London flat, and travelled back in time to Lenin's Russia. I like to study oppression in comfort. Close to my right hand on my modernist coffee table was a pile of books comprising the masterpieces of Soviet satire of the twenties. Over the course of a week, I picked them up one by one.

Confronted by a virgin political system and the efforts to impose it on an ill-informed and uneducated population, the imagination of Russia took off. A handful of astute writers quickly latched on to the shortcomings and contradictions of Communist theory and praxis, despite the fact that one of the Bolsheviks' first decrees in 1917 was to ban the opposition press. In this early phase of Communism the state had not yet sucesssfully imposed censorship on journalists and writers, so the dominant form of humour was sophisticated literary satire, rather than the more populist *anekdot*. First amidst the anarchy of the civil war, and then in the chaotic world of the New Economic Policy of the mid-twenties, a multiplicity of political views could still be expressed in newspapers, broadsheets, posters and books. Much of this took the form of the wryly humorous. Between 1922 and 1928 seven satirical magazines were published every week in Moscow and St Petersburg with a combined print run of half a million – the same as the daily edition of *Pravda*: this was the first flowering of Communist humour.

Mikhail Bulgakov is the best known of this generation of satirists today. In the twenties he produced a couple of allegorical science-fiction novellas. In the first, originally entitled *The Red Ray* (but now known as *The Fatal Eggs*), a professor invents a mysterious beam that increases the growth rate and size of animals. Armed with a wodge of papers and official permissions, a Soviet bureaucrat requisitions this machine to solve one of the many food shortages that were a permanent feature of Soviet Communism. In this instance, there are no eggs and no chickens in the shops because poultry is being wiped out by a mysterious disease. The official plans to use the machine on hens' eggs, but mistakenly zaps a crate of laboratory snake eggs with the red ray. Soon the country is overrun with a plague of monstrous serpents against which the Red Army is powerless. Russia is saved by a freak cold spell in the height of summer, which kills the plague. It is a parable, which condemns the Bolsheviks' solution to Russia's problems, suggesting they only make things worse.

The Red Ray was published in 1924 but Bulgakov's next short novel, *Heart of a Dog* (1925), was banned. The story goes: a surgeon transplants the testes and pituitary gland of a thief into a dog, who then comes to resemble a young Soviet zealot, who exhibits all the worst qualities of violence, drunkenness and lechery. Eventually the canine Commie turns on his creator and denounces him to the political police. Thus Bulgakov derides Communist efforts to transform the uneducated Russian masses into dedicated Marxist–Leninists. The surgeon says scathingly: 'In short, I ... would perform the most difficult feat of my whole career by ... turning a dog into a highly intelligent being. But what in heaven's name for?'

Bulgakov's most celebrated novel, *The Master and Margarita*, written in the early thirties, satirised the world of corrupt officials, neighbour-informants and political police of thirties Russia. In the book, the devil arrives in Moscow, accompanied by an enormous black cat and a ruthless assassin – all personifications of the Soviet apparatus of repression. There they perform black-magic tricks, which thrill and terrify its citizens, framing a handful of them for the anti-Soviet crime of possessing foreign currency. Although many of the devil's victims are themselves guilty of crimes such as bribe-taking, everyone is tainted in Bulgakov's hellish panorama of life in the pitiless Soviet capital. Consequently the novel was banned from publication until 1966, thirty years after Bulgakov's death.

Bulgakov was part of a mass movement. A decade before *The Master and Margarita*, at a time when Communism had barely begun, a handful of budding Russian writers began scribbling their own *Animal Farms* and *1984s*. Yevgeny Zamyatin, aged thirty-three in 1917, was one of them. His best-known novel, *We*, describes a society of numbers and a man whose humanity is revived by a passionate woman, and was written in 1920. It's amazing how quick off the mark Zamyatin was!

We is not really a humorous book, but Zamyatin also wrote short stories that parodied Bolshevism. In *The Last Tale About Phita* (1922) a mayor decides that, in order to make the inhabitants of his town happy, he will make everyone equal. He orders them to live together in a large barracks, then shaves every citizen's hair off to put them on a par with the bald, and makes them mentally disabled to equalise their intelligence. It's obvious, once again, that Orwell owes a debt to Zamyatin for *Animal Farm* as well as *1984*. In *Comrade Churygin Has the Floor* (1926) a group of peasants march to the estate of a rich landowner and demand to know what has happened following the death of their leader. In the midst of this, a fellow peasant arrives, bringing news of the Revolution: 'The Tsar Nikolai has been replaced and all kinds of nasty palaces have to be wiped off the face of the earth so there won't be any more rich people, and we'll all live like poor proletarians just like in the Bible, only now it's because of the science of our beloved Marx,' explains the peasant in a way that describes the ignorance of Marxism in the Russian countryside. Following the precepts of the Revolution, the peasants decide to destroy the estate starting with a classical statue. But when the landowner pleads with the mob, saying it's a statue of Mars, the peasants think he said Marx, and they doff their caps and pay homage to it.

Zamyatin emigrated to Paris in 1931 and died in poverty six years later.

Another major force in the satirical golden age was Yuri Olesha. In his short novel *Envy* (1927) he portrays a dedicated Bolshevik revolutionary, Babichev, who has risen rapidly in the expanding Soviet bureaucracy to the important position of Director of the Communal Kitchen. Here he has taken great pride in developing a new, more advanced form of sausage. His tenant, Kavalerov, a weak, reactionary young man, who narrates the novel, refuses to accept the materialist values of the Communist society represented by Babichev; yet he is envious of his confidence and success.

I was filled with spite. He, the ruler, the Communist, was building a new world. And in this new world, glory was sparked because a new kind of sausage had come from the sausage-maker's hands. I didn't understand this glory. What did it mean? Biographies, monuments, history had never told me of glory like this … Did this mean the nature of glory had changed? I did feel that this new world being built was the chief, triumphant world. I wasn't blind. I had a head on my shoulders. No need to teach or explain to me. I was literate. It was in this world that I wanted glory! I wanted to beam the way Babichev was beaming today. But a new type of sausage was not going to make me beam.

These satires have often been misinterpreted as hostile critiques of Communism, but this was not a counter-culture. On the one hand, even the most rabid party ideologues agreed that the new society had faults. On the other, many of the satirists were sympathetic to the new political creed, and they thought that if they made fun of the shortcomings of their emerging society, then it would improve. These optimistic Communists believed that lazy bureaucrats, selfish capitalists, backward peasants and deluded religious believers could be laughed, as well as persecuted, out of existence.

In *A Mayday Easter* Valentin Kataev set out to ridicule religion (although today it seems, in parts, to read as a mockery of Communism). The president of the local Workers' Council invites several guests for an Easter banquet, which coincides with May Day. The guests exchange the traditional greeting 'Christ is risen!' but then a Communist Party official unexpectedly arrives. 'What in the world is going on here, brother?' he asks. 'Isn't this an Easter table? Religious superstitions? Petty bourgeois guests? Oy vey! I didn't expect this from you, even though you aren't a Party member!' The Council president thinks a moment and then says that the party is, in fact, an agricultural production meeting. All the food items are production samples; and the initials Kh. V. *(Khristos Voskrese* – 'Christ has Risen') actually stand for *Khozyaystvennoe Vozrozhdenie* ('Economic Regeneration'). Then the guests get down to the important business of testing the food samples.

Novels constituted only a tiny fraction of the satirical output of twenties Russia; the overwhelming majority of ironic depictions of the new Soviet society took the form of satirical columns and short stories, which ranged from two thousand words down to a paragraph, the length of a joke, and were printed in the scores of newspapers that multiplied across the Soviet Union. Numerous freelance satirists earned a living mocking the official enemies of the Soviet state, among them the writing team Ilf and Petrov, who met in Moscow in the twenties. Here they both worked on the railwaymen's newspaper *The Train Whistle*, where they were in charge of sifting through the readers' letters expressing grievances about bureaucracy, injustices and shortages. Some they marked for publication; others they used as raw material for short humorous stories.

One of the characters of their first great novel *Twelve Chairs* (1928) is surely a self-portrait: Absolom Vladimirovich Iznurenkov is an official satirist who 'produced sixty first-rate jokes a month' for the printed press:

> He never made them without reason, just for the effect. He made them to order for humorous journals. On his shoulders he bore the responsibility for highly important campaigns and supplied most of the Moscow satirical journals with subjects for cartoons and humorous anecdotes ... He aimed his sting at bootlickers, apartment-block superintendents, owners of private property, hooligans, citizens reluctant to lower their prices and industrial executives who tried to avoid economy drives ...
>
> As soon as the journals came out, the jokes were repeated in the circus arena, reprinted in the evening press without reference to the source, and offered to audiences from the variety stage by 'entertainers writing their own words and music'.

The undisputed master of the genre of the satirical newspaper sketch was Mikhail Zoshchenko, little known outside Russia today, but back then more familiar to Russian readers than Gorky, Mandelstam, or Pasternak.

Zoshchenko fought for the Red Army in the civil war, but became a prolific writer in the twenties. His succinct tales catalogue the new human typologies and social values of Soviet towns. *A Dogged Sense of Smell* (1924) suggests that Russia has become a nation of petty criminals. A merchant calls the local police after having his coat stolen. The policeman arrives with his sniffer-dog. The dog dives into a crowd and singles out one person after another, who all spontaneously admit to different post-Revolutionary crimes. An old woman admits to brewing her own vodka; the Chairman of the Housing Committee concedes he has been skimming money off the service charges; a young man admits to dodging military service. The dog eventually turns on his owner, the policeman, who confesses, 'Citizen Dog, I received three ten-rouble notes for your dog food and took two for myself.'

A Victim of the Revolution (1923) mocks people who boast about their role in the October Revolution – a character, who claims to have been injured fighting with the Bolsheviks turns out to have had his

Fig. 5. Communal kitchen (*Kukrynitsi*, 1932) After the revolution, many Russian city, dwellers lived in croweded communal apartments with one family per room.

foot grazed by the wheel of a car sent to arrest an aristocrat. Another story describes cabbies who get lost on the streets of Russian cities, confused by all the newly named Karl Marx Squares and Lenin Avenues; on the same theme, a group of Russian holidaymakers on a cruise lose their ship every time it docks, because its name keeps being changed. In *The Galosh* (1927) the narrator loses a wellington boot in the rush hour. His attempt to find it in the lost-property depot leads him into the labyrinth of Soviet bureaucracy. He eventually recovers his boot – proof that the system works – only to find he has lost his other one in all the rushing about.

There was a chronic shortage of housing at the time, which got worse as the decade wore on. It was commonplace for ten families to live in a shared apartment, one per room (Fig. 5). Children would sleep under dining tables, grandmothers on them. By 1928 the average living space for a Moscow resident was under six square metres. In *The Crisis* (1925) Zoshchenko tells the story of a family that moves into a bathroom. The landlord tells his tenants: 'There's no windows, I grant you that. But there's a door. And running water's freely available.' The family are happy: 'The only inconvenient thing was that in the evenings the tenants of the communal apartment kept on barging into the bathroom to take baths.'

The new terminology for Communism's new political organisations is Zoshchenko's target in *Monkey Language* (1925). Two uneducated citizens are looking forward to a meeting – 'It's going to be really plenary today, just wait till you see the quorum that's present,' says one, before arguing over whether the meeting is 'concretely industrial' or 'concretely actual'. Newspaper headlines of the day were full of these unfamiliar political terms expressed with frantic enthusiasm – 'The *Peasant Gazette* sends Ardent Greetings to the Conference of Red Teachers,' said the eponymously titled paper one day in 1925. 'We Must Reform our Party Cell,' it exclaimed on another. Critics of these hectoring headlines branded them 'naked meetingism'.

The papers of the time printed daily articles extolling the advances of the Soviet economy. In Zoshchenko's *The Match* (1925) a delegate from the Matchmakers' Union gives a speech to an assembly of workers that parodies this language of Soviet success: 'Productivity, that foundation-stone of Soviet life, is improving. Total output is also bounding ahead. And the quality of goods is becoming wonderful.'

But when the speaker tries to light his cigarette the flaming tip of the poorly made match snaps off and hits him in the eye.

As the decade progressed, Communists became increasingly aware that their social Utopia required a total re-education of the Soviet population. This reality did not escape Zoshchenko. In *Electrification* (1924) the narrator complains that ever since the replacement of his kerosene lamps with electric lighting, he can now see in what squalor he lives. The story concludes: 'So you see, comrades, light's good, but even light has its problems. We've got to change every aspect of our lives. There must be cleanliness and order. We must decisively sweep away all that is rotten and revolting: what's good in the dark is bad in the light! Wouldn't you agree, comrades?'

The origins of this thought can be traced back to 1917 and Gorky, who observed, 'The new structure of political life demands from us a new structure of the soul.' Trotsky agreed: 'To produce a new "improved version" of man – that is the future task of Communism.' One of the key features of Communism is that the project transmuted instantly from a struggle to liberate the proletariat into a struggle to create an as yet non-existent social organism, the Soviet Man. Communism was a movement of social invention, not social transformation. And the Communist jokes are, in one sense, a meticulous breakdown of this social invention into its constituent parts, a long list of Communist inventions.

Like many other satirical writers, Zoshchenko found it difficult to get his material published by the end of the twenties. Nevertheless he remained a member of the Soviet Writers' Union until 1945, when he was expelled after publishing a short story in which a monkey escapes from a Soviet zoo, hit by a Fascist bomb. The ape spends a day in Soviet society, encountering queues, shortages and an aggressive population, finally concluding that 'it was silly to leave the zoo. You could breathe more peacefully in the cage.' Stalin's culture minister, Zhdanov, was furious!

Labyrinthine bureaucracy, a world of new artificial heroes, the political ignorance of the masses, low-quality manufacturing, an over-zealous police force, language that is meaningless ... Zoshchenko's brilliant stories established a set of themes that would dominate the next seven decades of Communist jokes, and they set a high benchmark for Communist humour – one of surprise, detail and breadth.

Zoshchenko was painting with a broad brush. His tales had a lot to do with the dawn of mass society and with the project of the rational organisation of this new phenomenon which both Communist and Capitalist states were undertaking. Notwithstanding this, the fact that the advent of the Communist society brought with it an instant golden age of satire, both in scale and quality, shows that humour was, from the start, a distinctive component of the Communist experience.

Print, though, was not to be the primary form that it took in the coming decades. Already in the mid-twenties logical arguments against satire were being formulated, and at the end of the decade, as Stalin established his monopoly of power, many satirical magazines and newspapers were closed down. Writers were persuaded to soften their tone; those who didn't found themselves without a publisher – like Yevgeny Zamyatin. In 1931 he wrote a begging letter to Stalin: 'To me as a writer, being deprived of the opportunity to write is a death sentence ... No creative activity is possible in an atmosphere of systematic persecution which increases in intensity from year to year.'

In 1934 the First Congress of Soviet Writers was held in the grand Hall of Columns, an eighteenth-century palace, which the Bolsheviks had given to the trades unions. It was decorated for the occasion with enormous portraits of Shakespeare, Tolstoy, Gogol, Cervantes, Heine, Pushkin and Balzac. The location was an indication of the importance of this event. Here Lenin had lain in state in 1924; here the Tsar had announced the emancipation of the serfs in 1861; and here George Bernard Shaw celebrated his seventy-fifth birthday in 1931. Over fifteen days, six hundred writers and politicians heard two hundred speeches. In the wings, delegations of workers, collective farmers, representatives of the Red Army and Communist Youth came and went.

The Congress was the first meeting of the subservient new Writers' Union that Stalin had set up in 1932. Its purpose was to ritualistically consolidate the state's control over the literary output of the Soviet Union, which included the repression of independent satirical magazines, and to transform that output so that it propagated a certain vision of the world. Socialist Realism – the depiction of Communism's 'marvels of heroism and of organised discipline, which have won the admiration of the whole world' in a nineteenth-century realist style – was declared the official artistic 'ism' of Communism. The imposition of this stylistic monopoly had an unanticipated side effect: it entrenched and accelerated the creation of an underground culture of anonymous political jokes.

Every important Soviet writer of the era attended the Congress: Maxim Gorky, Boris Pasternak, Mikhail Zhdanov, Ilya Ehrenburg, Karl Radek, Isaac Babel. Among the delegates was Mikhail Kol'tsov (Fig. 6), one of the leading Bolshevik journalists of the day, a member of *Pravda*'s editorial board and the founder of several satirical magazines, including, in 1922, *Krokodil*, which still exists to this day. His staff included his brother, the caricaturist Boris Yefimov, of whom I will write more in the next chapter.

Kol'tsov was a powerful pro-regime satirist, although today we would describe his style as invective. His bullying columns slavishly followed the Party line – just like his brother's cartoons – heaping scorn on imperialists, Christians, Tsarist émigrés, inefficient bureaucrats and greedy businessmen. In one example published in *Pravda* on New Year's Day 1924, Kol'tsov mocks the political opportunism of Soviet intellectuals. The article lists the New Year toasts pronounced by the same character from 1914 to 1924, which reveal how he changes from a loyal monarchist to a radical Communist, then emigrates, and becomes a vehement anti-Communist. Kol'tsov was no liberal and the newspapers he presided over were part of a system of propaganda and denunciation, in which satire played a part.

But now rivals wanted to sideline the *Pravda* editor, and they targeted his sense of humour. As he got up out of his seat in the enormous hall and walked towards the podium, Kol'tsov was about to defend the value of satire, not because he believed in freedom of the press but because this genre of writing was the source of his political power. He began his speech with an anecdote:

Fig. 6. Mikhail Kol'tsov by Boris Yefimov, 1920s

A Leningrad driver had driven drunk. When stopped by the police, he showed them his friend's ID. When this offence came to light the driver's workmates called a meeting to discuss what should be done with him. Some suggested he should be sacked and excluded from the trade union; others called for his immediate arrest; a third group, however – the most bloodthirsty – demanded that he be handed over to the writer Zoshchenko so that he could have a story written about him.

The audience laughed and clapped, but this was a bad joke in support of a weak argument. How could a writer's wit compete as a punishment with Soviet prison camps?

Satire had been under attack from certain elements of the Bolshevik Party since the mid-twenties. Vladimir Blium, a ponderous theatre critic, was the first to ask the serious question: could there really be jokes in a utopian society? In his 1925 article 'The Line of Least Resistance' he wrote that the fragile new Communist system was too delicate to bear the weight of satirical criticism: 'To mock the proletarian state through the use of old satirical devices and thereby to shake its foundations, to laugh at the first steps – albeit uncertain and clumsy – of the new Soviet society is at the very least unwise and ill-considered.'

Humour offered the early Communists the same philosophical conundrums that every other area of culture offered: what belonged to yesterday and what to tomorrow? Many argued that humour could be used to ridicule the old bourgeois habits that persisted ... But, said others, given that the Soviets were creating a perfect world, there would soon be nothing left to laugh at in Russian politics or society; ergo, the end of political and social humour ... No, said others with equal gravity: the liberation of the working classes meant that finally the masses could take control of the language of humour that used to be the preserve of the elite ... No, not quite, a third group of straight-faced critics theorised comically, there would still be laughter under Communism, but the new society would invent an entirely new sense of humour.

On the stand at the Writers' Congress of 1934 Kol'tsov repeated the contorted counter-arguments that had been presented in the last decade. Even if one day, when the system was perfect, he conceded, there would be no need for laughter, there was still a place for it now.

Even if the satire took the same forms as old-fashioned Tsarist humour, that was no reason to see it as reactionary. Since the working class were, according to Marxist–Leninist theory, the last class before the arrival of a classless society, their laughter was acceptable because, Kol'tsov said ingeniously, 'In the history of the class struggle, the working class will have the last laugh.'

It was a ritualised debate which is confusing to read today. Neither side was talking about *all* satire – no one thought for a minute that satire about Imperialism, Capitalism and bourgeois values outside Russia's borders should cease forthwith, though they did imagine that, with the worldwide victory of Communism, these forms would also eventually become obsolete. This was, primarily, a discussion about what could be criticised inside the Soviet Union, how strongly, and who was permitted to do it.

Kol'tsov sat down. He would shortly leave for Spain, where he would report on the Civil War. Other Congress delegates, such as the Soviet writer Panteleimon Romanov, won the day with a new theory of the future of laughter: 'I would like to express the wish that by the end of the third Five-Year Plan the need for satire will have disappeared in the Soviet Union, leaving only a great need for humour, for cheerful laughter.'

A new kind of laughter was imagined, which came to be known as 'positive humour'. The Soviet state would inculcate in the 'New Man' of Communism not only new attitudes to work, family, religion and society, but also a new sense of humour. There would be a new kind of joke, which would be greeted with a new kind of chuckle. In his speech, Romanov announced:

In the land of the Soviets a new type of comedy is being created – a comedy of positive heroes. A comedy that does not mock its heroes but depicts them so cheerfully, emphasises their positive qualities with such love and sympathy that the laughter of the audience is joyful and the members of the audience want to emulate the heroes of the comedy, they want to tackle life's problems with equal ease and optimism. This does not mean that there is no place in our literature for scathing satire; in our way of life there are still many ugly things, the remnants of Capitalism still make themselves felt, there are suitable subjects for the satirist's pen. But the laughter of the victors, laughter as refreshing as morning exercise, a laughter evoked not by mockery of the hero but by joy for him, is ringing out more and more loudly on our stage.

What Romanov meant was that humour had to become toothless, unless it was attacking the enemies of Communism. There could be no more ironic essays about overcrowded apartments, food shortages and Soviet neologisms.

The state could never engineer how people laughed or what they laughed at. Nevertheless it would try. By the time of the Congress, the outpouring of independent political comic writing in Russia of the twenties had been firmly brought to a close – its magazines closed down and its writers silenced. On his return from Spain, in 1938, Kol'tsov was arrested by Stalin and executed in 1940. But, as Romanov said and we shall see, laughter still remained essential to the Communists. There were now two kinds of humour: official and unofficial – the written and the spoken, the public and the private. In the censored void, a culture of the spoken joke would develop, a collective satirical work produced by the whole population.

Ariane appeared at the doorway of her living room, wearing her usual: a colourfully mismatched patterned dress, long purple socks

that came up over her knees and thick-soled black lace-up boots. It was squatter style and, though she now paid rent on her flat, she refused to abandon the look or the agenda. The outfit projected a curious mix of naïvety and violence – the same emotional

Fig. 7. Caricature of Mayakovsky by the *Kukrynitsi* cartoonists, 1928. Note the ballerina's legs in the painting on the wall, undoubtedly a reference to the poet's amorous adventures.

dialectic as fuelled early Soviet Communism. My wardrobe was so different: a mixture of blue, grey, black and white from designer labels bought in sales or on ebay. She always complained it was too monochrome.

She handed me a C90 cassette. I held its transparent plastic casing and looked at the thin grey reel of tape inside.

'You might find this useful,' she said.

Despite our differences, she still wanted to help me with my research, perhaps because she vaguely thought she could convert me to her cause. Her choice of recording format was evocative. I and my friends had long since thrown away our tape-players, with their clunky buttons and irritating hiss, and replaced them with iPods. But antiquated analogue was, it seemed, still in use in the former states of the Soviet Bloc. Technologically they were years behind. On Ariane's gift was an interview with Vladimir Kaminer, a best-selling young Russian writer, living in Berlin, about the Soviet poet Vladimir Mayakovsky. He had been speaking a fortnight before at a literary theme night held once a month in a bar in what was once East Berlin.

Born in 1893, Mayakovsky (Fig. 7) was one of the crusading cultural figures of the Russian Revolution, and was later named by Stalin as the greatest Soviet poet. Like the photographer Alexander Rodchenko and painter El Lissitzsky, he enthusiastically placed his skills at the service of the Revolution. Avant-garde art, he thought, could win over the masses to Communism. Today, in the eyes of many left-wing writers such as Kaminer, he is a literary Che Guevara, precious on two counts. First, he symbolises the free spirit of the Revolution – eccentric, avant-garde and counter-cultural – before it was polluted by Soviet politics. Secondly, he is one of the few artists whose work offers evidence of art's most outlandish claim to be capable of fighting political oppression. But Mayakovsky has a third significance. The arc of his career illustrates the inevitability of the Communist joke: he started off as an enthusiastic supporter of the ideology and ended up producing satire about it.

Speaking German in a thick Russian accent, Kaminer spoke about the era before the Revolution. Mayakovsky took part in Socialist demonstrations in Georgia, aged fourteen. When his family moved to Moscow, in 1906, Mayakovsky developed a passion for Marxist literature. He was imprisoned three times for his political activities while still under sixteen. In 1911 he joined the Moscow Art School and met the Russian Futurists, for whom he became a spokesperson. His first published verses appeared in the 1912 Futurist volume *A Slap in the Face of Public Taste*. He was in St Petersburg for the October Revolution and soon he was writing poems supporting the new regime, such as 'Left March! For the Red Marines: 1918', which he recited at naval theatres.

For the Red Marines: 1918

Does the eye of the eagle fade?
Shall we stare back to the old?
Proletarian fingers
the throat of the world
still tighter hold!
Chests out!
Shoulders straight!
Stick to the sky red flags adrift!
Who's marching there with the right?!!
LEFT!
LEFT!
LEFT! …

In 1919 Mayakovsky became a key member of Agitprop, the new propaganda ministry established to teach Communism to the Soviet Union, where hardly anyone had heard of the German political philosopher Marx. There were Agitprop departments within the central and regional committees of the Communist Party forming a nationwide network of information bureaus. There were Agitprop trains that toured the countryside and offices in major towns, all advertising the principles, merits and policies of Soviet Communism. They ran campaigns against religion, crime, vandalism, drunkenness, illiteracy, anti-Semitism and the landowning peasant. All kinds of artists and writers joined Agitprop. Artists swapped painting for poster design; poets gave up romantic verse, instead turning out catchy slogans by day and declaiming Communist couplets in public recitals at night. Newspaper journalists wrote articles designed to educate and motivate the population, not report on events.

Mayakovsky did it all. Employed at the Russian State Telegraph Agency, he wrote texts, designed posters, made films and composed an estimated twenty thousand poems. In 'Back Home' (1925), he declared ecstatically:

> I want
> A commissar
> With a decree
> To lean over the thought of the age ...
>
> I want the factory committee
> To lock
> My lips
> When the work is done
>
> Proletarians
>   Arrive at Communism
>   From below –
> By the low way of mines,
>   Sickles,
>   And pitchforks –
> But I from poetry's skies,
>   Plunge into Communism,
> Because
>   Without it
>   I feel no love.

Ariane, meanwhile, sat sewing a blindfold, like the ones you get free on long-distance flights but made out of small multicoloured bits of cloth. Like most female former citizens of East Germany, she had learned how to make her own clothes, because she didn't want to wear the dowdy fashions that were on sale. 'In the DDR you could never buy any nice clothes,' she told me. 'The trousers in the shops were all the same and they fitted terribly. If a shipment of nice skirts arrived, the word went round so fast that they sold out in an afternoon.'

I needed the blindfold because there were no curtains on my girlfriend's bedroom windows. Her alternative lifestyle meant she wasn't woken up by the light of the rising sun, but I was used to the luxury of sleeping in darkness.

On the tape, behind Kaminer's voice, I could hear the muffled noise of the audience, whispering and drinking. His story was interrupted every ten minutes or so by a musical interlude, in which a DJ called

'Doc Choc' played either a Soviet anthem or songs by obscure German punk groups. Lenin would have found this melange of twentieth-century revolutionary spirit rather confusing.

Mayakovsky was one of the Revolution's loose cannons. He drove around Moscow in a limo with young ballerinas and wrote thousands of love letters, often recycling exactly the same material for different women. He threw oranges at Soviet officials and punched the Swedish ambassador at a reception. A lung disease in his youth meant that he could never smoke, yet in his publicity photographs he insisted he coolly hold a cigarette, said Kaminer on the cassette recording.

Mayakovsky designed the blueprints for the Soviet stereotypes of Western leaders as warmongering greedy capitalists. In his play 'Championship Tournament of the World Class Struggle', a crown, a large gold coin and a sack labelled 'The Profits from Imperialistic Massacres' are thrown into the ring. The British and French prime ministers of the day tussle over the sack. The American president grapples with a speculator (bourgeois Russia) over the gold coin. In a plot twist, that is execrable even by the low standards of Soviet propaganda, when the Revolution enters the ring, no one wants to fight and the Entente, the alliance of Western liberal regimes of the day, asks for a ten-minute intermission!

Clunking storylines like these have left Mayakovsky with only a limited literary reputation, but that was not something that Vladimir Kaminer pointed up. Along with his newspaper columns and several nostalgic novels about Communism, Kaminer had recently published 'The Socialist Cookbook' – recipes of what people ate under Communism – co-authored with his wife. For him Mayakovsky remained delicious revolutionary fare, despite his suicide in 1930. There was applause and the tape ended.

Perhaps Kaminer had simply run out of time, but he didn't explain that by the end of the twenties Mayakovsky was disillusioned. Stalin had sidelined the poet. His avant-garde plans for the celebrations of the tenth anniversary of the foundation of the Soviet Republic in 1927 had been rejected. A poem from 1930 concludes

> When I appear
> Before the CCC
> Of the coming
> Bright years,

By way of my Bolshevik Party card,
    I'll raise
Above the heads
    Of a gang of self-seeking
        Poets and rogues
All the hundred volumes
    Of my
        Communist-committed books.

In 1929 Mayakovsky wrote 'The Bedbug', a satire against Communism. The stage directions in scene 5 imagine a vast party conference, which is no longer attended by delegates; in their place are rows and rows of loudspeakers:

> Fifty years later. An immense amphitheatre for conferences. Instead of human voters, radio loudspeakers equipped with arms like directional signals on an automobile. Above each loudspeaker, coloured electrical lights; just below the ceiling there are movie screens. In the centre of the hall a dais with a microphone, flanked by control panels and switches for sound and light ...

Two technicians are tinkering around in the darkened hall; one tells the other to 'check up on the voting apparatus of the agricultural zones and give it a spot of oil'. His colleague responds, 'He must tighten up the arms of the metropolitan auxiliary personnel – they're deviating a bit – the right arm tangles with the left one.' Then the President of the Institute for Human Resurrection enters and ascends the podium. He announces that a frozen human figure has been discovered under the ice and: 'The Institute considers that the life of every worker must be utilised until the very last second.' So he asks for a vote on resurrection. It's a futuristic vision of a dehumanised world where proletarian democracy has mutated into industrial slavery – exactly what would happen in the 1930s.

'The Revolution, Communism was a great thing, but it got perverted by Stalin,' Ariane said, handing me my finished patchwork blindfold.

I put it on and it fitted. I stuck out my arms, trying to find her and embrace her. 'I can't see anything now,' I said.

'Doesn't matter,' she said. 'You look much more colourful.' She wound her hands into mine and then slipped them through my arms and behind my back.

On 14 April 1930 Mayakovsky committed suicide. Shortly after his death a joke appeared:

What were Mayakovsky's last words before he committed suicide?
'Comrades, don't shoot!'

Thus the progression was established from the hymns of ardent faith to the satire of disillusionment and, following the elimination of that, to jokes.

TWO

Stalin and the Grim Grin

Stalin made terrible jokes about his Terror, in which, by the latest sensible estimates, twenty-four million Soviet citizens, a tenth of the total population, were exiled, imprisoned, sentenced to forced labour or killed.

He developed a running gag with one of his commissars, Vladimir Nosenko, responsible for shipbuilding. It began some time before the Second World War when, passing him in the corridor, Stalin exclaimed: 'Comrade Nosenko, why haven't you been arrested yet?' According to his colleagues, Nosenko spent many sleepless nights waiting for the knock on the door. Over the next few years, whenever Stalin met Nosenko he would joke: 'I thought I had you shot.' Finally he talked to Nosenko at the celebrations for victory in World War II. 'What really brought us victory?' Stalin asked. 'Was it our superior Socialist technology? Was it our dedication to the motherland? Was it our proletarian consciousness? Yes. It was all these things. But mainly it was our sense of humour. Wasn't it, Comrade Nosenko?'

In 1932, during the interval in a performance of Bulgakov's play *The Days of the Turbins* Stalin emerged from what had once been the royal box, and went to talk to the cast.

The leading actor asked him: 'I'm about to go on holiday; where would you recommend?'

'Why ask me?' Stalin replied coldly.

The actor bravely replied, 'You come from the south; you would know.'

'You should go to Turukhansk,' Stalin said, referring to the desolate place, north of the Arctic Circle, to which the Tsar had exiled him in 1913.

The actor, strangely uncowed, continued his questioning: 'So why did you leave then?'

Stalin said, 'The food went downhill.'

On another occasion, Stalin received the Minister for Cinema, Bolshakov, wearing his gleaming white marshal's uniform. Bolshakov took out his pen to sign a document, but it wasn't working. He shook it, and the ink splattered everywhere, including on Stalin's pristine white jacket. The terrified Bolshakov apologised profusely.

Stalin said nothing and simply left the room.

Bolshakov sat there quivering, so the story goes, for what seemed like the proverbial eternity, and then Stalin suddenly re-entered in a clean jacket.

He looked at his guest and said: 'So you thought I only had one marshal's uniform.'

Stalin liked to make jokes about his power and his kindness. There's a similar binary structure to them all, in which he ironically admits the violence of his rule but then supplies a punchline suggesting his magnanimity ... or vice versa.

Once the opera singer Ivan Kozlovsky, the lead tenor at the Bolshoi 1926–54, was giving one of his many private performances at the Kremlin. Members of the Politburo clamoured for a particular song. Kozlovsky hesitated.

Stalin said, 'Let's not put Comrade Kozlovsky under any pressure, gentlemen; let him sing what he wants.' He paused for a moment and continued, 'And I think he wants to sing Lensky's aria from *Onegin*.'

In December 1944, at the close of the war, the future French president Charles de Gaulle flew to Moscow to sign a treaty with Stalin. At a state banquet, the drunken Soviet leader introduced him to the other guests, the members of the Politburo. He raised his glass to 'Iron' Lazar Kaganovich, whose enforcement of collectivisation in the Ukraine and brutal management of Soviet railroads and heavy industry made him personally responsible for thousands of arrests, deportations and deaths by starvation and execution. 'A brave man,' Stalin said. 'He knows that if the trains do not run on time, we shall shoot him!' Stalin clinked glasses with Kaganovich. He toasted the health of the Quarter-Master General of the Red Army, Khrulev, who had performed logistical miracles in the Second World War. 'He'd better do his best or he'll be hanged for it. That's the way we do things in our country!' Stalin then looked at Novikov, the brilliant Air Force Commander, who helped turn the tide of the war at Stalingrad with innovations such as tank-buster bombs, night fighters and low-level bombing. Stalin said: 'Let's drink to him and if he doesn't do his job properly we'll hang him.' Stalin caught a look of disgust on de Gaulle's face and said to him, 'People say I'm a monster, but as you can see, I make a joke out of it. Maybe I'm not so nasty after all.' Shortly thereafter Novikov was arrested, tortured and sentenced to fifteen years' hard labour.

Many Communist jokes bear a close resemblance to these true anecdotes.

Stalin is giving a speech to an assembly of workers in a big factory. 'The thing we hold most precious in the Soviet Union is a human life,' he says.

Suddenly someone in the audience has a fit of coughing.

'Who is coughing?' bellows Stalin.

Silence.

'Okay, call in the NKVD,' says the dictator.

Stalin's political police, the NKVD, rush in with semi-automatic weapons blazing. Soon only seven men are left standing.

Stalin asks again: 'Who coughed?'

One man raises his hand.

'That's a terrible cold you've got,' says Stalin. 'Take my car and go to hospital.'

Another popular joke went a step further and mocked Stalin's clemency.

A Georgian delegation has come to visit Stalin. They come, they talk with him in his study and they leave.

No sooner have they disappeared down the corridor than Stalin starts looking for his pipe. He opens drawers, moves papers, but he can't find it anywhere. He shouts down the corridor for the head of his political police, Lavrenti Beria. 'Beria,' he says, 'I've lost my pipe. Go after the Georgian delegation and see if you can find if one of them took it.'

Beria bustles off down the corridor. Stalin carries on looking for his pipe. After five minutes he looks under his desk and finds it on the floor. He recalls Beria. 'It's okay,' he says, 'I found my pipe. You can let the Georgians go.'

'It's a little too late for that,' Beria replies. 'Half the delegation admitted they took your pipe and the other half died during questioning.'

In Russia, I was told, a handful of the people who had told these jokes were still alive. I booked a flight to Moscow – Aeroflot of course. Just my luck, the plane turned out to be a clanking Russian-made Tupolev, not one of the airline's new Airbuses. In my Capitalist imagination, the flight seemed bumpier than usual, and the take-off and landing noises more alarming, as if passengers from ex-Communist countries required less soothing than Capitalist ones. I blanked out my anxiety by focusing on a humorological problem: how should one interpret the fact that Stalin cracked the same kind of jokes about himself as his enemies were whispering? The problem was that no one knew which came first, Stalin's cruel jokes, or the jokes about cruel Stalin.

These two scenarios had different implications. If Stalin's repartee came first, it meant that his sense of humour, not just his actions, inspired jokes invented against him. And since he persecuted joke-tellers, that meant, in turn, that Stalin was opposed to, or – to use the language of Marxism – *alienated* from his own sense of humour.

If the reverse was true – that people's jokes came first and Stalin adapted them in his own conversation – another reading was possible. Although I remembered little of the Marxist cultural theory, popular when I went to university in the eighties, this would perhaps be called an appropriation or 'co-opting' of the joke. In those days left-wing professors used to complain that any attempt to critique Capitalism was co-opted by dominant ideology, which meant the state. They typically complained that works of art that were critical of Capitalism were usually sold for large amounts of money. Stalin appeared to be able to do the same thing, standing at the other end of the political spectrum, with the jokes.

By retelling them himself, Stalin was adding a layer of cynicism to the brutality of his regime, which only joking could provide. He indicated that he was not looking for a moral justification for his actions but was celebrating their arbitrariness. The flaw of the Communist joke, as Stalin's wit suggested, was that it was a weapon that could be turned against the person who wielded it.

Hard as I tried, I would never find out which of the two scenarios for Stalin's joke-telling was true, but the fact that the question had arisen had its own meaning. It was an early indication that the dividing line between the humour of the oppressed and that of oppressors had been exaggerated by my predecessors in this field of cultural studies.

*

Under Stalin, a large and distinctive new group of jokes emerged that reflected not only the new social conditions of Stalinism but also the new mood of the people. The age-old genre of gallows humour, in which a person threatened with death and misfortune makes light of his impending doom, achieved an unprecedented scale and depth in the popular Communist jokes of Stalinism.

In 1922 Lenin assigned Stalin an administrative position whose political potential he had overlooked: General Secretary of the Communist Party – in modern corporate parlance, head of human resources for the Bolsheviks. Stalin methodically filled up vacancies in the ever-expanding state apparatus with his supporters. A year later Lenin had a stroke, putting him out of the political picture, and a year after that he died. He was embalmed, the pharaoh of the proletariat, and exhibited in his own mausoleum, where you can still inspect him to this day, prompting the following joke:

For the next four years, Stalin jostled for power with rivals, the best known of whom was Leon Trotsky. In 1927, he engineered Trotsky's expulsion from the Party and sidelined the others. Stalin held power until his death in 1953. At the beginning of his regime, the Soviet Union was still the pluralist society of the New Economic Policy, a collage of booming private businesses and lumbering state factories, of farmers' markets and peasant collectives and, at the political level, of factions and splinter groups inside the Bolshevik monolith. Ten years later the state had a monopoly on all political, economic and cultural power, and on violence. Oral humour followed a similar trajectory. At the beginning of Stalin's rule, there was a chaotic variety of political jokes; by his death these had consolidated into the new homogeneous entity of the Communist joke.

Stalin's solution to the economic backwardness of his country was size, centralisation and Siberia. In 1929, under the slogan of 'The Great Break', he brought to an end the limited free market of the New Economic Policy, and replaced it with a programme of industrialisation and collectivisation, organised in the first of many Five-Year Plans.

As happened under Lenin, the second attempt to create a state-run economy was a disaster. This system was reasonably successful at building big factories, canals or dams (albeit with forced labour), but it couldn't stimulate agriculture or replicate the intricate distribution system of the free market. The results were shortages, poverty and starvation.

Stalin is in his limo, alone with his driver. 'Let me ask you a question,' he says to the chauffeur. 'Tell me honestly, have you become more or less happy since the Revolution?'

'In truth, less happy,' says the driver.

'Why is that?' asks Stalin, his hackles raised.

'Well, before the Revolution I had two suits. Now I only have one.'

'You should be pleased,' says Stalin. 'Don't you know that in Africa they run around completely naked?'

'Really?' the chauffeur replies. 'So how long ago did they have their revolution?'

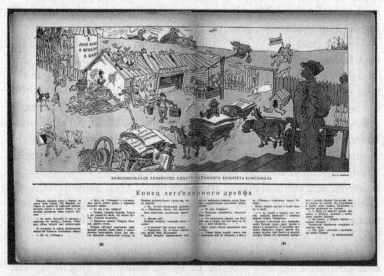

Fig. 8. One of the cartoons published weekly in the *Krokodil* in the 1930s, which idealised life on the collective farm, I. Semenov, 1938

In 1929 Stalin launched a collectivisation campaign, in which, as one party activist put it, 'the last decaying remnant of Capitalist farming must be wiped out at any cost'. The impact of Stalin's social re-engineering is impossible to conceive today. In the first two months of 1930 half of all the Soviet peasants – sixty million people in a hundred thousand villages – were absorbed into collective farms (Fig. 8). The party aimed to destroy the largely imaginary class of rich peasant they called the 'kulak'. They set performance targets: in January 1930 sixty thousand 'malicious kulaks' were to be sent to labour camps and 150,000 other 'kulak' households were to be exiled to northern Siberia, the Urals and Khazakhstan. Two million 'kulaks' were deported in the 'dekulakisation' campaign of 1930–1.

Far from making Soviet agriculture more efficient, the result was a disaster. The number of cattle in the Soviet Union halved between 1928 and 1930. By 1933 famine was affecting half the Soviet population. Three million people starved to death in the Great Famine of the Ukraine, 1932–3. This catastrophic failure of Communist economics was commemorated in the following sardonic jokes:

> One day Stalin is in his office in the Kremlin and notices that there are mice in his study. He complains to President Kalinin about this.
> The President thinks for a moment and then suggests: 'Why don't you put up a sign reading "Collective Farm"? Half the mice will die of hunger and the other half will run away.'

> Two skeletons meet on the streets of Kiev. 'Hey,' says one. 'When did you die?'
> 'In 1932, in the Great Famine,' the other replies. 'How about you?'
> 'Oh I'm still alive, thank God.'
> 'Shhhh! Don't you know that nowadays you can't thank God, you must thank Stalin.'
> 'And what should I do when he dies?'
> 'Then you can thank God.'

The overwhelming majority of the emerging Communist jokes concerned Stalin's Gulag – the system of arrests, imprisonments, deportations, exile and labour camps by which he enforced his programme of change. The Gulag was not a means of law enforcement, it was an all-encompassing economic policy. Collectivisation was enforced through the deportation of peasants to forced-labour and resettlement camps. Stalin's strategy of crash industrialisation relied on a similar procedure, applied to people from all walks of life: the big mineral-extraction projects in Siberia and inside the Arctic Circle were in places far too cold and inhospitable, and the working conditions too uncomfortable, to attract volunteer labour at a price the Soviet state could afford. The solution was to build camps there and send 'kulaks', other 'bourgeois elements' and 'political' prisoners to carry out the work as slaves. This was, as the governor of one camp put it, 'an experimental form of industrial development'. This is how Stalin built industrial cities such as Magnitogorsk and Norilsk, the Moscow–Volga and White Sea canals, the Moscow Metro and the Dneprostoi dam, the largest hydro-electric installation in the world, which was in operation by 1932.

The population of the Gulag rose from twenty thousand in 1928 to one million by 1934, and eventually around eighteen million people were sent there. Another six million were deported or condemned to internal exile in remote parts of the Soviet Union. A flood of jokes ensued that described every aspect of Stalin's police state: the denunciations, arbitrary arrests, atmosphere of mistrust and fear, show trials, imprisonment, deportations, forced labour and Stalin's purges of his own party.

A man knocks on the door of his neighbour's apartment: 'Quick, quick, get up, get dressed.' Inside he hears the screams of fear. 'Don't worry,' he continues, 'it's nothing serious. I'm not the NKVD. I just want to tell you that your flat is on fire.'

A flock of sheep are stopped by frontier guards at the Russo-Finnish border. 'Why do you wish to leave Russia?' the guards ask them.

'It's the NKVD,' reply the terrified sheep. 'Beria's ordered them to arrest all elephants.'

'But you aren't elephants!' the guards point out.

'Try telling that to the NKVD!'

One legendary Terror joke concerned Karl Radek, a leading Communist who fell out and in and out again with Stalin and was eventually sentenced in 1937 for counter-revolution (Fig. 9).

At a concentration camp in Siberia, several inmates are talking with each other about why they are in the camp. One says, 'I am here for saying that Karl Radek was a counter-revolutionary.'

The second says, 'Isn't that interesting? I am here for saying that

he was not a counter-revolutionary.' They turned to the third man and asked, 'What are you here for?'
   He answered: 'I am Karl Radek.'

Born in 1885 in Warsaw, Radek lived in Switzerland in the early years of the century and had contact with Bolshevik émigrés, including Lenin, before the Revolution. After 1917 he joined the Central Committee and became one of Lenin's closest advisers. He had powerful connections to German and Polish Communists and became a leading figure in the Comintern, the Communist International, responsible for fomenting revolution abroad. Radek was in Berlin in 1918–19, encouraging the failed German Communist revolution. Here he tried, unsuccessfully, to convince Rosa Luxemburg that terror, which would one day consume him, was an acceptable way of waging world revolution, 'to make up for lost time'.

More than just the subject of a classic joke, Radek is one of the only individuals credited with inventing Communist jokes, and they show how the experience of Communism was producing a similar, classless sense of humour from the level of ordinary citizens right up to the Soviet leadership. A brilliant and witty journalist, Radek's

articles for *Izvestia* earned him the title 'Megaphone of the Revolution', but that didn't stop him turning his pen on his masters: he renamed Lenin's 'Electrification Plan' the 'Electrifiction Plan'. His verbal repartee was as good as his written material. At one of the first congresses of the Comintern, a delegate asked Radek why there was no one there from the Zulu Communist Party. Radek is said to have replied: 'We couldn't find any Jews prepared to put rings through

Fig. 9. Karl Radek, drawn by Bukharin.

their noses' – a reference to the prominence of Jews in Communist parties, on the one hand and, on the other, to the disappointing attendance at these conferences and the specious claims made for Communism's swift advance across the globe. Radek spoke many languages and translated many of the speeches of foreign delegates at the congresses. A visitor asked him, 'How come you can understand so many languages and translate so fluently?'

'What do you mean?' Radek replied. 'I just know what the people here are allowed to say.'

These lines were transformed into popular jokes. The noses rejoinder, for example, became:

> Why was the African delegation late for the Second International?
> They were just waiting for the black paint to dry on Rabinovich.

Jokes, by their nature, appear to emerge collectively and anonymously, and no more obviously collectively than under Communism; so to be able to point to an author like Radek is an almost unique event. Colleagues from his office testified that he came up with what may be the most definitive *anekdot* of them all.

> What is the definition of Capitalism?
> The exploitation of man by man.
> And what is the definition of Communism?
> The exact opposite.

Radek's political sympathies lay with Trotsky and that spelt his doom, after Lenin's death. At the Twelfth Congress of the Soviet Communist Party, Stalinist loyalist and Soviet General Marshal Voroshilov was at the podium as Trotsky entered, followed by Radek. 'Oh look, here comes the lion, followed by his tail,' Voroshilov sneered.

Radek answered: 'Better to be Trotsky's tail than Stalin's arse.'

Stalin heard about this and when he next met Radek, he asked him if this was one of his jokes.

'Yes,' Radek said. 'But I didn't invent the one about you being the leader of the International Proletariat.'

Reckless Radek became the only person known to have told a Stalin joke to Stalin's face. His line became the template for an evergreen Communist joke told about every leader and in every era.

> A Communist ruler [take your pick] hears that there is one person

who is responsible for 99% of the jokes about him and the Communist system. He summons him for a meeting at his opulent offices. A huge banquet has been laid out. 'One day,' says the leader, 'every Communist citizen will be eating like this.'

'Hey, I thought I was the one who told the jokes,' says the guest.

In 1925 Stalin sidelined Radek, giving him the uninspiring job of rector of a college for Asian Communists. A German Communist, Erich Wollenberg, recalls:

Radek was in discussion with a group of students, when Stalin came to visit the college with some aides. He asked Radek if he was once again spreading new jokes about him.

'No,' Radek said. 'We are speaking at the moment about the redistribution of power after the next coup.'

'And will I end up in jail?' asked Stalin.

'No,' said Radek. 'We have decided to found a Jewish university and make you the rector.' Everyone laughed.

Molotov, Stalin's unofficial second-in-command, stuttered: 'But Comrade Stalin is not a Jew.'

Radek replied: 'Am I Chinese?'

In 1927 Stalin exiled Radek to Siberia with Trotsky. A year later Radek disowned Trotsky and was allowed to return to Moscow. He performed the ritual of public 'self-criticism' in front of an audience of a hundred at the *Izvestia* newspaper offices, obsequiously admitting his 'crimes' against the Revolution. Stalin permitted him once again to write for the newspapers and advise on foreign affairs. But by the mid-thirties Stalin's campaign against Trotsky was reaching new heights; the newspapers were full of denunciations and caricatures. The writer Bulgakov records another of Radek's jokes in his memoirs, from this time.

Trotsky wakes up in the morning.
'How are you?' an assistant asks.
'I don't know,' he says. 'I haven't read the papers yet.'

In 1936 Stalin re-arrested Radek. He was urged once again to confess to being a Trotskyite 'for the sake of the Party'. He held out and eventually Moltshanov, the head of the secret police in Moscow, interrogated him. Radek made him an offer: he would admit that he wanted to murder all the members of the Politburo and crown Hitler in the Kremlin on condition that Moltshanov admitted that he was an accomplice in this plot. If it was so much in the interests of the Party to obtain a confession from him, Radek reasoned, then the party would also be happy to sacrifice a dozen Moltshanovs. Eventually Stalin met Radek himself and a deal was struck. In a theatrical show trial in 1937, Radek admitted he had plotted with Trotsky to overthrow Communism. His life was spared, but only for a few years: he had disappeared without trace by 1942.

From 1917 to 1953, Soviet Communism was one long era of social trauma. Two-thirds of Soviet families contained members who were caught up in the Soviet machinery of punishment. Nevertheless, the average Gulag population at any one time was between only one and two million, which is explained by the swift turnover, thanks to amnesties, the completion of sentences and, annually, thousands of escapes. The Party replenished the Gulag population and kept its power over those outside it, and the leader maintained his position over the Party, by constantly renewed waves of repression. Lenin began with his 'Red Terror', which was mirrored by the other side in the civil war with the 'White Terror', and Stalin continued to arrest and deport hundreds of thousands of people after the end of the Second World War in the lesser-known 'Little Terror'. The Gulag population peaked – at around two and a half million – only in 1952. Nevertheless the Great Terror of 1937 to 1938 was the most terrifying of them all. Stalin turned on his own, conducting large-scale purges of the Party. Ninety per cent of all executions under Stalin took place during the Great Terror – a total calculated by the NKVD at under seven hundred thousand. It was a kind of political cannibalism in which the monster consumed its kind – many of the original generation of camp commanders and senior NKVD officers were killed in these years. Future Soviet leaders Khrushchev and Brezhnev both got their first career break filling the shoes of a Party official who'd been removed. One joke celebrated the speed at which party officials could be promoted and then 'liquidated'.

An international magicians' competition.

An Indian appears. He shows his empty hand: 'Nothing in my hand. Abracadabra!' He waves his clenched hand in the air and opens it – an egg appears. 'Abracadabra!' He closes and opens his fist again and there's a chick. 'Abracadabra! Nothing there.' He opens and closes his hand and it's empty again.

Next up is an American. Following the same routine he produces a lump of steel, a wheel, a model car and then nothing again.

Finally a Soviet magician enters. 'Nothing in my hand now,' he says, following the same trick. 'Abracadabra! A City Committee Secretary! Abracadabra! A Regional Committee Secretary. Abracadabra! A Central Committee Secretary ... and once more! Abracadabra! Nothing there.'

The regime did not claim that this ghastly society was the Communist Utopia, only the forgiveable means to achieve it. Following Marx's description of the evolution of Communism, Lenin, Stalin and their successors developed a present-tense narrative in which the Soviet Union was always *progressing* towards 'full Communism' from Capitalism via various oddly defined transitional phases of Socialism. Stalin claimed to have laid 'the foundations' of Socialism, while Brezhnev later announced 'developed Socialism', and the East German state coined the phrase 'Real-time Socialism' (*Realexistierende Sozialismus*). That's why the word 'Communism' was rarely used by post-war Soviet states. In the official ending of this myth, there would be a society of plenty. Jokers mocked this implausible prediction.

Daddy, have we achieved full Communism or are things going to get a lot worse?

It is a hundred years later. Communism was reached a long time ago. A young boy asks his grandmother what a 'queue' is.

'They used to have queues in Socialism. People would stand in a row one after another, and they gave them butter or sausage.'

'Grandma, what are butter and sausage?'

Once full Communism had been achieved, Soviet theorists promised, there would be no more hunger, money would no longer be necessary, the state would 'wither away' and the police would cease to exist.

Will there still be a police force when we have achieved full Communism?

No, by then people will have learned how to arrest themselves.

The themes of Communist jokes were emerging. The political police and state terror were two; political theory another, and state propaganda a fourth.

Stalin dies and he's not certain whether he wants to go to Heaven or to Hell. He asks for a tour of each. In Heaven, he sees people engaged in quiet prayers and meditation; in Hell people are eating, drinking, dancing and generally having a good time. Stalin opts for Hell. He is led through a series of labyrinths into an area with boiling cauldrons. Several devils grab him. Stalin begins to protest and points out that on his tour he was shown people enjoying themselves.

'That,' replies a devil, 'was just propaganda.'

One group of jokes mocked state slogans. 'Catch Up and Overtake the West' proved particularly vulnerable to sardonic remarks, such as: 'When we catch up, can we stay there?'

The state created its own worker-celebrities, an elite of ultra-productive labourers known as Stakhanovites, after the first one, the miner Aleksei Stakhanov, who dug up a record amount of coal in 1935. The Stakhanovites could be factory workers, teachers or collective-farm workers; what they had in common was that they appeared to have exceeded production targets and set records, though often this image was manufactured by newspaper feature writers or ambitious local officials. The Stakhanovites were given medals, homes and financial privileges, were written up in the papers and attended specific Stakhanovite conferences. Some became members of the Supreme Soviet. The jokes about them bear the hallmarks not only of scepticism but also of jealousy.

An old housewife joins a queue: 'What are they giving out?'
Person in queue: 'A slap in the face.'
Old housewife: 'To everyone? Or just Stakhanovites?'

Another joke concerned the awarding of prizes to Stakhanovite milkmaids. The first gets a radio receiver, the second a gramophone, the third a bicycle. Then comes the fourth, the 'leading pig-tender' of the collective farm. The collective-farm director presents him with the 'Complete Works of Our Beloved Comrade Stalin'.

A voice is heard from the back: 'Just what the bitch deserves.'

If it were a mathematical equation, Stalinism would equal Communism times Nationalism. The internationalism of Leninism was gone, the dream of quickly spreading the faith to the rest of the world abandoned. In its place came a hysterical nationalism that was both messianic and paranoid. It was an easy transition, since Communism was, at this time, confined within the borders of one nation.

The messianic logic ran that since Communism was the world's most advanced political and social system, Russia would now lead the world in every field. As one newspaper explained in 1949: 'It may be seen in the history of mankind how ... the world's languages succeed one another. Latin was the language of antiquity ... French was the language of feudalism. English became the language of imperialism. And if we look into the future, we see the Russian language emerging as the world language of Socialism.'

The meritocracy of Communism, in which the proletariat now received equal educational opportunities, meant that the Soviet Union, so the papers proclaimed, was producing a new generation of scientific geniuses. The best known of these was Timofei Lysenko, a Ukrainian peasant, who attracted attention at the end of the twenties with claims of success planting a pea crop in winter. Beset by famines, the Soviet leadership were susceptible to radical Communist solutions to agricultural problems. Lysenko had them: he condemned the internationally regarded science of genetics as reactionary and sent hundreds of decent Soviet scientists who opposed him to the Gulag, in an agronomic version of the Great Terror. Communist zeal was all that science needed. 'In order to obtain a certain result, you must want to obtain precisely that result; if you want to obtain a certain result, you will obtain it ... I need only such people as will obtain the results I need,' he said. Lysenko rose to become the head of the Academy of Agricultural Sciences, advocating a hotch-potch of esoteric farming methods often based on hybridisation (Fig. 10).

Who invented barbed wire?
Lysenko, who crossed a snake with a hedgehog.

Did you hear that Comrade Lysenko had an accident? He fell off a ladder plucking parsley.

Somewhat contradictorily, but all the more nationalistically, Soviet greatness was backdated to Tsarist Russia: all great technological inventions, including the radio and the steam engine, were shown to be the work of home-grown talent.

Who discovered the electric razor?

It was discovered by Ivan Petrovich Sidorov ... in the dustbin behind the American Embassy.

There were two portraits on the museum wall, one of the scientist Ivanov who invented the locomotive, the steamship and the aeroplane, and the other of scientist Petrov, who invented the scientist Ivanov.

The paranoia worked the other way from the messianism: it was isolationist, not evangelical. The Soviet Union was now a lonely outpost of Communism threatened by – to use the official terminology – 'hostile Capitalist encirclement'. Within the country, numerous foreign 'saboteurs' were hard at work to disrupt economic growth. A worker who accidentally damaged a machine in a factory, or one on whose shift a machine broke down, could be sentenced to hard labour in the Gulag.

Somewhere in Siberia three prisoners are sitting together and they finally get to talking about why they were deported. 'I'm here because I always arrived at the factory five minutes late – so they charged me with sabotage,' says the first one.

'That's strange,' says the second. 'I'm here because I always arrived at work five minutes early, so they convicted me of spying.'

'No,' says the third in surprise. 'I'm here because I kept arriving at the factory on time, every day, and then they found out that I owned a Western watch.'

Stalin's anti-Western campaigns climaxed in a witch hunt against Jewish professors, scientists and researchers, which was brought to an abrupt end only by his death in 1953.

So what was different, if anything, about the new Communist joke that emerged under Stalinism?

This is easy to answer in a couple of ways. There were noticeably more jokes than ever before. The Stalinist journalist Mikhail Kol'tsov, whom we encountered in the previous chapter, wrote about this in one of his satirical columns, 'Ivan Vadimovitch Buries a Comrade', in 1933. The garrulous narrator is walking in a funeral procession and chatting to a friend:

Fig. 10. 'Interruption in an institute of Scientific Research'. W. Litvinenko, *Krokodil*, 1952. Contempt of the regime for conventional agricultural experts is shown in this cartoon from the fifties. Farmyard animals poke their heads through the window at a meeting of scientists, who are holding papers on arcane and irrelevant research subjects: 'The Use of Zebras as Beasts of Burden'. 'The Problems of Rearing Ostriches in the Northern Ukraine'. 'The Qualities of the Hooves of Antelopes'.

Remind me afterwards to tell you the joke about the two Jews who went to see Kalinin [the Soviet President]. Counter-revolutionary, but very funny. Be interesting to find out who thinks up all these jokes ... No, I can't tell you now, there are too many people looking at us. Better on the way back ...

People's laughter also had a distinct motivation. Gulag survivor Lev Razgon was arrested in the Great Terror and spent seventeen years in labour camps. The principal charge against him was having friends who had already been arrested. In his memoirs, he wrote: 'We used every means to disguise our fear, driving it deep within. We joked about it, told funny stories, and in our private conversations "They" appeared not only cruel but also stupid.'

There was one quality, which pre-dated Communism and existed in other jokes, but which came to dominate the Communist ones: the joke-tellers spoke about their *own* plight. Most political jokes in other social systems are told about an *other* – Jews, Arabs, Irishmen. Communist joke-tellers overwhelmingly told jokes about themselves.

Humorological pedants argue that the novelty of Communist jokes under Stalin derived from the novelty of the situations the jokes described, not a new *style* of joking. Admittedly, it's difficult to demonstrate convincingly that different eras have different senses of humour, but sometimes when I recite the jokes aloud in my head I think I detect a new tone: they are dry and cynical, usually pithy (short enough to be whispered quickly) and pitiless. Perhaps you can see a difference between the old and the new if I compare a traditional political joke that was updated for Stalin with an entirely new one. The following *anekdot* has a pedigree that goes back at least as far as the Austro-Hungarian Empire.

Two friends are walking down the street. 'What do you think of Stalin?' the first asks the second.

'I can't tell you here. We have to go somewhere private.' He leads his friend into a side street.

'Now, you can tell me here,' says the first.

'No. It's not safe. Follow me.' They turn into a yard of an apartment block.

'Okay. Here then.'

'No. It's too public. Follow me.' The two friends head down some stairs into the dark basement of the block.

'No one will be able to hear us here. Now here you really can tell me what you think of Stalin.'

'Okay. I quite like him, actually.'

And here is a new joke:

> The Politburo is discussing how to commemorate the anniversary of the October Revolution. Eventually Stalin speaks: 'I propose that the day of the October Anniversary be declared a day of collective flagellation.'
>
> Fellow members of the Politburo are horrified, but too scared to object. On the day of the October Anniversary they assemble in the Kremlin, fearing the worst. Then they hear the hubbub of a crowd, approaching.
>
> An excited security officer enters the room. 'Comrade Stalin,' he says breathlessly, 'a delegation of workers in the arts has broken into the grounds of the Kremlin. They are demanding to be flogged first.'

The Austro-Hungarian joke is endearingly slapstick, but the Stalinist one has an unfeeling cynicism.

The NKVD, Stalin's political police, pursued the joke-tellers. Under the Roman and Chinese emperors, as under Europe's absolutist monarchs, there are plenty of documented cases of writers and orators who were arrested, imprisoned and occasionally executed for lampooning their rulers. When, in the fourth century BC, the Greek King Antigonus offered to pardon the poet Theocritus of Chios if he would 'stand before the eyes of the King' Theocritus, knowing the King had only one eye, responded: 'Well, then, reprieve is impossible.' He was executed for this line. In the third century BC, Sotades of Maroneia told King Ptolemy II Philadelphus (308–246 BCE) that, by marrying his sister, 'he had thrust his dick into an unholy hole'. The King had Sotades sealed inside a leaden jar and dropped into the sea. Caracalla executed thousands of citizens in Alexandria because of the jokes they made about his fratricide. Ovid spent the last years of his life in exile on the Danube because of his satires about Augustus. In eighteenth-century France, Molière was arrested for his jokes; in eighteenth- and nineteenth-century Russia, tsars imprisoned editors of satirical newspapers and sent satirical poets into exile.

But the persecution of joke-tellers under Communism was different on two counts. For the first time since Caracalla, large numbers of ordinary people were imprisoned for telling jokes about their leader. And for the first time ever, people were sentenced and imprisoned for telling jokes *about a political system*, rather than about a head of state. The political police prosecuted joke-tellers under a clause in the criminal code, article 58 paragraph 10, for 'anti-Soviet propaganda'. This covered a spectrum of anti-Soviet utterances, from insults, offhand remarks, curses, cartoons, graffiti, pamphlets and flyers, to jokes. Under this clause it was forbidden to tell jokes, listen to jokes or write them down.

Significant arrests for joke-telling probably began in 1933, when '*anekdot*-telling' is first described as an anti-Soviet activity in the proceedings of the Communist Party at the Central Committee Plenum of January 1933. One ambitious Stalinist zealot and future member of the Central Committee, Matvei Shkiriatov, gave a speech, which presaged the purges of the Great Terror, warning of 'those within our ranks who ... go about clandestinely organising operations against the party'. Among the activities of these unwelcome Communists, he declared,

I would like to speak of one other anti-Party method of operation, namely, the so-called jokes [*anekdoty*]. What are these jokes? Jokes against the Party constitute agitation against the Party. Who among us Bolsheviks does not know how we fought against Tsarism in the old days, how we told jokes in order to undermine the authority of the existing system? ... [Now] this has also been employed as a keen weapon against the Central Committee of the Party.

The arrest of joke-tellers began, and joke-tellers imagined the following logical scenario:

A clerk hears laughing behind the door of a courtroom. He opens the door. At the other end of the room, the judge is sitting on the podium convulsed in laughter.
'What's so funny?' asks the clerk.
'I just heard the funniest joke of my life,' says the judge.
'Tell it to me.'
'I can't.'
'Why not?'
'I just sentenced someone to five years' hard labour for doing that.'

The NKVD's statistics for the 58/10 arrests were not collected in a methodical way, which limits what they reveal about arrests of joke-tellers, but the numbers are shocking. In 1935, three years before the Great Terror, 43,686 people were arrested for 'counter-revolutionary propaganda' or 'anti-Soviet agitation', and there were another 15,122 arrests listed in the category of hooligans and socially dangerous elements. In 1936 and 1937 there are no records specifically for arrests under Clause 58/10, but one might expect similar or higher figures. After the war Stalin's police were still arresting ten to fifteen thousand people a year for 'anti-Soviet propaganda'. In 1949 15,633 people were arrested for anti-Soviet propaganda, of which 5,707 were for oral propaganda. In 1951 3,974 people were arrested for oral propaganda.

Three million files of people sent to Stalin's Gulag lie in Russian state archives, but they were only declassified in 1999 and are so vast that they have not yet been examined. No one knows how many of them specifically mention jokes. I came across only one example, unearthed by archivists in Perm: Ivan Burylov, a bee-keeper, wrote 'comedy' on his Soviet election ballot paper and was sentenced to eight years (Fig. 11).

The absence of documented cases of joke-tellers means that one must rely on personal testimony from Gulag survivors. For a few days

Fig. 11. Ivan Burylov and, right, his defaced ballot paper

I taxied around Moscow to meet a few men in their seventies and eighties who'd been imprisoned in the camps after the Second World

War. They lived alone in little flats in run-down Moscow apartment blocks. The Russian state had never offered much compensation for being sent to the Gulag – in the sixties the standard pay-out was a couple of months' wages at 1938 levels. On the dark-hued walls of the homes of these former slave labourers hung black-and-white photographs of parents and weddings above small shelves of frayed books. They were poor, but spoke with acuity and dignity.

One of them remembered how his mother had witnessed an arrest for a careless aside. She was queuing for fish in the small village where the family had a dacha. 'Why are your anchovies so mangy and smelly?' a woman in the queue asked the fishmonger. Another customer said sarcastically: 'Because they're Stalin's anchovies.' She was denounced and sent to the Gulag.

Another survivor told me he met people in the camps who'd been imprisoned for listening to jokes and not reporting them. There was a classic joke about exactly this crime:

Two Gulag inmates are talking about why they got put away. 'I'm here for laziness,' says one.

'What do you mean? Did you fail to turn up for work?' asks the other.

'No. I was sitting with a friend telling jokes all night, and I thought, at the end, I'll go to bed, I can report him to the police in the morning.'

'And why was that so lazy?'

'He did it the same evening.'

A third survivor met someone in the camps who'd made a joke that took advantage of the fact that Russians use the verb 'to step on' to mean 'to join': in the joke someone asks Rabinovich, 'Have you joined the Communist Party?' He lifts up his foot and looks at the sole of his shoe and says, 'No I haven't stepped in anything.' This joke-teller got ten years.

In the camps themselves, I was told, few people told jokes, because they were full of informers, and no one wanted to risk getting a second sentence.

A new inmate arrives at a prison camp, where the fearful inmates have devised a system of telling a joke by simply stating a number. The new arrival sits down with a group of them in a barrack.

'Forty-three,' says one, and everyone roars with laughter.

'Fifty-seven,' says another, and there is another burst of giggling.

The new inmate joins in. 'Thirty-two,' he says. Silence. No one laughs. 'Thirty-three,' he tries. 'Thirty-four ... Thirty-five.' Still silence.

He looks at his new companions: 'What did I do wrong? Why aren't you laughing?'

'It's nothing personal,' says one to him, 'just the way that you tell them.'

Yet, as I travelled around Moscow recording interviews, I began to learn that joke-telling was not as serious a crime as I had imagined.

Shortly before his death I met Marlen Korallov, one of many former middle-class tradesmen imprisoned in the 1940s on suspicion of economic sabotage. He had been a real political prisoner and he had little time for the idea of my eastern European friends that jokes were a form of resistance. In the camps, he told me, fellow prisoners spoke dismissively of a special category of inmates called *anekdotchniks* who were not considered real 'enemies of the people'. This gave rise to a subgroup of jokes about sentences for joke-telling:

A new convict arrived at a prison camp. The inmates began questioning him about the length of his sentence.

'Twenty-five years,' replied the newcomer.

'What for?'

'Nothing. Didn't do a thing; I am innocent.'

'Don't give us that story. The innocent only get five years.'

A factory worker is sentenced to fifteen years in prison for calling the secretary of the local party an idiot. After the sentence is read out, his lawyer protests that the penal code calls for only a maximum of five years for insults of this kind.

The judge corrects him: 'We didn't sentence the defendant for offending the secretary, but for divulging a state secret.'

My search for clues to the scale of these arrests turned up one more address. One eighty-year-old Russian historian, I was told, once had particular access to Gulag statistics for arrested joke-tellers. I drove to the outskirts of Moscow to meet him. The roads were crowded with Ladas from old Soviet production lines and the 4x4s of the New Russians. Reliefs of hammer-and-sickles on the façades of Stalin-era blocks, a figure of the space hero Yuri Gagarin, atop a fifty-metre column, ads for mobile phones and make-up drifted past. We pulled up outside a blue-painted wooden dacha, the home of Roy Medvedev. The garden was full of apple trees dripping with fruit. He led me into his dimly lit study, lined with uneven, crowded shelves.

After Stalin's death, in 1953, hundreds of thousands of Gulag inmates were released and rehabilitated. Between 1953 and 1962, Medvedev, a conviction Communist, had been given special access to the committee established to oversee this process. Medvedev had been authorised to write a critical biography of Stalin, which was eventually published as *Let History Judge*.

'When rehabilitation began, the first official directive sent by telegram to the camps ordered the release of all the wives and family members of men caught up in the purges. The second carried the simple message to set free all those jailed for *anekdoty*,' said Medvedev. 'As far as I know I was the only person the committee members talked to about these things. They told me they were surprised by the number of people imprisoned for telling anecdotes and said that there were around two hundred thousand of them.'

This figure, Medvedev reminded me, did not include those who would have been arrested for telling jokes but who had previously been released or had died in the camps. But was it a lot, I wondered? I had imagined there would have been many hundreds of thousands of them. After all I knew the joke:

Who dug the White Sea canal?
The right bank was dug by those who told jokes ...
And the left bank?
By those who listened.

I did some quick maths. There were around two and a half million people in the Gulag at the time of Stalin's death – only two hundred thousand of them were jokers. That was a modest 12.5% of people sent to the Gulag. My heart sank. My calibration of Stalinist evil was in millions – twenty-one million deaths for which Stalin was responsible, eighteen million sent to the Gulag ... Surely, if jokes were a significant form of resistance, then millions would have been arrested for them?

Medvedev added another tiny detail: jokes were for beginners – for both sides. Medvedev had a friend who had trained to join the NKVD in the thirties and who had told him how he and his fellow students had been sent on practice assignments to public libraries and smoking rooms and told to hang around and listen if anybody told jokes about Stalin.

What is the difference between Stalin and Roosevelt?
Roosevelt collects the jokes that people tell about him, and Stalin collects the people who tell jokes about him.

Disappointed student of Communist jokes that I was, I was prepared to face up to the facts. I suggested to Medvedev that the small percentage of people imprisoned for telling jokes, and the lightness of the sentences, showed that jokes were not an important crime in Stalin's Russia. But Medvedev corrected me: the reverse was true. The state's repression of joke-tellers was a fundamental part of Stalin's machinery of state terror. It was the first line of transgression between the state and its opponents. It showed that the state would not tolerate even the most casual or light-hearted expression of dissent. The prosecution of joke-tellers was a powerful way for the state to demonstrate to the population its own ruthlessness and all-pervasiveness. Jokes – together with the criminalisation of spreading rumours and cursing Soviet leaders – were the closest Communism got to the Orwellian notion of *thought-crime*.

The state repressed one kind of humour, but it promoted another which had been outlined at the 1934 Writers' Congress. The anonymous Communist joke, critical of the regime, was countered by the

Fig. 12. *Krokodil* cartoon of self-criticism, 1950s. The caption for it ran: 'I think that this criticism is justified and I promise that I will correct my mistakes.' 'But you have promised us that twenty times already.' 'I also consider this criticism justified and will correct this mistake.'

state's own production of wit. Contrary to the urban myth, the Communist machine had comedy in its cogs. The Party cracked jokes, and it did so deliberately and strategically.

Even in this political system without democracy or 'free speech', the state permitted – indeed, it desired – criticism, of a certain kind. The expression of disaffection could take three forms. The first was letters of complaint addressed to newspapers and to politicians, from local Party officials right up to Stalin. Thousands of these letters, effectively denunciations, were posted, drawing attention to supposedly incompetent officials and businesses. The second form of criticism was self-criticism, in which individuals or groups of them would admit their own mistakes in public (Fig. 12). Instead of parliamentary votes, official inquiries or legal evidence, the Soviets relied on this form of confession. This reached its apogee in Stalin's show trials of the mid-thirties, in which leading Party members and military staff were arrested and tortured, and then admitted charges of espionage and sabotage in court. And thirdly there was official humour. Despite the grand-sounding pronouncements of the end of satire at the 1934 Writers' Congress, it survived in certain politically desirable forms. This satire, taking the form of essays and cartoons, was the only possible generalised form of criticism – as opposed to that targeted at individuals. As such it was the most important component of what formed an *ersatz* alternative system to democratic debate.

In the satirical magazines and supplements, many of the categories of the underground jokes were taboo – there were no gags about the leadership, ideology or Party. Instead the official humorists had a set of topics that the underground jokers never bothered with – namely, jokes about Western imperialism and Capitalism, and 'positive satire' – jokes which celebrated the Revolution or

Fig. 13. 'Faulty New World' by L. Gench, 1939. 'There's one drawback about our whole town having been built since the Revolution – we've not got one historic revolutionary spot to celebrate.'

Fig. 14. 'What would it be like if the workers of the clothing factory wore the dresses they were making?'
A cartoon from *Krokodil*, which suggests that the workers would produce better goods, if they were using them themselves.

Underground Joke

A factory manager is showing a group of visiting American businessmen his production line, which is producing metal plates. 'This is our most successful product,' he says. 'In our first year we made 500 units. In our second, 5,000, and in our third 500,000.'

'Wow,' says one American visitor. 'What do you manufacture?'

The manager hands him one of the metal plates.

The visitor flips it over and sees it is a sign bearing the words 'Out of Order!'

An underground joke on the subject of shoddy manufacturing.

sought to improve the behaviour of the workers. These were far more difficult to produce than the unofficial jokes, and the writers and cartoonists should be congratulated for their achievement. Not all the jokes are flat and even the ones that are are beautifully drawn or written.

Alcoholism and the marvel of Soviet construction programmes

were popular subjects for the kind of positive humour that was called for by the 1934 Writers' Congress. In one cartoon, two young Soviet citizens observe the new construction in their town, remarking, 'There's one drawback about our whole town having been built since the Revolution – we've not got one historic revolutionary spot to celebrate.' (Fig. 13) In another a drunk bends over and whispers in the ear of a statue of a discus-thrower, 'Can you direct me to the nearest beer hall?'

The line between state and popular humour was blurred and ever-shifting. There were several topics which they shared. The low quality of goods produced by the state factories was one. Yet, in these cases, the difference emerged in the punchlines. The state-sanctioned

БЕЗВЫХОДНЫЙ ВЫХОДНОЙ

Fig. 15. This is a cartoon about shortages, by the famous trio of cartoonists, the Kukrynitsi, published in *Krokodil* in 1937. The sign outside the café has a list of drinks for sale with everything crossed out except vodka. On the right the cinema has a padlock across it and a sign saying there will be no more screenings until the electricity supply is restored. There was an original text underneath the cartoon which blamed the local officials and denounced one chairman by name. 'As for the town council and its chairman, Comrade Kasatkin, the Kukrynitsi have decided not to draw them because their existence has no effect on the town's life.'

jokes about shoddy manufacturing blame the lazy workers, the popular ones ridicule the dysfunctional economy (Figs. 14 and 16).

There was one area of overlap between the underground and the official humorists that dwarfed all others: the bureaucracy (Fig. 15).

From the 1930s until the end of Communism, official humour publications were crammed with cartoons and satirical essays about Communist bureaucracy. It was a very strategic kind of gag, designed to blame the endemic problems of the system, the shortages in the shops, the corruption in the administration and the deception of the propaganda not on the political leaders but on the people who worked for them.

An endless stream of cartoons and satirical essays was produced about bureaucracy from the thirties through to the eighties, which all

"We grow the tallest corn in the region."

Figs. 16 and 17. (Left) Various groups of people are being given a guided tour of a factory. The implication is that the workers aren't working hard enough. The caption underneath read, 'In the space of five days one textile factory was visited by nursing students, polytechnic students, delegations from various industries from the environs of Moscow and employees of the Society to Assist Aviation and Chemical Defence. The standard excuse for the visits was "sharing the experience".' K. Rotov, *Krokodil*, 1939.

— Товарищи, в работе нашего месткома есть один существенный недостаток: уж очень много мы говорим и мало делаем! Вот об этом давайте подробно поговорим...

Fig. 18. The caption reads: 'Comrades, in our business meetings we are talking too much and doing too little, so let's have a discussion about this.' W. Dobrovolsky, *Krokodil*, 1951.

carried the same thought – that incompetent and dishonest officials and red tape were holding back the Soviet economy (Figs. 17 and 18). The humour about Soviet bureaucracy found its sharpest formulation in 1938 in the hit musical comedy film *Volga, Volga*, directed by Mikhail Romm and starring Igor Ilinsky, one of the most famous actors in the Soviet Union at the time. The film provides a marvellously unforgiving portrait of a provincial bureaucrat, Byalov, whose door bears the brass sign: 'Head of the Manufacturing Department' and who never puts down his briefcase. He manages a small musical-instrument factory in a remote town, but has only one ambition: to rise in the Soviet state apparatus. In the first scene his sycophantic secretary remarks: 'I have been with you for five years now, during which we have changed our place of work over twenty times in an effort to get closer to Moscow and suddenly, when we have only three or four thousand kilometres to go, they take such an extraordinary man as you and put him in this dump.'

A shoddy-goods joke puts in an early appearance when an employee knocks on Byalov's door and complains that the balalaikas they are manufacturing don't have a good tone. 'Listen, comrade,'

Byalov replies: 'This is mass production. We can't check every single instrument. Understand?' As the film begins, the long-awaited invitation to Moscow arrives, but it is not the one Byalov hoped for. Instead he has been requested to bring his most artistically talented workers to the capital for a music-and-dance competition. Against Byalov's best efforts, the workers make it to Moscow, with many an adventure and song-and-dance routine on the way. There they perform an original song written by the heroine of the film, a poor but honest labourer, and win the competition. Just before the credits roll they announce that they will sing a song, which 'contains the message of the story':

> You won't find too many bureaucrats like Byalov
> But sometimes a blockhead like him ends up in charge.
> Laughter is the best defence,
> With laughter you can conquer evil ...

Here is an unmistakeable expression of the Soviet use for humour. Humour, it was recognised as early as the thirties, was the acceptable face of opposition. The state claimed that citizens could improve the system by joking rather than by any other kind of reforming activity. Moreover, it urged its citizens to make light of the problems.

Stalin loved *Volga, Volga*. After it was released in cinemas, the star, Ilinsky, was invited to sing at the Kremlin to celebrate the anniversary of the Bolshevik Revolution. Ilinsky was very nervous while performing because Stalin was sitting in the front row, didn't look at him

Fig. 19. Ilinsky plays Byalov in *Volga, Volga*.

and instead talked throughout in a loud voice, drinking and eating with the others at his table. Ilinksy finished and went to sit down.

Later Stalin got up and started mingling with the other guests. Before long, he came to Ilinsky's table. One of the people at the table was a famous opera singer. Stalin said to her: 'You sing pretty well, but you have to work on your upper C.' He then turned to his aide and said, pointing to Ilinsky: 'Who is this person?'

The aide said: 'The famous actor Igor Ilinsky.'

Stalin replied: 'What's he famous for? I've never heard of him.' Ilinsky turned white.

Stalin's aides explained that Ilinsky played Byalov in *Volga, Volga*. Stalin reacted: 'Ah, Byalov! Why didn't you tell me before?' Stalin turned to Ilinsky, now with a broad smile on his face: 'Comrade Byalov? We bureaucrats, we understand each other, don't we? Enjoy yourself.' He shook Ilinsky's trembling hand and walked off.

Historians of facts like to say that Communism 'tolerated no dissent' or denied 'free speech'. The historian of jokes knows this was not the case. The unofficial jokes show that it is always impossible to eradicate free speech; the official ones show that certain kinds of criticism could be spoken. From the beginning, the battle was not one between jokers and a humourless regime, but between two sides who each had their own kind of tactical jokes and who had both agreed to fight a battle on the terrain of laughter.

In 1934 the unknown author of an essay entitled 'Self Criticism in Soviet Cartoons', published in *New Masses* (1934), wrote:

The first Five-Year Plan turned out a splendid success. If collectivisation has won glorious victories, if industrial production is growing at an unprecedented rate, the ruthless and at times almost savage way in which the Bolsheviks criticise themselves had a great deal to do with it. To take a nation of backward individualist peasants, and mould them within a short time into efficient, cultured, and responsible industrial workers and collective farmers is a colossal task. In this the Soviet writers and artists have played a magnificent part. Cartoons are proving a most powerful weapon in satirising foibles and criticising failures. Small wonder there has been an efflorescence of the art of cartooning in the Soviet Union.

Communist caricature generated a few artists of international

Fig. 20. Left: Boris Efimov holds one of his caricatures of Brezhnev.
Fig. 21. Right: Cartoon by Boris Efimov: an American capitalist counts his money on an abacus made of skulls.

stature, chief among them Boris Efimov. Efimov was one of the greatest cartoonists of the twentieth century (Fig. 20). I met him in his flat on the seventh floor of a sixties modernist Moscow block. His son opened the door and reminded me of the fee. Efimov no longer sketched but did charge $500 an hour for his well-rehearsed interview. He was born in 1900 in Kiev, the second son of a Jewish shoemaker. From an early age Efimov was drawn to caricature – he read the weekly *Satyricon*, one of the best Russian pre-Revolutionary satirical magazines, at school. He studied and copied pictures and sometimes

whole pages from the magazine. Efimov drew his first political caricatures for the Communists in Kiev in the months after the Revolution – 'I drew anyone who wasn't a Red,' he said. Some were published in the army news-sheets.

In 1921, Efimov moved

Fig. 22. Caricature of capitalist by Boris Efimov

to Moscow after his brother, Mikhail Kol'tsov, an editor for *Pravda* whom we encountered in the previous chapter, offered him a job drawing political cartoons. His caricatures of every leading Bolshevik were published, except for one.

'It was popular at the time to draw friendly, harmless cartoons of famous political figures, even those with whom you sympathised,' he told me. 'One day in the office the question of Stalin came up. Should we make a caricature of him? We knew Stalin did not take kindly to jokes, but I was assigned to draw a picture of him. I drew it as any other caricature, emphasising all of Stalin's features to the maximum. It was decided that it was a little risky to publish this without checking first. Advice was sought from Lenin's sister. She looked at the picture

Fig. 23. Above, Fig. 24. Above right, and Fig. 25. Examples of Boris Efimov's anti-Nazi cartoons from the late thirties

without a hint of a smile, said she wasn't sure and sent it on to Stalin's adviser. Two days later it was returned with the annotation "DO NOT PRINT". So it was never published.'

Efimov's first collection of cartoons was published in 1924 and included a foreword by Leon Trotsky. But by the end of the twenties Efimov was portraying Trotsky as a traitor and fascist, in an effort to please Stalin.

In the early thirties, Efimov produced scores of savage cartoons of fat cigar- smoking American Capitalists and Western political leaders (Figs. 21 and 22). One of his cartoons of Chamberlain so outraged the British embassy that they sent a protest note to the Soviet government. From the late 1930s onwards Efimov produced merciless cartoons against the Nazis (Figs 23, 24 and 25).

Then, one day in 1938, Kol'tsov was arrested. Efimov tells the story of how the night after this arrest he packed his rucksack with some warm clothes and waited for the knock on the door. In those days it was rare for one member of a family to be arrested without others suffering a similar fate. 'When they arrested my brother, I prepared myself for my own arrest, since I was as guilty as he. But it never happened. I was left in freedom. For roughly a year and a half I was unemployed. They sacked me from the newspapers and magazines where I worked, because I was the brother of an enemy of the people. But at the same time as my brother's case ended, and he was executed, I was asked to go back to work. It was a gruesome kind of reckoning. I could have refused. I could, out of principle, have said, "No! You killed my brother; I'm not going to work." But they would have sent me to the same place. I had a wife; I had a young son. If I had done that, they would all have died. So I went back to work.'

Stalin saw himself as a man of the arts. He maintained correspondence with many Russian writers, playwrights, poets and artists. He occasionally instructed his political police to spare them from the latest round of arrests. Often he would solicit manuscripts and would make his own pedantic suggestions for improvements. Efimov occasionally got the call and he loves to tell one story of one of his cartoons from 1949, in the early days of the Cold War:

'One day in the late 1940s I got invited to a meeting with Andrei Zhdanov, the Minister of Culture member of the Politburo. He greeted me very cordially, asked me to sit down and said: "This is why we

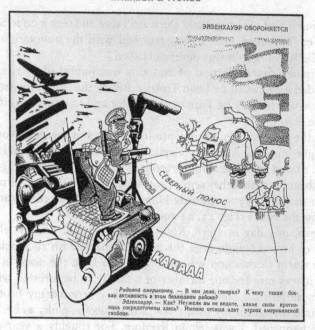

Fig. 26. Caricature of Eisenhower by Boris Efimov (1949)

bothered you. You may well have seen in the press that American military forces are being sent to the Arctic, apparently due to the fact that from there they are being threatened by the Russian menace." I said: "Yes, yes, I have read about it." He said: "So, Comrade Stalin said that we have to fight this situation with laughter. Comrade Stalin remembered you and asked us to discuss with you whether you would be willing to draw a cartoon on this subject." Well, I have to say that when I heard his words about Stalin, "He remembered you," my heart suddenly went cold. To be among those whom Stalin remembered, to be one of those whom he paid attention to – this presented a threat to one's life. It meant that if you made a single mistake, if he was disappointed with you in any way, you would be killed.

'Zhdanov told me exactly how Stalin envisaged this picture: General Eisenhower, with a massive army, is bursting to get into the Arctic. Next to him a common American bystander asks what the problem is. Eisenhower replies: "Can't you see the Russian threat from here?"

'Of course, outwardly, I gave the impression that this was a great honour for me, I was very proud, etc. I simply said: "Could I just ask when you would like this to be done by?" At this point, Zhdanov said: "Well, we are not going to hurry you, but you must not dawdle either ... Good luck." I left and on the way home I tried to figure out what this meant. "We are not going to hurry you, but you must not dawdle either." It meant: if I draw this caricature for tomorrow or the day after, they will say: "He hurried. He did not understand the importance of the task which Comrade Stalin had set him." That would be very dangerous. If I gave them the caricature three or four days later, they might say: "He dawdled. He did not understand the urgency of the task Comrade Stalin had set him. He was negligent." The next day I sat down and by lunch time the whole sketch was almost finished.

'I had to show in a humorous way that the so-called "Russian menace" which Eisenhower perceived didn't exist in reality. I had Eisenhower on a tank, arriving in the Arctic with his army, as Stalin suggested, and I drew an Eskimo's igloo, and next to it, an Eskimo who is looking in disbelief at this terrible American show of force. Next to him there's a little Eskimo boy, who is holding an "Eskimo" ice cream, which were very popular at the time in the Soviet Union (Fig. 26).

'Zhdanov greeted me very warmly in his enormous office, put his arm around me, led me to the big table on which my caricature was lying and he said: "Well then, we've looked it over and there are changes to be made. We have no criticisms of the picture. Some members of the Politburo said that Eisenhower's arse was too exaggerated, but Comrade Stalin did not think this was important. But the changes to the caption underneath have been made in Comrade Stalin's own hand." So I looked down at the text to read it. Next to Eisenhower I had drawn an ordinary American, who was asking him: "General, why is there such an active military presence in this peaceful area?" And Eisenhower answers: "Can't you see that even here we are threatened by the Russian menace? One of our enemies is about to throw a hand grenade at us." I was referring to the little Eskimo who was holding an "Eskimo" ice-cream lolly. Comrade Stalin crossed out the whole sentence about the hand grenade, and instead he wrote: "Can't you see that even here there is a threat to American freedom?"'

After the end of the Second World War, Efimov went on to become the chief editor at Agitprop, and worked with *Pravda* until the eighties. Like everyone else who survived that period and worked for the state, he has some skeletons in his cupboard – in the 1930s he made grotesque caricatures of the accused in the show trials, depicting them as snakes.

I asked Efimov how he felt today about the decades he had spent producing Soviet propaganda. 'In those days, it was better,' he said, giving me the unreformed Communist perspective. 'There was only one propaganda, so people had only one thing to believe. Now people are confused because there are so many different kinds of propaganda coming from so many different sources.'

A third player entered the field of Communist jokes shortly after the end of World War II: the Capitalists.

The West discovered the abundance of Communist jokes, and the repression of them, via a major study, known as *The Project on the Soviet Social Systems*, commissioned by the American government from Harvard's sociology department. Between 1950 and 1951, Harvard University graduates under the leadership of Alex Inkeles and Raymond Bauer, interviewed around six hundred citizens of the Soviet Union who were at the time in refugee camps in Western Europe. The researchers noted with surprise that their interviewees, when asked to describe life in a Communist system, often quoted a joke. They noted five categories: those about Stalin, those critical of the regime or Soviet life in general, ones featuring the NKVD, anti-Semitic jokes and dirty jokes.

The respondents not only told the jokes, but gave explanations about them as well. For instance:

'Why did Lenin always wear shoes, but Stalin wore boots? Because Lenin always walked around puddles while Stalin walked straight through them.' Or: 'Why did Lenin wear a shirt and tie whereas Stalin did not? Because Lenin knew where he was going but Stalin didn't.' The respondent explained: 'People considered Lenin as flexible in politics, while Stalin barged ahead.'

Some of the people who took part in the survey were ex-NKVD. One of them told the famous orphan joke:

A teacher asks his class: 'Who is your mother and who is your father?'

A pupil replies: 'My mother is Russia and my father is Stalin.'
'Very good,' says the teacher. 'And what would you like to be when you grow up?'
'An orphan.'

There were also reports of the punishments handed out to people who told jokes about Stalin. One respondent said: 'I had a friend in Stalingrad who was drunk and walking in the street. He saw a man who looked like a Party worker. He jostled him as he pushed past him and said, "I am in a hurry because I have to fulfil the Five-Year Plan." He was arrested and received a three-year sentence for making fun of the Five-Year Plan.'

Probably inspired by this research, the editors of the weekend magazine supplement of the *New York Times* began to publish small selections of Communist jokes, often collected from refugee camps. The first such collection I found was printed on 2 October 1949. Its author, David Dallin, had been a moderate member of the Moscow Soviet in the early years of the Revolution, before fleeing the threats of the Cheka in 1921. 'During a recent prolonged stay in Western Germany,' he wrote, 'the writer had occasion to meet a considerable number of refugees from the Soviet Union. In the course of many conversations, numerous anti-Soviet anecdotes were told as being current in countries behind the Iron Curtain.' Such as . . .

The peasant back from Moscow, entranced with what he has seen, enlarges on the wonderful progress of the capital. 'Why,' he says, 'there are great buildings there which were built in two or three months. Formerly they would have taken two or three years!'

'That's nothing,' retorts a neighbour; 'look at our cemetery. Once we would have needed fifty years to fill it. Now it will be full in two years.'

'It is still risky to tell jokes in the satellite countries,' begins another newspaper feature, 'Laughter Behind the Iron Curtain', from 2 September 1956, 'but the people's enthusiasm for telling them in many cases outweighs the danger.' Its author Flora Lewis, the 'wife of Sydney Gruson, *New York Times* correspondent in Prague, Czechoslovakia', lists a couple of jokes from different Soviet Bloc countries, observing that there were similar jokes in every country.

An old woman has formed the daily habit of hurrying to the news-

stand early in the morning to get the first copy of Scinteia *[Romanian newspaper]. She buys it, takes a glimpse at the front-page headlines, crumples it up in disgust and tramples on it. She does this every day.*

Finally the newsvendor can no longer restrain his curiosity. 'If you don't want to read the paper, why do you rush down to buy it every morning? Newspapers are expensive.'

'I'm looking for a death notice,' explains the old woman.

'No wonder you never find it, silly old woman,' says the vendor. 'Don't you know death notices are always printed on the back page?'

'Not the one I am looking for,' says the woman. 'It would be on the front page!'

Thus, from the late forties until Ronald Reagan, Communist jokes had an impact not only at home but abroad. The West's interpretation of the significance of these jokes was always the same: 'A bitter humour with a strong sense of irony but no pity ... has served to keep up the spirits of the people during ... Communist rule,' wrote a

Fig. 27. Spot the difference! (Right) The original cartoon published in the Hungarian satirical magazine *Ludas Matyi*, 12 October 1961. The title of the cartoon is: 'Autumn ploughing in the "Negligence Co-operative"'. The caption underneath says: 'The tractor doesn't work but we have to use it anyway.' (Below) The cartoon reprinted and translated in the American journal *East Europe* (Jan/Feb 1962) minus the title caption. Thus a cartoon about the incompetent management of the collective farm is transformed into one that appears to be directed against official policies.

journalist in the *New York Times* magazine in 1956. Occasionally Western journalists reprinted the anti-bureaucratic cartoons in *Krokodil*, under the mistaken impression that they were anti-Soviet.

Sometimes there was not only misunderstanding but also manipulation. The editors twisted or dropped parts of the captions in order to misrepresent the material as anti-Communist. One instance of this occurred a little further on in our timeline, in 1962, when an American journal about Eastern Europe reprinted a Hungarian cartoon in which a tractor is pulled by a horse. 'The tractor doesn't work, but we have to use it anyway,' says the farmer at the wheel. It seems to imply that there are orders from the top forcing this kind of absurd pretence on ordinary citizens. But in the original cartoon published in the Hungarian satirical magazine there was a title caption at the top of the cartoon which implies blame for the instruction to the farm managers – it says 'Autumn ploughing in the "Negligence Co-operative."' (Fig. 27).

In the popular Capitalist imagination the jokes were taken as proof that Communism was stupid and awful and that the people who lived under it thought so too. This, as we shall see, was both a simplification and a misinterpretation. Yet this leaping to conclusions gave the jokes an additional role in the history of Communism: they now played a part in reinforcing the opposition of Western states to Communism. Invented as a counterweight to Soviet propaganda, the jokes became part of the armoury of Capitalist propaganda.

America had to wait another two decades, until June 1978, for the first academic conference on Soviet jokes, held at the Kerman Institute for Advanced Russian studies in Washington. 'Marxism was serious for three minutes and it's been funny ever since,' said Professor Stephen S. Cohen of Princeton.

Stalin was not yet dead, and already I knew I would be humorologically a historical revisionist. The further I progressed along the Soviet timeline, the more my understanding of political humour under Communism diverged from the existing consensus.

They were right about the proliferation and criminalisation of jokes, but the jokers were not fighting an unsmiling regime. Instead there were two sides, each competing with a different kind of humour. At the same time there was not a clear dividing line between them: Stalin laughed at the same kind of jokes as the people he was oppressing. And the Soviet state seemed to think that if people told the right kind of jokes – and this excluded ones about Stalin or the Party – then they might become more accepting of Communism. The idea that the jokes revealed widespread popular opposition to Communism was quite probably a myth spread by organs of American propaganda, with the encouragement of disaffected Soviet émigrés.

Ariane asked me to come down to the studio to help her assemble the larger collages. These new works would form her first solo show in a leading New York gallery. She had white boards, larger than she was, laid out on the cold floor, alongside her grainy magnified photocopies of Communist propaganda.

She lifted up a corner of a large picture showing a gallery full of Social-Realist paintings, empty except for two posed visitors, and began to spray adhesive on the underside.

'What is the difference between Impressionism, Expressionism and Social-Realism?' I asked, adding without waiting for an answer: 'The Impressionists paint what they see; the Expressionists paint how they feel, and the Social-Realists paint what they are told to.'

Ariane gave me a calculatedly blank stare. I saved up my worst Communist jokes for her. She had brought her pile of *Soviet Life* propaganda magazines down to the studio too. Still spraying, she waved at them and asked me: 'Can you see any other images I could use?'

I found a photo story from the seventies about the newly con-structed oil refineries and gasworks in Siberia. A shining grid of silvery steel piping gleamed amidst clouds of white steam.

'These industrial pictures would be good,' I suggested. 'These are the things Putin is using to enrich his cronies, blackmail the West and launch a new Cold War. You know about that?'

She ignored me. She wasn't looking for contemporary relevance. I helped her position some of her own selections onto one of the three-metre-by-two-metre mounts, carefully holding the edges of a flimsy cut-out in which there was a high shot of children standing in a playground, the tarmac of which was covered in chalked equations. It was a story about a maths competition among Soviet schoolchildren.

'Did you hear about the school kids who are tested on maths? The schoolteacher asks the first pupil, "What's two times two?" "Four," the pupil answers. "Try again," says the teacher. "Five," says the pupil. "And again," says the teacher. "Hmmm ... six?" The teacher writes down in his report, "Promising young Communist. Stupid, but is making progress." He asks a second pupil the same question. "Four" is the first answer once again, and "Five" the second answer; but after that the pupil sticks to "Five". The teacher writes down in his report: "Promising young Communist. Stupid, but determined." The teacher puts the question to a third pupil, who answers "Four" resolutely each time. The teacher notes: "Keep this child under observation. He appears to be an intellectual."'

Over the playground of numbers we laid a cut-out of a Soviet space probe in sharp focus, behind it another circle, this time of the blurred Earth. I knew a joke for every hackneyed image in her magazines.

'A Romanian cosmonaut goes to the moon,' I said. 'He leaves a note for his mother on the kitchen table: "Gone to the Moon, back in a week." He comes back and the house is empty. There's a note on the table from his mother: "Gone to buy cheese. Don't know when I'll be back."'

'You shouldn't be so cynical,' she said. 'It makes you less attractive.'

THREE

Nazi Jokes vs Communist Jokes

At 3.15 a.m. on 22 June 1941 Nazi tank-commanders switched on the ignition keys of thousands of Panzers, assembled along the River Bug and rolled into the Soviet Union, just as they did in the Hollywood war movies that used to be on television on Sunday afternoons. As the historical cliché continues, the Germans crushed everything in their path. Soviet tank divisions were decimated, villages were razed to the ground, Jews and civilians were massacred and the Red Army sent into headlong retreat. But there was one other thing the Nazis vanquished that historians have overlooked: Communist jokes. For the next four years, until the Russians occupied central and eastern Europe, Nazi jokes eradicated Communist jokes. I have found only one joke about Communism from this period, and that is significantly only half of its theme:

Trotsky and Lenin are travelling through a small town in Russia. Children run out and greet them with the chant: 'We know who you are! We know who you are!'

'Look,' says Trotsky. 'The Revolution has made us famous. Even children recognise us'

But before Lenin can respond, the children chorus: 'You're Jews, you're Jews.'

The reason for the collapse of Communist jokes is contained in this joke. It wasn't that the Nazi jokes were better equipped, more advanced or had the element of surprise; it was that the Nazis much preferred to tell jokes about the Jews than the Communists. The Communists, meanwhile, fending off the Nazi invasion, stopped telling jokes about themselves and united to make fun of their enemy.

A student of Communist jokes should not be disappointed by the Nazi jokes. Their shortcomings offer the devotee his best arguments against those straight-faced sociologists who consider Communist

94

jokes an unexceptional reversioning of the traditional previously existing body of 'gallows humour' jokes. These academics point out that there is a collection of gags which are repeated by the residents of every and any dictatorship and totalitarian state. Therefore, they say, we can learn very little about Communism from the jokes.

True, there is something generic about jokes that exist between the oppressed and the oppressor, which can be found across history and cultures. Communist jokes were not an entirely new genre, but the humour of Communist oppression was honed and textured into something special, and one way to show that is to compare it with that of its most obvious competitor, a contemporary system of totalitarian rule as brutal if not more brutal, yet lacking the wit. Thanks to the Nazis, we can test the negative thesis on Communist jokes empirically.

The Germans had been telling occasional Nazi jokes since the early thirties. Like Communist jokes, they have fortunately been exhaustively catalogued by historians since the seventies. There are perhaps less than one hundred original Nazi jokes. This indicates the first difference: there were far fewer Nazi jokes. The Third Reich lasted a sixth as long as Soviet Communism – twelve years compared to seventy-two – so logically one might expect a sixth of the jokes, which would add up to around 166–250, but we have around half that figure.

As with Communist jokes, major political events generated political jokes. After the Reichstag was set on fire, in 1933, people made jokes about how the Nazis pretended not to be involved.

On the evening of 27 February, Goering's adjutant rushes into the office of his superior. 'Herr Ministerpraesident,' he says, 'the Reichstag's on fire!'

Goering looks at his watch and shakes his head in amazement: 'Already!'

After the Night of the Long Knives, when Hitler purged the SA, many jokes emerged about the homosexuality of its leader, Ernst Röhm.

Now, at last, people understand what Chief of Staff Ernst Röhm meant when he told young men that there could be an SA officer inside everyone of them.

*

And so the jokes went on, just like the Communist jokes, charting the events of the Third Reich, but with less frequency.

The second obvious difference between the jokes of the two ideologies is quality. For those of us familiar with the enduring wit of Communist jokes, Nazi jokes make unentertaining reading, and I should apologise for the almost sadistic way I am subjecting you to them. However, it would not be right to draw an easy conclusion and blame the German sense of humour – their Communist jokes, as we shall see in the post-war era, were often hilarious. Among the better Nazi ones were those that laughed at the proliferation of medals on Goering's uniform.

Goering's adjutant bursts into the office and tells him of an emergency in the building: 'A pipe has burst in the Air Ministry!'
Goering replies: 'Quick! Bring me my admiral's uniform!'

Goering has attached a diagonal arrow to the front of his uniform underneath all his medals – it says: 'Continued on the reverse.'

A third fundamental difference between the jokes of the Nazis and Communists is *themes*. Communist jokes cover every politically important characteristic of the system; the Nazi jokes avoid them. The Germans did not tell jokes about Hitler's racist ideology; neither the Nazis' bizarre rituals nor their mass meetings were made the subject of jokes. I know of no contemporaneous German joke about the goose step or Hitler's moustache. There were, in fact, astonishingly few gags about Hitler, of which the following is the best known:

Hitler visits a lunatic asylum. The patients give the Hitler salute. As he passes down the line he comes across a man who isn't saluting. 'Why aren't you saluting like the others?' Hitler asks.
'Mein Führer, I'm the nurse,' comes the answer. 'I'm not crazy!'

Until the advent of the Final Solution there were only a couple of concentration-camp jokes, which a Scottish humour analyst, if one existed, would file under 'soft-as-shite'. The stand-up comedian Weiss Ferdl, who occasionally – strange but true – did a warm-up for Hitler, recounted in the mid-thirties how he had 'made a little trip to Dachau. It looked amazing: barbed wire, machine guns, barbed wire, more machine guns and yet more barbed wire. But I'll tell you one thing: if I want to get into the place, I'll find a way.' At first I read this joke as a sarcastic jibe, but I was mistaken: Weiss Ferdl was an enthusiastic member of the Nazi Party, and convicted after the war of collaboration.

On the streets people swapped another camp joke:

Two men meet in a bar. 'Nice to see you free again! How was it in the concentration camp?' asks one.

'Fabulous,' says the other. 'In the morning we had breakfast in bed, fresh coffee, then sport. At lunch, soup, meat and dessert, and then we played parlour games till tea time. There was a little light snack in the evening and afterwards we watched a film.'

The man is amazed: 'Wow. How I was lied to! I just spoke to Meyer the other day, who was also inside, and he told me such tall stories!'

The other nods seriously: 'Yes, they took him away again!'

Only at the end of the war do traces of contempt and bitterness creep into the Nazi jokes. As Allied bombers flattened their cities, Germans joked,

'Tell me, what are you doing after the war?'
'I am taking a trip through Greater Germany.'
'And what are you doing in the afternoon?'

And after the surrender they told the following, one of the few really good ones:

The war is over. Judgement has been handed down. Hitler, Goering and Goebbels are hanging from the gallows. Goering turns to Goebbels and says: 'You see, I always told you this thing would be decided in the air.'

'How time flies when you are enjoying yourself!' Goebbels replies before the noose tightens; 'a thousand years have gone so quickly!'

That is a witty and cynical joke, but it still does not take issue with Nazi ideology, which indicates the most fundamental difference between the two joke cultures. Even if the German population's jokes belatedly came to show contempt for their rulers, they did not collectively attack their ideas or the activities of the repressive state apparatus in their jokes, as the citizens of the Soviet Union did. On the contrary, one of the reasons why there were so few new jokes was that both the regime and its citizens recycled so many of the old ones about the Jews.

'It is unsatisfactory to reduce the humour of the Third Reich to regime-critical whispered jokes,' writes Rudolf Herzog, the latest historian of Nazi humour, who like other humorologists has a bizarre biography, as the former producer of a reality-TV series involving gang heists and as the son of German film director Werner Herzog. 'The majority of the jokes that have a relation to the contemporary moment were totally harmless and had no political direction,' he concludes. So, compared to Communist jokes, the Nazi jokes are sporadic in occurrence, weak in ideological content, poor in quality and patchy in socio-political coverage.

Admittedly Stalin had more social targets than Hitler, who tried to exterminate the Jews but had nothing against landowning farmers, businessmen and Capitalists. Nevertheless, the Nazis sent millions of young German men to their deaths, brought destruction down on most German cities and persecuted intellectuals and journalists who disagreed with them. So it's surprising there weren't more virulently anti-Nazi jokes circulated by native Germans. The dearth of jokes supports the views of those historians who say that much of the German population had Nazi sympathies.

One section of the German population did produce bitterly clever jokes against the Nazis: the Jews. From the early thirties, the illogicalities of Nazi ideology, the violence of their supporters and finally the horrors of their camps were described with dignified irony.

In the jungles of the Congo, Levi and Weinstein meet by chance, each carrying a heavy rucksack on his shoulder. Great joy! 'How are you? What are you doing here?' Levi asks Weinstein.

'I have an ivory workshop in Alexandria and to cheapen the production costs I shoot the elephants myself, and you?' replies Weinstein.

'Very similar – I have a crocodile-leather-goods factory in Port Said and I am here shooting crocodiles. How's our mutual friend Simon?' Levi asks.

'Oy vey! he's a real adventurer. He stayed in Berlin.'

Several storm troopers enter an evangelical church during a Sunday morning service. 'My fellow Germans,' begins their leader, 'I am here in the interests of racial purity. We have tolerated non-Aryans long enough, and must now get rid of them. I am ordering all those here whose fathers are Jews to leave this church at once.'

Several worshippers get up and leave.

'And now I am ordering out all those whose mothers are Jewish.'

At this, the pastor jumps up, takes hold of the crucifix and says, 'Brother, now it's time for you and me to get out.'

Goebbels was touring German schools. At one, he asked the students to call out patriotic slogans.

'Heil Hitler,' shouted one child.

'Very good,' said Goebbels.

'Deutschland über alles,' another called out.

'Excellent. How about a stronger slogan?'

A hand shot up, and Goebbels nodded. 'Our people shall live for ever,' the little boy said.

'Wonderful,' exclaimed Goebbels. 'What is your name, young man?'

'Israel Goldberg.'

Jakob is walking through the park, when he spots his friend Chaim sitting on a bench reading a newspaper. As he gets close he sees that he is actually holding a copy of the anti-Semitic Nazi newspaper Der Sturmer.

'How can you read that, Chaim?' he asks.

'Well,' says Chaim, 'you know what a bad time we are having now. Our businesses are being closed down. We are beaten and kicked in the streets. Our possessions are being seized. But I open the pages of Der Sturmer, and I read that we are still rolling in money and that we control the world!'

Two Jews had a plan to assassinate Hitler. They learned that he drove by a certain corner at noon each day, and they waited for him there with their guns well hidden.

At exactly noon they were ready to shoot, but there was no sign of Hitler. Five minutes later, nothing. Another five minutes went by, but no sign of Hitler. By 12.15 they had started to give up hope.

'My goodness,' said one of the men. 'I hope nothing has happened to him.'

What's the difference between Jewish optimists and Jewish pessimists?

The Jewish pessimists are in exile, while the optimists are in concentration camps.

Scores of Communist jokes were appropriated by opponents of the regime, Jewish and other, who then substituted the name of Hitler for Stalin. Most of the time this was nothing more than plagiarism, but I found one interesting example of a joke whose meaning was altered through this process while the syntax remained identical.

It's late in the war. In a concentration camp two Jews are sentenced to be shot. But on the day of their execution, a guard informs them that the sentence has been changed to death by hanging.

'We are so lucky!' says one Jew to the other. 'They are running out of bullets.'

In this Nazi version, the absence of bullets suggests imminent Allied victory, but in the analogous Communist one it is simply a joke about shortages.

The different ways the two totalitarian ideologies of the last century punished joke-tellers offers further material for comparison. Until recently the historical consensus was that the Nazi state reacted with ruthless brutality against Nazi jokes, indicated by the German term for these kind of gags: *Flüsterwitze* – 'whispered jokes'. A joker, it was said, could reckon on imprisonment in a concentration camp or death, if he was overheard. Yet new research has overturned this view. From 1933 until 1943 Nazi jokers rarely received a prison sentence. One could tell jokes 'freely, publicly and without fear of penalty', writes Rudolf Herzog. The statistics of joke arrests show that in 61% of trials for joke-telling the defendant was let off with a warning. Alcohol was often cited as a mitigating circumstance. In a few isolated cases the accused was fined, and in 22% the jokers were sentenced to prison, but usually with a term of under five months.

It was a somewhat different story with jokes performed in public. German comedians fought dangerous skirmishes with the authorities over what could be joked about on stage and endured similar experiences to their Soviet Bloc counterparts after the war – a mixture of warnings, work bans and short prison sentences. If they were Jewish comedians, their fate was worse.

One circus artist trained his monkeys to give the Nazi salute whenever they saw someone in a uniform. When the Nazis learned about this trick, they threatened to kill the monkeys if they ever did it again. The monkeys quickly desisted. But other comedians were bolder.

In Berlin, Werner Finck, who survived the war, concluded the nightly cabaret show with a political stand-up full of the most oblique anti-Nazi jokes. 'It's strange,' he remarked onstage one night in 1933; 'it's spring but already the leaves are turning brown' – a reference to Hitler's brown-shirted paramilitaries. 'Did you hear about the guy who went to the dentist? The dentist says, "Open your mouth." The man says, "I can't do that. I hardly know you!"' In one sketch, performed just after all state offices were ordered to hang a photograph of Hitler on the wall, Finck's sidekick entered the stage carrying a picture of which the audience could only see the reverse. As he walked on, he almost dropped it. Finck, in mock panic, dived forward and just saved it from crashing to the ground. In another sketch, he went to a tailor to buy a new suit. 'How about something with stripes?' the tailor suggested, referring to the prison uniform of the day. A heckler accused Finck of being a 'Jewboy'. 'No,' he responded, 'I just look that intelligent.' When he spotted Nazi officials in the audience, who'd come to monitor his show, he asked, 'Shall I speak more slowly? Are you following me? Or should I follow you?' In 1935 the Katakomben was closed down and Finck was arrested and sent to a concentration camp for six weeks. Here he performed routines for the inmates, fragments of which have been preserved.

Comrades. We want to cheer you up. Our sense of humour will help us to do that – although we have never experienced humour and the gallows living so close to each other … You will wonder how we can be so cheerful and happy here. Now there's a reason for this, comrades. In Berlin we didn't feel like that. On the contrary, wherever we performed we had an unpleasant feeling in our back. That was the fear of ending up in the camps. And look, now we don't need to be afraid any more. We're already inside.

Several Jewish comics died in Nazi camps, but Finck was luckier – freed at the intercession of one of Goering's mistresses. Within a couple of years he was back performing on another stage in Berlin, until 1939, when he was again forbidden to perform. 'We will eradicate the political joke,' wrote Goebbels in his diary at the time. Unable to leave the country, Finck outsmarted his enemies by volunteering for the army. He served in the war as radio operator on the Western and Eastern Fronts, winning the Iron Cross, Second Class. He also performed comedy for the troops and claims that he was protected from Goebbels by sympathetic officers.

In the later years of the war, after the tide had turned, a small number of people were executed for telling jokes, sentenced by Judge Freisler, a Nazi zealot, who ran the *Volksgerichtshof*, dealing with political crimes against Hitler. In 1943 a war widow and female worker in an armaments factory was arrested for telling the following joke:

> *Hitler and Goering are standing on the Berlin Radio Tower. Hitler says: 'I want to make Berlin happy.'*
> *Goering says: 'Well just jump off the tower.'*

She was tried by Freisler, condemned to death and guillotined. The film star Robert Dorsay was also executed the same year, sentenced by the same court. Among the jokes attributed to him:

> *One day when the Führer visits a town, a group of small girls come to greet him with a bouquet of flowers. One of them stretches out a bouquet of plain green reeds*
> *'What shall I do with that?' Hitler asks.*
> *'Eat it,' the little girl says. 'People say that good times will return only when the Führer is chewing grass.'*

These grim individual cases offer further evidence for the *différence*, as a French post-structuralist might say, of the Communist joke. Unlike the Nazis' mostly lenient treatment of joke-tellers, the Soviet authorities sent tens of thousands of their citizens to the Gulag for this crime. But, although you were much less likely to get hauled up and tried for telling jokes under Hitler than you were under Stalin, if the authorities decided to make an example of you, you could suffer a much nastier fate: there is no known instance of a Soviet citizen being sentenced to death for telling a joke.

This tells us something about the contrast between these two totalitarian ideologies. If one sets aside the Great Terror for a moment, the Communists, it can be said, believed in the possibility of redemption and thought they could save all mankind. Through forced labour, the 'kulak', speculator and joke-teller would be converted to the cause. The Nazis, on the other hand, considered most of mankind beyond repair. So they enforced obedience by making gruesome examples of individuals.

Ariane lived in one of the few unrestored apartment blocks left in Berlin whose old masonry still bore shrapnel damage from the last war.

We cycled past Goering's Air Ministry and the Reichstag with Norman Foster's new glass dome, which preserved the contribution of other Brits to the building's architecture, namely the impact of Allied air attacks. We glided gently downhill, past Eisenman's enormous Holocaust Memorial, a ghostly miniature city of grey concrete. The evening sun reflected off the golden dome of the restored synagogue in Oranienburgerstrasse, which was sometimes visible in the distance between apartment blocks. Its finely polished surface gleamed with the unnatural brightness of historical overcompensation. We were on our way to see a new film, but you could never get away from the war in Berlin.

We parked our bikes near the Philharmonie, bought a couple of tickets and sat down on deckchairs in an open-air cinema in the forecourt of the Museum for Applied Arts. It was a warm summer night. To the right of the screen, rising up in the background, were the thin, illuminated skyscrapers of Potsdamer Platz, a futuristic collection of pinnacles like a back-projection from *Total Recall*. A neon Mercedes logo revolved slowly on top of one building. Berlin was like that – it offered up in the same breath remnants of a shattered history and a low-cost hi-tech lifestyle. The film was by a young German director, barely out of college, already making his second feature, the story of a German student who performs *Zivildienst* – the alternative to compulsory military service – by becoming an assistant in Auschwitz. He is assigned to a cantankerous camp survivor, and a love–hate relationship ensues. It didn't hold my attention. Over fifty years later the Germans were still finding ever more leaden ways to reformulate their discomfort with their Nazi past.

'Once, when I was twelve,' Ariane recalled afterwards, 'I told my family that I was going to visit my grandmother. She lived forty-five kilometres from my home town, near the industrial town of Altenburg. I had a specific question I wanted to ask her – but I didn't tell my parents that.

'"Grandma?" – "Yes my child?" – "Who did you vote for in 1933?" She lowered her magazine and peered over her bifocals and said gruffly: "Hitler."

'I just looked back at her. Then she said several times: "He ruined my life, he ruined my life." I asked: "Why did you vote for him?" "He gave us work," she said. That's all she said: "He gave us work."'

It was a little story, but it explained why Ariane, and so many young Germans like her, have a soft spot for Communism; and it explained why, after the war, out of all the countries occupied by the Soviet Union, Communism got perhaps its warmest reception in East Germany: it was an ideological insurance policy. If Hitler had been English, I might have been a Communist too.

'When the thousand-bomber raids took place – and they targeted Altenburg because it was an industrial centre – my grandma used to walk to the top of a nearby hill with other women and they would look through binoculars to see where the bombs fell, so they could go and loot afterwards,' Ariane remembered, in an attempt to rehabilitate her relative.

Fig. 28. Anti-Hitler collage from *Krokodil*, 1938

I had my own story from that period in history. On my mother's side my family had been Berlin Jews. All of my sixteen great-uncles and great-aunts and my great-grandparents died in the camps – except for the great-grandfather who had a heart attack in 1939.

'Do you think your granny ever told any Nazi jokes?' I asked.

Ariane gave me a half-smile.

So far, we have been talking about jokes inside Germany, but beyond its borders people had plenty of incentive to come up with anti-Nazi jokes. From Hollywood came Charlie Chaplin's *Great Dictator* and Ernst Lubitsch's *To Be or Not To Be*. The BBC broadcast a satirical programme in which the actor Johann Mueller performed daft monologues in a perfect imitation of Hitler's voice. Inside Russia, cartoonists such as Boris Yefimov and the *Kukrynitsi* trio had been hard at work since the early thirties, churning out vicious caricatures of the ranting, bloated Nazi leadership and their cruel, cowardly soldiers (Plate 1, Figs. 29 and 30). But the geography of jokes that will most interest us is the map of Nazi-occupied Europe. A serious comparative study of jokes is more complicated than it looks. It must consider not only jokes told by Germans about the Nazis but also the jokes told by non-Germans living under occupation. We must look ahead, and compare these jokes with the ones which would be told in coming decades in countries that would be occupied by the Soviets.

In Nazi-occupied Europe there were the same ingredients as the societies of the post-war Communist Bloc: an unwelcome occupying force, an alien political ideology, a repressive, often brutal police state, shortages of basic foodstuffs. So did they come up with similar jokes? Well, it depends where you look.

In Norway, invaded by Hitler in April 1940, the answer is no. Here, the jokes, often adaptations from timeless peasant wit, emphasised the superior intelligence of the occupied people, and often climaxed in basic insults.

Do you know the difference between a bucket of manure and a Nazi?
The bucket.

Why is Hitler safest on the toilet?
Because there he has the brown masses right below him.

Figs. 29 and 30. Two cartoons
by the legendary trio of Soviet
cartoonists, the *Kukrynitsi*.
Above, the evil Nazi
leadership is thrown out of the
Soviet satirical magazine
Krokodil and into the dustbin
by its editorial team (1945). On
the right Hitler talks to a
General (1944).

There was a sub-genre of cruel jokes about Norwegian girls who slept with German soldiers:

Why is one only allowed to take pictures of Norwegian girls from the waist up?
Because it's illegal to photograph military targets.

A German asks: 'Are there only stupid women in Norway?'
A Norwegian replies: 'No, only the ones who go out with you Germans.'

There were queues for food but only a few jokes about food shortages:

At a movie theatre they are showing a German propaganda film of a ship unloading cheese and meat at a Norwegian port. A man shouts out: 'They're running the film backwards.'

The international jokes circulating about the war reached Norwegian tongues and ears:

Do you know why Hitler wears a diving suit?
To inspect his fleet.

Hearing that Mussolini's offensive against Greece is failing, Hitler rings him up and asks: 'Won't you be in Athens soon?'
Mussolini answers: 'And I suppose you are calling from London.'

In 1945, the Norwegians asked:

Why has Rommel been recalled to defend Berlin?
Because he is an expert in desert warfare.

Have you heard that the Germans and Russians have become friends? That's why the Russians are following them all the way back to Berlin.

Communist jokes rarely show the superiority of the occupied people; instead they ironically portray their impotence and submissiveness. The cocky Norwegians, on the other hand, told this joke about the occupying Germans:

A German soldier stops a Norwegian on the street and asks the way. The Norwegian feigns ignorance in a haughty tone. Enraged, the officer says, 'You Norwegians treat us as shamelessly as you treat your dogs!'

'But we do not treat our dogs shamelessly,' the Norwegian replies.

But after the war, the eastern Europeans told this joke about Soviet soldiers.

A Czech tells his friend: 'You know what happened to me last night? I came home and found my wife in bed with a Russian officer.'
'What did you do?' asks the friend.
'Tiptoed out, of course. I was lucky: he didn't see me.'

As the Norwegian scholar of Nazi jokes, Kathleen Stokker, observes: 'While the Norwegian material has a predilection for portraying Norwegians delighting in overtly disrespectful replies to Nazi authorities, the humour of the former Communist regimes tends towards almost the exact opposite mechanism of highlighting the individual's terror of expressing any opinion that could possibly be construed as critical of the regime.'

Norway, of course, was never occupied by the Soviets. But if we turn to the jokes told in the Czech Nazi state, we move several steps closer to the Communist joke. Czech jokes about the Nazis were reported to the government-in-exile in London by secret agents. In 1939 one informant wrote to London that the Czechs 'live from jokes and innumerable anecdotes that travel like an avalanche from Prague to the countryside'. In 1944 another informant wrote that 5% of the Czechs were 'downright traitors', while another 20% 'tended to blow with the wind, for financial, personal or family reasons', but the remaining 75% remained opponents of the Nazis, 'instantly identifiable by their smiling faces'. The Prague intellectual Oskar Krejcí collected hundreds of jokes before being arrested by the Gestapo in 1944. 'Our only weapon was the joke,' wrote another collector, Josef Gruss, 'which like a beetle gnawed away at the feeble foundations of that monstrous colossus.'

The jokes the Czechs told about the Nazi occupation were different from the ones they told about Russians, but they share common characteristics. Here at last is a spectrum of jokes that takes on the whole Nazi system. First, its racist ideology:

What should the ideal Nazi look like?
For the protection of the race and in the interests of the nation's

population, he must have as many children as Hitler. He must be racially pure, like Leni Riefenstahl; have a slim, resilient frame, like Goering. He must speak truthfully, like Goebbels; and be true to the cause, like Hess.

Second, the censorship:

Grandma Hanacka enters the tram in Prague with a heavy sack and a suitcase. While stowing her baggage, she does something that no lady in polite company would normally do. The Germans in the car hold their noses in disgust. Granny turns to her Czech fellow-travellers: 'They've shut our mouths, but they can't do the same to our arses.'

Third target: German bureaucracy:

A worker is telling a colleague how he went to a government building in search of the office that will award him a pay rise. When he enters the entrance hall, he finds two doors, one marked 'Germans', a second marked 'Others'. He enters the second. Beyond it lie two more doors, one with a sign reading 'Married', the other with a sign reading 'Single'. He enters the first. Then there are more doors, each marked 'One Child', 'Two Children', and so on. He enters the appropriate door; the adventure continues.

'So what happened?' a co-worker hearing the story asks.

'Nothing,' the worker responds, 'but that's what I call organisation!'

Fourth target, the occupying army:

What is the difference between the Romans and the Germans?

The Romans put hopeless miscreants on the cross. The Germans put crosses [i.e. Iron Crosses, the highest award for bravery] on hopeless miscreants.

As in Soviet-era jokes, the Czechs mocked their own impotent subservience. They daubed anti-Nazi graffiti at the cemetery – 'Czechs arise ... to make room for the Germans' – and they mocked their puppet president, Emil Hácha:

When Hácha was in Berlin, they had to give him something to eat. So he sat next to Goering, who gave him a menu. Hácha took it, gave it a quick glance and asked where he should sign.

Like future Communist jokes, the Czech Nazi jokes feign an acquiescence in the rules of the occupying power. Many jokes concerned the Czech language, which few Germans could understand.

One morning the Czech state's leading Nazi official, Karl Hermann Frank, looks out of his castle window towards the opposite wall and sees painted a slogan in Czech in huge letters. 'Hitler is an ass!' it says – and that much he can understand. Apopleptic with rage the Reichsminister goes straight to the offices of the Czech puppet, President Hácha, and launches into a furious speech about the disloyalty of the Czechs.

Hácha takes his cigar out of his mouth and waves apologetically towards the Nazi: 'These people, these people,' he says. 'How many times do I have to tell them, "Everything in German, everything in German!"'

The similar ambition of Czech Nazi and Soviet Communist jokes shows that the latter were a product of both culture and politics. Central and eastern Europeans, unlike Norwegians, were apparently predisposed to criticise a political system with jokes broadly in the genre of 'gallows humour'. Thus the distinctiveness of the Communist joke was partly the product of historical conditions and partly the product of its geographical context. After the war, different national traditions of humour from central and eastern Europe came together and enriched the Communist joke, which already benefited from the culture of Jewish humour and the Russian *anekdot*. The result was the emergence of a new breed of super-jokes, perhaps the best that had ever existed in history.

If you will permit me to suspend my narrative for a moment, I will tell you about a relevant comparative study of humour, which I came across by chance in an obscure folklore journal. Between September 1987 and June 1988 sociologist Mary Beth Stein conducted 'fieldwork' on both sides of the Berlin Wall, the three-metre-high concrete border erected by the East Germans in 1961 to prevent the exodus of their citizens. Stein was looking for Berlin Wall jokes. She was told many on the Eastern, Soviet side.

Why are the East Berliners dumber than the East Friesians?
They built a wall and placed themselves on the wrong side.

When does a good border guard fire the warning shot?
At the end of the second clip of ammunition.

Why is there no smog alarm in East Berlin when there is one in West Berlin?
Our borders are secure!

Walter Ulbricht, the first Communist leader of East Germany, is sitting in a restaurant. One of the waitresses who serves him flirts with him. Ulbricht is entranced. 'I will grant you one wish,' he says. She thinks and says, 'Then open the Wall for just one day.' Ulbricht winks at her: 'So you just want to be alone with me?'

On the Western side the American sociologist found some political graffiti that used lines from East German jokes. 'Honecker please turn off the lights' is the punchline of an East German joke in which Honecker comes back to East Berlin after a diplomatic visit and discovers that everyone has left the country. He finds only a Post-it note on the door of his office with that line written on it. Another graffito – I am the Berlin–Rostock Motorway. I have been placed here as a result of a management error – comes from the East German joke that the Berlin Wall is actually a new motorway hung up to dry. Other scribbled lines, while not deriving obviously from East German jokes, preserve their spirit. Stein came across a number that imitated German traffic signs: 'Keep the Exit Clear', 'Passage Temporarily Closed', 'Open House Day Tomorrow', 'East German High Jump Training Area'.

But, hard as she tried, Mary Beth Stein heard no jokes about the Berlin Wall in West Berlin. What greater evidence could there be of the peculiarity of the Communist joke than the fact that, when confronted by exactly the same bizarre phenomenon, the Communists invented scores of jokes about it, the Capitalists none?

FOUR

The Soviet Bloc

The Treptower Park War Memorial is the finest Soviet monument of them all. It is located in the suburbs of Berlin in the middle of a large park, so it remains off the tourist trail. Knowledge of it guarantees you entry to the select club of Connoisseurs of Communism.

You enter between two towering constructivist triangles of pink marble, resembling frozen curtains, at the base of which kneel a pair of sculptures of Russian soldiers, double life size. In front of you is an area the size of a football pitch, bisected by pathways. Tens of thousands of Soviet soldiers, who died in the battle for Berlin in spring 1945, are buried here in mass graves, each topped with a neat lawn. A cycle of magnificent marble reliefs describing the Soviet version of World War II lines the edges. At the other end of this rectangular space, in the distance, a giant statue of a Russian soldier, twelve metres high, rises up. He is cradling a baby in his arms and stamping a large swastika underfoot. This is a sledgehammer of a sculpture with an obvious message, and yet – in an effect the Soviets never anticipated – the scale of this sentimental boast generates a wave of disbelief in the onlooker. Pop artists understood and used this principle years later: a small tube of toothpaste or a box of matches means very little, but when it's twenty times life size it becomes a critique of consumer culture. That's why first-time visitors to this landmark can feel not only their eyes opening wide in astonishment but the corners of their mouths turning up in an irrepressible smile of cynicism.

As I walked lopsidedly down the over-large steps into the long sunken arena of the memorial, I spotted the person I had agreed to meet. He was short and had a close but untidy dark beard. This, I thought, was how émigré Hungarian authors of books of Communist jokes were meant to look. Like other early joke-compilers, György

Dalos was a writer of novels himself, best known for *1985*, a sequel to *1984*, published in 1982. This prophetic book anticipated the demise of Communism. It's 1985, the story goes, Big Brother has just died. Oppressive Oceania's air force gets annihilated by democratic Eurasia's. Orwell's Oceanian NKVD, the 'Thought Police', go soft and start promoting reforms that bear an uncanny similarity to Perestroika and Glasnost, and in the happy ending a fairer political system begins to emerge.

'After the Soviets occupied eastern and central Europe, they plastered it with monuments to Lenin, Stalin and their victory, and these inspired many kinds of jokes,' said György. 'For a start, we had monument jokes. You know the famous one about Stalin and the Lenin statue? A monument to Lenin was planned, but no monument could be erected without Stalin's approval. The architect showed him the project plan – a huge statue of Lenin, five times life size. Stalin said, "I think there is something missing. Think a bit more about it." The architect came back with a new project: Lenin, and beside him a young Stalin. Stalin said this was much better but that there was still something unbalanced about the composition. The architect, after careful thought, produced a third version: Stalin, seated and reading one of Lenin's books. "Now that will do," Stalin said.'

The barrage of jokes had begun. From now on, Communist jokes were no longer restricted to their Russian heartlands. The victory of the Red Army in the Great Patriotic War, as the Soviets called World War II, took Communist jokes to a whole new audience. The Communists celebrated their acquisition of half of Europe, but all that territory came at a price: they were also acquiring tens of millions of potential Communist jokers, armed with the rich traditions of humour from central and eastern Europe. The Czechs were known for their surrealist wit, the Romanians for their dry irony, eastern European Jews for their inventiveness and sardonicism, and the Poles, apparently, for their Catholic analogies.

'All the eastern European nations contributed to the superstructure of the Communist joke, yet each had its speciality. The Poles, naturally, told the best religious Communist jokes,' György explained, 'like the one about the party secretary who's talking to a farmer:

'"I've heard that you go to church every day," says the official.'

'"Yes, that's right," says the farmer; "I've been doing it since my childhood."'

'"I have been told," the Party secretary continues, "that each time you kneel in front of the cross and kiss the feet of Jesus."'

'"That's right. It's a Catholic ritual," says the farmer.'

'"But you are a member of the Party. Would you also kiss the feet of the leader of our Party?"'

'"Yes – as long as he was nailed to a crucifix."'

Above all, the occupation produced a whole new genre of Communist jokes that put to use the powerful tradition of racist humour – eastern Europeans could now make Communist jokes about the Russians, and György knew them all.

We walked round the mass graves and looked at the reliefs. One had ranks of Soviet soldiers, arranged in a strong diagonal, rifles drawn, marching west towards Berlin under a flag bearing Lenin's portrait. 'There were many jokes about the "liberation",' György continued. 'Listen to this one from Hungary, which we can date to around April 1945, the month the Russians came in: Two Hungarians are talking to each other as the bombs are falling, and one says to the other, "I had a wonderful dream." "What?" says the other. "That the Germans left and no one arrived." Later we asked ourselves: "What is the proof that Hungary is the biggest country in the world?" – "Because the Russians arrived a decade ago and they are still trying to find their way out." Or years into the occupation: "Why are the Soviets still here? Because they are still trying to find the people who invited them."

'The Poles had their own special joke for the end of the war:

'A German, a Russian and a Pole are sitting drinking tea. Suddenly a genie appears out of the teapot. "I will grant each of you a wish," he says.

'"I would like the Soviet Union to be completely wiped out," the German says.

'"I would like Germany to be razed to the ground," says the Russian.

'They both turn to the Pole, who sighs, "And I would like a nice cup of coffee."'

In the texts on the sides of the reliefs the Russians described themselves as the 'brothers' of the working classes of the countries they occupied. Yet historians estimate that at the same time as the Americans were investing $14 billion in Western Europe in the Marshall Plan, Stalin was extracting the same amount from Eastern

Europe in gold reserves, raw materials, machinery and grossly exploit-
ative trading agreements (Plate 4).

'There was to be fifty years of fraternal greetings and fraternal
jokes,' György continued. 'The granddaddy of these jokes is: Are the
Russians our brothers or our friends? Answer: Our brothers, because
you can choose your friends.'

The reliefs in the official Social-Realist style were beautiful in their
own sentimental way. Aeroplanes and explosions were etched into
the marble, alongside weeping Russian mothers and children, bidding
their soldier sons farewell. Red Army heroes hurled grenades at tanks
crashing through the rubble of Stalingrad or some other bombed-
out Russian city. I was enjoying the artwork so much that I was
disappointed to see that both sides of the memorial had exactly the
same scenes – evidence of the limits of the official imagination. I
expressed my artistic appreciation to György. 'This kind of art inspired
another genre of joke,' he said quickly. 'What's the definition of Social
Realism? A portrait of a leading political personage in a style they
can understand.'

I don't recall every joke György cracked that afternoon. I remember
that one of his favourites was prompted by a relief in which the
German mothers and children greet victorious Red Army soldiers
with flowers and kisses. The joke was about a Soviet literary prize.
The Fraternal Union of International Socialist Writers had announced
a shortlist for the Lenin award for the best book ever written about
elephants. The five entries were: from France, 'The Love Life of the
Elephant'; from the United States, the best-seller 'The Fastest Way to
Become an Elephant'; from England, 'The Elephant and the Empire';
from the Soviet Union, ten volumes, entitled 'Russia is the Motherland
of Elephants'; and from the DDR, 'The East German Elephant: Best
Friend of the Soviet Elephant'.

We approached the towering statue of the soldier erected at
one end of the arena in the same position as a crucifix in a
cathedral.

'The scale of this memorial gives you a sense of how ordinary
people felt dwarfed and overwhelmed by the propaganda. I wanted
to meet you here because I wanted you to get that feeling,' György
told me. 'The jokes were a kind of counter-propaganda. They were a
way to undermine the enormity and uniformity of Soviet propaganda.
Told over decades, they gradually broke down the prestige and moral

authority of the regime. In a sense you could say that Communism was laughed out of existence.'

Laughed out of existence? That was a good turn of phrase. György offered the most extreme formulation of the maximalist position on the jokes I had encountered. He believed the myth, and its corollary – that people risked their freedom to tell jokes. The introduction to his own collection of jokes, *Workers of the World, Forgive Me*, included a couple of abbreviated names of Hungarian students who'd been arrested for telling jokes in the fifties. I asked him if he knew how to contact them.

'No idea. That was a long time ago,' said Dalos. He'd been shown some documents once, but he couldn't remember where or by whom. His tone changed, irritated by my search for proof.

'But did you hear the one about the Soviets giving the Hungarians three hundred thousand pairs of shoes ... to re-heel?' he said.

The jokes were starting to pall, as they always did when I was told more than fifteen in an hour. I faked a look at my watch and said my goodbyes.

'One more fraternal joke – the best,' Dalos offered. I smiled, shook my head and walked slowly away. Behind me, I could hear, fading into the distance:

'A train from Moscow arrives at Warsaw station. A fat man appears at the window. He calls out to a baggage carrier, "Are you a porter?" – "Yes." – "Where are your colleagues?" – "Over there." – "Call them all ... quickly." The Warsaw luggage boy runs to his colleagues. "Boys, there's a Russian who must have loads of cases. He wants us all to help him." All the porters run to the window of the Russian's compartment. "Where's your luggage?" they ask. "What luggage?" says the Russian. "Is this all of you?" – "Yes." – "Well, Comrade Baggage Carriers of Warsaw, as the Chairman of the Moscow Baggage Carriers, I have the pleasure of extending to you Greetings from Moscow."'

Later that evening I learned from my Communist girlfriend that in the DDR, as late as the eighties, East German schoolchildren were set the task of writing an essay in appreciation of the Treptower Monument.

'We had to say how the statue was based on the true story of how a Red Army soldier rescued a small child from the rubble of Berlin,'

Ariane told me. 'It showed how the Soviet soldiers, unlike Capitalist ones, didn't fight for money, but for peace. The children with good memories would add that the soldier was not holding his weapon, yet it remained ready at his side – a sign that he was not an aggressor, but was always ready to defend Socialism. We were asked to write this essay every five years!'

Surely, I thought, that was enough to make one despise the DDR. But Ariane had been an enthusiastic pupil, who, to her parents' shock, had volunteered to join the Russian class, which contained only the children of Party members and wannabe Stasi officers.

My memories of my own school years were different but equally symbolic. I remembered a spelling test at my primary school, aged seven. I was the only pupil who spelt the word 'laugh' right. As a teenager I won a reputation for coming top in German, History and Latin and for making bad jokes in class, which would make everyone groan.

Ariane was making me dinner. She was, in every way, like a walking museum and she still cooked the same food she ate in East Germany, with pride. *Hefeklösse*, East German semolina-like dumplings, were on the menu tonight. They were my favourite – not, of course, because they tasted good, but because they tasted of Communism. They were white and bland with the texture of an old sponge, over which Ariane would pour a warm plum compote.

Sometimes I'd cook my Capitalist food, usually Italian.

'How do you make such a delicious tomato sauce?' she asked once, in a charming tone of amazement.

'I just pour in loads of olive oil,' I said nonchalantly. 'That's the secret. I don't suppose you had a lot of olive oil in the DDR?'

'We didn't have *any*.'

Her shiny, curly, black hair fell forward so that I couldn't see the expression on her face, but it felt like a sad moment. For the first time, I'd pinpointed something that she regretted the DDR didn't have. It didn't bother her to have lived in a state where there was no freedom of speech, but she was upset about having experienced half her life without a decent pasta sauce. I came up behind her and pushed my face into the tangle where her neck would be, and breathed out warm air.

I wanted to cheer her up. 'I know that some things were better in East Germany than in the West,' I said.

'Oh yeah?' she said doubtfully.

'Like the dwarves,' I continued. 'Did you hear about the British dwarf and the East German dwarf who both live on the tenth floor of big apartment blocks. The British dwarf can only reach the button for the eighth floor, so he has to walk up two floors; but the East German dwarf is tall enough to press the twelfth-floor button, so he proudly always gets out there and walks down two floors. And do you know why that is? Because the East Germans have the tallest dwarves in the world!'

Despite the Hungarian joke-collector's lack of leads, I soon found myself on a plane to Budapest, an atrocity tourist in search of the people whose lives had been ruined by the Communist jokes they had told.

I had attempted to get inside several political-police archives in other Eastern European countries, without success. In Romania the files were too poorly organised to be able to find specific jokes cases. In East Germany, the privacy laws presented a catch-22: I needed the permission of the individuals concerned to read their files, yet without seeing the names in the files I couldn't seek permission. In Russia the bureaucracy was so dense, the rules so arcane and the system of favours so costly that I barely tried. In Poland, laws prevented most people from looking at political-police files, to avoid the embarrassing revelations about Catholic bishops and Solidarity activists that are now surfacing. But in Hungary it was different. An archivist offered to look through the files for me, for a modest fee that reflected not only the favourable exchange rates of former Communist countries but also the antiquated respect for serious intellectual enquiry that still persists in central Europe, long after the end of the era in which chain-smoking intellectuals talking about poetry in cafés constituted Communist society's most highly regarded leisure activity.

Unlike Warsaw or Bucharest, Budapest is one of those cities that look as if they never had Communism, and were never meant to. The size of the estates on the edge of town is modest. The few Communist-era buildings in the centre are built in the inconspicuous style of Stalinist classicism. Budapest, with its avenues of neoclassical and art-nouveau palaces, was never bulldozed to make way for apartment blocks. One of its grand buildings houses the archive of the Hungarian political police. I ascended a small stone staircase, opened a door and found myself, Alice-like, on the other side of history. The room was long and thin, with low ceilings. Cheap metal shelving in military grey or green supported brown folders and box files bursting with yellowed paper. Card indexes were dotted with frayed scraps that stuck out and had a year written on them: 1945, 1952, until 1989. This was Hungarian Communism's archive of unhappiness. Between 1948 and 1953 over 10% of the Hungarian population were arrested, prosecuted, imprisoned or deported, some of them for jokes.

I was greeted by a middle-aged blonde female archivist. I couldn't wait for her to show me the files she had found.

By May 1945 the Russians had liberated and occupied Hungary, Poland and most of Czechoslovakia. Within five years these countries, along with Bulgaria, East Germany and Romania became satellite states of Russia, constituting the Soviet Bloc. As the British Foreign Minister Bevin put it, central and eastern Europe were destined to 'exchange one set of crooks for another'.

The Communists gained power in every satellite state with the same diverse set of tactics, which ranged from straightforward democratic participation, through persuasion and manipulation to coercion and execution.

The gradualist road to power of the Hungarian Communists is exemplary. Led by Rakosi, the inventor of 'salami tactics' (which meant getting rid of one's

Fig. 31. 'Please leave your bombs in the waiting room.' Polish *Szpilki* cartoon against Western militarism, 1958 (German reproduction).

enemies slice by slice), they did their best to discredit the agricultural Smallholders' Party as fascists in the aftermath of the war. Nevertheless, the latter still became the largest party in the parliament in the elections of November 1945. The Communists then formed an alliance with the Socialists and voted to expel a handful of Smallholder politicians from parliament. The Smallholders' leader was charged with espionage and exiled to Siberia. The Communists took the key Ministry of the Interior, which allowed them to falsify the results of the next election, though there were limits to what could be achieved: they still ended up with only 22% of the vote, and the Smallholders with 15%. Now the Communists formed a grand alliance of leftist parties, with themselves at the helm, and in May 1949 this unity party polled 95% of the vote. In the new government the other left-wing parties were palmed off with uninfluential positions, like president.

And so it went in every other Soviet Bloc country, except Czechoslovakia, where the Communist Party managed to win a third of the vote in May 1946; but even here a coup was launched in 1948.

The new regimes were carbon copies of Stalin's Russia. Farms were collectivised (except in Poland). Huge industrialisation projects were initiated. Private businesses of any size were nationalised through punitive taxes and penalties. The bureaucracy, with appointments controlled by the Party, was expanded. A powerful political-police

force was recruited. And satirical magazines were set up – *Szpilki* in Poland, *Dikobraz* in Czechoslovakia, *Ludas Matyi* in Hungary, *Eulenspiegel* in Germany – which began to churn out the same anti-Western 'positive humour' as the Soviet *Krokodil*. In the cartoons of the fifties Western leaders were depicted as aggressive Nazis; anthropomorphic warmongering missiles

Fig. 32. How the West writes responses to Soviet suggestions, *Szpilki*, 1950s.

Fig. 33 (above left). Bureaucrat out hunting – 'I report an instance of a hare in the field of vision ... urgently await instructions' (W. Tichanovich, *Krokodil*, 1950s).

Fig. 34 (above right). 'Portrait of a bureaucrat: He hears no evil, sees no evil, speaks no evil' (*Dikobraz*, 1961).

Fig. 35 (left). 'Modern Fairy Tale – The Mermaid' (Y. Ganf, *Krokodil*,1951).

admired themselves vainly in mirrors; young children drowned in floods of violent American magazines and films; doves of peace searched for a place to land in America; and anything that went wrong was the fault of the bureaucrats (Plates 2 and 3; Figs. 31–6).

The editors of these new satirical undertakings faced the same exhausting conundrums as all the other Communist satirists before them. Arnold Mostowicz, the chief editor of *Szpilki*, recalled these early days in an essay in *Szpilki and its Draughtsmen*, an official publication, in 1962:

It has to be said that satire didn't find it easy in the new social

Fig. 36. A cartoon about the violence of American popular culture
and its influence on the young (B. Leo, *Krokodil, circa* 1960)

order and under the new conditions ... What content should satire
have if it is meant to target all shortcomings, all the faults of human
praxis but without targeting the system which is in the process of
formation? What content shall it have to help this system, without
painting it in pretty colours or sweetening reality and thereby losing
that sharpness and uncompromising quality which distinguish true
satire ... Satirists did not find the answers to these questions easily
... Even today, fifteen years later, the answer has not been clearly
formulated. The time of the search for new content and new forms
for satire is not yet over, and the question remains if an end to the
search will ever come in sight.

The cartoons in the satirical magazines weren't the only jokes in town. The blonde archivist pushed a pile of papers in my direction. For the first time I was to see contemporary documentation of Communist joke-tellers and read about their fate.

The archivist spoke quickly and breathlessly, as if she was worried my attention might falter before she'd delivered all the information she had accumulated. Just like their Soviet counterparts, the Hungarian political police did not charge people with telling jokes as such, but with 'anti-Communist propaganda'. They were looking out for opponents of the state, she said, and joke-telling was a convenient way of identifying suspects who hadn't yet committed greater crimes. The majority of the archive's documents relating to jokes come from one Hungarian city, Szeged, but one couldn't draw any conclusions from this. It might suggest that the number of arrests depended mostly on the nervousness of the local political-police chief and his network of informers; on the other hand, many files were destroyed over the years, so the Szeged files might have survived by luck.

'If we look at the period around forty-eight to fifty-three, it was much easier to get rid of a joke-teller using the incitement laws than it was to prove that the young man in question was *persona non grata*, a kulak, a social democrat or the son of an industrialist. Under Hungarian law, he could be prosecuted for incitement if two people or more overheard the joke. But it is also very important to focus on the documents, because in the internment camps many people claimed they were in there for telling jokes, because they didn't want others to know their more serious crimes.'

The file of one Jozsef Ebinger was the first she talked me through. An informer reported to the police on 6 April 1949:

In March 1949 Jozsef Ebinger, who lives in Kubekhaza, came into the pub. After a short while, he turned to me and said: 'What would you say, Mrs Szeles, if one of Rakosi's ears was cut off?' I asked who he meant – 'The Rakosi whose bar has just been closed?' Ebinger said, 'No, I mean Matyas Rakosi, the General Secretary of the Hungarian Communist Party. If one of his ears was cut off he'd look like a chamber pot!'

The political police investigated Ebinger promptly and filed the following report a week later on 12 April, in a process that would be often repeated:

> Jozsef Ebinger, born at Kubekhaza 1924 April 1, father: Jozsef Ebinger, mother: Ilona Reininger, lives Kubekhaza Arpad str 249. His name is registered in our files under 18965/–1948. He owns 31 acres of land, and half a house. He earns 700–800 Forints per month on top of the farm production. Party leaning: he was not a member of any party in the past, after the liberation he worked in the MKP [Communist Party] and the Social Democrat Party but he also joined the Smallholders Party. Later he started a destabilising process among the youth. He is not reliable politically. He has anti-Semitic views and keeps contact with similar 'kulak' elements.

Ebinger was arrested the same day, interrogated and appears to have confessed immediately: 'I confess that at the end of March 1949 I was once in Szeged and heard that joke which I then told someone else. But I can't remember whom I heard it from.'

On 28 April the police handed over their evidence to the prosecutor, 'The People's Court', describing Ebinger's offence: 'Reason: He described one of the leaders of our Party in unfavourable terms in front of four people, in a way designed to arouse contempt from those listening.' In June 1949 the case came to trial. Ebinger was found guilty on 25 June, and here is the text of the original sentence:

> Ebinger (personal data as before) is guilty of the crime of incitement (1946/VII/2), therefore the court sentences him to 2 years imprisonment. The court also bans him from public affairs for 5 years and orders the confiscation of 2 of his 3 properties, and the confiscation of his tractor, if he has one. The defendant is also obliged to pay all the costs to the state treasury.

The court noted: 'The Defendant defended himself by saying that he did not make these statements out of bad will but he was just joking while he was drinking some wine ... [but] the People's Court did not accept the defence because such statements go far beyond jokes.'

Ebinger's lawyer appealed, whereupon the court ruled generously that only one of his properties should be confiscated and that, instead of the ban on participating in public affairs, his political rights would be suspended for ten years.

In the months after Stalin's death, in 1953, the archivist said, the number of arrests for jokes shot up, and there are records of two hundred cases from this period. People may have thought that Stalin's death would bring with it a reduction in the power of the state or perhaps there was a spontaneous outbreak of good humour celebrating his demise. At any rate, this wave of repression took place against a background of unrest across the whole Soviet Bloc. In East Germany four hundred thousand workers went on strike in the 17 June Uprising (Fig. 37). Soviet and East German forces shot three hundred dead on the streets. Several thousand were arrested, fourteen hundred imprisoned and two hundred later executed. Meanwhile, in Russia there were revolts in the labour camps in Siberia and Kazakhstan.

The archivist ran me through some more prosecutions closely following Stalin's death: 'There was a case against someone who thought that it was a bad day because he couldn't go out dancing. Or there is the case of a young man who went into the human-resources

Fig. 37. Vicious East German cartoon by Kurt Poltiniak, depicting the protesters of the 17 June Uprising in Berlin as violent terrorists, armed with American weapons, who are setting fire to themselves (*Eulenspiegel*, 1953)

division and told them that they would be partying that day. When he was asked why, he said that they would discover what had happened – that comrade Stalin had died. And later he joked, also in this company, that when Stalin died, he was embalmed, but when they touched his face, it turned out that he was not really dead, so then the embalmers said that if he was already dead, he should stay dead and hit him in the head with a stone. This young man was sentenced to almost two years in prison and all of his possessions were confiscated.'

Among those arrested were three waiters from the Tisza restaurant in Szeged. Janos Harangozo, aged thirty-three, Pal Kovacs, aged fifty-three, and Laszlo Albertovics, aged forty-nine. Informers reported that the day after Stalin's death, they told eight jokes about him.

One of the waiters, Janos Harangozo, was arrested, on 18 March 1953 and a confession not obtained until 14 July:

> I confess that I have anti-democracy views, as a result of which I have repeatedly spread insulting and gross anti-democracy and anti-Soviet jokes, and made insulting statements about public services. I made disgusting and gross jokes about the death of the leader of the Soviet Union, and made insulting statements when the workers were in deep mourning. Two of my colleagues, Pal Kovacs and Laszlo Albertovics, have similar anti-democracy views to mine, and we jointly and regularly expressed our hopes of regime change to the clients of the restaurant. I confess that by committing the above crimes, I severely hurt the interests of the working people and the laws of the People's Republic. I don't wish to add anything else. I confirm my confession with my signature.

Harangozo got a three-year sentence, and his two colleagues slightly shorter ones.

The political police of Szeged were on the lookout for any anti-Stalinist japes in 1953. Eighteen-year-old Attila Szijarto got one year in prison for drawing a gallows on a Stalin picture. The political police file says: 'In the cultural hall of the workshop, Attila Szijarto abused the picture of one of the leaders of the Soviet Union with graffitti. He did not remove the drawing upon the request of co-workers but kept embellishing it.'

Szijjarto was held in the same cell as Imre Pal, a heating engineer, who, as the records state, on 10, 11 and 12 March 'repeatedly abused ... our democratic leaders' by throwing potato stew over a Stalin statue'. On 19 June 1953, Szijarto and Pal were found 'guilty of the crime of incitement of hatred against the democratic state' and sentenced to a year in a prison for young offenders, a 200 forint fine, and a two-year ban from public affairs.

There was little uniformity to the sentences. Twenty-seven-year-old Sandor Tülkös, for example, was sentenced to three and a half years for asking his friend for a Stalin picture to put up in his toilet. Others got off more lightly. In September 1953 Endre Toth was joking amongst friends. They were talking about how cold the autumn was. 'Never mind,' said Toth, 'it will be warm in Hell because Stalin is already there, and wherever he is things are very hot.' A woman present reported Toth to the state security, but all he got was a knock on the door and a warning.

The joke trials had virtually disappeared by the end of the decade. Hungarian historians of humour, such as György Dalos, think this was part of the effect of the uprising in 1956, which was crushed by Soviet tanks – 'It made the authorities realise that jokes weren't a problem, but people marching on the street was.' Over 2,500 Hungarians and 722 Soviet troops were killed and thousands more were wounded. Following that, the number of joke trials dipped, but there were occasional prosecutions, if a particularly enthusiastic joke-teller was uncovered. One such man was a journalist, Istvan Deli, who was caught up in the sweep following the uprising.

The main charge against Deli was that he had taken part in the 1956 revolution. When police searched his home they found a gun and the earliest known book of Communist jokes, handwritten, inside Eastern Europe. So the prosecutor brought a secondary charge of incitement. The pale-green notebook, held in the Hungarian archive, contains sixteen jokes. On the inside page is Deli's signed confession: 'It was me who wrote these jokes down based on how I heard them. I wrote them down because I liked them, and I told them to some of my acquaintances.' This statement is marked with a stamp authenticating Deli's authorship from the 'Capital Court Handwriting Expert'.

Here are some of Deli's jokes:

An outsider arrives in Soroksar and sees that huge statue bases are being assembled. He asks a local: 'Tell me, whose statues will be placed on these bases?'

'Well, the first will have Rakosi, the second Stalin, the third Mindszenty and the fourth Eisenhower.'

'Well, this is a very strange selection.'

'Yes, but the statues are being erected with public money and the public wish was that, instead of a name, a sentence from the Lord's Prayer would be written on each base so that if someone didn't know these people by their faces, they would still recognise who the statues were of.'

'But how do you do that?'

'Under Rakosi we write: "Our Father,"; on Stalin: "Which art in heaven"; on Mindszenty: "Hallowed be thy name"; and on Eisenhower: "Thy kingdom come."

The simple kosher Jew goes to see the rabbi and tells him, 'Rabbi, the world is in turmoil; they're preparing for a new war. You are so wise, tell me: can we really not avoid war?'

'War? No, there will be no war, my son. But the fight for peace will be so bad that no stone will be left standing.'

Very nasty jokes about Rakosi are being reported and one day he overhears one. He gets very angry and tells his political police to find the person who is spreading the jokes. A little later he gets the report that the joke started off from an old Jew who lives in Dob street 12, and pays people for jokes: 5 forints for a bad joke, 10 forints for a better one, and 20 forints for a very good one. Rakosi immediately gets into a car, drives there and asks the old Jew angrily: 'Tell me, aren't you ashamed to spread such jokes about me – I, who have nine million people's support?' On which the old Jew tells his wife: 'Hey, Suzy, give this man 20 forints!'

A new phenomenon has appeared these days: even party secretaries and cadres are telling reactionary jokes. Do you know why this is?

Why?

Because they want to stay close to the masses.

Rakosi is surprised to learn that the stamps issued for his birthday are not selling. He goes incognito into the Filatelia stamp shop on Stalin Road. 'I'd like to have a 40 filler Rakosi stamp, please.' He is

given the stamp, licks it, sticks it on an envelope and asks the woman:
'Tell me, why aren't these stamps selling?'
  'Because they don't stick.'
  'But this sticks very well.'
  'Yes, but the others are spitting on the other side.'

Delli was treated relatively leniently – his sentence was only ten months, on the grounds that he was a 'mistaken worker'.

I had seen the files, but I wanted to find out if anyone mentioned in them was still alive to interview. I searched phone books and cold-called people with the same names as those listed, but almost everyone arrested for telling jokes seemed to be dead already. Only two names belonged to living people. One of them was the widow of an arrested joke-teller, Gyula Kormos.

She lived in one of those small apartments whose décor hadn't changed for thirty years. The deep-brown veneer of the wooden sideboard, the lace table covers and curtains, the frayed oriental carpet and framed black-and-white photographs of her humorous husband propelled me back in time.

'He told a lot of jokes, because in that era there were a lot of jokes, not like nowadays, when we tell so few,' she began. 'My husband was working at the film studio as an assistant. One time they had hired a load of American cars in for a film and it was the time of the elections, and my husband suggested they drive round town in these cars handing out leaflets saying "Vote for the Communists". But his big mistake was to make a joke at the expense of the famous actor Imre Sos, who was the one who reported him in 1950. One day the actor and his actress girlfriend missed the obligatory ideological training hour, known as a "seminar" after work. My husband said they were probably at a "semen-ar" down by the river. The actor got very angry when he heard about this.

'My husband was charged with being an Enemy of the People's Republic. A few days later the political police came in the morning and deported us to the eastern plain in Konyar.' Mrs Kormos's tears were beginning to flow as she recalled her punishment. 'I was heavily pregnant and because of the shock I gave birth the same day. My baby only weighed two kilograms. My husband took a job as an agricultural labourer. The police knocked on our door every other night in the middle of the night to make sure we hadn't absconded. My child was so weak at six months that a doctor advised me to leave the resettlement village, but the police arrested me when I tried to go, and sent me to an internment camp.'

The couple had to live there for a couple of years, and her husband wasn't allowed to work as a driver until 1956. That year he was allowed back to the film studios. While Mrs Kormos was crying, I found myself calculating: a deportation ... a premature birth ... perhaps a narrowly missed miscarriage. It wasn't the horrific story of persecution I was looking for; I felt ashamed of my disappointment.

'There was such oppression,' the widow said, 'that we had a joke saying that there are three kinds of people in Hungary, the ones who already have been in prison, the ones who are in prison, and those who will be going to prison.'

I managed to track down just one bona fide arrested joke-teller who was still alive. I made the two-hour journey to meet him in a plain, small village outside Budapest. The train trundled in an old-fashioned side-to-side rhythm along unmodernised track. In another apartment with lace, veneer and oriental carpets, Janos Szabo told me how, when he had been at university in the fifties, he and his class had been sent to work in a co-operative picking turnips. All schoolchildren and students across the Soviet Bloc were sent out to help with the harvest, a symbol of the proletarian solidarity of Communist societies. The work was hard and universally unpopular. Szabo joked to his schoolfriends: 'I feel like Moricka; I would like to get a slap from President Truman.' This was a reference to a well-known political joke featuring a regular character in Hungarian humour, a smart-arse kid called Moricka. The joke went:

'*What would you like to have for your birthday, Moricka?*'
'*A slap in the face from President Truman.*'
'*Are you crazy? Why?*'
'*Because then either he would be here or I would be there.*'

Next day young Szabo was called in by the university authorities and informed that he would be expelled. The student parliament had discussed his case and he was charged with 'wanting to invite over President Truman'.

'You can't imagine today how important the jokes were for

us,' he told me; 'they were our way of standing up for ourselves.'

I had finally met face to face a man arrested for telling a Communist joke; yet I felt somewhat unsatisfied. There wasn't the avalanche of cases I had expected. That could be explained away by the destruction of court records. But there was nothing that could alter the fact that Szabo's sentence and those of others like him were relatively lenient. On the return journey to Budapest I took comfort in the thought that my research might lead to a new, more accurate history of the jokes, perhaps equally compelling.

At first sight, it appeared that Stalin's imposition of Communism on central and eastern Europe produced the same kinds of culture of humour as that in 1930s Russia. True, there were some similar kinds of Communist jokes, there were laws against joke-telling and there were organs of official humour, the satirical magazines. The humorous structure of Stalinism was thus replicated in the Soviet Bloc. But there were differences too: there was a prolific new kind of joke, arguably more hostile than any previously existing Soviet genre. It fused the much older tradition of jokes about a foreign *other* with Communist jokes and was directed against the Soviets as an occupying power.

Despite the danger of this new type of humour, the new regimes dealt with the people who expressed this kind of hostile sentiment in a less severe way than Stalin dealt with his own witty critics. Under Stalin, a convicted joke-teller would endure the life-threatening experience of the Gulag; in the fledgling Communist states the punishment was short-term and the sanctions economic and educational. Communism was already beginning its transition from the terrifying to the absurd, via the intermediary stage of the *vindictive*.

The stories of the jokers' arrests and punishments shed a certain light on the day-to-day administration of Communism in central Europe. I had come to Hungary expecting mass arrests and a methodical application of the law by a highly organised, ruthless centralised state. But the evidence of the jokers' arrests was of a haphazard and arbitrary system of small-scale punishments based on the personal predilections of police and judges. The jokers' trials show how unpredictable, not how omnipotent, the state was – scary but not for the reasons that historians generally suggest.

Spoken jokes were one of two kinds of oral humour in the post-war Soviet Bloc. The other was performed jokes – what today we would call stand-up comedy but was then known as cabaret.

Student and occasionally semi-professional cabaret troupes sprang up in the towns of central and eastern Europe. The Rat der Spötter from Leipzig was typical. Today two of its former student comics occupy important positions on the German cultural landscape. Ernst Röhl, born in 1937, contributed for two decades to the German satirical magazine *Eulenspiegel* and authored a dozen funny books both before and after the fall of the Wall. Peter Sodann, born in 1936, is best known in Germany today as the detective Kommissar Bruno Ehrlicher in the German crime series *Tatort*. He has played several roles in East German feature films and, when I met him, he was also still the director of the state theatre in Halle. In 2005 he was ousted because the town mayor found his plays too political.

I met Röhl and Sodann at the latter's theatre complex. I tried to make small talk about the world's most famous Communist playwright Bertholt Brecht, as thick black coffee was served to me in the fluted porcelain espresso cup indigenous to German offices.

Ernst Röhl greeted me with a selection of short and well-timed jokes:

> *One housewife to another: 'I hear there'll be snow tomorrow!'*
> *'Well I'm not queuing for that.'*

> *Why is a banana crooked?*
> *So it can make a big detour around East Germany.*

> *A guy is hopping across Red Square. 'Hey,' a friend calls out, 'have you lost a shoe?'*
> *'No, I found one!'*

'That was always my favourite joke when I was in jail,' he said.

In 1961 Röhl and Sodann both spent a year in prison, nine months of it in solitary confinement, for the Communist jokes they told. Despite this extreme experience they have a sympathy for the old DDR today that goes beyond nostalgia.

'Capitalism today is as bad as Communism was in those days. We East Germans like to say that we will bring down Capitalism in the same way we brought down Communism! I still believe in a Communist society in some form or other, if it's done right,' said Sodann.

He was a short man, with thick grey hair, who expected others to marvel at his achievements. To this end, he led me on a tour of the theatre, waving me through the auditoria and backstage areas at a speed that was calculated to indicate modesty, before walking me up to the roof, so that I could see the various interlinked buildings he lorded over, explaining how he had built it all up from a tiny regional theatre into a multi-stage complex.

Röhl, with his bald head and kind eyes, had exactly the opposite demeanour to that of his former colleague, but shared his politics. 'I think also the historical perspective today is not correct,' he said. 'I can't say that everyone in charge was a criminal. They were utopians with varying degrees of harshness in the means they employed to achieve their goals. Journalists today say proudly how they aren't censored. I don't believe that and I've often asked myself how censorship works today – and the answer is you just pay the journalists €20,000. I just wanted a fair society – not one in which some people have 50 million euros and others have trouble feeding their children.'

It is possible to understand these points of view psychologically, as the stubborn pride of a vanished nation; but the roots go deeper than this. Röhl and Sodann shared the opinion, which I encountered over and again in my travels in eastern Europe and Russia, that Communism could have worked, if it had had a bit more democracy and a bit less coercion. They both still liked the idea of a central government that forced people to share things, and stopped them buying too much or getting too rich. It was anti-materialistic, Christian, eye-of-the-needle stuff – Jesus with coercion. Communism tapped into, and still taps into, the primal New Testament morality of Europe. This attraction was captured in the following joke:

A man dies and goes to Hell. There he discovers that he has a choice: he can go to Capitalist Hell or to Communist Hell. Naturally, he wants to compare the two, so he goes over to Capitalist Hell. There outside the door is the devil, who looks a bit like Ronald Reagan. 'What's it like in there?' asks the visitor.

'Well,' the devil replies, 'in Capitalist Hell they flay you alive, then they boil you in oil and then they cut you up into small pieces with sharp knives.'

'That's terrible!' he gasps. 'I'm going to check out Communist Hell!'

He goes over to Communist Hell, where he discovers a huge queue of people waiting to get in. He waits in line. Eventually he gets to the front and there at the door to Communist Hell is a little old man who looks a bit like Karl Marx.

'I'm still in the free world, Karl,' he says, 'and before I come in, I want to know what it's like in there.'

'In Communist Hell,' says Marx impatiently, 'they flay you alive, then they boil you in oil, and then they cut you up into small pieces with sharp knives.'

'But ... but that's the same as Capitalist Hell!' protests the visitor. 'Why such a long queue?'

'Well,' sighs Marx, 'sometimes we're out of oil, sometimes we don't have knives, sometimes no hot water ...'

Röhl told me, 'The DDR had a special utopian attraction for young people after the end of the war. I thought we could turn it into a sensible country. I had seen some of the benefits of Communism close-up. My father, who hadn't a penny to his name, could suddenly feed his family. I came from a tiny village – in earlier times I would never have been able to go to university. I had reasons for my optimism. If you can't understand that, you can't understand the DDR. In our cabaret group we all agreed that we wanted to improve Communist society through comedy. We didn't want to escape to the West, like so many other people were doing.'

'Instead of Liberty, Equality, Fraternity, we used to say Liberty, Equality, Peppermint Tea!' Sodann added, a nonsensical refrain that asserted the Rat der Spötter's right to deviate from the Party slogans.

Like everyone else, the students inherited and adapted the old Nazi jokes and told them amongst themselves. 'We had this way of measuring the strength of the speeches of the big leaders in Moscow and Berlin,' Ernst Röhl remembers. 'For example, if there was a speech in Moscow by Khrushchev we rated that at ten Khrushches, like you measure electricity. In Berlin, when the East German leader Ulbricht gave a speech, we measured that at thirty Ulbs. We got the idea from an old Nazi joke – people used to talk about the unit of a Goeb, referring of course to the propaganda minister Joseph

Fig. 38. Rat der Spötter cabaret: left, Ernst Röhl, and right, Peter
Sodann, *circa* 1960

Goebbels. A Goeb was the amount of time it took from the beginning
of a speech by Joseph Goebbels until ten thousand radios were turned
off!'

The Rat der Spötter cabaret was set up in 1959 in the faculty for
journalism at Leipzig University (Fig. 38). For a while they were
allowed to perform unimpeded. In 1961 they began writing a new
sketch show, titled *Where the Dog's Buried*, a graphic German expression which describes a place of shame that no one likes to visit. They
meant East Germany. Röhl told me: '*Where the Dog's Buried* is a
metaphor. Our show was set in a cemetery at midnight. The grave-
digger appears and he begins to dig in the earth, looking for the
weaknesses and shortcomings of the DDR. The audience realise this
bit by bit. Ghosts appear and then explain why some people don't
like the DDR. The idea of our show was to explain to the audience
why people were leaving for the West. We wanted to suggest what
needed to be improved in East Germany, so people would stay.'

It never crossed this naïve group of students' minds that the authorities might take offence at the portrayal of their young country as a
canine cemetery. Perhaps they would have got away with it in other
times – Röhl and Sodann certainly think so – but East Germany was
reaching a watershed in its relations with the West. Twenty thousand

East Germans emigrated in June and the same number in July 1961. In August the authorities put up the Berlin Wall.

'Well, we were intending to make this our hardest-hitting show yet,' Sodann admits. 'The political situation was tougher and we were responding to that ...'

'And the Berlin Wall – that reminds me of another joke,' Röhl interrupted. 'It's my favourite joke. A father is sitting at the table with his son and asks him, "How was school?" "Today we wrote an essay about the Anti-Fascist Protection Wall" (which was the official East German term for the Berlin Wall), says the kid. A few days later the father asks his son, "How did you do in that essay?" "We got them back today," says the son, "and I got an A+." "Wow," says Dad. "How did everyone else do?" "I don't know yet – they're still all under arrest."'

Like every other show of the time, *Where the Dog's Buried* had to be previewed in front of a censorship committee, who included representatives of the university administration, youth movement, student unions and Stasi. The lights dimmed and the show began.

Among the sketches is one criticising the requisitioning of materials by the authorities. Two of the actors start dismantling a wall, brick by brick. 'What are you doing?' asks a third. 'We're tearing down the walls of the brick factory!' they reply. 'Why are you doing that? There's a shortage of bricks!' the other responds. 'Exactly,' say the two labourers, continuing with their work. 'That's why we're dismantling the walls!'

In another sketch Sodann is looking for his copy of the official East German newspaper *Neues Deutschland*. 'Maybe my dog's eaten it?' he says, and then reaches down and picks up a big fluffy toy dog. He reaches inside its mouth and pulls out a neatly rolled copy of the Communist Party paper – 'Hmmm, even my dog can't digest it.'

The script was amateurish, but that wasn't why the officials weren't laughing. The sketch that went down worst was one in which a sycophantic Party official, Pumpernickel, answers every question with a banal quotation from the East German President, Walter Ulbricht, 'just to be absolutely on the safe side'. 'People ... people,' the official intones. 'To persuade is a lengthy task. It requires much patience ...' The naïve young students conceived the scene as a criticism of bureaucrats who couldn't think for themselves, but it was easy to misinterpret it as an attack on the Ulbricht personality cult and on the Party line.

The show was greeted at first in silence, but by the end there were roars of outrage and raised fists from the audience. Two days later the entire comedy group was arrested.

You can read the official reports on *Where the Dog's Buried* in the Stasi archives: 'Instead of attacking the militarism of the West German state and flushing out the fifth column inside the Democratic Republic of East Germany,' wrote Jochem Bohme, the First Secretary of the District Administration, 'the show consisted of provocative defamations of the press, workers, Party officials, and youth leaders.' Agent Heinz Werner noted in his report: 'This is what the counter-revolution looks like: disgusting, artificial, totally spineless.'

The government was very nervous about how people would react to the construction of the Wall. Anyone who said anything suspicious was immmediately thrown into jail,' Röhl remembers. 'For a while I shared a cell with a seventeen-year-old who had spread the terrible lie that Khrushchev was a fatso!' Sodann shared his cell with the head of the Leipzig Market Hall. 'He was responsible for providing bananas for every trade fair – tropical fruit to impress the Western visitors. But bananas go off like any fruit and one day he drove a whole lorryload of overripe, rotting bananas to a pig farm. Someone informed on him and he was slung into prison.'

Several members of Rat der Spötter were soon moved into solitary confinement. The Stasi began a lengthy interrogation, in which they questioned the suspects about their 'so-called political jokes' (that was the official terminology since, following Soviet theory, there were no political jokes per se under Socialism). The Stasi were vindictive: Röhl was only told about the birth of his son fourteen days after his wife sent a telegram to the prison.

'You went out of your cell into the interrogation room in which you had to sit on a stool that was screwed into the floor so you couldn't use it as a weapon. You had to put your hands on your knees and then you were asked the strangest questions in the world,' Sodann told me. '"What do you think of the cultural politics of the DDR?" "Wonderful," I'd reply. "But you said the new opera house was bad …?" "Well, I imagined something that looked more modern, not so classical …" "So are you saying the opera house is a nonsensical building?" "No, I just thought it would look different." "Do you think that First Secretary Ulbricht gave the National Prize to the architect because he was stupid?" And then you are trapped, because Ulbricht is never wrong.

'They kept on asking me: What jokes did you tell?' Sodann continued, 'But they didn't need to ask me because they had files from informants quoting examples of the jokes I'd told. Later I read my files and the Stasi had seventy-seven different spies who reported on me.'

Nine months later, on 24 May 1962, a trial was held. The very same day the state issued a judicial decree that granted an amnesty to certain political prisoners. Consequently, people who'd been arrested for telling jokes were released on probation. Röhl and Sodann were convicted but the sentences commuted.

'I never left the DDR,' said Sodann, 'and I never wanted to. I had an interesting life. If you want to have an interesting life, let me give you the following advice: go to the Party Secretary. Say you want to join the Party of Socialist Unity. Let them make you a member and then tell them loudly what you think of everything. Then they will throw you out of the Party. And then you will have an interesting life.'

Röhl was similarly unbitter about his encounter with the violence of the state, despite being banned from university. 'After my release I went to work in an iron foundry. I was at the bottom. I had nothing left to lose. It was a great time. Soon I started writing stories for the official satirical magazine, *Eulenspiegel*.'

I drove my rented Volkswagen Passat up the wide, newly modernised motorway from Berlin to Leipzig. I was traversing one of those virtual landscapes, that French theorists call *non-places*. A grey, green and white combination of grassy verges, farmed forests, chevrons and road signs zipped past. I thought of the narrow two-lane potholed road that would have defined this part of the world under Communism and which Sodann and Röhl would have driven along.

Their empathetic, forgiving attitude to the regime that had imprisoned them made me realise that another revision needed to be made to the historical consensus on the Communist joke – to something that was not, as émigrés and Western academics had described it, exclusively an expression of opposition to Soviet Communism. The humour was more ambivalent and more universal than that. The jokes were also told by people who sympathised with, even romanticised Communism. Perhaps that was where the jokes acquired their tragic quality – the pathos that every great work of art contains. Behind the contempt, frustration and fear lay a note of attraction and forgiveness. However awful Communism was, the ideals and goals behind it never lost their allure.

I thought of Ariane's collages of Soviet propaganda with their layers of optimism and obsolescence, hubris and delusion. The jokes shared something with these works of art: they also contained many possible meanings.

'With my other boyfriends we always had discussions about how to improve the world,' Ariane said to me one morning as we lay in bed.

I imagined the series of handsome young anti-globalisation pro-testers who had once been where I was now, their tousled hair draped across the pillow, running their thin fingers, yellowed from a thousand hand-rolled cigarettes, up and down Ariane's back, while gazing at her with admiring dark eyes. I didn't feel any jealousy. I was enjoying thinking how she and her previous lovers must have competed to come up with ever more naïve ways of making the planet a better place.

'What solutions did you propose?' I asked. 'Getting rid of armies and governments? Back to the land? The abolition of money?'

'Yes, those ideas came up. How would you improve the world, then?' Ariane asked me.

'Maybe not try to improve it,' I said. 'Stop having dreams of big solutions and try to make it work better with a few more little laws. I dunno.'

Ariane was frustrated by my lack of conviction. Communism was all about building Utopias, but trendy Western European theorists now called our age *post-utopian*. Where I came from, a lack of convictions was one of one's most deeply held convictions.

'But how will you end exploitation, poverty, and environmental destruction?'

'Maybe they can't be ended,' I said. When Ariane and I talked politics it always made me think of an episode from an old science-fiction series. I felt that my spaceship had touched down on a remote part of the Earth. My ideas were like a Martian language to her.

'But doesn't it matter to you that the gap between the poor and the rich has been getting wider,' she asked, beginning to sound irritated.

'Oh, inequality is not such a bad thing. It doesn't matter that the gap between the rich and the poor gets bigger, as long as the poor are getting richer, which they are.'

'But don't you feel a sense of outrage at the millions of impoverished migrant workers in China and Asia, filling up the slums of the mega-cities and working in sweatshops to make toys for our children and shoes for our feet?'

'These people are playing catch-up after years of being held back by Communism. Anyway the alternative is that they stay where they came from, trying to keep the family goat alive on a barren hillside.'

I enjoyed watching Ariane's eyes opening wider and wider in astonishment, like a child in a Hollywood movie who opens her toy cupboard and sets eyes on an alien. 'It's really okay, if there are some incredibly rich people in the world' – I was on a roll. 'It's not a big crime. Anyway there's a limit to what you can do with all that money. Once you are flying first class and staying in big hotels and you've bought a yacht, there's nothing to do with it except give it away. Unless you want to buy art.' I zapped her a meaningful look. Her exhibition in New York was only a month away.

'Communists like yourself have never lived so well as they do now under Capitalism,' I concluded.

That was a disproportionate use of force. My belligerent arguments were vaporising our relationship. I asked myself: where had my sense of humour gone?

But it was too late to make jokes now. Ariane said nothing for a while. She was looking away. This was meant to be a conversation between two lovers about the world's problems, but I'd turned it into an ideological bloodbath.

'Sometimes with you, I am worried that I am going to lose my identity,' she said.

How did it look at the time from the other side, from the perspective of the regime? I wanted to know what people in the Party and bureaucracy thought now of the prosecution of joke-tellers in the fifties.

Every former Soviet Bloc country has its own associations of unrepentant Commies, and I arranged to spend an evening with the Hungarian variant – the Janos Kadar Appreciation Society, named after the moderate Communist leader of Hungary from 1956 to 1989. Among the unappealing fixtures on the calendar of this association is a wreath-laying at the Soviet Army Memorial on the anniversary of the Hungarian Uprising, to celebrate the crushing of the 'counter-revolution'. On May Day they set up a stall in the City Park alongside many other groups, where they display a portrait of Kadar, distribute leaflets, and sell T-shirts with their namesake's picture and a line below reading: 'Do you remember me?'

They hold monthly gatherings with guest speakers. The night I attended, the trade-union leader of the Dorog Coal Mine was speaking about the history of Hungarian mining, which had apparently been run down by post-Communist governments. I wanted to find out how the members of this society defended the persecution of joke-tellers, but as their guest it would have been rude not first to give them the chance to correct the historical misconceptions that Capitalists such as myself entertained about Hungarian post-war history.

'In 1945 Hungary was called the country of three million beggars,' said Attila Moravcszik, a former member of the leadership of the Hungarian Communist youth organisation and President of the Kadar Society. He was smiling benignly and speaking in a sweet tone, like a father to a ten-year-old son. 'There were eight million people living in Hungary then – Hitler had not given back some territories yet – and three million of them were starving and begging. This is what has to be understood, and then it will be clear why people chose the kinds of lives they did. Here, in Budapest, we were sharing a two-room flat with a kitchen with another family, we had never met before. There was no electricity in Budapest and we had to use a petroleum lamp, and this was only sixty years ago.'

The thrust was that the Communists brought prosperity and development to the lucky Hungarians. Attila introduced me to a severe-looking woman with tightly bound, wiry grey hair, Margit Forizs, an agrochemical engineer. 'People keep talking about all these Communist detention camps and all this persecution, and, of course, there were things like that too,' she said; 'but, considering the size of population of the country, this stuff only affected an insignificant minority.'

Then they both started on the Hungarian Uprising. 'The Russians only invaded in 1956 to save Socialism... The counter-revolutionaries had drawn up death lists with the names of leading Communists...'

My stomach turned. The unblinking brazenness with which these former Communists recited their mantra impressed me – not because of the strength of the arguments but because it had changed so little in three decades. I was familiar with their shortlist of excuses and their rhetorical style, one combining relativism and sentimental personal narrative. I had heard it so often as a teenager in interviews with apparatchiks on documentaries about the Soviet Bloc in the eighties. The responses were so uniform that the script had probably once been written for them by Moscow. I looked out of the window and tried to peer into the reflective windows of a nondescript office block opposite. I imagined it was home to a marketing firm run by young people in Adidas trainers. They were busy developing a campaign for a soft-drink brand for a country that was now a member of the European Union. My eyes returned to my interlocutors. These people are history, I thought. They asked: Didn't I remember McCarthyism, Vietnam, Agent Orange … ?

The old crimes-of-America ploy. They'd had their say; now it was time for me to try to fight back with the weapons used in days of old.

'What is your opinion? Were the Soviets your friends or your brothers?' I asked the representatives of the Janos Kadar Appreciation Society, citing the legendary joke. 'Answer: our brothers, because you can choose your friends.'

I emitted a loud, phony belly laugh, designed to irritate them. They didn't waver, but responded with a superbly pitched, condescending half-smile.

'Oh, we had lots of jokes like that,' said Karoly Krisko, whose sinister CV lists only one employer: he had been an agent for the Ministry of the Interior, from 1957, aged nineteen, until retirement. 'I will tell you another one: In the Warsaw Pact, a Hungarian and a Soviet soldier are digging a trench. The Hungarian's spade gets stuck in something, and he says, "Come on, Ivan, let's look at what's here." It is a box full of gold. The Russian says, "We'll share it fairly." The Hungarian replies, "No, Ivan. It'll be fifty-fifty." Nobody was punished for telling this joke, of course.'

I persisted: 'So were the Russians your brothers or your friends?'

They contradicted the famous joke. One said: 'In my estimation, yes, they were friends. I remember they arrived in a tank in the town where I lived ten or fourteen kilometres from Budapest and they brought wine in a bucket for my brother, who was a year younger than me and very scared of them. This is true, and not a joke. They saved us from the Germans.'

The jokes weren't working – yet. I attempted to increase the pressure with scatological humour. 'Do you know why,' I asked, 'despite the shortages under Communism, Hungarian toilet paper was always two-ply? . . . Because they had to send a copy of everything they did to Moscow.'

'Oh, yes,' came the disconcertingly enthusiastic reply, 'and there was one that went: Why can't we overtake Capitalism? Because then they would see that our bottoms are hanging out of our trousers. We knew these obvious jokes, but they weren't important. We took them as a joke. We heard them, we smiled, we carried on.'

'Why do you think there were so many political jokes in Hungary?' I asked.

'Because they were good times. We had no problems, neither political nor existential, so people invented jokes. Try to find a good joke nowadays.'

These people were real pros as far as the Western media were concerned. I thought of another tack. I asked the former Ministry of the Interior agent: 'Did you tell jokes to the people you interrogated?'

'Yes – to create a good atmosphere and to establish a relationship. We offered them cigarettes, and if they complained that the food was not good enough in the prison, we gave them some of ours. Often the convicts – I mean, suspects – told jokes to us. And we laughed at them too, because in that situation we had no reason to be angry. They told us jokes, and we liked them; this is the truth. Even police jokes . . .'

Time to go for the object of their veneration. I adapted an old Hitler joke into one about Kadar. 'So, Janos Kadar is sailing on a lake. He falls in and starts to drown. A peasant sees that he is in trouble and saves him. Kadar says, "I'm Janos Kadar; you saved my life. You can ask for anything as a reward." The peasant says, "Please, do only one thing: don't tell anyone that I saved your life."'

'Don't know that one,' said one of them. 'Me neither,' chipped in a second.

It had always been difficult to argue with Communists, and twenty years after the Cold War ended, I hadn't thought up any clever new ways of catching them out. Then I realised that, in all the obfuscation, I'd forgotten to mention the files of those sentenced for telling jokes. I told them about Janos Szabo, the old man I had met who had been thrown out of university for making the Truman joke.

'The Soviet Union had a great authority, and to joke in such a way about this authority – it showed this person was not a follower of the system,' said the female agro-economist. 'So why should he have been allowed to go to the Socialist university? Why should he study for free? Why should he be allowed to become an intellectual if he is not willing to serve the system that paid for his studies?'

At that piece of sophistry I found myself unable to suppress a cynical snort of laughter. My reaction was in itself meaningful. It answered anew the question: why the jokes?

The voices of my interviewees faded into the distance and everything went into slow motion, as I had a sudden revelation. There was a hypnotic logic to the agro-economist's answer. Since the Party wasn't elected, and since it controlled all educational opportunities, anyone who got an education had the Party to thank for it. There was a counter-argument – that Hungarian citizens funded the education system through taxation – but what was the point of flattering the absurdity of the reasoning of the state with debate?

That's where the jokes – at least some of them – came in. Instead of trying to argue with a Soviet absurdity, people came up with another absurdity. Instead of discussing Soviet sophistry, people came up with an alternative sophistry – a joke. The jokes were a specific discursive choice, as a French theorist would say. Through the jokes, the people could manufacture an alternative set of *reasons* that were as fantastic as the ones the Janos Kadar Appreciation Society were proposing.

Jokes are dense forms of literary expression and fully unpacking them is laborious to do and boring to read, but to give you one example: the joke about why the Soviet economies hadn't outperformed Capitalist ones replaces the official reason of 'saboteurs' with a new one – that the Soviet government didn't want Capitalists to see how poorly dressed its citizens were. The joke therefore appears to support one of the claims of the state – that it protects the dignity of its citizens. This daft explanation is made possible through a switch in meanings of the phrase 'catch up' from the metaphorical to the literal – an old joke strategy. Embedded in this explanation lies another implicit critique of the propaganda – that they would never fully catch up with the West, since even when they appeared to have caught up, they'd still be dressed in rags!

So far I have defined the ontology of a Communist joke mostly in terms of its quantity and legality. Now we can define its strategy. In an earlier chapter, Nazi jokes indicated a little of the distinctive humour of Communist jokes, namely that they feigned submissiveness and adherence: But the notion of the discursive choice of joking points the way to a more detailed analysis. Many jokes from other places and times are based on offering explanations, but the *explaining* in Communist jokes – not all, but very many of them – took a specific form: it recycled apparently faithfully the same ways of thinking as the state and turned them against it. Responding to the issue of the low birth rate in parts of Eastern Europe, the jokers asked:

Why is it not possible to control the birth rate in Soviet Bloc countries?
Because the means of production remain in private hands.

The members of the Janos Kadar Appreciation Society were still talking, but I wasn't listening. I had my first glimpse of a theory of the Communist joke. There were two related, inverted formulas at work. Sometimes, as above, the jokes applied the state's theories to explain inappropriate problems; sometimes inappropriate approaches were applied to official positions, as in the following:

Is Marxism–Leninism a science?
No. If it was, they would have tested it on animals first.

Thus the official mantra that Communism was 'a science' is disproved by inappropriate scientific methods. The same formula lies behind the joke about the Russians being friends or brothers, while its inverted corollary is used in the joke about the two-ply toilet paper. Admittedly – my mind was racing to test this hypothesis – these jokes were all too complex to be fully described by such simple rules – the joke about Marxism being a science applied a methodology that in other contexts would be applauded by the state, so the reasoning wasn't totally 'inappropriate'. The joke about the birth rate was an indirect condemnation of the power of the centralised state. And the one which I had told the Communists sitting opposite me, about rescuing Kadar from drowning, had nothing to do with official reasoning at all.

Clearly much cross-referencing remained to be done before I would be able to present papers on this subject at international symposia.

My mind returned to the interview. The Kadar enthusiasts were still talking, oblivious to the distant look in my eye. '... If the revolutions of 1989 hadn't happened,' they said, 'we have been told by experts that we would have needed three or four years to rethink, rework and reprocess the existing order, and then the Socialist experience could have got back on track. Unfortunately, there was no possibility of doing this, but this game is not over yet.'

FIVE

The Golden Age of Communist Jokes

In the years after Stalin's death the repression of joke-tellers was relaxed in unpredictable stops and starts. The loose alliance of Politburo members who took over – among them the vicious head of the NKVD, Lavrenti Beria, and the next Soviet leader, Nikita Khrushchev – immediately set up a commission to organise the release of inmates from the Gulag. The first directive telegrammed to the camps in 1953 liberated wives and relatives who had been imprisoned along with the male head of the family. A second ordered the release of all those convicted of 'oral propaganda' – that is, saying things against the regime, which included joking. Over one million people, out of a Gulag population of around 2.5 million were released in these amnesties.

A young man is sent to the camps before the war. Twenty years later his mother receives a telegram to meet him at the railroad station. As he steps out of the overcrowded train, she rushes into his arms.

'How did you recognise me after all this time, mum?'

'By your coat, darling.'

Lavrenty Beria's violent past made him a threatening figure for some colleagues, while his sudden new reformist zeal, which exceeded the rest of the leadership, antagonised others. For Khrushchev, Beria was simply a rival. He saw his chance and formed a cabal with Politburo members and army generals. Within a year, they arrested and summarily executed Beria. Thus Soviet leaders drew a line under Stalinist terror, with this last purge, and also indicated they wanted reform, but not too much.

What became known as Khrushchev's 'thaw' climaxed at the Twentieth Party Congress, on 25 February 1956, when the new Soviet leader gave an unprecedentedly forthright speech denouncing Stalin's personality cult and crimes. Stalin, he said bluntly, had 'put the Party and the NKVD up to the use of mass terror'. Stalin was guilty of 'mass arrests and deportations of many thousands of people, execution without trial and without normal investigation'. He showed 'his intolerance, his brutality and his abuse of power ... Many Party, Soviet and economic activists who in 1937–8 were branded "enemies" were actually never enemies, spies, wreckers, etc., but were always honest Communists.' Stalin was 'pathologically paranoid'. Khrushchev made a small joke on the podium. Referring to 'the mass deportations of entire nations from their places of origin', Khrushchev said, 'Ukrainians avoided meeting this fate only because there were too many of them and there was no place to put them. Otherwise, Stalin would have deported them too.'

The stenographers recorded the reaction of the conference: *laughter*. Leaders of the Soviet satellite states were among the stunned audience. Walter Ulbricht, the East German leader, was asked next day by an aide what he should tell the Party faithful. "You can just tell them that Stalin is no longer considered a classic,' he said drily.

Although it was dubbed a 'secret speech', within weeks copies of the text had been read to twenty-five million Party and Communist Youth League members. It was the biggest political U-turn in the twentieth century. For a brief moment the official satirical magazines were allowed to make fun of Stalin (Plate 5; Fig. 39).

First the two steps forwards, then the step backwards: Khrushchev's thaw turned out to be only a partial defrosting. The

Fig. 39. 'What a shame. How he would inspire me in my task of writing an essay criticising the personality cult' (*Eulenspiegel*, 1956). This is referring to the dark patch on the wall where a portrait of Stalin used to hang. When Khrushchev condemned Stalin in 1956, many of these ubiquitous portraits were taken down and cartoonists could make occasional jokes on the subject.

liberalisation led to uncertainty, unhappiness and unrest in many parts of the Soviet Bloc. There was an attempted democratic revolution in Hungary, which Khrushchev put down with tanks and live ammunition. Thousands of workers went on strike in Poznan in Poland, demanding 'Bread and Freedom'; the Polish army crushed them, killing fifty-three. Protest spread to the Soviet Union, where anonymous leaflets and graffiti supporting the Hungarian Uprising appeared. A special turn of phrase even appeared in Russian speech: 'He was imprisoned for Hungary.' Meanwhile, in Georgia, the birthplace of Stalin, the opposite happened: tens of thousands of people marched in defence of the reputation of the 'Great Leader'. Policemen were attacked, their stations ransacked. Some members of these crowds combined their 'hoorays for the Great Stalin' with ominous calls for Georgian independence.

The Politburo was alarmed by the scale of criticism and resistance that was surfacing. The reforms stopped. Hundreds of thousands of victims of Stalinist justice were left to remain in camps or exile (the sentences that forbade them to live in Russia's big cities). On 21 December 1956 a directive was issued ordering the strengthening of the fight against 'anti-Soviet elements'. A short-lived, repressive campaign ensued, in which almost 3,500 people were arrested for anti-Soviet propaganda. It was minuscule by Stalinist standards, but it did target the tellers of a new set of jokes about Khrushchev. Sentences ranged from two to six years in the camps.

These cases can be studied in much more detail than those under Stalin, thanks to improved record-keeping and more manageable numbers. The sources are a combination of KGB and camp archives, court records from the Minstry of Justice and a report from the Supreme Court from 1989 that analyses the cases of people arrested under article 58/10 in this period.

As previously under Stalin, the arrests were for a basket of activities that included off-the-cuff insults, recited jokes, remarks that 'denigrated the leaders of the Soviet Union' as well as the occasional pamphlet. Most of the records don't specify the exact nature of the transgression concerned, but unlike the material so far uncovered in Russia from Stalin's era, there are some documents which tell in fascinating detail the stories of the crimes and how they were dealt with. One file from 1957 concerns a citizen of Voronoj, who got drunk, went to the main street of the town and started shouting obscenities and 'speculating about the sex life' of Khrushchev and other members of the Politburo. He was immediately arrested and taken to the police station, where, still drunk, he told all present what he thought of the Soviet regime. He was sentenced to two years for anti-Soviet propaganda and drunkenness. Released early in 1959, he was quiet for a year, but then he got drunk again, repeated the same behaviour and was sentenced to four years. He was released in 1964 but did the same thing again, and received another seven years.

The campaign against anti-Soviet utterances died down in summer 1958 when certain Soviet legal institutions including the Soviet Supreme Court, began to criticise it. The mini-witch-hunt was formally closed in spring 1959. For the remaining period of Khrushchev's rule, only around two to three hundred people a year were arrested for oral and written criticism of the Soviet Union; yet, once again, it appears that the reduced numbers led to more detailed record-keeping.

In 1961 one bored remand prisoner took a piece of his bed sheet and drew a swastika, a dollar sign and a skull-and-crossbones on it, adding the slogan underneath: 'Revolt against Soviet Power'. He then hung it out of his cell window like a flag. On top of his three-year sentence for burglary he got seven years for anti-Soviet propaganda and for damage to the bed sheet. In 1962 a man was arrested in Perm. He had taken part in a strike, and 'complained about the hard material situation of people, expressed approval of the situation of people in the US, criticised social shortcomings in the Soviet Union, said the newspapers were lying, and told jokes discrediting Khrushchev'. In another incident, a number of prisoners were caught attaching notes with insults against Khrushchev to the legs of three pigeons they had caught. They received additional sentences.

In 1961 a member of the Communist Party, an intellectual, was arrested for counter-revolutionary propaganda in the city of Bryansk in western Russia. He got eight years. He was released in March 1962, after serving four years. On the second day after his release he arrived at the local train station and attempted to buy a ticket home, but he was told that there were no more trains to his choice of destination that day. Understandably exasperated, he bought some vodka, drank it and 'in the presence of many people he displayed his anti-Soviet humour and disparaged Soviet realities'. So he was re-arrested, having got no further than the camp's local train station, and sentenced for 'terrorist activities against Communists and other administrative departments' (which probably meant he swore at officials in the ticket office) and got another six years. He was finally released in 1967.

Gyoerg Botsokin, aged fifty-four, a worker in a central-heating factory and cabaret performer, was arrested in 1964. An informant reported that in conversations with him, he 'discredited the Soviet government, made insinuations against Soviet realities and the order prevailing in our country, relayed to his friends what he had heard on foreign radio broadcasts and told anecdotes with anti-Soviet content'. He was sentenced to three years, which he served in full.

There were many jokes that these convicts may have told. By the late fifties Nikita Khrushchev was a deeply unpopular leader. He'd been able to make little capital out of his denunciation of Stalin, his amnesties for political prisoners or the successes of the Soviet space programme, which sent the first man into orbit in 1961, preceded four years earlier by the first dog . . .

What are the key components of the Soviet space programme?
German technology, Czech uranium and a Russian dog.

On the economy, the Soviet message was that Capitalism was 'in crisis' and the growth rates of Communist economies would soon outstrip their ideological competitors. On 24 July 1959, at the opening of the American National Exhibition in Moscow, Khrushchev appeared on television in a 'kitchen debate' with the then American vice president Richard Nixon.

'How long has America existed? Three hundred years?' Khrushchev asked.

'One hundred and fifty years,' Nixon replied.

'One hundred and fifty years?' said Khrushchev. 'Well then we will say America has been in existence for a hundred and fifty years and this is the level she has reached. We have existed not quite forty-two years and in another seven years we will be on the same level as America. When we catch you up, in passing you by, we will wave to you.'

Joke-tellers didn't wait till 1966 to make jokes about this ludicrous prophecy.

Fig. 40. Cartoon suggesting that the Capitalists were attempting in vain to hold back Soviet economic growth (R. Verdini, *Krokodil*, 1957).

They say American Capitalism is on the edge of the abyss, and that in a few years Communism will overtake it.

Khrushchev was obsessed with Russian backwardness. Later on the same trip, he met the American President Eisenhower. Eisenhower made small talk, telling the Soviet President that the telephone kept ringing even when he was on vacation. Reading a little too much into the President's chit-chat, Khrushchev responded angrily that back in the Soviet Union telephones were even installed on the beach when he went swimming. Soon, he said, they would have more and better telephones in the USSR than there were in the USA. From Khrushchev onwards, the Soviet leadership would become ever more frustrated by Communism's failure to deliver the prosperity Marx had predicted (Fig. 40).

Khrushchev had made many public pledges that the Soviet good times were just around the corner, but he couldn't fulfil them. Without the repression and distraction of Stalin's vicious state apparatus, it appears that many Soviet citizens began to focus on their low standard of living.

Why isn't there any flour for sale?
Because they started adding it to bread.

What is the longest anekdot?
Khrushchev's speech at the Twenty-Second Party Congress about the raising of living standards.

There still weren't enough basic foodstuffs in the shops in the fifties. Soviet agriculture was unbelievably primitive – harvests were overall smaller than they had been before World War II and the livestock count was lower than in 1926. Khrushchev promised to solve the shortages with an outlandish scheme to grow corn in vast tracts of Siberia and Kazakhstan, the 'virgin lands'. Young volunteers were encouraged to go North and work on these new farms – three hundred thousand went in 1954 alone. But the plan didn't work. Milk, butter and meat were in permanently short supply, harvests shrunk. In an effort to encourage agricultural productivity, Khrushchev hiked prices by an enormous 35% in 1962, yet the main effect was to infuriate consumers, to whom Communism promised ever-cheaper goods: it was the classic double bind of the centrally planned economy. In 1963 the Soviets had to import tens of millions of tons of grain from Canada, America and even Romania. Jokers linked this crisis to the most obvious feature of Khrushchev's physiognomy, his baldness.

What is Khrushchev's hairstyle called?
The harvest of sixty-three.

What will the harvest of 1964 be like?
Average – worse than 1963 but better than 1965.

The Party viewed Khrushchev as unfavourably as did the people. They judged the Berlin Wall, antagonism with China and the Cuban Missile Crisis as foreign-policy failures and they blamed Khrushchev. Half a million East Germans fled to the West in the two years before the construction of the Wall, yet only two months before it went up, the East German leader Walter Ulbricht told an international press conference: 'No one intends to build a Wall.' In Cuba, Khrushchev had agreed to dismantle Soviet missiles, in return for the American withdrawal of their nuclear warheads from Turkey – but this second part of the deal was secret, so it looked like another Russian climbdown. And then there was China: in 1962 Khrushchev pulled almost all Soviet advisers and businesses out of China.

Lenin, Stalin and Putin have more in common than the last two letters of their names: Khrushchev was not the strong authoritarian Tsar-like leader that many Russians wanted and still want to see lead their country. A short, fat big-ears with – in Macmillan's words – 'pig eyes', Khrushchev was loud-mouthed, short-tempered and oafish. When he attended an art exhibition he told an artist that his work was 'dog shit ... a donkey could smear better than this with its tail'. He once informed the British ambassador at the Bolshoi that six hydrogen bombs would be 'quite enough' for Britain, and nine would do for France. In 1958, when he met an American senator from Minneapolis, he got up from his desk, went over to a big map of the USA on the wall and ostentatiously drew a circle in a thick blue pen around the city. 'That's so I don't forget to order them to spare the town when the rockets fly,' he said. He called Mao an 'old condom' in a bugged room in Beijing and in 1960 he famously took his shoe off in the middle of a speech at the UN and banged it on the table. This was all manna from heaven to joke-tellers.

Khrushchev is walking through the Kremlin, getting worked up about the Soviet Union's problems, and spits on the carpet in a gesture of disgust.

'Behave yourself, Nikita Sergeyevich,' admonishes his aide. 'Remember that the great Lenin walked through these halls!'

'Shut up,' responds Khrushchev. 'I can spit all I like here; the Queen of England gave me permission!'

'The Queen of England?'

'Yes! I spat on her carpet in Buckingham Palace too, and she said, "Mr Khrushchev, you can do that in the Kremlin if you wish, but you can't behave like this here ..."'

Khrushchev is inspecting a new exhibition of modern art. He scowls and sneers at everything until he pauses in front of a mirror; gazing in admiration, he says, 'What a wonderfully life-like statue of a pig.'

There was the saying:

During Stalin's time we had a personality cult; now we have a nonentity cult.

My driver parked his Lada outside one of the concertinas of twenty-storey apartment blocks that ring Moscow. They were built in the 1970s but remain in good condition; their cursory prefab construction has its own aesthetic. Wall sections with windows have a decorative grid of red tiles under the sill and the Lego-like geometry is tempered by thick squiggles of grey sealant that are visible between the sections. It was here I was to meet a former KGB colonel, who early in his career had been on the front line of a new softly-softly strategy against the jokes.

'They had to stop arresting people for telling jokes about Khrushchev,' Colonel Prelin told me dismissively; 'otherwise they would have had to lock up the whole country.'

Igor Prelin lived in one of Moscow's archetypal tiny Communist flats, which one can move through only by shuffling positions with the owner and any other guests present. I shuffled into the hallway, my host stepped back into the kitchen, I squeezed up against the coat stand, and my host shut the front door. He moved forwards. I took a step backwards into the bathroom; then I shuffled after him into the living room and he waved me to sit down on his built-in corner sofa, which I did by shuffling down behind his inappropriately large mirrored coffee table.

The room had an oppressively warm palette. The upholstery on the sofa was rust, the wallpaper, textured to look like an outdoor wall, was orange. The carpet was red. An unusual combination of ornaments was displayed. There were ledges supporting the silver cups Prelin had won in fencing tournaments, cheap African masks and several black-and-white photographs of my host, aged about forty, with a manly grey-black beard, wearing reflective aviator sunglasses and cradling a machine gun. These pictures looked like film stills from a James Bond film, but they were souvenirs from the most adventurous part of Colonel Prelin's career: he had been a Soviet agent in Africa in the seventies. But before that, between 1961 and 1967, he had been assigned to the local KGB office in the medium-sized town of Orenburg in the south Urals. In spring 1959 Khrushchev had delivered a speech to KGB officials in which he said that with regard to anti-Soviet propaganda the emphasis should be on 'preventative' measures not prosecution, ending the repressive campaign I have already described. This was elaborated as procedure over the next twelve months.

'We received a directive in 1961 ordering us not to arrest people for anti-Soviet activities, but instead telling us to have "conversations" with them. In this "preventative" method, we would explain to them the mistakes they were making – it was called "wrong evaluations of Soviet society". We would give them an official warning, which threatened arrest if they continued their activities. Sometimes the suspect would be asked to write a letter of apology, admitting his mistakes, addressed to "KGB, USSR". The letter had to say: "Today I was invited into the KGB offices for a conversation because I – for instance – told jokes discrediting one of the leaders of the Communist Party ... and it has been explained to me how I was mistaken and I promise not to do this again."'

Prelin estimated to me that his office, which covered half the town's population, conducted five of these talks per year. 'Sometimes if the conversation went very well, at the end of the letter they wrote: "I want to say thank you to the KGB who, instead of arresting me and applying criminal laws, were kind enough to talk to me."'

The Colonel, a remarkably trim seventy-year-old, recalled one of these important missions in great detail. 'In a big motor plant there was a highly qualified engineeer, aged forty, who was also the leader of the largest brass band ensemble in the region. We received information that he was telling anti-Soviet jokes in his place of work and during rehearsals at the local cultural centre. Other members of the KGB office collected signed witness statements from people in whose presence he had told jokes. After that my colleague wrote a report in which he explained the case and suggested we use the preventative procedures. The head of our department agreed.

'In 1961 I was the only person in the Orenburg local office who'd finished higher education, so I was always sent to talk to the better-educated transgressors, because you could only argue with intellectuals if you could talk to them on their level. It was very sophisticated work and you had to argue very skilfully. So my boss ordered me to take on this case.

'I prepared thoroughly for this meeting. I went to the place where the suspect was rehearsing. These preventative actions could take two forms: an open conversation in front of the suspect's peers, like a people's court, or alternatively a private one-on-one chat. We only used the first method for mistakes at work, such as ruining a machine (a crime for which you could have been sent to the Gulags under

Stalin). For jokes, the one-on-one approach was better because we didn't want everyone hearing the jokes. We had a joke at the KGB at the time: What's the difference between a dissident and a KGB agent? – The dissident invents the jokes, and the KGB agents spread them.

'This joke had a lot of truth in it because, if a KGB officer overheard someone telling jokes, he would have to write a report stating the jokes in it, and then that report would be copied and given to his superiors; then their secretaries would type up those reports and give them to officials higher up, and before you knew it fifty people had learned a new joke and told it to their wives ... That's the other reason why we stopped arresting people for telling jokes.

'So I had a meeting with this engineer, and at first he denied everything. I told him that we had several signed statements, so there was no sense denying it. Still he maintained his innocence. Then I said: "Listen, ten years ago you would have been sent to the Gulag for this; is this what you want to happen now? Be sensible." He was still resisting. I guess he knew that this was no longer a convincing threat. I continued, "Do you want to ruin your career with this silly behaviour?" That cracked him. He started to cry. "It's so stupid of me," he said; "I am an old fool." He was weeping uncontrollably, I recall. "Well," I said, "to finish this business off you should write a letter admitting what you did and apologising." But then he really broke down. He refused to write the letter. He got down on his knees in front of me, begging me through his tears not to have to write a letter. I realised he was afraid that I wanted to obtain a confession from him in writing so that he could be more severely punished. I knew he would never write the letter, so I was simply firm in my warning: if I ever heard he told another anti-Soviet joke again, he would end up behind bars.

'My superior was not happy because he wanted a letter, but we never heard from the suspect again.'

'My father had to write one of those letters,' Ariane said to me, catching me by surprise. We skyped each other every few days when I was out on the road on the trail of Communist jokes. I watched her blowing me a pixellated kiss on my computer screen.

'What – a letter of apology for telling jokes?' I asked, amazed at my good luck in going out with her.

'No, not for jokes – for speeding,' she said. 'I remember I was about thirteen, so it was the early eighties. It was Easter and he drove into town too fast and he was stopped by two *Vopos*.'

Vopo was East German slang for the *Volkspolizei*, the detested local police force. I immediately recalled a large number of jokes about them. Many were ubiquitous and universal cop jokes, but they were told with particular venom in the DDR.

Why do Vopos always travel in threes?
One who can read, one who can write, and one to keep his eye on the two intellectuals.

A moped-rider is stopped by a Vopo on a country road. 'Right, please unfasten your seatbelt and step out of the car,' the officer says.
The moped-rider looks at him and says, 'Would it be all right if I just wind down the window?'

Ariane continued her story. 'My father was furious and he totally lost it and started cursing the policemen. So they ordered him to write a letter of apology.'

'Why didn't they just fine him on the spot?' I asked.

'No, we didn't do it like that in Socialist countries,' she said. She remembered how her mother had tried in vain to persuade her father to write this letter. He had talked about it day after day. The problem seemed to go on for ever and he refused to write the letter. Then one day his boss called him in for a meeting. He said that if he didn't write the letter he would lose his job – but if he did write the letter he would get a 400 Ostmark bonus, equivalent to half a month's salary. Then my father wrote the letter.'

'So,' I said, spotting an opening in her defences, 'this Capitalist inducement finally persuaded your father to play ball.' The speed of my response was impressive, but I regretted it as soon as I'd said it. I'd forgotten that her father died young.

'My father was appalled by reunification,' she said. 'He had an important job in the DDR: he was a senior engineer, overseeing the central heating of all the apartment blocks and the electricity supply to the town where we lived. After the Wall came down they sacked everyone in the administration who had anything to do with the Stasi, which was the majority of the management; but there wasn't anyone else qualified to employ, so my father had to do all their work as well.

Fat West Germans from big energy companies would roll up in BMWs and take him out for lunch and try to persuade him to invest in their expensive technology. The pressure and the workload were too much. I think they contributed to his heart attack.'

In my memory, that was the moment the temperature changed in our relationship. At the time, I blamed it all on my lack of sensitivity towards her dad. But perhaps I was being too hard on myself. She could also have felt politically embarrassed – a consequence of my uncovering of the profit motive in the heart of her Communist family. Whatever the real cause, from this time on the fun somehow seemed to have gone out of our ideological disagreements. At breakfast she still gave me a historical choice of coffee cup – either one that bore the *Mitropa* logo of the old East German railway company, or a commemorative espresso cup with a tiny drawing of a Young Pioneer in a blue scarf helping with the harvest. But it wasn't the same. I felt Ariane was building her own Berlin Wall, her own – to use the official name given to it by the East German state – 'anti-fascist protection barrier'.

Most analysts of Communist jokes agree that the 1960s was the golden age of Communist jokes. A handful of factors lay behind this surge of jokes and joke-telling. Within the first few years of this decade, all regimes of the Soviet Bloc had more or less abandoned arresting and prosecuting joke-tellers. This new relaxation of oppression, the decay of the system yet the persistence of the old ideology and of Soviet domination, combined to produce – to use the parlance of our times – a tsunami of *anekdoty*. These jokes, which covered every aspect and dimension of life, built up piece by piece a complete alternative reality for citizens of Communist countries, a mirror image of the world the state presented on podiums, posters, television programmes and the printed page.

Imagine, if you will, twenty-four hours in jokes. We all know the legendary book by the Soviet dissident Alexander Solzhenitsyn, *A Day in the Life of Ivan Denisovich*, which describes the ordeals of daily life in the Gulag; but how many of us are familiar with the apocryphal manuscript of the author's younger brother, 'A Day in the Life of Ivan Zimpsonovich'? I had heard rumours of such a book but I'd never been able to get hold of a copy. In my fevered Capitalist imagination I found myself reconstructing it as an episode in an animated TV series, 'The Zimpsonoviches'. If there had been good Communist TV, perhaps this is what it would have been like:

The title sequence has the chords of a Communist anthem over which a chorus sings 'The Zimpsonovi-i-i-i-ches'. Each family member is rushing home in their own way – Zimpsonovich slips up as he crosses an iced-up street and as he falls, in an effort to regain his balance, he reaches out to try to grab hold of something. By chance a young Party activist is passing, holding a placard, which bears the slogan 'Full Speed towards Communism'. Zimpsonovich tumbles, the placard ends up underneath him and he slides on it on the ice all the way home. Mrs Zimpsonovich boards a terribly crowded tram, which she can only squeeze into by holding her breath for the entire journey. Her small daughter is marching with her Young Pioneer band, belting out a rousing Communist tune, and as they pass her home, she peels off, while still playing her part on her trumpet. The Zimpsonoviches' son is getting a lift home by hanging on to the back of a decrepit old Lada, which slithers across the slippery roads, while wearing his ice skates. They all arrive home together. As they throw themselves onto the sofa, you watch it sink, and hear the old springs ping. They turn on the telly and flick the channels, once, twice, thrice ... on every channel Khrushchev is giving a speech at a Party conference, until the fourth one, when a man in military uniform appears wagging his finger in disapproval. Zimpsonovich looks terrified and then his son runs up to the TV and twists the dial one more time to reveal a screen that says: 'The Zimpsonoviches'.

Mr Zimpsonovich lives with his wife and two children in a small apartment block in Leningrad. This weekday is like any other, and the Zimpsonoviches eat breakfast together. Ivan Zimpsonovich's son, Bartski, takes a piece of bread, picks up a knife and opens the fridge to look for some sausage, but there is no meat on the shelves.

'Daddy,' he says, 'I don't like Communism.'

'But, son, Communism's lovely,' says his father, enthusiastically.

'We haven't yet reached Communism,' his clever sister Elizaveta pipes up; 'we are still in the stage of Socialism.'

'Daddy,' he says, 'will there be sausage in the fridge when we reach Communism?'

'Yes,' says his father, 'and everyone will have their own aeroplane.'

'Why?' asks Bartski.

'Well,' says his father, 'for example: we live in Moscow, and if we hear that there is some sausage on sale in Vladivostok, we will be able to get into our aeroplane and zoom over and be the first in the queue.'

'Wow,' says Bartski, and grabs his rucksack. He and his sister go off to school.

'I can't wait for full Communism,' sighs Mrs Zimpsonovich. 'Today I am going to find some sausage.'

Like millions of his fellow countrymen, Mr Zimpsonovich goes to work in a factory that produces substandard and poorly made goods. In this case it's electric clocks, the quality of which the managers often boast about – 'the fastest watches in the world', they say proudly (by the eighties, this factory was producing electronic equipment and making 'the largest microchips in the world'). As Ivan Zimpsonovich is working away, several colleagues are standing around drinking tea in the corner. (Under the Soviet system there was always full employment, but that often meant people were not fully occupied.) One of the senior-management team comes round with a delegation from America.

'Wow what a big factory and what a massive workforce!' exclaims one American businessman. 'So how many people actually work here in total?'

Before his manager can answer, Zimpsonovich interjects: 'Oh, about half.' An instant later Zimpsonovich yelps. He's taken his eye off his machine for a moment and caught his hand in it. (Safety standards in Soviet factories were notoriously lax.) Zimpsonovich nurses his mangled hand.

The manager looks at him concerned, and then turns to the foreman and asks: 'How many times has this happened to Zimpsonovich this week?'

'This is the sixth time,' says the foreman.

The manager breathes a sigh of relief: 'Phew! We haven't yet exceeded our quota of accidents. Zimpsonovich, go home.'

Mrs Zimpsonovich, meanwhile, has gone to join something that is fifty metres long, moves very slowly and eats potatoes – a queue for sausage in Moscow. Queues were part of daily life in Communism, but there were many different kinds of queue. Depending on the era and country, citizens might be queuing for basics such as bread and meat, toilet paper and make-up, or luxury goods, such as tropical fruit and nice trousers. The reason for the queue could also vary – it might be because the factories weren't producing enough of a particular product to meet demand, or because it was all being exported to earn foreign currency; or, if they were imported goods, because the state couldn't afford to buy them. Or the problem might be that there was plenty of the product available but the distribution system was inefficient. Even if the shop shelves were full, there were still often several queues – one to select goods, another to pay for them, and a third for collection. Not that there was a shortage of everything. There were great surpluses too – of things that no one wanted to buy! In the later eighties Soviet factories were producing three pairs of shoes a year for every Soviet citizen, but they were styles that no one wanted to wear. Such were the pitfalls of the centrally planned economy. That's why queuing, even in relatively wealthy Communist countries, was a way of life.

Mrs Zimpsonovich has to queue for several hours but her neighbour is standing in front of her, so she has someone to talk to. 'I hear there'll be snow tomorrow,' she says to the old lady.

'Well, I'm not queuing for that!' the woman replies. 'But do you know, I'm getting so absent-minded: I left the house today, I shut the front door and looked at the empty bag in my hand and for a moment I couldn't remember if I was about to go shopping, or if I had just come back.'

By the time she gets to the front of the line, Mrs Zimpsonovich discovers the refrigeration units are empty. 'I see you don't have any sausage today,' she says to the shopkeeper.

'Oh no,' he replies, 'we're the shop with no cheese. The shop with no sausage is around the corner.'

Mr Zimpsonovich's children, Bartski and Liza, are at school. That day Bartski's first lesson is about the Russian space programme. The Soviets are far ahead of the Americans in the space race. Their cosmonauts have orbited the Earth, yet ordinary citizens are not usually allowed to travel outside the Soviet Bloc.

'Soon the successes of Communism will benefit the whole world. Sputniks are just the beginning. One day you will be able to go to Moscow airport and buy a ticket for the Moon or Venus,' says the teacher.

Bartski puts up his hand to ask a question: 'That's just fantastic, but will there be connecting flights from there to Paris or Hamburg?'

Meanwhile Elizaveta Zimpsonovich has to take a test in political theory. The paper contains three questions. *Describe the United States* is the first question. Liza writes: 'The United States is a Capitalist country which has millions of people unemployed and living in poverty and where thousands of young people are addicted to drugs.' The second question is: *What is the goal of the Soviet Union?* She writes: 'The goal of the Soviet Union is to catch up with the United States.' The third question is: *What is the evidence that proves that Communism is superior to Capitalism?* Liza, who always comes top of her class, writes: 'If there was such economic confusion and disorder under Capitalism as there is under Communism, Capitalism would have collapsed long ago.'

Bartski's second lesson is history, his worst subject. The teacher lifts a slim, tattered volume off his desk and waves it at the class. 'Who wrote this, the *Communist Manifesto?*'

No one says anything. Bartski is in the thickest class.

The teacher looks round; then he repeats the question in a firm voice. Still there is no answer. For a third time, he asks the question, this time angrily.

Bartski puts his hand up sheepishly and says, 'It wasn't me, sir.'

'That is counter-revolutionary stupidity,' says the teacher. 'I am sending you home now!'

Bartski leaves the class, downcast.

On his way back from school Bartski sees one of his friends, hurrying home, holding a roll of toilet paper. 'Hey, where did you get that from?' he asks.

'I just got it back from the dry-cleaner,' says his friend.

On his way back from work, Ivan Zimpsonovich pops into the local grocery store. 'I'd like a roll of toilet paper,' he says.

'No delivery till next week,' says the unhelpful shopkeeper.

'I can't wait that long,' says Zimpsonovich, and rushes out of the shop.

Father and son meet at home. Bartski tells his father what happened at school. 'I believe you,' says his father. 'I know you didn't write the *Communist Manifesto*. It must have been someone else in the class.'

Zimpsonovich wants to cheer up his son. He's just received a letter from Bartski's favourite uncle, an idealist who has gone off to Kazakhstan to help cultivate the 'virgin lands'. 'Hmm,' says Zimpsonovich, opening the letter, 'he told me if things were going badly out there, he'd write to me in red ink.' The letter is in blue ink. Zimpsonovich reads it: 'Dear Ivan, Marsha, Bartski and Liza, I am having a wonderful time in Kazakhstan. The weather is warm, I have a big apartment and plenty to eat ...'

He interrupts the letter, turns to his son and says, 'You see, Bartski, we are progressing along the road of Socialism ...' Then he reads the last line of the letter: 'There is only one problem – I can't find any red ink.'

A few hours later, Liza comes home to find the rest of her family watching the news on their TV. In a drab set, with a map of the world behind him, the newsreader announces:

'Today, following months of negotiations, the long-awaited hundred-metre sprint race between American President John Kennedy and Russian Premier Nikita Khrushchev finally took place. The Soviet First Secretary came in as a respectable silver medallist, while the American President was unfortunately second from last.

'Following the successful launch of the Soviet space satellite Sputnik, the President of the German Democratic Republic has announced that his country will also launch its own space probe. This will not, however, orbit the earth, but will instead be designed to circle round the Soviet satellite.'

Ivan Zimpsonovich changes the channel ... It's more news.

'Details are emerging of the hijack of an Aeroflot passenger jet. The plane was on a scheduled Moscow to London flight when an armed man overpowered the crew and forced it to land at Düsseldorf airport. There are three hundred and fifty hostages on board, all of them of eastern European origin. The hijacker has demanded the immediate delivery of his Lada, a three-bedroom apartment for his family and a guaranteed holiday on the Black Sea. He has said that if his demands are not met by 08.00 hours GMT, he will release a hostage every ten minutes.'

'Supper-time,' Mrs Zimpsonovich calls from the kitchen. 'Sausage soup,' she lies. She serves.

Bartski takes a spoonful of soup, but before he puts it in his mouth, he sees something black and rubbery on his spoon. 'Yuck, look, Mum,' he says, "there's a piece of tyre in my soup!'

'Eat it, Bartski,' says his father. 'This is another achievement of Socialism. Barely fifty-five years since the Revolution, and already we have almost completely replaced the horse with the automobile.'

Bartski's teacher, meanwhile, has gone home. He tells his wife the Bartski story of the day.

His wife says, 'Maybe the boy is telling the truth and it wasn't him.'

His wife's answer is so stupid that the teacher goes off to have a drink with a friend of his who is a KGB officer. He tells him about the question he put to his class and the answer he got from Bartski. 'Can you believe it?' he says to the secret policeman.

'Don't worry,' says the policeman; 'give me a couple of hours and I'll find out who really wrote it!'

The policeman goes to visit the Zimpsonoviches. 'You and I should step outside to have a little talk,' says the policeman to Ivan Zimpsonovich.

Mrs Zimpsonovich is alone. She turns on the radio. She listens to a live advice show on Radio Yerevan from Armenia.

The Radio Yerevan jokes could be about any of the main topics of Communist jokes, but they took a specific form. There were no live phone-in radio shows in the Soviet Union – yet more proof of the state's lack of interest in the views of its citizens; nevertheless, the Radio Yerevan jokes imagined exactly this scenario.

'Caller on line one,' says the radio presenter, 'what is your question?'

'Is it true that in the Soviet Union no one lacks a stereo system?'

'In principle, yes,' says the presenter. 'You hear the same from all sides here.'

He takes another call. 'Yes, Boris from Vladivostok, what do you want to say?'

'Is it true that half of the members of the Central Committee are idiots?'

'No, that is rubbish, Boris. Half of the Central Committee are not idiots.'

'Can a pig become bald?'

'Sorry, we do not answer political questions.'

'We have time for one more call before the break. Masha, I hope you have a more sensible question than our previous caller.'

'What is the difference between a Communist optimist and a Communist pessimist?' a voice crackles down the phone line from Minsk.

'Good question! A Communist pessimist says things can't get any worse; a Communist optimist says yes, they can,' the presenter replies.

Another caller, another question: 'I had a big row with my wife last night. I told her that Comrade Khrushchev was the best leader we've ever had. She disagreed with me. Was I right?'

Suddenly the programme is interrupted by the loud hiss of interference. Mrs Zimpsonovich tuts to herself and goes over to the radio to retune it. She finds the show just in time to hear the presenter say, '... apologise for the temporary loss of reception.'

After an interlude of marching music, the radio presenter reads out some of the mountain of letters he receives ...

'Dear Radio Yerevan, I don't know what's the matter with me. I don't love the Party any more. What should I do?'

'Please send us your name and address,' says the presenter.

The jingles roll: 'Radio Yere-e-e-e' – (for the final syllable the melody goes up an octave) – 'v-a-a-a-an.' Mrs Zimpsonovich goes to the window and throws a small pebble against a window a floor down at the opposite side of the yard. Then she goes into the bathroom and takes out her lipstick. In the background the radio show continues:

'Are there any historical precedents for the Soviet system of elections?'

'In principle, yes, in the story of the Creation. God made Eve, put her in the Garden of Eden, and said to Adam: "Now choose a woman."'

Meanwhile, Mr Zimpsonovich is in the local pub with the KGB agent. The agent pats him on the back in a friendly way and invites him to a vodka. 'Your son is in a lot of trouble,' he says, raising his glass to Zimpsonovich's. They down them and the agent orders another.

'He didn't do it,' says Zimpsonovich. 'I know my Bartski. He never wrote no manifesto.'

'Of course not,' says the agent. They continue drinking.

Alcoholism was a widespread problem in the Soviet Union, and people used to say:

What is the stage that comes between Socialism and the arrival of full Communism?
Alcoholism.

Zimpsonovich, of course, loses his guard when he is tipsy. He says to the agent, 'I heard a wonderful political joke yesterday.'

Ten years earlier this story would have ended tragically here. Mr Zimpsonovich would have been arrested and deported to Siberia. But times are different now. The KGB monitor the jokes, and write reports on them for the Ministry of the Interior, in order to evaluate the public mood. 'May I remind you that I am a KGB officer,' says the agent.

'Don't worry,' says Zimpsonovich; 'I'll tell it slowly.'

'I don't want to have to arrest your son,' says the agent, returning to the matter in hand.

'No, no,' says Zimpsonovich, his eyes filling with tears; 'I'll do anything, but don't arrest my son.'

'You know, Zimpsonovich, the KGB likes to solve its cases.'

Zimpsonovich says nothing.

'I know where your wife can buy sausage tomorrow morning,' says the agent.

Zimpsonovich's face lights up.

Zimpsonovich stumbles home late at night, drunk. He clambers up the stairs – the lift isn't working, nor are the lights. He enters his flat, opens the bedroom door and finds his wife in bed with his best friend. 'You can't do that!' he says to her. 'You need to get some sleep. Tomorrow you have to get up early because I heard there'll be sausage at the grocer's.'

The KGB agent meanwhile gets into his Lada to drive to the teacher's apartment. He rings the doorbell. The lights slowly turn on inside.

The teacher opens his door in his dressing gown. 'Why have you woken me up?'

'I've solved the case. It wasn't the boy. His father has confessed.'

Roll music and credits: 'The Zimpsoooooonoviches . . .'

There are other legendary episodes. The Zimpsonoviches are Jewish, of course, and one storyline from the early seventies is about their doomed attempts to emigrate, at a time when growing numbers of Soviet Jews were beginning to obtain visas. It has a scene in which Zimpsonovich goes to the synagogue. After the service, there's a chat over kiddush:

'Hey, Jakob, how come I didn't see you at the last Party meeting?' asks Zimpsonovich.

'Well Ivan, if I'd known it was the last one, I would have been sure to have been there,' Jakob replies.

'So anyway, Jakob, how's your son Joseph?'

'He's living in Warsaw and building Socialism.'

'And didn't you have a daughter, Judith – how's she doing?'

'She's well too – living in Moscow and building a Communist future.'

'And your older brother Bernie ...'

'Oh, he moved to Israel.'

'And is he building Socialism there too?'

'What, are you crazy? Do you think he'd do that in his own country!'

It is winter. A rumour goes round that there has been a meat delivery. Zimpsonovich joins a long queue outside the butcher's shop, early in the morning. After three hours have passed the shop door opens and the manager announces: 'Friends, we have meat but not enough for everyone; would the Jews please leave.'

Mr Zimpsonovich and half of the queue leave; the line gets shorter. Two hours later the door opens again: 'Comrades, we have meat but not enough for everyone. Would all those who didn't take part in the Great Patriotic War please leave.'

Another large part of the queue sidles off, muttering. Three hours later the door opens again: 'Comrades, we have meat but not enough for everyone. Would all those who didn't take part in the overthrow of Tsarism please leave.'

There are now only three half-frozen old men left. At eight o'clock the door opens once more: 'Comrades, there won't be any meat today.'

The old men move off, grumbling, 'You see, the Jews get the best deal.'

It's this kind of anti-Semitism that leads Zimpsonovich to apply for a visa to emigrate. He goes to see the emigration officer.

'What are your reasons for emigrating?' asks the Soviet bureaucrat.

'Well I have two reasons,' says Zimpsonovich. 'The first is that if the Soviet government collapses, everyone's going to blame us Jews ...'

'That won't be a problem,' says the official. 'I can guarantee to you that the Soviet government won't collapse any time soon ...'

'... And that's the second reason,' says Zimpsonovich.

Zimpsonovich is reading a book in Hebrew in the park. A KGB agent passes by. 'What is that strange writing?' he asks Zimpsonovich.

'This is Hebrew,' he says. 'It's the language of Israel.'

'Why bother?' says the agent. 'You'll never get a visa to go to Israel.'

'I'm going to America,' says Zimpsonovich proudly. 'But Hebrew is also the language of Heaven.'

The agent replies, 'What makes you so sure you're going to Heaven and not to Hell?'

'Maybe I'm not so sure, but I already know Russian.'

Despite the agent's pessimism, Zimpsonovich gets his visa – the Soviet authorities are only too pleased to get rid of one of their dimmest citizens. The week before he leaves, Zimpsonovich takes his family to visit the city's museum. They stop to admire a painting of Adam and Eve. Next to them are two foreigners.

'Look,' says one in a French accent, 'you can see they are French: they are naked and beautiful.'

'No,' replies the other in an educated English accent, 'you can tell they are English: they are shy and modest.'

Despite his religion, Zimpsonovich still feels some national pride and now he cannot restrain himself. In his limited English, he says to them: 'You are both wrong. You can see Adam and Eve are Russian: they have no clothes on, they have only an apple to eat, and yet they are being told they live in paradise.'

The Zimpsonoviches have a farewell party. They eat and sit around swapping jokes over vodka. That night the best one is:

Everyone knows about the seven wonders of the world – but what about the seven wonders of Communism.

1. Under Communism there's no unemployment.

2. Although there's no unemployment, only half the population has to work.

3. Although only half the population works, the Five-Year Plans are always fulfilled.

4. Although the Five-Year Plans are always fulfilled, there's never anything to buy.

5. Although there's never anything to buy, everyone is happy and contented.

6. *Although everyone is happy and contented, there are frequent demonstrations.*

7. *Although there are frequent demonstrations, the government is always re-elected with 99.9% of the vote.*

The next day the Zimpsonoviches fly to New York. Zimpsonovich is interviewed by an immigration official:

'Tell me, what is the political situation in your country?' asks the American official.

'Oh, I can't complain,' says Zimpsonovich.

'Okay,' says the official, confused, 'what is the human-rights situation in your country?'

'Well, to tell you the truth, I can't complain.'

'All right, how about the economic situation there?'

'I really can't complain,' comes the reply again.

'Well,' says the exasperated officer, 'why do you wish to leave the Soviet Union, then?'

'I can't complain!' says Zimpsonovich.

The Zimpsonoviches' application for asylum is turned down and they are sent back to the Soviet Union on the next plane.

As the plane approaches its destination, the stewardess announces: 'We are about to begin our descent to Moscow airport. Please extinguish your cigarettes, put your seat backs upright, fasten your seat belts and wind your clocks back ten years ...'

Is there any other age or place in history where one could narrate in such detail the daily life of its citizens through jokes? That's a rhetorical question and the answer is – of course not. The sheer scale and variety of Communist jokes puts them in a category of their own. And yet these very qualities have also been the greatest impediment to a deeper definition in terms of its style of humour. Humorologists have been either too cautious or too overwhelmed to come up with an aesthetics of the Communist joke. Until now.

I had begun to develop a tentative theory of the Communist joke, based on its reuse and distortion of Marxist–Leninist modes of explanation. Now, in the sixties' panoply of jokes, I could see if this hastily conceived notion held up.

The Communist humour of the life of the Zimpsonoviches reveals that a core group of Communist jokes engaged with the thinking of the regime. The jokes, firstly, feign fidelity to and enthusiasm for Communism. The one about being able to travel to the West via the Moon, for example, accepts the laws preventing ordinary Soviet citizens from travelling to Capitalist countries, but finds a possible way around the regulations, based on the technological achievements the state was so proud of. The joke about the manifesto shows the KGB rapidly solving crimes, and another shows them tolerating joke-telling – preferably slowly.

But alongside an enthusiasm for Communism is a subsequent or simultaneous critique often using the language and legitimations of the system. When he seeks asylum, Zimpsonovich agrees with the official Soviet line that there is nothing to complain about in his country, but that is also why he wants to emigrate. His friend's children are all good Communists dedicated to 'building Socialism' but not in their homeland. The claims of Soviet propaganda that Russia had played a leading role in history meant that even Adam and Eve were Russians – though the reasons why are not those the state would offer.

One would not expect any theory about these jokes to be all-inclusive. Many rely for their humour on a simplified description of daily life – like the potato-eating queue for meat – or clever insults against those in power – hence Russian is the language of Hell. There are too many jokes to be covered by one overarching definition, and there are too many different traditions of humour that influenced the Communist joke – the Tsarist *anekdot*, Russian peasant folklore, Jewish humour, the wit of each Soviet Bloc state and the ancient genre of gallows humour, to name a few I have already mentioned. But it is not enough to define the unique quality of Communist jokes as an amalgam of all these different cultures. No other kinds of jokes impersonated their targets with the same precision as Communist jokes, or used the logic of the state to discredit its ideology. This was a unique collective satirical project.

The humour of the Communist joke erupts from the explosive tension between embrace and unmasking, devotion and disabuse, affection and contempt.

My theory, which, just like Monty Python's Miss Anne Elke, is mine and belongs to me, goes as follows: the Communist joke is obsequious at one end, much more ambiguous in the middle, and antagonistic at the other end.

*

While many Soviet Bloc citizens, like the Zimpsonoviches, believed their derision of Communism would bring the end of the system a step closer, the state had now developed its own diametrically opposed theory of the power of Communist jokes. The Politburos of the Soviet Bloc thought that as long as people expressed their opposition in terms of jokes instead of marches and riots, its power would be secure. A new theory of the power of Communist jokes was emerging: that their telling would actually help to preserve the system.

It wasn't easy to find high-ranking Politburo members from the sixties alive, but one of them lived in retirement in Bucharest: Romania's former Minister of Propaganda, Paul Niculescu Mizil*. I rang the buzzer of his modest 1950s villa. He was short, with thick, grey hair and a mischievous smile. He looked like everyone's favourite grandfather; yet it was he who had been responsible for thirty years of lies about the Romanian harvest, the quality of Romanian apartment blocks and the country's economic growth.

Mizil was one of the longest-serving ministers in the history of Communism. Born in 1923, he had received training in Moscow and became a member of the Romanian Central Committee in 1955 under the violent dictator Gheorgiu Dej. In 1957 he became Minister for Propaganda, a position he retained until 1973 under Dej's incompetent successor Nicolae Ceauşescu. Thereafter he worked in the industrial department of the economics ministry. He remained in power and one of a *troika* of ministers closest to the Ceauşescus until 1981, when he was sidelined. He led me down to his dark basement, which was lined with the kind of cheap books acquired by people who want to give the impression of scholarly endeavour – monographs on Monet with poor reproductions, volumes of national poetry by men whose names end in *-escu*, and his own defensive memoirs.

I was lucky to get an interview with him on the subject of humour under Communism. It gave away my political position immediately, but I could guess the calculations that had led him to agree to meet me. When he first read my request, he would have thought that I wanted to make a fool of him; but then, wily old fox, he would have smiled to himself as the thought dawned on him that an amateur English historian of jokes would be putty in his hands.

* Paul Niculescu Mizil died in 2008.

'Did Ceauşescu have a sense of humour?' I began by asking.

'I can say that he was a particularly human person who showed great openness to other people's problems and needs. Let me tell you the story of a trip taken to the Soviet Union around 1955 in the company of Ceauşescu ... I fell very ill one night. My colleagues came to see me and one of them even informed Ceauşescu that I was unwell. I remember that the following morning at 7 a.m. sharp Ceauşescu came to see me. I was sitting in the hotel lobby; he came to me and asked what was wrong with me. I told him that I was feeling unwell and that I was also affected by the fact that I had been away from home for a long time and left my pregnant wife alone in Bucharest. I confessed that I felt as if I couldn't bear to stay in Russia any longer. And do you know what he replied? He said: "Actually, I can't stay either." The very same day he declared the diplomatic visit closed, although some events were scheduled for the following days. The very same day we went back to Bucharest.'

It was a mind-numbing story, but to be expected. By now I had some experience of interviews with old Commies, so I knew the games they played. Mizil was bombarding me with three Communist interview strategies in one: ignore the question, tell a long, dull, sentimental tale about the leader and reveal that one is a family man. I interrupted: 'Yes but did Ceauşescu tell any jokes?'

'Well, when it came to international competitions, no matter what the sport, Ceauşescu would always support the Romanian team. I remember one time when we were in Moscow for the annual inter-national Congress of Communist Parties. That meeting took place at the same time as the European Boxing Championship – it was a Romanian versus a West German. I remember that Ceauşescu got all the Romanian delegation together to watch the match. While we were watching it, we were caught up in the fight and kept shouting out: "Beat him. Beat the reactionary." Then, at some point, he turned to the Russian officer and said to him: "I expect you to mention in your report that we are against reactionary types of behaviour."'

'Very funny,' I said, trying to make him feel at ease. 'But weren't you worried about all the political jokes that were being made against Communism by ordinary people, while you were propaganda minister?'

Mizil gave me a cheeky smile that indicated he had anticipated this question and had a clever answer to it. Mizil said: 'By the way, do you know the joke about Nikita Khrushchev that refers to the congress at which Khrushchev condemned the crimes committed by Stalin? After he finished his speech, one voice from the audience asked him: "Comrade Khrushchev, where were you when Stalin was committing all those crimes?" On hearing that, Khrushchev went mad and stamped on the table. "Where is the one who dared to ask me such a question?" Everybody in the hall was terrified and nobody dared to stand up. "See, that's exactly where I was," said Khrushchev.'

Of course, how stupid of me! Romanian Communists were against Soviet domination. Ceauşescu had condemned the invasion of Czechoslovakia in 1968 and he refused to allow Warsaw Pact military exercises on Romanian territory. So Mizil would have no objection to the genre of anti-Soviet Romanian jokes. 'Apart from jokes about Russians, weren't you worried by all the jokes that made fun of the system?' I asked.

'No. Many of them expressed support for our policies,' said Mizil. 'Listen to this one:

'Question to Radio Yerevan from a listener: "Can Socialism be built in the desert?"

'Reply from Radio Yerevan: "Yes, that is possible, but not advisable. After some time they will have to start importing sand."

'That actually fitted the politics of the Romanian Communist Party: we did not want a Socialism built "in the desert"; we wanted a Socialism that was adapted to the local circumstances.'

I wanted to say, 'But what about jokes like . . .?' But I'd lost the will.

'We didn't worry about the jokes,' Mizil sighed, giving me a sympathetic look. 'Political jokes expressed the discontent of the population. However, this particular way of expressing their position was actually a way to avoid taking responsibility. The jokes were good for us. They were a way for the population to let off steam, nothing more.'

Mizil was expressing a verdict on Communist jokes that I hadn't heard before, but that I would encounter frequently, from now on, among unapologetic former Communist officials and some ultra-conservative sociologists. It was an extreme formulation of the minimalist position that amounted to joke denial. If the maximalists argued that the jokes brought down Communism, and the minimalists considered that they were only an expression of public opinion, the deniers said that the jokes actually helped prolong Communism. In their theory, joke-telling was an impotent activity that gave those practising it the false impression that they were fighting the system. This 'wrong evaluation' of the impact of the *anekdoty* meant that people were expending their energies harmlessly instead of pursuing strategies that would actually destabilise the regimes.

Mizil concluded: 'I do not think that political jokes are an efficient form of protest against a hostile political environment.'

Across the Soviet Bloc, from the sixties onwards, the Politburos simply did not see the flood of jokes as a danger. Unchecked, the number of jokes grew and grew. Once in a blue moon, a party official or judge would try to put his finger in the dyke.

The archives of Radio Free Europe, the anti-Communist Cold War broadcaster, contain scores of records of jokes that listeners sent in or refugees brought in, and which were subsequently read out on air. It's very difficult to find evidence of trials for joke-telling after 1960, but I came across documentation for one prosecution in Czecho-slovakia in 1967 in these archives. A refugee brought the news that a worker in a liquor factory had been arrested for telling the following joke:

> *Why is the price of lard not going up in Hungary?*
> *So that the workers can have lard on bread for their Sunday lunch.*

This rather weedy joke was a reference to the price of meat. The implication was that, since meat had become so expensive, instead of a Sunday roast, workers would be spreading pig fat on sandwiches. The joke had been overheard by the Party secretary of the factory, who had immediately reported the worker. The joke-teller had been arrested on charges of 'incitement and defamation against the People's Democracy'. After six hearings, he had been fired. The sentence was relatively lenient because the co-workers all stood by the employee, saying that the Party secretary had not heard the phrase the accused had used to preface the offending material, which was: 'I heard a very stupid joke yesterday ...'

The odd trial was not the only way some lone figures in the Party attempted to turn off the tap of wit. I found a remarkable letter published in *Izvestia* in early 1964, under the headline: 'We Should Fight for It!' It purported to have been written by a miner from a remote industrial town, but I think we should take that with a pinch of salt. Full of the flowery language of Soviet propaganda, with its anachronistic romanticisation of industrialisation, it was probably written by someone high up in the Party. It deplored the growth of jokes and joke-telling, looked nostalgically back to the era in which joke-tellers were sent to the camps, and warned that the policy of tolerance could undermine the system.

Dear Editors!

Ten days ago I went to the local bank. In front of the clerk's window there were five people waiting for their turn. I was waiting as well. And while standing there I heard too much ... Two well-dressed people stood in front of me – they looked well fed and healthy. One of them had the demeanour of a man of culture, the other had a wrinkled face. There they stood in a public place, and with a pronounced insolent casualness they 'did their best' as regards the anecdotes. They spoke in a mocking tone about the bad harvest and talked sarcastically about our shortages.

I felt as if they were sticking pins into me, as they told these nasty things to each other and roared with laughter. Here we are, they say, we do not care a damn about it ... Behind their grins I saw something slippery, grey, disgusting. It was vulgarity personified.

It was repugnant but I simply turned away. Later I thought that I should not have left. I am for fighting back! Because what I overheard concerns all our lives, and deserves to be defended. All these 'fruits of wittiness' are nurtured and bred by someone with a certain goal – to attract the support of the lacklustre leaders of the anti-Party group, who are presented by some as political 'stars'. Some people insist that we should not pay attention to these jokes. They say people will stop this idle talk the same way they started it. Today no one is put into prison for this kind of chit-chat.

Some tell me: don't get wound up! After all, you can't shut everyone's mouth, and the times are different now ... We have to regard these jokes as 'splashes of life'. This is how far it can go! But sometimes, you see, these anecdotes are not funny at all. Sometimes anecdotes cross over into the offensive ...

So, how should one deal with all these mudslingers? ... How can I restrain myself in front of the 'joker' who tells me mockingly a 'new anecdote'. Nothing is sacred for him. He is ready to spit upon everything! I am ready to fight with anyone who pretends that this verbal filth is just an innocent joke. I would have gathered three dozen of these ill-minded people, put them in the train and sent them far away. No, not to the jail, not to the camps, but on a tour. I would have given each of them papers, pencils, set them by the window in the train from Moscow to Nakhodka. I would have forced them to watch everything, to count everything, to write it down, the prices, kilometres, money, items, everything. Houses, bricks, column cranes, streets, restless trains, high-voltage transmission lines and elevators. I would have brought them to Magadan. Let them see our capital, let them count everything. From Magadan to our regional centre, let them write about it as well. How many aeroplanes take off and land daily, from where and with which cargo.

But what can we do with these toadstools that I think about all the time? The toadstools are bad words of angry and dangerous people. There are not many of them, but they stink. How can we treat these people? We can not behave as our woodcutter used to do, when he pretended to be a gardener. But we have to fight them; it is necessary to defame, shame and dishonour them in front of the honest people. I know what should happen to a person who cannot tell the difference between freedom of speech and freedom of dirt. We are for criticisms of the imperfections, for sharp but helpful critique. But we are against the spiteful critics, whose wanton words suit well only our enemies ...

With deep respect,
Nikolai Kuritsin
Miner, external student
Kadykchan village

From that letter, you might think that there was a sharp dividing line between the jokes told by ordinary people and the official humour of a humourless political system. That's certainly what the jokers imagined. They read letters like Nikolai Kuritsin's, and thought that their jokes were a thorn in the side of Communism. Yet, as in the thirties, there were many areas of overlap and subtle differences of degree between the jokes of the state and the jokes against the state.

Eulenspiegel, the German satirical magazine, serves as a case study in this complexity. It was founded in 1954 on the say-so of the East German Politburo. It inherited its name from another post-war satirical magazine called *Ulenspiegel*, which had been banned in 1950. But four years later, in the aftermath of the uprising of 17 June 1953, the state thought it wise to have some form of comic expression: students were authorised to establish cabarets in Berlin, Dresden and Leipzig (including the Rat der Spötter we encountered in the previous chapter) and the satirical magazine was relaunched. The magazine had the same brief as its other Communist counterparts. In 1956 the Central Committee spelt out that the construction of Socialism could 'never be a subject for comedy or ridicule', but that 'the most urgent task of satire in our time is to give Capitalism a defeat without precedent', which included, of course, exposing 'backward thinking [and] holding on to old ideologies'. Every Thursday, the editor of *Eulenspiegel* went to the weekly Agitation Commission meeting in the Central Committee building in Berlin. There in the company of all the DDR's other leading newsmen, he was advised by officials of the interests, themes and mood of the Party that week, which he and his team were to translate into cartoons and comic essays in their magazine. There was always a demand for cartoons with doves of peace.

In the 1950s *Eulenspiegel*'s print run was three hundred thousand, rising to half a million in the eighties – but they could have sold many more copies if there hadn't been a permanent shortage of printing paper in the DDR. Despite the vast circulation, it was actually quite difficult to find a copy. The DDR had seventeen million citizens and *Eulenspiegel* was the only place where they could read even veiled criticism of the state they lived in.

Eulenspiegel was not simply the mouthpiece of the state; the situation was more complex than that. The state needed to employ the most talented humorists of the time, and they wanted to tackle the problems inside their society as well as in the West. Many of these humorists, though they were members of the Party and believed in Communism, also wanted to make it better. They saw the magazine as a chance to do this from within. Among these wannabe fifth columnists was Ernst Röhl, the former member of the Leipzig cabaret troupe Rat der Spötter, now the domestic-affairs editor of *Eulenspiegel* 1965–97. He'd begun writing for the magazine shortly after he was released from prison in 1962.

'*Eulenspiegel* existed so Ulbricht could say: look we have a democracy, we have a satirical magazine; but we used that crack in the system, its weakest point, as a Trojan Horse,' said Ernst Röhl to me.

From the sixties onwards the battle was not simply between official and underground jokers. There was a fifth column inside the bureaucracy of official humour – a Maquis of witty double agents – who were working behind enemy lines to bring the system into disrepute.

'I could have jumped over the Wall,' said Ernst Röhl, 'and got shot; but I had a family. No one would do that. One had to find a way to exist behind the Wall. I thought: maybe I can improve things. I am of the opinion that the whole erosion of the DDR happened because of the work of *Eulenspiegel*, because sooner or later one saw that it couldn't go on, one had to stop DDR-ing.'

I searched volumes of *Eulenspiegels* to find essays by Röhl that might have chipped away at the DDR. I came across 'Now we have salad' from 1970:

Man doesn't live from bread and ham alone. He needs something green. And green things have been in short supply for a long time. Cabbage has been more the subject of discussion than digestion. And the Adam's apple is the closest one gets to fruit at the dinner table. But this year Mother Nature has been particularly green. Cucumbers are no longer the shoemaker's bribe. Onions no longer bring laughs in cabaret sketches . . .

Röhl's article was the equivalent of one of the jokes about queues and shortages – yet, writing for an official magazine, Röhl had to couch his satire on the failings of the economy in terms of a success story. At a push it's possible to see the inversion here as adding an extra dose of biting satire, but it read to me like a sop to the regime.

'I'm in favour of a certain pragmatism in life, even if that means I am morally damned. I always tried to expand the relevance of the themes we were meant to deal with in *Eulenspiegel*. I know people understood our hidden messages,' Röhl said.

I found other articles by Röhl that were fairly unexceptional satires on petty corruption.

In my bathroom the pipe's been leaking for three weeks. Despite several visits I hadn't managed to catch the repair man when he was in until yesterday. With sad eyes he looked at me. 'What can I do?' he said. 'I have a thousand jobs and only two hands. Calculate for yourself, my good man, when it'll be your turn.' 'Perhaps we can agree on an appointment. My wife bakes an exceptionally good apple cake' ... 'Of course I will come, but not before—' 'Excuse me for interrupting you, but I also have an acquaintance in a premises which has just received a delivery of Budweiser beer.' 'Of course I'll come,' the plumber said, 'but not before—' 'I hope you will permit me to interrupt you again,' I said. 'I have taken the precaution of writing your name on this envelope.' The plumber looked down at the envelope which contained some attractive greenish notes. 'That's not necessary,' he says. 'Let me see – it's now 11 o'clock. Of course I'll come, but not before 12.30.'

But Röhl could also, admittedly, produce hilarious mockeries of Communism, as in this meditation on a very common German surname and the names of Communist businesses.

What's in a name? Not much, some people say, but I beg to differ. Three weeks ago my surname was 'Bestmiller'. But doesn't that sound incredibly arrogant? As if one wanted to declare oneself superior to all the ordinary hard-working Millers? I am thinking of changing my surname to the name of the company I work for – the People's Collective for Cold-Pressed South East Saxon Vegetable Oil. Some spoilers find the name too long just because they need to take a few breaths as they say it, but I take a more positive view: no word is excessive. The name is as short and precise as is required. It avoids any confusion with the Semi-Nationalised Collective for North West Thuringen Rapeseed Oil. This trend of Socialist renaming poses the biggest threat to those of a poetic inclination who aren't interested in the exactitude of the name but just want something with a nice ring to it. Luckily these poetic names cannot resist the force of Praxis. The Berlin laundry 'White Blossoms' had its name changed to REWATEX years ago so that its customers didn't get confused ...

Was Röhl deluded? Many minds greater than mine have tried to work out if the official humour was subversive in any way, shape or form. Certain subjects were always off limits – such as criticism of the leadership. This was the Achilles heel of champions of Communist satire and it was cunningly exposed by West German satirists in an exchange in 1963. In that year, the editors of *Eulenspiegel* approached their West German counterpart magazine *Pardon* and suggested a collaboration. The West Germans replied succinctly that it would be possible, if *Eulenspiegel* would write about Walter Ulbricht, the leader of the DDR, as critically as the Western satirists wrote about their own leader, West German Chancellor Konrad Adenauer. The suggestion, to which there was no reasonable Communist answer, stung *Eulenspiegel* into an extraordinary self-incriminating essay, entitled 'How We Write about Walter Ulbricht'.

We are proud of the fact that Socialist satirists don't feel compelled to lash out in every direction in order to make profits for Capitalism … The transparency of our state makes it not only difficult, but simply impossible to write satire about its representatives. Where there is nothing to uncover and expose, the satirist has nothing to look for. Where no masks are worn, there can be no demasking. So, how do we write about Walter Ulbricht? We satirists are obliged to analyse the world in order to improve it. We therefore send birthday greetings on 30 June to the First Secretary of the Central Committee of the Party.

Still wondering, perhaps too generously, if *Eulenspiegel* was subversive or sycophantic, I took a train to Leipzig to see a major exhibition of East German cartoons: *Unterm Strich: Karikatur und Zensur in der DDR*, which can be translated as: 'The thick red pen: caricature and censorship in the DDR'. Perhaps if I acquired an overview of the cartoons of *Eulenspiegel*, I would at least acquire an impression of which side the magazine was on.

The exhibition was installed in the Zeitgeschichtliches Forum, one of the handful of worthy museums dedicated to the history of the DDR that have sprung up in former East Germany. I walked dutifully through the rooms of vitrines and framed exhibits and breathed in that uniquely sawdusty and under-oxygenated museum air. I felt tired immediately, as I looked at the creased blue uniforms of the FDJ, the East German Communist youth movement, and reconstructions of *Westpakete*, the parcels of goodies that West Germans were allowed

Fig. 41. American soldiers in Germany look up and see a flock of birds forming the message 'Americans Go Home' (Karl Schrader, *Eulenspiegel*, 1953).

Fig. 42. An American tank, its barrel pointing towards the border with East Germany, is disguised as a cute cottage (Peter Dittrich, *Eulenspiegel*, 1968).

to send to their relatives on the other side of the Iron Curtain. There were the bright colours and geometric graphics of propaganda posters, which still gave me a little Ecstasy-like rush of utopian euphoria. A world without poverty and inequality where everyone agreed with each other and the state knew best! There were leaden wall texts about the people who had died in the custody of the Stasi, the world's largest ever political-police force, if one measures it as a percentage of the population. And in the exhibition I had come to see there were neat rows of utterly beautiful framed cartoons and caricatures – many of which should be reclassified as works of art and exhibited in national galleries – spanning the whole history of East Germany.

It was apparent that in the *Eulenspiegel* cartoons the traditional themes of official humour were still in demand right until 1989. Hardly an issue went by without a cartoon about bureaucracy – a

Fig. 43. The Evolution of Man, Frank Leuchte, *Eulenspiegel*, 1979.

Fig. 44. 'Artze, you go to the meat counter, Jacqueline go and queue for the veg, and Kelle go and stand in the checkout queue.' Karl Schrader, *Eulenspiegel*, 1974.

worker collapses with exhaustion at the desk of an official, set in an idyllic landscape: he's raced over hill and dale just to get a stamp. A dragon finds himself stamped by a bureaucrat 'File Closed' rather than attacked by a knight. There were gratingly obvious swipes at the West in which birds in the sky form the words 'Americans Go Home'; a dove of peace floats around the hammer-and-sickle, a skeleton carries a placard saying 'I like Nixon' and West German politicians are dogs in Nazi uniforms. A portrait of the American President Kennedy is drawn in Archimboldo-style composed not of fruit and vegetables but of weapons; an American tank is concealed behind the neatly curtained windows of a West German cottage (Fig. 42).

It was fine to criticise lazy workers – the state didn't connect their reluctance to work with the lack of free-market competition: the low quality of service is lampooned in a cartoon of the evolution of man that shows the transformation of an ape first into a standing man and then into one on his knees before an imperious waiter (Fig. 43). Cartoons on shortages were also permitted. A housewife uses her children in the supermarket to beat the queues by sending each to stand in a different one (Fig. 44). As in this cartoon, in material on this subject there is usually an ambiguity about the target – it is not clear if it is against greedy consumers or badly stocked shops.

I could see a line of development. The early cartoons had an angry propaganda tone, targeting the first Chancellor of West Germany, Konrad Adenauer, and other West German leaders. Then, in the

second half of the sixties, the system became more porous. From time to time it allowed editors and cartoonists to sail incredibly close to the Communist wind, especially if the material was on the inside pages (Plate 6). In one cartoon, a man fails his eye test. In the caption, the opticians says: 'Don't worry.

Fig. 45. 'Don't worry, You can still get a job in the quality-control department of a factory.' Karl Schrader, *Eulenspiegel*, 1962.

You can still get a job in the quality-control department of a factory' (Fig. 45). In the seventies there's a notable number of cartoons that point out the discrepancy between promise and reality. The quality of East German construction is ridiculed in one that shows a family moving into a new home and being given a spanner instead of a set of keys (Fig. 46). These were cartoons on subjects that the state had always tolerated – but they had acquired a new level of satirical intensity.

Did this material show Ernst Röhl had a point, and that the cartoonists were slowly pushing back the state, slowly but surely shaving away at the Party's taboos?

Another way of assessing the critical value of the *Eulenspiegel*'s cartoons is to look at what got stopped. Unlike other Soviet Bloc satirical magazines, *Eulenspiegel* was not proof-read by a censor before it was published. East Germany was unique in the Soviet Bloc in that it had no office of press censorship, which made it possible for the state to claim it had freedom of speech. This carried the dis-advantage that it was difficult for officials to act before the event. For historians it has the benefit that the mistakes were occasionally produced in full colour before they could be corrected.

In the fifties and early sixties several editors came and went, when they overestimated what the Party could take. The cartoonists themselves were never punished – though they might be shouted at, as some remember, for 'pandering to the class enemy'. The editor who lost his job most unusually was Heinz Schmidt. In 1958 he allowed himself to be photographed for a news-paper article standing behind a desk strewn with papers and

Fig. 46. ' . . . and it is with great pleasure that I can now give you the keys to your new home' (Barbara Henniger, *Eulenspiegel*, 1985). The couple are receiving a spanner instead of a set of keys, implying that the construction of their flat has been faulty and careless.

Fig. 47. Banned *Eulenspiegel* cover. The text reads: 'I always thought you were a drop-out!' (Heinz Behling, 1969). The message of the cartoonist was that all young people could find a place in the Youth Movement, but the East German leadership thought the cartoon supported hippies.

Fig. 48. Another banned cover, from 1981. The butcher says: 'Just between you and me, this is of course your standard sausage, but thanks to the additional two knots it has acquired totally new properties.'

Fig. 49. Willi Moese, *Neue Berliner Illustrierten*, 1970.

cartoons. He is absent-mindedly holding a caricature of Walter Ulbricht, which had already been banned from publication. Underneath the photo there was an interview in which he told the newspaper journalist, 'So many problems can be solved simply tidying up one's desk.'

On two occasions a whole edition had to be recalled and pulped. In 1969 the editors published a cartoon on the cover that depicted a meeting of the East German Communist youth movement, the FDJ. The two youth leaders in the foreground were drawn with long hair, in the style of West German hippies (Fig. 47). Long hair was frowned on in East Germany at the time, and children who disobeyed were given forcible haircuts. The Central Committee raised the alarm as soon as they saw the image ... but it was too late: the magazine had already been posted to hundreds of thousands of subscribers. Undaunted, the government ordered all the copies that had been sent out to be collected in. Every little post office had to fetch back those it had delivered to their individual destinations. All the collected magazines were then handed in to the local police station, the numbers were passed on to the magazine staff in Berlin and they had to compile

Fig. 50. Typewriter, Willi Moese, 1977.

a table of what had been retrieved. Finally a new edition was printed with a different cover.

Two decades later, in 1981, another edition was pulped as the result of an offending cover concerning price-fixing. One of the holy tenets of post-war Communism was that there was no inflation, unlike in the West. Thus in East Germany a loaf of bread cost the same in 1989 as it had done in 1949. Maintaining price stability like this involved huge subsidies and was in many instances impossible to finance. Hence the practice evolved of altering the original product in some spurious way and then increasing the price. The offending cartoon showed a butcher with a new kind of sausage, which had the irrelevant addition of an extra knot at either end – two instead of the usual one – and cost one mark, instead of the usual eighty pfennigs (Fig. 48). 'We just managed to save the deputy editor his job,' remembers a staff writer at the time, Jürgen Nowak.

Nor was it only *Eulenspiegel* that could make mistakes that would lead to the pulping of an entire edition. In 1970 a cartoon by Willy Moese in the weekly *Neue Berliner Illustrierten* consigned the entire edition to the bin – it showed a man running into a cellar with a newspaper so that he could laugh out loud at it – the first cartoon translation of a joke that went back to Hitler (Fig. 49).

The show of cartoons in Leipzig had one more great exhibit: a typewriter with three keys (Fig. 50). In 1977 Honecker visited the

Eighth Art Exhibition of the DDR in Dresden, and viewed this object. 'I learned how to type on one of these,' Honecker said cheerfully. His companions laughed politely – the letters on the keys spelt: b-l-a.

On the train back to Ariane in Berlin I scribbled down a balance sheet. Gags about Communist hippies, stealthy price hikes and the First Secretary were out; but biting jokes about queues, shoddy goods and construction were in. I thought I could weigh up what was allowed against what was banned, but I had to give up because I couldn't work out an accurate system of measurement. The unspoken 'rules' about what kind of subjects official humorists could or could not deal with, and with what severity or lightness of tone, were impenetrable. Beyond that was an even larger ontological obstacle: there was that quality of satire that it could gain in strength the more it feigned to be on the side of those it criticised. That meant that one could never safely damn *Eulenspiegel*'s cartoons as sops.

There was one more aspect of *Eulenspiegel* on which its editorial staff prided themselves. The East German state permitted serious – that is, non-humorous – criticism to be aired in public in two locations. One was a weekly TV consumer show called *Prisma*; the other was in the national organ of humour.

'We were the opposition. We were the critical voice in the country,' Gerd Nagel told me. Nagel had edited *Eulenspiegel* from the late sixties until 1989. His thinning grey hair was trimmed into a high Mao-style bob. We met on Alexanderplatz, the former central square of East Berlin. In the old times, this had been an empty, windy expanse of concrete in the middle of which stood a blue-tinged Interhotel skyscraper and a department store with an ostentatious façade of an intricate concrete lattice. Some way off, the edges of the plaza were lined with cheap apartment blocks, like an audience of workers watching an athletic display of luxury. Now this space was filled up with a new shopping centre and the ground floors of most buildings had been converted into tasteless tourist cafés. We sat down in one and Gerd Nagel ordered tea with schnapps.

'People wrote to us when things went wrong – when the roof leaked, when they had problems with builders and plumbers, they wrote to us in the hope that we'd write an article about it, and we often did. We had slots for these pieces called "A Fairly Open Letter" and "I have a question about that ..." Then, from 1972 onwards, we started a section called *Quittiertes* ("Resolved") where the persons criticised, the director of a company or such like, had to write a reply. Sometimes we published the most grovelling apologies,' he said with relish.

Eulenspiegel's tip-offs did not come only from their readers. The magazine had a close relationship with the DDR's inspectorate, a department called ABI (Arbeiter und Bauer Inspektion – 'Worker and Construction Inspectorate', which was the organisation that checked that the DDR was running properly. They supervised construction organisations, light and heavy industry, businesses and trade, services, children's education – everything, really. The ABI, Gerd Nagel explained, fed *Eulenspiegel* information, which they turned into critical satirical articles. Four times a year he would meet the head of the ABI, who would advise him what investigations they were conducting over the next four months.

'What was in it for the ABI?' I asked naïvely.

'They were desperate to leak their reports to us,' said Nagel. 'It was the only way they had of getting anyone inside government or industry to take notice of their recommendations. Do you think these big unaccountable state-owned industries or businesses would have cared what they were doing wrong if they hadn't been ridiculed in *Eulenspiegel*? We were the pressure for change.'

Thus the state recognised the need for some kind of critical dynamic to keep everything running. They gave *Eulenspiegel* – humour – that responsibility.

Nagel pulled a pile of old magazines out of his bag and showed me the magazine section he meant. It consisted of consumer complaints, an East German version of *That's Life*. I glanced over the responses of the businesses the magazine fingered:

The criticisms from citizen Werner Romrig from Erfurt are completely justified. Some staff members used the meeting to extend the duration of their official break. This gross contravention of the rules and hospitality of the establishment led to a critical collective discussion. Colleagues who seek to damage the reputation of socialist gastronomy must be held to account ...

In response to the charges made against him, the relevant Number 40 bus-driver explains that in the specified time-frame of the incident significant disturbances to the normal operating procedures were caused by other undisciplined road-users who parked their vehicles in the turning zone of Robert Koch Square despite the parking ban ...

Our investigations reveal that the repairs specified on the repair sheet were duly carried out. The fault in the tape recorder occurred during the transit from the technician via the storage depot to the collection counter ...

There was something pathetic about the way Nagel's concept of 'opposition' had not got beyond Esther Rantzen. It was as if he had never understood what politics was.

'How could you see yourself as a kind of opposition, when all you were doing was producing consumer exposés?' I asked him.

He sipped his fortified tea. I thought I noticed his facial muscles tightening. 'There could be no *Systemkritik*,' said Nagel, using one of those concise and crunchy German words that carries more weight in its original language than in translation. 'We could not criticise the shortcomings of Socialism, and the criticisms we made had to be concrete criticisms that could be substantiated.'

'And why were you happy with this rule of no criticism of the system?'

'I saw no alternative to the system.'

Other members of the *Eulenspiegel* staff had told me how, at editorial meetings, Nagel vetoed scores of cartoons (Fig. 51). 'Do you remember any cartoons that you rejected?'

'No.'

'But members of your editorial staff told me that you often rejected images.'

'I don't recall banning any cartoons for their political content,' he said. 'I suggested small changes or had other kinds of objections.'

Nagel was apparently also vigilant with the articles his staff wrote. One writer told me that his essay about sheep-dog trials was spiked because the editor thought the way the dogs managed the sheep might be understood as a criticism of the leadership of East Germany. Another staff member had told me: 'We were always being summoned by the Central Committee and told: "You can't say that ... That's two one-sided ... That is too broad a criticism, whereas the problems are individual ... You can write about individual cases but not give the impression that everything is rubbish in the DDR."'

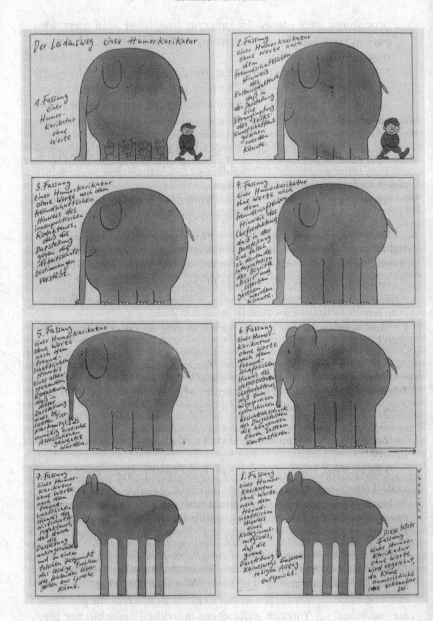

Fig. 51.

'The Trials and Tribulations of a Cartoonist' (Manfred Bofinger, *Eulenspiegel*, 1977). This cartoon by a brilliant *Eulenspiegel* caricaturist suggests what it might have been like working for Gerd Nagel. The text, from left to right and top to bottom, of course, reads:

1 First version of a humorous cartoon without words.
2 Second version of a humorous cartoon without words after the friendly advice of the arts editor that the image could be interpreted as a denigration of the creativity of ordinary people.
3 Third version of a humorous cartoon without words after the friendly advice of the domestic affairs editor that the image contravenes the health and safety laws.
4 Fourth version of a humorous cartoon without words after the friendly advice of the editor-in-chief that the image could be seen as a false interpretation of the concepts of 'base' and 'superstructure'.
5 Fifth version of a humorous cartoon without words after the friendly advice of a freelance female contributor that undesirable erotic associations could be awakened by this image of a popular resident of the zoo.
6 Sixth version of a humorous cartoon without words after the friendly advice of the deputy editor that the drooping ears look odd in view of the notably happy facial expression.
7 Seventh version of a humorous cartoon without words after the friendly advice of the economics correspondent that it might – unwisely and at the wrong time – raise the question of the regrettable problem of a shortage of outsized clothing in the shops.
8 Eighth version of a humorous cartoon without words after the friendly advice of a local councillor that the grey hue of the image in no way corresponds to the colourful reality of our lives … This last version of a humorous cartoon was refused because no humorous content could be identified in it.

There were only two occasions in the whole history of the DDR in which the 'opposition' named ministers. In 1980 *Eulenspiegel* called on the Deputy Minister for Construction to correct a defect in the planned economy – a company that made products from aluminium waste had complained that another company that made aluminium windows was not providing the promised quota of secondary material. The windows company responded that, following government directives, it had found a more economical way to manufacture the fittings, which produced less waste. In 1982 *Eulenspiegel* addressed the Minister for Construction himself about leaking apartment blocks that had remained unrepaired for three years. The buildings were fixed, but the Politburo then banned any further articles naming politicians, and after 1986 they ended the inspectorate's relationship with the satirists. Nevertheless, Nagel thought that, as editor of *Eulenspiegel*, he had been working for the improvement – for the reform – of East German Communism.

'Did you ever wonder if this was a system that *could* be reformed?' I asked. 'Did you have any days of doubt?'

'No.'

'Did you ever have any afternoons or mornings of doubt?'

'No.'

I could have asked him for more explanation, but I knew the rest. He'd signed the Faustian pact of Communism, along with every other adherent of that ideology. He had been prepared to forgo a large measure of free speech and truthfulness in return for the creation of a just society. Unfortunately, the devil hadn't kept his side of the bargain.

Some people collect works of art, others jokes. Ariane collected old coat hooks. She was nailing another one – probably of German origin, late nineteenth century – to the uneven row of them she had in her hallway when I walked in. 'How did it go?' she asked.

'Great, really great,' I said, trying to pick my words so as not to sound like a victorious Capitalist returning from battle. 'We talked about how he worked with a close group of caricaturists over many years, and how they saw themselves as the voice of criticism inside the DDR ...'

I could see her hackles rise, just at the tone in which I spoke the words 'voice of criticism' ... 'I asked him if he thought it was odd that the only place where one could express criticism in the DDR was on the terrain of humour, and he just didn't have an answer for me ...'

'Why should he?' she asked.

I ignored the question and continued, 'I asked him: did you ever have any days of doubts, at the time? No, he said. Just no. I couldn't believe it.'

Ariane exploded. 'You just wanted a statement of regret,' she said, waving the hammer in her right hand and holding the coat hook in her left, which for a moment resembled a small sickle. 'That's what people from the West writing about the DDR always want. You just want them to say how guilty they feel about their actions and how they got it all wrong. How can you expect him to say sorry to you, a stranger?'

'No, I wasn't looking for an apology. This man spent twenty-five years thinking that he could use satire to improve the system from within. He was working in an environment where there was no free speech. By his own admission, only his magazine could express criticism. There was that joke about the guy who's asked if he has a personal opinion of the political situation – Yes, he says, but I don't agree with it. I just wanted to know if he ever, at the time – not now, at the time – wondered if the system could be changed or was worth attempting to change.'

'Why should these people have doubts? They were building a state they believed in. He was trying to change the system.'

'But this was a state that shot people who tried to leave it,' I said, referring to the 190 DDR citizens who were killed trying to cross the Berlin Wall, and the four hundred more murdered trying to leave at other points of the East–West German border. 'You know the joke about the two East German border guards. One says to the other, 'Are you thinking the same as me? – Well then, I am going to have to shoot you.''

'Why do people always bring up the handful of *Mauertöte*?' – in German, there is, predictably, a concise word for these victims of the DDR, the 'Wall-dead' – 'What about the ordinary people killed in imperialistic wars by Western soldiers?'

'The Soviet state also launched wars of imperialism, but Western states did not shoot people who wanted to leave,' I said. I thought to myself: *Ever heard the one about the East German Communist squatter who dated a West European middle-class intellectual? No? Oh well, it's a really short one.*

The next morning, I decided it was time to go. I packed my bags. I walked heavily down the three flights of stairs from Ariane's flat, lugging a suitcase full of books of Communist jokes. When my friends asked me why we'd split up, I told them it was 'political differences'. They looked at me as if I was mad.

*

In 1968 the Czech Prime Minister Alexander Dubček began an experiment in political freedom under Communism, known as 'Socialism with a human face', otherwise known as the Prague Spring. For the first time, a government inside the Soviet Bloc permitted criticism of the system in non-humorous form in newspapers and public meetings.

Freedom of speech led quickly to the emergence of opposition voices in the newspapers and calls for multi-party politics and elections, which, if they had been held, as they were twenty-one years later, would immediately have ended the Communist Party's monopoly of power – and the Soviets knew it. The experiment proved Communism and Democracy were incompatible – the former relied for its survival on a one-party state, and in Europe, at least, that was not possible without the enforced repression of public dissent.

In 1964 Khrushchev had been replaced by Leonid Brezhnev, the second-longest-serving First Secretary, who held power for eighteen years, 1964–82. Brezhnev gave speeches rehabilitating Stalin, which led to jokes comparing Brezhnev's most distinctive facial feature, his bushy eyebrows, with Stalin's, his moustache.

Brezhnev gets dressed in the morning. He grasps one eyebrow in the fingers of each hand, pulls them off his forehead and rearranges them under his nose. 'The joke's over,' he says to himself.

In the last week of August 1968 Brezhnev took action. Russian tanks rolled across the Czech border, with the weak excuse of an 'invitation' from concerned local Communists. Military-resistance was not an option. Jokes became the Czechs' weapon of choice – not that they had any choice. A sting of apposite invasion jokes appeared, which may be filed as a sub-genre: *Eastern European Jokes about the Russians – Invasion Jokes – Prague '68*. Many of these jokes recycled the wit of the Hungary Uprising in 1956. Then, as in 1968, the Soviet army arrived claiming it was coming to help its Socialist 'brothers'; hence:

How do the Russians visit their friends?
In tanks.

Is it true that the Czech patriots appealed to the Red Army for help?
Yes, it is true, but they appealed in 1939 and help arrived only in 1968.

How do the Czechs know that the Earth is round?
In 1945 the imperialists were driven out to the west and in 1968 they returned from the east.

What is the shortest and most beautiful Czech fairy tale?
'They have gone!'

The Czechs also made a number of new additions to the canon. Some linked their experience to the latest theory of international relations, the diplomatic principle of 'non-interference', which was then in vogue with the Chinese and the Russians, as a new riposte to criticism of their disregard for human rights:

Which is the most neutral nation in the world?
Czechoslovakia. It does not even interfere in its own internal affairs.

What is the most secure country in the world?
Israel, because it has no friendly neighbours.

What is black and knocking at the door?
The Future.

One apocryphal graffiti joke centred on the posters which proclaim that a certain day of a certain month is 'A Day of Soviet Czech [or Soviet–Hungarian, or Soviet–Polish] Friendship', to which someone scribbles '... and not a minute longer!'

The graffiti did not exist only in spoken jokes. During the first week of the invasion, Czech resisters turned Prague's central square into an ever-changing open-air gallery of anti-Soviet humour, which was captured on camera by underground photographers and film-makers. They wrote on walls – 'Soviet State Circus back in town: new attractions'; 'Soviet School for Special Needs Children, End of Term Outing'; they drew an image of the hammer-and-sickle in chalk with the sickle as a snake, and they put up cartoon posters. The most popular symbol was a circular road sign with the customary red border and a tank in the middle with a line through it. Early in the morning, young Czechs would make lightning dashes into the square to paste up new cartoons and slogans. In the evenings, Soviet soldiers would tear down the photos and burn them. One night the statues around Wenceslas Square had their mouths taped over (Figs 52–6).

Fig. 52. 'No tanks' road sign, the most popular symbol
of opposition to the Soviet invasion

Fig. 53. 'Soviet State Circus back in town: new attractions'

Fig. 54. Statue of a saint with her   Fig. 55. Chalked graffiti in central Prague
mouth taped over

Fig. 56. Putting up anti-Soviet posters in Prague, 1968

Fig. 57. Soviet soldiers tear down anti-Soviet posters in central Prague

'In 1968 the humour which until then had only appeared in newspapers or in conversations between friends flowed out onto the streets,' remembers one member of this underground resistance, Ivan Hanousek. Hanousek had been working for a Prague newspaper, but 'Russian soldiers armed with AK47s came and occupied our offices, so we set up an underground press and carried on publishing our paper from there.'

It took several months for the Soviets to wind the clock back, because it entailed the closure or purging of the whole of the Czech media. Consequently, between August 1968 and May 1969 an anti-Soviet press remained active. Underground printers produced leaflets and newspapers with texts and cartoons. Even the official satirical magazine *Dikobraz* could publish dark caricatures of the invasion.

The temporary absence of censorship led to the creation of a brilliant corpus of visual jokes, unique in the genre of Communist humour. Among the masterpieces produced in this period are Ivan Steiger's series of tanks. Steiger (Fig. 58), already an established critical caricaturist, fled to Munich the day after the Russians invaded. A chauffeur from a sympathetic member of the Central Committee paid him a visit on the evening of the invasion and told him that he was 'number sixteen' on the arrest list. He was able to cross the border

Fig. 58. Ivan Steiger selecting cartoon drawings for *Prague Diary* (Munich, 1968)

with ease because he had obtained a visa months before with an entirely different purpose in mind – 'I was a caricaturist and caricaturists always criticise things. But I didn't want to criticise Dubček's fledgling democratic government. It was young and fragile and didn't need any undermining. So I planned to go to Germany to work,' he told me.

In Munich, Steiger drew scores of cartoons, all using the tank as an absurdist image of the Soviet invasion. He drew tanks inside a cheese dish, tanks blooming on trees, tanks flying in formation like emigrating birds, tank jack-in-the-boxes, and so on. In one typically lateral drawing, a tank parachutes down, and lands with a thud on the top of an apartment block. You can see the inhabitant inside the apartment below hitting the ceiling with her broom – the traditional way flat-dwellers protested against noisy neighbours (Figs 59–62).

Steiger's cartoons were reproduced in the Czech newspapers that had gone underground (*Liternai Noveni*) and in newspapers across the world. In Czech cities, protesters drew them on the pavements, painted them on walls and printed them up as posters. Three weeks after the invasion, Steiger published them in a book, *Prague Diary*, one of the forgotten masterpieces of Communist humour, which

Fig. 59.   Fig. 60. Tanks, Ivan Steiger,
                           Prague Diary, 1968.

ironised the ubiquity of Soviet armoured vehicles in Prague and took the strategy of exaggerating the state's own propaganda – in this case, that its use of force was 'friendly' – to a new level.

A variety of the 1968 cartoons and *samizdat** material is kept in an obscure and impoverished eastern European archive in Prague, 'the Institute for Underground Literature', lovingly preserved and catalogued by bearded and impoverished former dissidents such as Jiri Gruntorat.

When I came to visit, Gruntorat fetched a large cardboard box, gently levered the lid off and pulled out a page covered in the wobbly text of a cheap old Soviet Bloc typewriter. He translated the title at the top for me: 'What You Still do not Know about the Theory and Practice of the Building of Communism in our Country'. During these months of occupation, he explained, normal life seemed to be

---

* Describes banned books, illegal news-sheets and pamphlets, published underground.

suspended. Economic activity slowed down. There was often little to be done in Czech offices. Bored secretaries did their bit for the humour underground by typing up sheets of A4 paper with jokes, such as the document we had in front of us.

'It's got fifteen. Some of them are absolutely perfect,' he said with an unmistakeable shiver of emotion in his voice. His eyes read from the page. 'Starting from the top: Why are we building Socialism? Because it's easier than working ... Which are the biggest enemies of

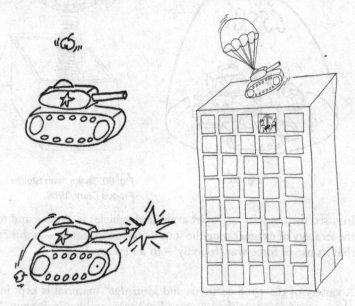

Fig. 61.   Fig. 62. Tanks, Ivan Steiger, *Prague Diary*, 1968.

Socialism? Spring, summer, autumn, winter and imperialism ... And here's another that's almost impossible to translate: When will Socialism be achieved in Czechoslovakia? When everybody has had enough of everything – This is exactly the double meaning you will never be able to translate into English.' That was not so difficult to translate, but the idea that it was was revealing. This was joke *pride*.

'I am convinced that the humour, at the very least, showed our intellectual superiority,' Mr Gruntorat told me, visibly inhaling and pushing his chest out. 'If this had been in a different country, the response would have looked different. Maybe the Yugoslavians would have put up a fight, but we here – we showed them our intellectual superiority and not a shot was fired. I don't know if this is good or bad, but this is how I see it.'

The jokes have another function for those people who suffered under Communism today, I realised. They are proof that they weren't simply lost years. They are evidence that some kind of soul came out of that era and that they have something that we in the West never had and will never have. Jokes were eastern Europe's jazz, the music of the oppressed.

SIX

Stagnating Jokes

By the end of the 1960s official satirists and Communist jokers had been battling it out for four decades. But who was winning this fight?

This was not the conflict that the existing literature on the subject had led me to imagine. In my zigzagging trips across the Soviet Bloc I had made many heretical discoveries that shook to its foundations the gospel of Communist jokes. I had seen that, as far back as the thirties, this was not a battle between one side without a sense of humour and another side with one. The Communists had their own sense of fun, too. The notion that jokes were the only tools of resistance for opponents of the regime was exposed as a mirage in the fifties: in truth, they could also print pamphlets, strike and riot. To make matters more complicated, in the sixties in Soviet-occupied Europe, the ranks of official humorists had been infiltrated by double agents, determined to sabotage 'positive satire' from within. Ultimately we know who won the war: the joke-tellers, in 1989, but it was a long-drawn-out conflict with many phases, in which the advantage swung back and forth.

By the beginning of the seventies there is extraordinary evidence that the joke-tellers had gained the upper hand, but at the beginning of the sixties, it's an entirely different story. Regarding these years, I made a discovery more blasphemous than any other. One of the holy tenets of the historiography of Communist jokes is that the state's humour was leaden and impotent, while the people's was lithe and persuasive. But there is material from the early sixties which suggests that at this time the official humorists were winning. Many Soviet citizens appear to have been persuaded by Stalin's satire, and it follows that many of the so-called Communist jokes being told in this period weren't actually *against* Communism.

Admittedly, there's little documentary evidence about the politics of joke-tellers, but there are files that tell us about the motivations of other related opposition to Khrushchev.

Teams of historians working on KGB and Interior Ministry documents declassified since 1999 have uncovered a surprising level of popular unrest against Khrushchev between 1953 and 1962. Much of this opposition was expressed under the influence of large quantities of vodka, reflecting the truth of the Russian proverb: *What the sober have on their mind, the drunk have on their tongue.* It ranged from expletives directed at the government, to assaults on police officers, marches, riots, looting, occasionally strikes and, of course, jokes.

Over the course of the fifties there were several riots and protests in the 'virgin lands'. Young workers who had moved there were enraged by the lack of running water and electricity and they attacked the offices of the local management. In September 1955 two thousand workers in Kemerevo went on strike against delayed payment of wages and extended working hours. Eleven workers were shot in one incident at Temirtau in August 1959, at the peak of which 25,000 workers didn't turn up for work. But few of these protesters were apparently anti-Communist. A pamphlet produced in the town of Kiselevsk by one Ivan Trofimovich, a Party member and deputy head of department of the Interior Ministry, revealed how protest did not imply *ideological* disillusionment. He wrote:

'Comrade miners, workers! ... The basic law of Soviet Power is that everything is for the good of the people. So they say in speeches and write in the newspapers. What does this mean in reality? ... In reality, the riches are enjoyed by a small clique of people – the Soviet bourgeoisie and their toadies.'

Between 1961 and 1962 these expressions of opposition – 'hostile phenomena', as they were officially termed – trebled; 34,600 anonymous texts were distributed in 1962, including 23,213 leaflets, saying things like: 'Khrushchev, you windbag, where is the abundance you promised?' – which relates perhaps to the joke:

Is it possible to wrap an elephant in newspaper?
Yes, if the paper contains a speech by Khrushchev.

All this occurred against a background of a breakdown in law and order – a doubling of arrests for 'hooliganism', which meant drunkenness, brawls and other antisocial behaviour.

In January 1961 there were two days of riots in Krasnodar against what one anonymous flyer called 'Soviet Capitalism'. The most significant unrest occurred at Novocherkassk at the Budenny Electric Locomotive Construction Works in June 1962, following the announcement of price increases and an effective pay cut of 30% for some workers. They held up a train, beat up local policemen, then marched on and ransacked the local government offices before they were stopped by soldiers firing live ammunition. The workers marched under a slogan: 'We want meat, milk, and a wage increase.' Strikers tore down portraits of Khrushchev, inveighed against 'false Leninists' and looked back fondly to Stalin's time, 'when we were moving consistently towards Communism', as one leaflet put it. The unrest shows that many Soviet citizens had actually been persuaded by the propaganda. The protesters often blamed the 'Soviet bourgeoisie' – by which they meant a corrupt bureaucracy – for the faults of the system, just as the official satirical magazine *Krokodil* did, and they blamed Stalin's successors, not him, for their economic plight.

The logical implications for the joke-tellers of the Khrushchev protests are fascinating. If people who joined protests against the state were not bent on bringing down Communism, it follows that the people who told the jokes must also have retained a belief in the ideology. Many people saw the faults in the system, but they wanted to correct them, not launch a counter-revolution. In other words, the 'Cold Warriors', the Soviet émigrés who put together joke books, the American journalists who printed the *anekdoty* in newspapers and all the rest who saw in the jokes the *will* of the people to bring down the system, were jumping to conclusions . . . .

So much for the beginning of the sixties; what about the end of them? By this time there had been more or less a decade of unrepressed joke-telling. The Soviet Bloc regimes were convinced that the jokes were not a political threat and that by tolerating them they might even be strengthening their regimes by providing a 'release mechanism'. But there is evidence that they got it wrong; and that evidence consists of the appearance of a new theme in the joking: Lenin. For the first time, joke-tellers breached the inner sanctum of Communism.

Nineteen seventy was the centenary of Lenin's birth. Preparations for the celebrations – the largest propaganda campaign ever mounted in the Soviet Union – began over a year earlier. It generated a flood of jokes ...

Leonid Brezhnev wanted to commission a portrait to be entitled 'Lenin in Poland'. Russian painters, being schooled strictly in the Realist school, were unable to paint an event that had never actually occurred.

'Comrade Brezhnev, we would like to do it, but we cannot. It goes against our training,' replied each of the many artists approached by Brezhnev. Finally, in desperation, Brezhnev was forced to ask the old Jewish painter Levy.

'Of course, I prefer to portray actual events, but I'll do the painting for you, comrade. It would be my great honour.' Levy commenced work on the painting.

Finally, the day of the unveiling arrived. Everyone gasped as the cloth was removed to reveal a picture of a man in bed with a woman who looked like Lenin's wife.

Brezhnev asked, horrified, 'Who is that man?'

'That's Trotsky,' said the artist.

'And who,' Brezhnev enquired, 'is that woman?'

'That is Lenin's wife, Comrade Brezhnev.'

'But where is Lenin?'

'He's in Poland,' Levy explained.

Under the slogan 'Lenin Lives', the Soviet Union experienced a deluge of school projects, lectures, films, billboards, songs, classical compositions, plays, lapel buttons, candy bars, and books (over eight hundred of them!), all funded by Moscow, who even financed the Antipodean commemorative volume of essays *Lenin – Through Australian Eyes*. A *New York Times* journalist wrote: 'It is fashionable in Moscow to ridicule the massive Lenin campaign – to point to the rows of unsold Lenin books and the banal Lenin posters that hang from every street corner, to the lifeless oratory, to the insensitivity to Lenin as a person that characterises the drive.'

The year 2000. The loudspeaker in the subway car squawks: 'Lenin Station with connections here for the Lenin Line and the Lenin Line. Next stop: Lenin Station.'

The doctors are interviewing a patient in the mental hospital:
'What is your name?' they ask.

'Doooh ...'

'Where are you from?'

'Duuh ...'

'What mental condition do you suffer from?'

'Daaah ...'

'Do you know what year this is?'

'Lenin's Jubilee.'

On the day itself, 24 April 1970, there were parades, displays and concerts all over the Soviet Bloc. The Soviet navy conducted special manoeuvres. In Moscow, six thousand delegates attended a rally at which Brezhnev gave a three-hour speech concluding with the thought: 'Lenin lived, Lenin lives and Lenin will live.'

'But at least he only has one one-hundredth birthday,' muttered the jokers.

Schoolchildren come to visit Lenin's widow, Nadia Krupskaia.
'Granny Nadia, tell us a story about Lenin,' they ask.

'You know, children, about Lenin's great kindness,' she says dewy-eyed. 'I remember once when a group of children came to visit Vladimir Ilich while he was shaving. "Play with us, granddad Lenin," they said. "Fuck off, you little bastards," he told them. His eyes were so kind.'

When we say Lenin, we mean Party. When we say Party, we mean Lenin. And this is how we deal with everything. We say one thing, we mean something else.

And then they came out with a bed that sleeps three, because, like the slogan says, Lenin is always with us.

Nineteen seventy-seven was the sixtieth anniversary of the Revolution and the same jokes could be dusted off, and if necessary polished up.

In Moscow in 1977 there was a competition for the best cuckoo clock. The third prize went to the clock in which on every hour a cuckoo came out and said: 'Lenin, Lenin.' The second prize went to a clock that said, on the hour, 'Lenin lives, Lenin lives.' The first prize went to a clock out of which Lenin himself appeared and said, 'Cuckoo, cuckoo.'

These jokes are significant not only because they are the first batch of Communist jokes about Lenin, but also because of their tone: they are lazy and cynical. Just compare them with the two or three jokes about Lenin that we know were invented before this period, such as these, the first probably from the twenties, the second from the fifties:

A man goes to visit Lenin's tomb. The guard says to him with gravity, 'Lenin is dead but his ideas will live for ever.'
'I just wish it was the other way round,' says the visitor.

A man visits Hell and he sees different punishments being inflicted on Hitler and Stalin. He asks the devil, 'Why does Hitler stand up to his neck in shit, while Stalin is only up to his waist?'
The devil answers, 'Because Stalin is standing on Lenin's shoulders.'

The punchlines of some of the new Lenin jokes are fundamentally different from those of the old. Instead of the ironic political statement that refers unmistakably to Communism in the older *anekdoty*, the new Lenin jokes – like many of the later Brezhnev jokes – offer crude ridicule, often with expletives and toilet or sexual humour. Thus, Lenin is not supporting Stalin on his shoulders, he is a hedgehog or a cuckoo clock, or someone is having sex with his wife. The Lenin jokes are dismissive. At this moment, one might theorise, Soviet citizens abandoned all faith in Lenin and his ideology, Communism.

If jokes really did help bring down Communism, then one would logically expect an uprising to follow the appearance of the Lenin jokes. The last bastion of Communist orthodoxy had been breached by humour; the next step would be counter-revolution; 1989 should have happened in 1971.

But it didn't. Instead the reverse took place. An era of inertia followed, which Mikhail Gorbachev christened the 'era of stagnation' and in which there were three different kinds of stagnating: economic, political and humorous.

By the end of the decade economic growth had ground to a halt in the Soviet Union and most other Soviet states. By the eighties the Polish and Czechoslovak economies were contracting.

What are the most constant problems facing the Soviet economy?
Temporary problems.

Despite their lack of resources, Soviet Bloc regimes offered their citizens a wan version of West European affluence. In West Germany they called it the 'economic miracle'; in Hungary it was known as 'goulash Communism'. Electronic goods were manufactured in larger quantities and sold at affordable prices. At the beginning of the seventies only a quarter of households in the Soviet Union had a television, and even fewer had a fridge; by the end of the decade over three-quarters had both.

But this pallid prosperity came at an unsustainable cost. The low prices and domestic appliances were funded by loans from Western banks. The Czech hard currency debt rose twelve-fold in the seventies, and Poland's thirty-fold. Between 1971 and 1980 the Polish hard currency debt increased from $1 billion to $20 billion, but you could still queue half a day for a loaf of bread.

How will the problem of queues in shops be solved when we reach
full Communism?
There will be nothing left to queue up for.

In Poland the Western money funded imports of goods, a new social-insurance programme for peasants and a price freeze for food at 1965 levels. East Germany, meanwhile, was spending 60% of its foreign-export earnings paying the interest on its debt to the West, despite the favourable rates offered by the West Germans. Soviet imports of food, mostly grain from America, tripled in the seventies.

Brezhnev gives his radio address to the Russian people: 'Comrades!
I have two important announcements for you – one joyful and one
sad. The difficult news is that during the next seven years we'll eat
nothing but shit. And the joyful news is that there will be an abundance
of it.'

The only productive parts of the Communist economies were the places where laws of state ownership had been relaxed: small businesses were legalised in Hungary and by the early eighties 84,000

Hungarian artisans were meeting nearly 60% of local demand for services.

The Soviet leadership was not short of advice about the urgency of change – they just ignored it. Handfuls of state-funded think tanks, established in the 'thaw' of the sixties, with plain-sounding names such as the Novosibirsk Institute of Economics and Industrial Organisation, the Central Economic–Mathematical Institute and the Institute for the World Economy and International Relations, produced classified reports urging the Politburo to introduce market reforms and expressed alarm at how far behind the West the USSR was in technology and living standards. Instead of following their recommendations, Brezhnev periodically purged these organisations of the voices of sanity.

Instead of imprisoning every rebellious citizen, the governments of East Germany and the Soviet Union allowed some of them to emigrate. The West German state bought visas for East German dissidents with hard currency, and by 1989 they had handed over the astronomical sum of around a billion West German marks for this purpose. In the 1970s, there was unprecedented Jewish emigration from the Soviet Union; 250,000 were permitted to leave, probably as a consequence of the pressure Western governments could exert through their loans.

How does a clever Russian Jew talk to a stupid Russian Jew?
By telephone from New York.

Internationally East–West relations offered a slight appearance of improvement. There was more diplomatic negotiation and a little less military antagonism: détente replaced deterrence, in the diplomatic terminology of the day. Brezhnev held summits first with Nixon and then with Carter to discuss reducing their nuclear arsenals.

Brezhnev visits Nixon; he sees a red telephone on his desk and asks him what it's for.
'Oh I can call up the devil with that phone,' says Nixon. Brezhnev asks him to prove it. Nixon tells one of his aides to call the number. The aide gets the devil on the line, hands the telephone to the American President, who talks to the devil for fifteen minutes and hangs up. Brezhnev is impressed. An aide comes in and says, 'Mr President,

you spoke for fifteen minutes; that will cost the American taxpayer $1,500.'

Brezhnev goes back to Moscow, and says to his aides, 'Get me the devil on the telephone. If the United States can do it, the Soviet Union can do it.' And so the aide gets the devil on the line and hands the telephone to Brezhnev, who speaks for about fifteen minutes. He hangs up, and the Soviet leader looks at the aide and says, 'How much did that cost.?'

The aide replies, 'Well, that cost two kopeks.'

Brezhnev is amazed – 'What? Two kopeks? You mean about five cents? The Americans paid $1,500, and we're only paying five cents?'

And the aide says, 'Yeah, you have to understand that, when you call the devil from Moscow, it's a local call. When you call from Washington, it's long distance.'

There were increased cultural and economic contacts. East Germans watched West German TV; Polish workers went to Germany to earn foreign currency; Soviet artists travelled abroad, leading to the joke:

What is the definition of a Russian string quartet?
A Soviet orchestra back from a US tour.

The West Germans launched Ostpolitik. They signed a treaty of friendship with the Poles, which led to a rapid decline in anti-German cartoons of people in Nazi uniforms in the Polish satirical magazine *Szpilki.* In other agreements, the West Germans recognised the existence of East Germany as a state for the first time. In return the Soviets signed the Helsinki Accords in 1975, which contained pledges to observe human rights.

But nothing seemed to change. Helsinki only confirmed the status quo. The disarmament talks led nowhere. By the end of the decade the Soviet Union had launched a new expansionist war with an invasion of Afghanistan. In response the Americans refused to ratify the SALT disarmament treaty. People spoke of a second Cold War.

At home, political apathy spread. As Khrushchev was deposed, the mass unrest died down. In the first five months of 1964 the KGB catalogued three thousand leaflets and letters with anti-Soviet content – but this was only a quarter of the eleven thousand items that they found in the second half of 1963. From 1969 to 1977, in the era of stagnation, not a single instance of mass unrest is recorded in the Soviet Union.

These were bleak years for Communism and bleak years for Communist jokes. There were fewer new jokes, and even fewer good new jokes. There was even a joke about it:

> *Why aren't there any new jokes nowadays?*
> *Rabinovich has emigrated.*

The punchlines were less punchy and, as if to conceal that, the jokes became much longer than those of past eras. Their style recalls the excess of decoration that afflicts art in the last phase of a declining civilisation. Then there was the tone: most of them, good or bad, carried a dispiriting mood of ennui. Perhaps the historical formulation is too neat to be plausible, but the jokes were stagnating, quantitatively and qualitatively, too.

> *Brezhnev was at his dacha on the Black Sea. Early one morning he went out onto the beach. The weather was beautiful and the sun was shining. Suddenly the sun began to talk to him. 'Good morning, dear Comrade Brezhnev. Don't be afraid; you may go bathing now. I've already warmed up the water for you.'*
>
> *So Brezhnev went for a swim and then lay down on the sand.*
>
> *'Now, why not go and have a snack, Comrade Brezhnev? You can come back in a while; I'll wait for you and chase the clouds away.'*
>
> *Brezhnev went to have some lunch, and soon returned to the shore.*
>
> *'Now then,' the sun said softly, 'turn over on your side and sleep for a while. Don't worry, I'll give you a nice beautiful tan.'*
>
> *Brezhnev listened to the sun and turned over.*
>
> *'Now once again, wake up,' the sun said to him sweetly, 'and go and eat dinner.'*
>
> *When Brezhnev came back to the shore in the evening, the sun had begun to set, and was already close to the horizon.*
>
> *'Well,' said Brezhnev, 'what should I do now?'*
>
> *The sun did not answer his question.*
>
> *'Why don't you answer me?' asked Brezhnev.*
>
> *'Kiss my ass,' said the sun; 'I'm in the West now!'*

The jokes continued to provide an alternative news service, ticking the boxes of every important historical development in the period, but not as hilariously as they once had done. Among the new ones, one that referenced the aging of the leaders of the Soviet Bloc, was this tired riddle:

What has forty teeth and four legs?
A crocodile.
What has four teeth and forty legs?
The Central Committee of the Communist Party.

The average age of the Soviet Politburo had been fifty-eight in 1966, but it was seventy in 1981. Brezhnev had one stroke in 1974 – which one may take as the start date for the era of stagnation – and another in 1976.

The government of the Union of Soviet Socialist Republics has announced with great regret that, following a long illness and without regaining consciousness, the General Secretary of the Central Committee of the Communist Party and the President of the highest Soviet, Comrade Leonid Brezhnev, has resumed his governmental duties.

After the strokes Brezhnev had to be helped to and from the podium and could barely read a speech.

Brezhnev is reading a speech: 'Who says that I only ever read from a piece of paper? Ha-hyphen-ha-hyphen-ha-hyphen-ha.'

How is it that Brezhnev became First Secretary of the Central Committee of the Communist Party of the Soviet Union?
According to the constitution of the Party, any member can hold the office.

Brezhnev showered himself with awards, and by the time of his death he had acquired 260 of them. His jacket eventually carried 110 medals, leading to a revival of decoration jokes not heard since the days of Hermann Goering. When they ran out of new accolades to give Brezhnev, they just gave him the old ones again – he received Hero of the Soviet Union, the highest honour of the nation, four times, though Stalin had set a maximum of three for this particular gong.

The Brezhnev family is having dinner and suddenly the whole building shakes like an earthquake. 'Oh my God, what's that?' asks his daughter Galina.

'Don't worry,' says her mother, 'that's just your father's jacket falling on the floor.'

The Soviet leader had expensive habits. He had a fleet of eighty cars and he also collected antiques, carpets and hunting weapons, which led to this groaner:

Brezhnev dies and winds up in Hell. The devil comes up to him and says: 'You, Leonid, are a prominent Communist, a man of great importance. Therefore, you may choose your own torture.'

Walking along in Hell, Brezhnev sees Adolf Hitler bathing in a tub of boiling oil and Josef Stalin stretched out on the rack. Suddenly he notices Nikita Khrushchev with Brigitte Bardot sitting on his lap. 'Well,' exclaims Brezhnev joyfully. 'That's the one! I want the same torture as Khrushchev!'

'No no, that can't be,' says the devil. 'It's not Khrushchev who's being tortured; it's Bardot.'

After the Americans landed on the Moon, in 1969, the Soviet Union lost its leadership of the space race, the only field in which it had been able to surpass technologically its rival superpower, prompting what is surely the worst Communist joke ever recorded:

Brezhnev calls in all the Soviet cosmonauts, and announces, 'Comrades, I have a plan to overtake the US in space exploration – you will land on the Sun!'

'But Comrade Brezhnev,' the cosmonauts protest, 'we'll burn up!'

'Do you take me for a fool?' Brezhnev replies. 'You'll be landing at night!'

Relations with China, which had broken down under Khrushchev did not improve – in March 1969 a battle at the border left eight hundred Chinese soldiers and sixty Soviet troops dead – nor did the jokes about them. Some jokes ingeniously combined China and Jewry.

Brezhnev has consulted a renowned sleep specialist after having a recurring nightmare: he sees a Pole sitting in Red Square eating matzo with chopsticks.

Tolstikov [leader of the Leningrad Party Committee and well known for his anti-Semitism] was appointed Soviet ambassador to China. When his plane landed in Peking, he walked from the cabin onto the tarmac, where a group of Chinese dignitaries awaited him. He looked at them and said: 'Ah, you kikes ... always something. Now you're squinting.'

In Leningrad there is a rumour that the schools will soon teach three foreign languages: English and Hebrew for those who plan to leave, and Chinese for those who plan to stay.

A couple of the better jokes tracked the new propaganda clichés. In Brezhnev's era the old Leninist terminology of 'bourgeois speculators' had been long forgotten, and Stalin's 'hostile Capitalist encirclement' was rarely mentioned. In their place came a range of new bland phrases. Among these were the perpetual thanks that factory committees and visiting delegations were obliged to offer the Soviets, which aroused popular suspicion because they were always expressed with exactly the same phrase:

What is the sixth sense that the entire Soviet population has developed?
A deep sense of gratitude to the Party.

In a churlish attempt to conceal the leader's incapacity, official communiqués and newspaper articles frequently added the word *personally*, before or after Brezhnev's name. Brezhnev 'personally congratulated' writers and actors, while ambassadors 'informed him personally' and he himself invariably 'personally intervened' to solve the problems of the day. Thus arose the joke:

Did you hear that Brezhnev has died?
What – personally?

Despite his mental and physical incapacity, it seemed that Brezhnev would never die.

Brezhnev is walking with his grandson. 'Granddad, when I grow up, will I be General Secretary?'
'What are you saying, boy? How could there be two general secretaries?'

But he did die, finally, in 1982, to be followed by two short-lived general secretaries, Chernenko and Andropov, under whose tenure the jokes did not improve.

What were Brezhnev's last words?
'Leave the plug alone, Yuri.'

How many people now rule the Soviet Union?
One and a half. Lenin, who lives for ever, and the half-alive Chernenko.

Andropov died in February 1984, his successor Chernenko in March the following year.

Two Party apparatchiks meet at Andropov's funeral. 'How did you get in?'
'I got sent an invitation. How about you?'
'Oh, I've got a season ticket.'

If the Soviet people were too lazy to tell good jokes, the authorities were also too lazy to arrest them. Brezhnev was once informed that people were joking that he was having chest expansion surgery to make room for all his medals. He is said to have replied, 'If' they are telling jokes about me, it means they love me.'

Under Brezhnev, the Soviet regime lost interest in prosecuting people for insulting and mocking the Soviet Union, focusing instead on individual prominent dissidents. Only around three thousand people were arrested for anti-Soviet propaganda during the entire eighteen years of Brezhnev's rule, and the majority of the cases concerned the publication of critical *samizdat* pamphlets. In 1974 the Central Committee even sent an official letter to the head of the KGB and future leader of the Soviet Union, Yuri Andropov, suggesting that he was arresting *too many* people for anti-Soviet propaganda. Andropov replied indignantly that as many people were arrested in the two and a half years of Khrushchev's thaw as in the first ten years of Brezhnev's rule.

There is no mention of *anekdoty* in the court archives between 1964 and 1981. The isolated cases from 1981 to 1983 show how the state became worried about the expression of anti-Soviet opinion only when there was also another serious political threat – in this case the Solidarity protests in Poland. In 1981 *Krokodil* received a number of letters containing political jokes. Magazine staff passed them on to the KGB, as was only sensible, since they might have been a provocation from state agents. The KGB launched a six-month investigation and finally tracked down the source: a woman who was involved in dissident circles. She was arrested and charged with collecting political jokes and she got a five-year sentence in July 1982 with an additional five years of exile. No one knows what jokes her letters contained, but maybe this one:

> *What do freedom of speech and oral sex have in common?*
> *One slip of the tongue and you get it in the arse.*

The producers of official humour struggled on, much as they had done before, to push the limits of what could be said and drawn, mostly without noticeable success. The Polish cartoonist Andrei Krauze fled to Britain in 1979 and made an international reputation over the following decade with his cartoons, printed regularly in the *Guardian* newspaper, about Solidarity and the situation in Poland. But in the seventies, he lived and sketched in Warsaw, fighting a constant battle with the censors. He estimates that about half of the cartoons he drew were turned down by the state. Among these was one of a sinister-looking bald man – obviously a Party official – giving a thumbs-up and saying: 'It's great' – a catchphrase of Poland's prime minister, Edward Gierek (Fig. 63).

Poland was the most tolerant of all the Soviet Bloc states. Through the seventies scores of cartoons by Krauze were published which used a cast of anthropomorphic animal characters to offer allegorical criticism of the state. Many images depicted Communism as a love-in between sheep and wolves (Figs 64 and 65). Others featured men in macs and trilbies, the uniform of the apparatchik,

Fig. 63. 'It's great!' Andrei Krauze, 1970s, Poland

Figs. 64 and 65. Cartoons by Andrei Krauze, 1970s, Poland

lording over an innocent world of animals (Figs. 66 and 67). Such obvious allegorical critiques of the state would have been impossible to print in any other Soviet Bloc state – or in Poland a decade earlier – but they indicated that the censors were getting lazier, not that the citizens were getting bolder.

In the Soviet Union comics and circus clowns experimented with occasional forays into mildly critical humour. Millions of citizens went to the circus every month and there was a big top in every reasonably sized city. Rather than whole circuses touring, acts would move from town to town, among them the clowns. Around the mid-seventies – it's difficult to be specific with dates in circus history – some clowns attempted jokes about the shortages of basic foodstuffs.

Figs. 66 and 67. Andrei Krauze's apparatchiks in their trademark hats

If there were local shortages, the clowns would perform a sketch that mocked Soviet propaganda about the heroism of the Red Army in the Second World War. A clown-wife sends her husband to war. She is crying. They embrace and he leaves ... Then there is the sound of battle ... He returns to the stage with torn clothes, but in one hand he holds a war trophy: a big bag of onions.

The legendary Russian clown Karandash had another sketch in which he appeared onstage with a whole sausage and proudly started eating it in front of the audience. He swiftly buckled over in pain with a terrible stomach ache – a joke which could be interpreted as a reference to the lack of sausages, or to the poor quality of the sausages available. Two other clowns appear dressed as doctors with a stretcher. They try to put him on it, but Karandash is so fat from the sausage that he falls through it and rolls off the linen. Finally they drag him away by his feet. During this sketch, a member of the circus troop always shouted offstage, 'Where did you get this sausage?' and Karandash would say the name of the town where he was performing. This sketch was apparently only performed briefly. Wherever Karandash did it, the local KGB would react by calling him in for questioning. He was eventually threatened with the termination of his career, unless he abandoned the routine.

Across the Soviet Bloc, stand-up comedians peddled their occasional, watered-down and ambiguous criticisms of the regime in shows whose scripts had passed the censors. Arkady Raikin (1911–87) was the best known of these in the Soviet Union. He had been performing in Moscow and Leningrad since the forties and was admired by Stalin, Khrushchev and Brezhnev. In 1968 he was given the coveted title of People's Artist of the USSR. In 1980 he won a Lenin Prize, and in 1981 he was made a Hero of Socialist Labour, the Soviet Union's highest civilian award.

In the course of the seventies he exploited the amount of official recognition he had garnered to present slightly more critical material than his contemporaries. One of his catchphrases was: 'We have everything, of course. But not for everyone.' Often he began his show with the thought, 'Oh, maybe it's not worth it. Maybe we should just keep silent tonight. We're all so good at keeping silent, and they say silence is golden. I could, for instance, just keep my mouth shut tonight for three hours plus the intermission. That way, we won't take any risks.'

But the risks he took were modest. Bureaucrats remained the number one target. In one sketch an official walks onto the stage and stops short in shocked surprise. 'What's going on here?' he says, pointing an accusing finger at the comedian. 'We have gigantic successes, colossal achievements, and you find it funny?' Raikin, repeating exactly the same justification for satire used by Kol'tsov in the 1930s, explains to him that his humour deals with society's flaws, defects and shortcomings, but the 'man who never laughs' does not back down. 'You mean, we have shortcomings, and you find it funny?' he says. In another uncontroversial sketch, a bureaucrat, who only makes people's lives more complicated, is offered a salary just to stay home in bed. But once in a while Raikin pointed the finger of blame a little higher – as in a scene in which a committee earnestly discusses the choice of a new chairman. Whatever their choices, a large hand with a raised index finger drops down from above to waggle a decisive yes or no. In another moderately critical moment, he attacked the planned economy, describing a factory that turned out seventy bows for every violin.

There's no evidence that he got into trouble with the authorities over his material, but in an interview in 1984 he told the *New York Times* disingenuously, 'The sharper the criticism is, the less pleasant for the person you are laughing at. If that person holds a high post, he might get angry, and people have often been angry at me. But what can you do? That's democracy.'

Christie Davies opened the door of his semi-detached house in a Reading suburb, a stone's throw from the university where he taught sociology, specialising in humour. We sat down in his living room on two decrepit old armchairs with uncomfortable wooden armrests. I felt the springs pressing on my thighs. Behind the emeritus professor were floor-to-ceiling shelves, on which mounds of papers and paperbacks, files and folders and hardbacks were piled up like one of Braque's most complicated Cubist paintings. The academic – bearded, of course – went off to make a cup of tea, which I already knew from the interior décor would be far too milky. My eyes scanned the shelves and I was pleased to see that we both owned many of the same collections of Communist jokes.

'The Communist economy was very bad at producing everything – except jokes. They were very good at jokes,' he said, coming back into the room with a mug of tea for me.

Davies was a founder member of the editorial board of *Humor*, the international journal of humour research, and he was also on the committee of the International Society for Humor Studies. In the early eighties he went on undercover missions to Bulgaria and Slovakia to collect jokes. 'I'd written a lot about humour and I asked the British Council to send me to Eastern Europe to work on jokes there. Now obviously I couldn't say to the authorities in Eastern Europe: "Well, I'm coming over to study jokes that are hostile to you," and so I said I was studying something else ...'

Davies was the first and perhaps only joke spy. His cover story was that he was researching ethnic humour. 'When I went to Slovakia I went there to look at "fool towns" – that is, jokes about the people from particular towns being stupid. Over there they had jokes that were very similar to jokes told in England about the Irish. Officially I was conducting a comparative study, but that was just what I did in the daytime. In the evening I would talk to people whom I'd met in the day but in quiet places – and they would tell me a different kind of joke; so I was doing two totally different pieces of research at the same time.'

I had come to visit the professor in the hope that his undercover work would have led him to unearth some unknown gems of Communist humour in the era of stagnation. But I was to be disappointed.

'At the Moscow Olympics in 1980,' Davies began, 'Brezhnev starts a speech "Oh ... Ooooh ... Oh ... Ooh ... Ooohh." An aide walks up quietly behind him and whispers in his ear—'

I couldn't resist joining in for the punchline: 'That's the Olympic logo, General Secretary,' I said.

Professor Davies tried another:

Nixon, Pompidou and Brezhnev meet God and God says they can each ask Him a question.

'When will Americans have everything?' Nixon says.

God replies: 'In five years' time.'

'So sadly not within my term of office,' says Nixon, shaking his head.

'When will the French become rich?' asks the French president.

God answers, 'In fifteen years.'

'So sadly not within my term of office,' says Pompidou.

'When will everything be all right in the Soviet Union?' asks Brezhnev.

I burst in: 'God responds, "Oh, sadly not during my term of office,"' we chorused together.

He told me the one about the crocodile and the Central Committee, and the one about Stalin on Lenin's shoulders, and the one about Lenin shaving while a little boy watched.

'I know all these jokes,' I said disappointedly. 'A spy is meant to uncover secrets.'

Now it was my turn. I couldn't resist showing off my own recently acquired encyclopedic knowledge in front of this acknowledged master. I opted for the classic 'Would it be possible to introduce Communism to ...' series. We were like two tennis players rallying jokes at each other, and now it was my turn to serve. 'Would it be possible to introduce Communism into the Netherlands?' I asked.

'Yes,' said the professor, 'but what have the Dutch ever done to you?'

'Would it be possible to introduce Communism to Switzerland?' I tried.

Davies said: 'Yes, but it would be a shame.'

'Would it be possible to introduce Communism to America?' I countered.

'Yes, but then where would we get our grain from?' – The ball came right back low over the net at me.

'Would it be possible to introduce Communism to Liechtenstein?'

'Yes, but why such a great honour for such a small country?' Davies laughed triumphantly.

'Would it be possible to introduce Communism to France?' I was running out of nation-states.

'No, because they have it already,' he said – that wasn't actually a Communist joke, at least not officially, but it worked.

I abandoned the jokes and asked him if he'd uncovered any evidence, while undercover, that the jokes had an impact on the demise of Communism.

'No,' he said. 'In retrospect, I don't think the jokes had any effect. It's a tricky one. I mean Orwell says, "All jokes are a tiny revolution," as if somehow, if they accumulate, it will undermine the system. On the other hand, other people say it's a safety valve and that telling the jokes reduces people's discontent. My view is that jokes may well do both, but the effect – the consequences – of jokes are so small in comparison with other social forces that you might as well forget about it. The jokes are a thermometer; they're not a thermostat.'

Yet more disappointment! Professor Davies, one of the world experts on jokes, turned out to be a proponent of the minimalist position. As I left him, I imagined that I was only the latest in a long line of students of Communist jokes who'd made the pilgrimage to his untidy terraced house full of hope and left, an hour later, with a dose of scholarly realism.

I had another kind of problem when I paid a call on a German academic, the distinguished social historian of the DDR, Stefan Wolle.

We sat in a bleached lecture hall on a campus on the outskirts of Berlin. I admitted to him how jaded I was feeling about the jokes of the seventies.

'At the time the jokes hit so hard that you would almost split your sides laughing,' said Wolle, who had been an East German teenager during that decade. 'That was how it was, but it's a bit difficult to reproduce that today.'

'So I shouldn't make the accusation that the jokes weren't very funny?' I asked.

'Well,' said Wolle, 'if you measured them by how much they were laughed over, then they really were very funny. People laughed at them a lot.' Wolle then launched into his own series of jokes. As with his counterpart in Reading, I had heard them before, but this time I recognised them all from previous Communist epochs.

'During a break in the summit meeting in Helsinki President Carter asks Brezhnev whether he collects stories against himself,' Professor Wolle began. '"I certainly do," replies Brezhnev. "Do you have many?" asks Carter. "Two camps full," says Brezhnev.'

'That joke is not historically accurate,' I complained. 'You couldn't fill one of your lecture halls with the people Brezhnev arrested for telling jokes.'

He tried again: 'Two soldiers are standing at the border and one asks the other: "Are you thinking what I am thinking?"'

'" . . . Well then I am going to have to shoot you,"' I burst in with the punchline. 'That one goes back to the thirties at the latest.'

'Honecker is going round a museum and after he sees the show he turns to an aide and says, "I loved the sculpture of the goat best." "Oh, no," says the aide—'

'"That was a mirror, Comrade General Secretary,"' I said quickly. 'They told that one about Khrushchev.'

'Okay, do you know the one about Erich Honecker and his Minister for the Economy, Guenther Mittag, who are standing on top of the Radio Tower and they both want to jump off . . .'

'I don't know it, but it's got a good beginning,' I said – which is also the punchline for this joke, which has a long history involving any number of different world leaders and tall buildings.

'Oh, I remember another good Brezhnev joke,' he said, still attempting to rise to the challenge I was posing. 'The German Chancellor Helmut Schmidt, the French President Giscard d'Estaing, and Leonid Brezhnev are showing off their expensive gifts. Schmidt displays an exquisite snuff box with an inscription reading: "To dear Helmut, from your loving wife". D'Estaing has a distinctive pipe that reads: "To dear Giscard, from a patriotic Frenchwoman". Brezhnev pulls out a gold cigarette box encrusted with diamonds with an inscription that reads: "To Count Uvarov, from Grand Prince Sergei Aleksandrovich".'

'Actually, the first documented instance of that joke is in Yevgeny Andreevich's book of Communist jokes, *The Kremlin and the People*, published in 1951,' I said snootily. 'It was told about the British Labour leader Ernest Bevin, Stalin's deputy Vyacheslav Molotov and two other contemporary Western political figures.'

'Look,' said Wolle, 'if you want to be strictly historically accurate, a vast number – perhaps the majority – of these jokes aren't Communist jokes or Stalin jokes or jokes from the twentieth century at all – they are nineteenth-century, French Revolution, or even ancient Roman jokes. Take the one about Brezhnev talking to his right-hand man Kosygin: Brezhnev says to Kosygin: "I think we should expel all the Jews and the Swedes." Kosygin says, "Why the Swedes?" Brezhnev says, "I knew no one would care about the Jews." That joke had a previous reincarnation as a Nazi joke but it originated as a nineteenth-century Jewish joke: "It's all the fault of the Jews," an anti-Semite says to a Jew. The Jew says, "And of the cyclists." "Why the cyclists?" says the anti-Semite. "Why the Jews?" says the Jew.'

Wolle's historical perspective hit me like a thunderbolt. The implications for my research project were more catastrophic than anything Davies had said. I knew that a few of the Communist jokes had precedents in the nineteenth century, but what if most of the Communist jokes weren't actually Communist jokes at all? Where did that leave the first central premise of Communist humorology – that the citizens of the Soviet Bloc reacted to the environment they were living in by creating their own corpus of original jokes?

I dug my British Library reading pass out of the back of my wallet and began a few days of tormented research. The news was not good. The classic joke about the guy-paid-to-sit-on-the-Kremlin-wall-and-look-out-for-the-world-revolution-being-a-job-for-life, which Yevgeny Andreevich had attributed to the early 1920s, was in fact a joke told by the Jacobins in the French Revolution, and by the Jews about the Messiah.

A Jew talking to his friend: 'My son Moses and I are doing very fine. Moisha works in the Comintern as a black African Communist, while I sit in the Kremlin, at the top of Ivan the Great Bell Tower, waiting to ring the bell for the World Revolution.'

'Well, it must be a rather dull job to wait for the World Revolution,' his friend says.

'Oh yes, but it is a job for life.'

The classic Stalinist joke:

What is the difference between life in the time of Jesus and life under Stalin?

Well, in those days one man suffered for us all, but today we all suffer for one man.

began life at least as early as the British Industrial Revolution:

A manufacturer is showing his friend round a new factory. 'It looks to me like the Passion in reverse,' said the visitor.

'What do you mean?' asks the factory owner.

'Well in the Passion one man suffered for everybody and here everybody suffers for one man.'

My Communist jokes were falling like flies. I wanted to seek consolation from my fellow readers. They had surely also encountered disappointments as they became ever more knowledgeable about their subjects. On my left a female art student with red hair was reading about eighteenth-century French cheese-making. On my right a young man in a corduroy jacket was working through a pile of books comprising equally Enid Blyton novels and journals on particle physics. In the event, I was too shy to talk about my problems. I began to realise that if jokes had a religion they would be Hindu – they had scores of previous reincarnations, no one knew how many. None of the Communist humorologists whom I'd read had dared to fully investigate this issue, limiting themselves to the occasional admission of precedents in a concise subordinate clause. Now I was learning why. Even the most Soviet-sounding jokes had an ancient provenance, like this familiar one, from Stalin's time:

It's 1933. A group of sheep arrive at the Soviet border anxious to escape Stalin. A border guard stops them. 'Why do you want to leave Russia?' he asks.

'It's the political police,' they say; 'Stalin has ordered them to arrest all the elephants.'

'But you aren't elephants,' says the border guard.

'Try telling that to the political police,' say the sheep.

This joke can be traced to twelfth-century Arabia, when the great Persian poet of the Seljuk period, Anvari, wrote in a poem:

> A fox was running away in fear of his life.
> Another fox saw him in the state of flight.
> He said: 'May it be of good omen, what is new?'
> 'The King has ordered all the donkeys to be taken away
>   [for forced labour].'
> 'You are not a donkey; why are you afraid?'
> 'That is true, but human beings
> Are not able to discern or make distinctions.
> To them a donkey and a fox are the same.
> They do not distinguish donkeys from foxes,
> These ignorant assholes.
> I am afraid, O Brother, that they will saddle us up like
>   asses.'

It was difficult for me to progress beyond the accumulation of a handful of isolated examples. We will never know exactly how many truly Communist jokes there were – that is, jokes that originated in Communist times – since there is no equivalent of an etymological dictionary of jokes. Nor is it only a question of the limited amount of research that exists; it's also about the limits of possible research, since, as the Czech writer Karel Čapek has put it, 'No one was ever present at the birth of a joke.'

One simply could not argue that one of the fundamental characteristics of the Communist joke was that it was invented by Communist citizens in Communist times. The distinctiveness of this cultural phenomenon resided far more in how it was perceived. If the idea of *Communist* jokes was largely an illusion, it was an illusion shared by the entire population, a kind of mass psychosis.

I could no longer locate the importance of the culture of Communist jokes in either the originality of the material – the distinctive expression of public opinion under Communism, as the minimalists had it – nor, for the moment, in the maximalist idea of a crescendo of humour that grew, by 1989, into Revolution. And these disappointments raised other problems that required explanation, such as why the jokes went into decline.

One possible theory concerns the ever-increasing absurdity of everyday life under Communism. One could argue that reality was by now surpassing any witticism the human mind could conceive, or that Communism had now reached a level of absurdity that made jokes obsolete.

Take East Germany. A wall cut through the capital city, across old roads and train lines, a metre and a half taller than the average height of a man, keeping Capitalism out of view. Yet, by the late seventies, East German Communism couldn't survive without Western hard currency – money which, according to the school curriculum and satirical magazines, came from the imperialist exploitation of the developing world.

East Berliners could take the metro to Friedrichstrasse in the centre of town and that was the end of the world as they knew it. It ended with planks and nails. But on the other side of the fencing was another Friedrichstrasse, the West German half of the train station, and through the hoardings – before the place was soundproofed – East German commuters could hear the announcements for the West German trains coming from the other side – 'train from Hamburg' or 'train to Munich'. If you walked or worked on certain streets in East Berlin you could see the LED ticker-tape headlines running round the top of the West German Springer office block. When there were coal shortages in the winter in Berlin, the city authorities turned off the street lights, but they kept the Wall lit up to prevent people from trying to escape. The result was a deeply ironic ethereal glow over the whole of the city, which looked like the Northern Lights.

In 1979 they put up a neon sign on an office block on the central square of East Berlin, which read: '30 Years of the DDR – 30 Years of Prosperity'. But after a few days the electronics malfunctioned and the '3' on the second '30' stopped working. As Stefan Wolle wrote in his book *Everyday Life in the DDR*, 'The DDR did not get better or worse, simply more ridiculous.'

Communist products were unreliable, shoddy and ugly and you couldn't get a decent espresso in a Soviet Bloc café. But high-quality goods were available, as long as you paid for them with the currencies of Capitalism. There were special shops where this trade was conducted; in East Germany they were called 'Intershop'. East German children would always ask their parents: 'Can't we go to the shop which smells so nice?' because the shops carried the aroma of good-quality soap and real coffee.

Communism appeared, like the old joke said, to be the exact opposite of Capitalism. Inside factories, production-line workers earned more than managers. In the high streets, the customer was not king. The absence of financial incentives for workers outside factories made it the responsibility of the client to talk them into doing their job. Official taxi-drivers would pull up at a taxi queue and announce the destination to which they wanted to go, and see who came forward. Handymen, plumbers and builders had to be persuaded to visit with bribes. No advertising billboards were allowed in East Germany, but there was much 'negative advertising' in shop windows – signs were put up that said: 'No Jeans', or 'No Corduroys', or 'No Hot Lunches' and 'No Coffee and Cake'; 'Shop Closed for Technical Reasons'.

There was a vibrant black market. The real economy took place after work and in the classified sections of newspapers, which were full of illegal ads for second-hand cars, electrical goods, many imported, and apartments for rent. In this topsy-turvy world, 'old' was more expensive than 'new'. If they bought a new car, East Germans had to wait twelve to seventeen years for delivery. Consequently, a second-hand fifteen-year-old Trabant with 50,000 kilometres on the clock could be sold for roughly the same price as a brand-new model. An investigation by the Stasi revealed that in the second half of the seventies, one canny unemployed East German used the small ads to run a used-car business with a two-million-Ostmark turnover. His profit was the unheard-of sum of 379,000 Ostmarks.

Censorship produced an inverted cultural order. The DDR was crammed with poets who'd never had a poem published, artists who'd never had an exhibition, philosophers who had no publisher. Yet these were all badges of honour and proof of excellence, since the state – at least in the popular imagination – would only permit the publication of the blandest and most conformist cultural products.

There were good things about the DDR, compared to the West, which its fans and apologists remember: there was no unemployment, no asylum seekers, no homeless, no drug addicts and no beggars. Instead of unemployment there was an ever-present shortage of labour. But this was not the perfect state of being that so many Western Socialists imagined. It created a breakdown of discipline at work. Punishments for theft or laziness were light, because workers were difficult to sack and replace. It was commonplace to head for the showers half an hour before the end of the shift. At closing time everyone would already be at the door. People took tools and materials home with them, joking that, since private property had been abolished, this was 'common ownership'. Alcohol was popular with night-shift workers. Ask anyone across the whole of the Soviet Bloc to describe what the economy was like in those days, and they all cite the same aphoristic joke: *They pretend to pay us and we pretend to work.*

It was impossible to get a visa to travel to the West, but every night East German households got away, by tuning in to West German television. The only place in the DDR where you couldn't get reception was around Dresden, which led jokers to rename the area 'The Valley of the Clueless'. For the thousands of West Germans who visited their relatives in the East, the trip was like time travel. Telephones still had the old-fashioned, rattling ring they had had in the West in the fifties. Television sets' volume and channels were controlled by dials not buttons. The young children of West German families would ask wide-eyed questions such as: 'Mummy, why does everyone in East Germany drive the same car?'

Soviet politicians made the opposite kind of observations when they visited West Germany. The Soviet President Nikolai Podgorny made a state visit to Austria in the mid-seventies. He was shown the bustling market of Vienna by his hosts. 'Look how well they set things up for my visit,' he remarked to his aides, indicating that he thought the abundance had been put on as a display for foreign visitors, as it would have been in his own country. The correspondence of reality to the form of a joke is illustrated by the number of jokes that paraphrase Podgorny's remark:

A Soviet citizen returns from a trip to the West. His friends crowd round him with questions. 'Is it true,' says one, 'that Capitalism is rotting?'

'Oh, it may well be rotting,' says the man with a sigh, 'but what a lovely smell!'

'And is Capitalism on its deathbed?' asks another friend.

'Yes definitely,' he says, 'but it's dying a magnificent death.'

'And is there any evidence that people are rich or poor there?' asks a third.

'They must be poor – they can't afford to buy anything,' he says. 'I passed hundreds of shops and their windows were full of all kinds of exotic fruits, delicious sausages and beautiful clothes, but there were no queues.'

The upside-down logic of the Soviet Bloc was completed by their own theory about why there was so much more humour in their part of the world, which was the opposite of the Capitalist theory. As the Czech newspaper *Rude Pravo* wrote on 27 January 1979:

Creating humour in Capitalist countries is apparently no fun. The governments and military complexes there take it very seriously and immediately see in it the desire for revolutionary aims or even a Communist threat ... For the representatives of the defence industries, who exercise their influence in NATO and in so many bourgeois governments, humour is undesirable. The meaningful influence that these centres of propaganda exert on the bourgeois press has led to the fact that humour has, so to speak, disappeared from the pages of the bourgeois press. The editors of many of the newspapers simply do not publish the jokes that are sent in.

Thus both sides, East and West, agreed that there was more humour in the Soviet Bloc and both sides explained this by the suppression of freedom of speech ... but in each other's country!

More evidence of the decline of the importance of humour is provided by the new kind of opposition that emerged against Communism over the course of the seventies: the dissidents.

The dissident movement consisted of intellectuals opposed to Communism. They used press and publishing contacts abroad and a variety of underground printing techniques ranging from Xerox and carbon copies to illegal printing presses in order to publicise human rights abuses, the crimes of the Gulag and contraventions of the law by Soviet states. They numbered only a few hundred across the whole of the Soviet Bloc, but they were, at least in the minds of the KGB, highly active. The Soviet political police reported to Brezhnev that between 1972 and 1979 the leading Soviet dissident Sakharov visited foreign embassies eighty times, had over six hundred meetings with other foreigners, held a hundred and fifty 'press conferences', and that Western radio stations broadcast twelve hundred anti-Soviet reports based on material he supplied.

The underground publishing of *samizdat* grew enormously in this period.

Now, not only leaflets but often whole banned books were typed up. The common practice was to squeeze eight sheets of thin carbon-copy paper around the roller to produce a small edition. A joke tells how great the demand was for this kind of reading material:

A woman brings a copy of War and Peace *to a typist to copy.*
'What for?' she asks. 'You can buy this in the book store.'
'I know, but I want my children to read it.'

The Soviet campaign against dissidents began in 1966 with the trial of Yuli Daniel and Andrei Sinyavksy, whose satirical novels about the Soviet Union had been smuggled out and published in the West. They were sentenced to five years' hard labour. Other dissidents, such as Vladimir Bukowksy, were sent to secure psychiatric institutions, since Soviet psychologists had defined opposition to Communism as a mental illness called 'creeping schizophrenia', in which 'most frequently ideas about a "struggle for truth and justice" are formed by personalities with a paranoid structure ... A characteristic feature ... is the patient's conviction of his own righteousness, an obsession with asserting his trampled rights, and the significance of these feelings for the patient's personality.'

The signing of the Helsinki Accords in 1975 was a spur to dissident activity. Across the Soviet Bloc they formed human rights 'monitoring' groups, of which the best known was the Czech association Charter 77, led by Václav Havel. Charter 77 was the name given to a document signed by 243 Czech intellectuals and published in a West German newspaper criticising their government for failing to implement the human-rights provisions of the Czech Constitution, the Helsinki Accords and UN covenants on political, civil, economic and cultural rights. The Czech state condemned the signatories as 'renegades and traitors' and persecuted many of them, arresting them, beating them up and evicting them from their jobs. The dissidents went on to form another group, VONS, dedicated to helping defend colleagues charged with political crimes. Five of them were tried in 1979, including Václav Havel, and sentenced to up to five years.

The dissidents differed from previous opponents of Communism in one important respect, above all: they did not use humour. True, Havel had written satirical plays since the sixties, inventing his own Communist take on the Theatre of the Absurd, mocking its rationalism and bureaucracy. In *The Memorandum* (1966), for example, an ambitious bureaucrat introduces a new language 'built on a strictly scientific basis' in which the lengths of words are calculated according to the frequency of their usage, 'the more common the meaning, the shorter the word'. Hence the shortest word is 'gh', meaning 'whatever', and the longest, with 341 letters, means 'wombat'. But, however ironic his plays were, when it came to opposition, Havel left the jokes behind. His best-known political essay, 'The Power of the Powerless', was humourless. Instead it urged each citizen to begin their own low-intensity campaign of civil disobedience, using as its famous example a greengrocer who stops hanging a sign 'Workers of the World Unite!' in his shop window.

Joke-tellers, it would seem, picked up the dissidents' lack of humour with the following *anekdot*:

A dissident walks out of his house. It's starting to rain. He looks up and says in indignation: 'They always do just what they want.'

The next day when the dissident walks out the sun is shining brightly. He looks up and says in indignation, 'Of course. For this they find the money!'

I swapped emails with Ariane. The exhibition for which she had been making her paintings and collages had opened in New York. She wrote to tell me what a success it had been and how everything had been sold before the show opened. There was evidently money to be made out of Communism nowadays. I googled for the reviews. Next to JPEGs of her overpainted photocopies of Soviet dance troupes and Social-Realist exhibitions, her gallery biog burbled in artspeak, 'Ariane started out as a "classic" painter who would choose a subject and turn it into a painting. Those days are now past. These days, she sees her artistic career in terms of a double collage, building up an *oeuvre* via the interplay of various elements.' A critic wrote: '[Her] practice resembles this process of constructing the world from the small kernel of one's own dreams. And she is well aware that, although having faith in rebuilding a reality destroyed by the void is utopian, sometimes it still yields positive results.'

Ariane's nostalgia was all the rage in the inflated art world. Artists were meant to look back critically at Modernism, which they defined as the twentieth-century ambition of solving social problems through central government or a universal theory. Her pictures slotted right into this discourse. One critic wrote: '[Her work] confronts the dream of novelty without losing sight of its long history.' Another enthused: 'Trains of optimism, fed by nostalgia and focusing attention on the social possibilities of art, may be seen to persist in her practice ... The whole thing may sound somewhat naïve, but in the way that your wise grandmother can be naïve, when she wields the renegade historical authority of nostalgia.'

I was jealous of Ariane's success. Her romanticisation of Communism was bringing her fame and fortune. By contrast, my exploration of the popular criticism of it was leading to a dead end.

I was on a train to Poland, leaning my head against the cold window pane and daydreaming.

I imagined I was taking part in a British television quiz show, *Mastermind*. I think it was some time in the mid-seventies. At any rate, I was aged about fourteen and wearing my school uniform – dark-grey trousers, black DMs (not regulation school wear, but you could get away with it), black blazer with a little fish on the lapel indicating I was a scholar (which meant that my parents got a small discount on the astronomical school fees), and for some reason a cap, although I don't remember wearing that very often. It was like one of those common nightmares that adults endure in which they have to sit their O-level exams again.

There was stiff competition. I was up against Stalin and Marx. They were both on before me, and as the studio lights went up on the famous high-backed *Mastermind* chair, I wondered how warm their buttocks would have made its soft black leather by the time I sat on it.

My dream was historically accurate. Magnus Magnusson was still presenting. 'Name?' I heard him say.

'Joseph Vissarionovich Stalin.' Stalin was wearing his typical green army uniform with his trousers tucked into his high boots.

'Can you confirm your specialist subject,' said Magnusson.

'Stalinism,' said Stalin.

'You now have two minutes to answer questions on your chosen subject,' said Magnusson. 'First question: how many people were executed in the Great Terror?'

'Nine hundred and seventy-five thousand, five hundred and fifty-four.'

'I can let you have that,' said Magnusson, adding quickly, 'It's around three hundred thousand more than the figures the KGB produced themselves, but you should know ... How many people were arrested for counter-Revolutionary propaganda under Article 58/10 in 1935?'

Stalin paused for a moment. Then he said: 'Forty-three thousand, six hundred and eighty-six.'

'Correct. And in 1936?'

I knew there were no statistics for this category of crime in 1936 or 1937. Stalin paused, as if trying to remember; then he said: 'Pass.'

'How many people died building the White Sea canal?'

Stalin seemed to be almost angry. His colleagues always said that he never showed emotion, but his eyes became smaller, tighter, more opaque. He may have suspected that the *Mastermind* trophy was being used to tempt him into providing answers to some of the mysteries of his crimes. Behind him in the shadows I could see a large section of the audience were NKVD officers in their trademark black-leather coats, fashionable amongst Bolsheviks in the thirties. They shuffled in their chairs and threw enquiring glances at their leader, as if asking if they should march Magnusson off the set. Stalin made a tiny gesture with his hand, indicating that they should remain in their seats, and he answered the question.

The figures rolled on, and the names: 'Who authorised the poisoning of the Russian writer Maxim Gorky?'

The *Mastermind* siren went off, indicating the end of the two minutes of questions. 'I've started so I'll finish,' said the compère.

'I did,' said Stalin.

Karl Marx took the chair next.

'Name?'

'Karl Marx.

'Please confirm your specialist subject.'

I expected Marx to say Dialectical Materialism, but he said: 'British Rave Culture, 1988–92.'

The audience gasped. In my dream I felt a wave of relief – this was surely something Karl Marx could know little about.

'Name the young British entrepreneur who organised orbital rave parties in secret locations around the M25.'

'Tony Colston-Hayter,' said Marx, with a German accent.

'Correct.'

'What was the slang word for pills containing the drug MDMA at acid-house parties in the late—'

Before the question was finished Marx replied coolly: 'Disco biscuits.'

'Correct.'

'Which artist recorded the early nineties garage anthem "Where Love Lives"?'

'Alison Limerick.'

'Correct.' And so it went on.

I felt a wave of jealousy. I could have got all these questions right too. This was a subject about which I was a real expert. In the nineties I had been a dedicated 'raver'. I took Ecstasy every weekend, worked at MTV, interviewed DJs and wrote about dance music for the magazines. This was my speciality, not Karl's.

'Karl Marx, you have fourteen points.'

Suddenly it was my turn.

'Name?'

'Ben Lewis.'

'What is your specialist subject?'

'Communist humour.'

'You have two minutes to answer questions on Communist humour, starting now ...' The clock began ticking. 'What was the prototype for a Communist election?' Magnusson was asking me a Communist joke.

'No, because if it was, they would have tested it on animals first,' I replied.

'Wrong,' said Magnusson. 'It was when God created Eve and then said to Adam: "Now choose a wife."'

I bit my lip: I had given the punchline to another joke.

'What is the first line of the joke that ends with the punchline: "No, we are the shop with no cheese"?'

It was as if I couldn't control my mouth. This time I offered the wrong question: 'Are the Russians our brothers or our friends?'

'Wrong. It's: "I see you don't have any meat today."'. . . Is Marxism a science?' he asked.

'Because Soviet dwarves are the biggest dwarves in the world.'

'No,' said the compère. 'It's: "If it was, they would have tested it on animals first!"'

I thought I had memorised every Communist joke I had collected. I had known I'd be asked these questions, but I was collapsing under the heat of the studio lights. Everyone could see what an intellectual charlatan I was. No one from the field of Communist jokes would ever take me seriously again.

At the end of the two minutes my score was a dismal five points. I would never make it into the second round. Karl Marx had invented a new political system. Stalin had enslaved tens of millions of people and become the world's most murderous dictator. The contribution I wanted to make to the history of mankind was modest by comparison. All I had ever wanted was to become an expert on Communist jokes, and I had failed.

The dream ended.

No one has come up with a convincing explanation of why the Soviet Union remained so stagnant in the 'era of stagnation'.

Historians suggest that the state cut its citizens a mysterious unspoken and unwritten deal, in which a minimum standard of living was offered in return for political quiescence. Certainly the standard of living in the Soviet bloc was rising in the seventies. According to this historical interpretation, all the regimes offered their populations just enough domestic appliances and new-build apartments to defuse protest. The East Germans allowed their population to watch just enough Western television and receive just enough decent coffee, clothing and electronic goods from their relatives in the West. The Polish government permitted its workers to travel abroad and earn just enough foreign currency to support their families, in order to dissuade large numbers of them from taking to the street. The Hungarians permitted their entrepreneurial population to run their own small businesses and farms. Even the West was involved in this exchange: the Soviets offered us just enough human-rights agreements to ensure we would keep providing them with just enough hard currency.

This is one of the vaguest historical explanations in history, but contemporary Soviet citizens didn't have a better theory. The opinions expressed in a *samizdat* book of interviews with Soviet women published in the West in 1979 were typical. Vera Golubeva lived in Archangel, which was neither a remote village nor a provincial backwater but an economically successful city in northern Russia with a population of half a million. Nevertheless the food shortages were unrelenting:

> According to the newspapers, we have no unsolved economic problems. And there probably are no problems, if you ignore the fact that in the city of Archangel people simply have nothing to eat. The stores in the city lack even the most essential goods. There is no butter or meat or milk ... there is no sausage or cheese or fish, although the city is a large bustling port. Every day for breakfast, lunch and dinner the Soviet people are served hefty portions of slogans which people have heard for so long that they are fed up to the back teeth with them. People are compelled almost forcibly to march [in official parades]. On rare occasions, usually before the holidays, meat and poultry may appear.

Vera Golubeva wondered with her interviewers why there was no resistance.

> Yet the question keeps arising: why do people so passively and indifferently eke out a miserable existence? I think the answer could be this. The corrupt system of our supposedly Socialist state has alienated the masses – the majority of the population. For this society fosters in its citizens an incapacity for united action and a lifestyle that encourages the pursuit of self-interests.

Another woman, Alla Sariban from Leningrad, told her interlocutors, 'The total certainty that one can change nothing is the character of the consciousness of the Soviet people. Anyone can participate in the Theatre of the Absurd, which is what Soviet life is.'

Thus these women explained the stagnation through apathy, which was almost tautological. The only half-decent explanation for the stagnation came from the jokers, though they were possibly recycling an old Jewish joke.

A dissident arrives at a remote village, to which he has been exiled.

Everywhere seems deserted, but as he gets towards the centre of town he notices an overpowering horrible smell. In the main square he comes across a big crowd of people standing quietly in a lake of sewage coming up to their chins. Suddenly he falls in. He starts flailing his arms and shouting in disgust, 'Yuk! I cannot stand this! How can you people just stand here not doing anything?'

They reply, 'Shut up and keep still, you are making waves.'

The joke suggests that no one tried to change anything because they were worried that what would result might be worse than what they were already experiencing. The history of Russia since 1989 shows that this was a reasonable if not astute position.

Some historians have argued that in the eighties the deal between citizens and state broke down, because Soviet states could no longer finance their largesse through foreign loans; but, as we shall see, the apathy persisted through most of this decade in most of the states of the Soviet Bloc. In fact, it was the population's commitment to apathy, their determination to stagnate – which had political, economic and humorous manifestations – that eventually goaded Soviet leaders towards reform.

By 1979 the era of joking appeared to be over.

Far from finding the missing link between the jokes and the end of Communism, my commitment to fact-based research was leading me to the conclusion that the jokes had nothing to do with the end of the system. Quite the reverse: the decline of jokes appeared to precede change and by a considerable period of time. Yet I had one last card up my sleeve – the joker in the pack – which was every historian's last resort: perhaps my methodology was to blame, not the facts themselves? Perhaps my theoretical framework was producing this negative verdict on the jokes, rather than the history of the jokes itself? It was time for self-criticism, in the Communist tradition. I had been simple-minded, counting the number of jokes and rating their funniness, and looking at how they were used by the opponents of Communism. Instead, I reflected, I should adopt a phenomenological approach to the Communist joke, and consider the whole context in which the joke was uttered. I should evaluate not just what was said and how often, but who was telling it and to whom it was told (principally in terms of their social class and profession, where it was told (in locations of varying public prominence), and how it was received there (with handcuffs or handclaps). I would begin a new decade with a new approach.

SEVEN

The End is Wry

Conventional historians, when asked to pick the date when Communism contracted its terminal illness usually choose 14 August 1980, the day Lech Walesa took over leadership of the Gdansk shipyard strike. As a historian of jokes, however, I would pick a moment a few months earlier, also in Poland, one evening in late June: the date of the broadcast of the TV special of the Opole Music Festival, hosted by the brilliant Polish comic Zenon Laskowik.

Laskowik, the John Cleese of Communist jokes, had been performing for decades at a small theatre in Poznan under the name of Cabaret Tey. Here his political jokes reached a devoted but small audience. He also starred in sitcoms on Polish television, which made him a household name, though they were free of any political gags. The Christmas Special was a different ball game: for the first time the political jokes of his cabaret reached a national television audience.

Laskowik began by leading the audience in an oath. The crowd repeated each line with a roar of laughter.

> 'We promise to be strong though all we have to eat is potato water.'
> 'Oh potato water, oh potato water!'
> 'We swear we don't want a bacon sandwich.'
> 'And we are quite happy with cabbage.'

'Jokes like these showed that we didn't turn our backs on the system. We accepted it as a Utopia,' Zenon Laskowik told me, explaining his gentle irony with gentle irony. He was a thin man with a sensitive face, in his early fifties. He had the slightly crumpled features and asymmetrical speech rhythms of someone who'd drunk a little too much in their life, and my Polish friends confirmed to me later that his appearance was not deceptive. 'If someone wants to try to live in Utopia, why not let them try? We didn't want to act like rebels who were trying to use words to destroy the system. No, we were trying to show on our stage how beautiful a dream Communism was!'

One of Laskowik's best-loved comic creations from Cabaret Tey was set in the back of a small grocer's store. Laskowik plays the shopkeeper, who takes deliveries from Bolek, and has an assistant called Smolen. The view is always through the back of the shop out across the counter, but there is rarely any food and rarely any customers. The shop sketches were performed on TV for the first time in 1980.

BOLEK: No deliveries today because the tractor is defective.

LASKOWIK: Don't say the tractor is defective. Say the wheel is defective. Only the wheel is defective.

BOLEK: That's boll—

LASKOWIK: Okay, you're not on a building site now.

BOLEK: ... Without a wheel the tractor doesn't work.

LASKOWIK: Wait a second. How many wheels does a tractor have?

BOLEK: Four.

LASKOWIK: How many wheels are broken?

BOLEK: Only one.

LASKOWIK: How many wheels are in good condition?

BOLEK: Three.

LASKOWIK: Why didn't you first say that three wheels were functioning?

SMOLEN: Don't talk so much. Come and help me peel potatoes, because people are coming soon with coupons for tomatoes.

LASKOWIK: Ah, Bolek! ... Bring me some red paint. We're gonna start making tomatoes.

The simple content of Laskowik's jokes will be familiar to any student of Communist humour. They could have been written in the twenties by the first Soviet satirists. The joke-deniers – those who say the number of jokes has been grossly exaggerated and their historical importance equally overstated – would argue that Laskowik's show simply illustrates how boring and ineffectual the jokes had become. They were so harmless that they could run on TV.

But, in the light of future events in the eighties – especially the rise of Solidarity – and the fact that this kind of material only appeared once on TV until Glasnost was in full swing, this argument is unsustainable. If one only looks at the content of these jokes, then it is true, they look old; but those of us who have patience to study the material carefully – and I have played the old, low-quality VHS I obtained of the show over and again, in stop-frame and slow motion – will observe two significant differences from what had gone before.

The first is the delivery. Although this will hardly be apparent from the printed page, Laskowik delays every punchline. With a look of complete innocence, he gives the audience a moment to predict what's coming next and then wonder if he's going to deliver what they expect. This timing contains within itself a Communist joke – one about knowing all the Communist jokes. The point is: *the jokes aren't new.* Laskowik's TV special shows how, by the eighties, the lexicon of jokes has a quasi-biblical familiarity, and their telling has become a ritual that unites people with a common belief, like stories from the Old and New Testaments recited in church and synagogue.

CUSTOMER: *Do you have prunes?*
SMOLEN: *No.*
CUSTOMER: *Well, do you have pears?*
SMOLEN: *No.*
CUSTOMER: *Do you have tropical fruits?*
SMOLEN: *No.*
CUSTOMER: *What have you got?*
SMOLEN: *We've got a stock list.*
CUSTOMER: *Why don't you have anything?*
SMOLEN: *Because it's the afternoon.*
CUSTOMER: *Okay, give me the complaints book.*
SMOLEN: *Which one – the old one or the new one?*
CUSTOMER: *Any will do.*
SMOLEN: *We've lost the old one, and we're still waiting for the new one.*

The second distinguishing characteristic of Laskowik's jokes is, of course, where they are being told. Not every sketch Laskowik put forward made it to the final show, and the rejected material shows just how radical a move it was to get this kind of humour onto national television. 'I remember one gag with mustard,' Laskowik said, his eyes glistening – it could have been with emotion or with an inebriated glow. 'The set was an office with a desk, at Christmas time. Now in Poland at this time of year everyone has a "Christmas fish" for his family in the drawer of his desk at the office. In the sketch I am interviewing someone and want to take something from a drawer.

In my excitement I put my hand into a pot of mustard, which is also in the drawer. Then I look for a towel to wipe my hand on. I see the fish and try to wipe my hand on the fish. The censors forbade us to play that scene because they saw it as a comment on the shortage of meat in Poland, mustard being something you eat with meat, not fish.'

Well worn and well censored as the content of Laskowik's show might have been, it still contained Communist jokes spoken in the central institution of state propaganda. The vast majority of Communist jokes had been invented to mock the claims made by the state on television and in newspapers. Now those jokes had crossed the line, for the first time since 1917. Not that Laskowik thought that analytically about this moment in his career: 'We concentrated on the state's propaganda. We saw the difference between the reality of life and what was said in the media.'

SMOLEN: *Look at this potato.*
LASKOWIK: *Put this one aside. I will take it to the TV station. Maybe when they see it, they will start to tell the truth about the state of Polish agriculture.*

But this was the first and last time that this kind of material was performed on television anywhere in the Soviet Bloc. Laskowik was not permitted to make political jokes on television again. The Opole Music Festival continued to host stand-up comics who mocked Polish Communism, but their routines were not televised.

Laskowik was not one of the victors of 1989. After the end of the regime he gave up comedy and took a job as a postman. People say it was because of the bottle, but he has a different story, which, like his humour, is funnier and more touching: 'It's 1989, the year of change, and I am listening to the news and they announce that a new government will be formed but General Jaruzelski will still remain President of Poland ...' – in 1989 Solidarity and Jaruzelski had round-table discussions and the Communists and Solidarity agreed to form a unity government with Jaruzelski remaining temporarily in his position until elections – ' ... And I am thinking to myself: I'm still drunk. How is this possible? I waited till I got sober and then I started thinking that these were bad compromises and who knows where they would lead? And at exactly that moment a postman came to my door with a new uniform on with a Polish crowned eagle on his cap.

I liked that – finally our national postal service looked truly Polish – and I told him that. He asked me if I wanted a hat like his: "What are you going to wear then?" I asked. "Well, if you come to work for us," he says, "we'll give you one." He says: "There is a job at the post office. It's a part-time job and no one wants it." I said to my wife: "Did you hear that? Capitalism's come to Poland and no one wants a job!" There's money to be made! I said to myself. Okay I'm going to take that job and I'm going to live out the new ideology that we've all been dreaming about all this time.'

Lech Walesa, the Hercules of the fall of Communism, still lives in Gdansk. I arranged to meet him there in the Solidarity Museum, located in one former warehouse deep in the shipyard. I arrived early, and I looked round the exhibition while I waited for the former Polish President and Nobel Peace Prize winner, who Americans think brought down Communism single-handedly. An array of Solidarity badges, flags and other merchandise in vitrines was exhibited in reverentially subdued lighting. Solidarity was the best-branded revolutionary movement in history, its graffiti-style *Solidarnosc* logo ranking alongside the screen-printed face of Che Guevara and the hammer-and-sickle as Communism's most recognised symbols. Along some walls were massively enlarged photographs of Polish armoured vehicles training their water cannon on thousands of workers – iconic images of the eighties. Grainy phalanxes of militia in riot gear stood at intervals along a broad road; thirty metres away from them, protesters in jeans were frozen in blurred poses, half-obscured by clouds of tear gas, as they lobbed a stone, waved a banner or dived for the protection of a doorway. I wished I had lived a life as exciting as theirs. At the far end of the museum stood the odd climax of the exhibition: the original podium, with its long desk and old-fashioned microphones, from which Walesa and other Solidarity leaders had made statements to the world's media. It was an unlikely yet inspired object of reverence, worthy of a conceptual artist – one that looked more like a minimalist altar of obsolete communication technology than a relic of the struggle for freedom.

The joke-deniers would say that it was only coincidence that a few months after Zenon Laskowik's show Solidarity was formed and the streets of Gdansk filled with marching shipyard workers led by Walesa. They have a point. A year before the cameras rolled on Laskowik, Pope Jean Paul II had arrived in Warsaw on his first

Fig. 68. Solidarity, Andrei Krauze, 1981

pilgrimage to Poland, attracting huge crowds and making thinly veiled criticisms of the Communist state. The shipyard workers of Gdansk had staged protests against the regime in 1970, when eighty workers had been killed by the army, and in 1976 – so 1980 was another chapter of a book that had already been started. And it was neither the Pope nor Laskowik, but a price hike for meat that led to the historic wave of strikes in every major Polish city in July 1979. The state first tried to arrest the strike-leaders, then negotiate with them. The strike organisations consolidated themselves into one union and on 18 November 1980 Solidarity was formed, the first ever independent trade union in a Communist country, with ten million members (Fig. 68). In February the following year General Jaruzelski, who had led the Polish military contribution to the invasion of Czechoslovakia in 1968, took charge. In December 1981 he declared martial law, after the Soviets turned down his request for military assistance. Solidarity was banned, scores of members were arrested, but its leadership survived underground (Fig. 69). Throughout the eighties they were still able to publish newspapers and pamphlets, give press statements to the Western media, and hold anti-government demonstrations on public holidays such as 1 May.

There was still time to kill. I went outside and headed towards a warehouse the size of a small stadium, and climbed an oily staircase at one end. From a height I watched a scattering of workmen below

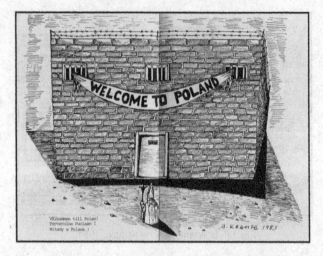

Fig. 69. 'Welcome to Poland.' Andrei Krauze, 1983

dismantling a vast cargo ship with blowtorches, a team of little Davids dismembering a Goliath, just – I was daydreaming in uninspiring metaphors – as they had dismembered Communism. Nowadays in Gdansk they are both shipbreakers and shipmakers. In the early nineties the shipyard almost went bankrupt, but the growth of global trade and international environmental laws played into their hands, even if it still looks like one of the last outposts of the centrally planned industrial Communist economy.

I was approached by three grey-haired workers, former Solidarity activists who still worked at the shipyard. I asked them about the Communist jokes.

'Some people thought the jokes we used to laugh at were enough – they even saw them as some kind of revolution. But for people like us, of course we used to tell jokes and stuff like that, but it wasn't enough,' they said clearly. 'We wanted to fight the Soviet system, so we decided to form an illegal opposition. We felt cheated. Something was wrong. Where did all the goods we produced disappear to? We wanted to shout out loud about all those lies. We didn't want to laugh about the situation. We wanted to fight for justice and our rights.'

Here was the minimalist theory of the Communist joke from the mouths of what had been the advance guard of the revolution. It was something that had kept up people's spirits in hard times, they had said, but it had little to do with the actual downfall of the state – that required an abandonment of joking.

'Mr President,' I asked Lech Walesa, 'did you use to tell any Communist jokes?'

'I am a politician and a revolutionary,' he replied icily. 'Don't ask me such questions.' Walesa was sitting uncomfortably, an old man on a small wooden chair. His son had persuaded him to talk to me. He might as well have been wearing a T-shirt that said 'Bruised Ego', or 'Former Political Hero – Please Do Not Touch'; but he wasn't: he was wearing a grey jacket and striped tie. He had been elected Polish President in 1990, in the elation that had followed the fall of Communism; but he lost power five years later, his term in office being generally considered a failure on account of his limited intellectual abilities. Since then he had attempted several political comebacks without success. Now he was standing for president yet again. It was a sign of his desperation – or his son's – that he imagined I might play a small part in his campaign. At any rate, he didn't seem to have been properly informed of the subject of my enquries. 'I listened to these jokes sometimes, but they didn't amuse me at all. Ask me some serious questions,' he said.

But I didn't have any serious questions. Walesa was an example of someone who had led real political change, but he said he didn't crack jokes. I couldn't tell if he was telling the truth or if he thought enjoying the subject might make him look like a lightweight. His mood went from bad to worse. He must have thought I was treating one of the most important political transformations of the twentieth century as a joke. I could see why this suspicion might arise, but I didn't mean it like that.

'Did you know the one about what would happen if Communism was introduced to Saudi Arabia?' I asked. 'Nothing at first, but soon there'd be a shortage of sand.'

Walesa grimaced. Like the shipyard workers who had followed him he belonged in the other camp of people, who thought the jokes were a silly diversion which kept the whole system going. He wasn't going to say that to me directly: that would already have been to take the jokes seriously and to exercise analytic powers that he didn't possess. He rehearsed for me the brief statesmanlike history of Poland since the eighties that he must have given a thousand times. He was a man of action not theories, he said. He decided to fight Communism, inspired by Pope John Paul II, and he won, largely thanks to God. After 1989 the Poles discovered that Capitalism had many faults, though not as many as Communism. He was sorry about all the problems that Capitalism created – inflation, unemployment, inequality – but that was because the Communists had run the economy into the ground. On autopilot Walesa was defending his own political record to me, as if I was another Polish journalist. Perhaps Walesa never had had a sense of humour, or perhaps years of mockery by Jerzy Urban (see below) had beaten it out of him. I tried to draw the conversation back to where I wanted. I knew a vaguely appropriate joke.

'Did you hear the one about the definition of Capitalism and Communism – that Capitalism was the exploitation of man by man and Communism was the opposite?'

'Yes I can agree with that,' he said to me humourlessly, but then he thought for a moment and added: 'Making Communism out of Capitalism is like making a fish soup out of an aquarium. You just need to boil the aquarium. Doing the opposite – making Capitalism out of Communism – is a bit more difficult.'

So he did know the jokes after all; he even knew one I didn't!

Walesa and Solidarity supported the minimalist theory of the Communist joke: it was something that had kept up people's spirits in hard times, but it had little to do with the actual downfall of the state. But that was only how it looked from the side of the opposition at the time. The state had not given up on the power of humour.

In August 1981 General Jaruzelski appointed a new government spokesman: Jerzy Urban was a renowned Polish satirist and professional maverick, 'the sort of man who ostentatiously and deliberately breaks wind in living rooms and watches the reaction of other guests', as one Polish journalist described him in the national newspapers in the eighties.

A professional, anti-authoritarian wind-up merchant, Urban wrote witty columns for the satirical magazine *Szpilki* and other Polish newspapers in the sixties and seventies. In 1967 he typically picked up a story from the papers that gave a glowing account of a chauffeur who reported on his boss – who would have been the manager of a state business and Party member – for using his company car for private purposes. Urban wrote:

The moral of this story is very important and all the managers who read it will be thankful for this lesson. Gentlemen, you may scream in your office at your underlings, you may make nasty jokes to your wives, you may abuse your lovers. I know people who live well even if they are at war with their bosses. But you must not do one thing: you must not make your driver angry. Your driver, gentlemen, is more important than wife, mistress and boss all put together.

While he had never been a vociferous critic of Communism, the views Urban had expressed in print had nevertheless been strong enough to lead the government to ban him periodically from being published (though he still wrote under a pseudonym). He had also never been a member of the Party. Now a kind of Communist joke-teller was hired to write press releases for a Soviet satellite state. Things had come full circle. 'I was searching for a spokesman who would be communicative, authentic, whom people would listen to, not another bureaucrat who'd read formal speeches,' General Jaruzelski told me once.

I met Urban at his offices in town. He drove me back to his villa in a wooded Warsaw suburb. He was a short man with hilariously large ears and he could barely see out of the window of his large black Mercedes. Nevertheless, he steered the vehicle neatly into his garage. We got out and he showed me through a side door that opened onto his heated indoor swimming pool. A charming host, whose eyes glittered with friendliness while at the same time searching my face for signs of character flaws, he took me into an enormous open-plan area, dotted with a dozen, sleek, early nineties designer Italian armchairs, arranged in pairs. On the walls hung six-foot pornographic oil paintings of orgies, and they made me ache to be invited to Urban's next party. His maid brought in a huge silver platter, dotted with Belgian pralines. I took one; he said: 'Political jokes in Poland and in the Soviet Union were huge. People made contact with each other by telling one another political jokes. When I look around today, I see that there is no such thing as a political joke. There are some jokes made by professionals such as myself. We attempt to tell them with cartoons, articles and essays in magazines, or on TV, but there is no such thing as a society sharing political jokes socially. Sex is left as the subject for jokes.'

'Do you remember any good jokes?' I asked.

'I don't even remember jokes I heard yesterday or the day before, but I do remember once when I was in a restaurant talking with a well-known professor of philosophy and he told me good jokes. I knew I wouldn't remember them, so I excused myself, left the table and started to make notes. A waiter saw me writing and warned the professor to be careful talking to me because I was writing down every word he said.'

Urban was living well. He had made millions since 1990 running a satirical magazine called *Niet*, a Polish version of *Private Eye* but immeasurably more vicious. 'I like Capitalism a lot,' he was quoted as saying in 1990. 'When I was in the government, I was never so rich and I never had the chance to play such a fascinating game as I do now.' There had been a remarkable continuity to Urban's career before and after the end of Communism. In the eighties, as government spokesperson, he had mocked Solidarity and Lech Walesa in numerous press conferences. After Communism his targets remained the same, only now the positions were reversed – Walesa was President and Urban one of the most powerful opposition voices, speaking through his satirical magazine. His most notorious remark concerned Walesa's autobiography, which, he said, was the first time a book had been written by someone who had never read one.

Through the eighties Urban's terse put-downs and brazenly unapologetic defence of the embattled Polish Communist regime entertained the enormous international press corps, who were following Solidarity's every move. Typically the journalists would receive statements from Solidarity spokesmen and then ask Urban for a response. Thus, throughout the whole of this decade, Poland was the only Communist country with anything like a government-and-opposition, an embryonic democracy in waiting.

Most of the time Urban was trotting out the well-established formulas of Soviet Bloc doublespeak, but the gay abandon, smiling confidence and zesty hyperbole with which he delivered his repudiations and accusations made them sound tongue-in-cheek, an acknowledgement of the comedy of Communism. He called the repression of Solidarity a 'policy of normalisation' and said that the banned trade union 'didn't exist'. Martial law had been declared to defeat attempts to 'isolate Poland'. The Western media were naturally guilty of 'bias', while America was 'meddling in Poland's internal affairs'. He ridiculed wherever possible the strong religious component in the opposition – 'It's either us or the Black Madonna of Czeschtochowa,' he once said, referring to Poland's most sacred site of Marian pilgrimage. 'But does it always have to be one or the other?' He turned his press conferences into a classroom by habitually commenting on, and even issuing grades for, articles published by journalists who came to his briefings. International politics took on the flavour of a theatrical farce, thanks to his straight-faced pettiness – when Reagan refused to meet Jaruzelski on a trip to New York in 1985, he won headlines by accusing America of 'bad manners'. 'We certainly are not straining on any door handles in Washington,' he added. A journalist once asked him if he was telling the truth. 'Is this the first time you've ever been to a press conference?' Urban replied. As the *New York Times* Polish correspondent wrote in 1985: 'While the party chiefs debate and skirmish in secret, Mr Urban jousts openly, usually joyfully and often cynically, with foreign journalists and through them with political dissenters, Western governments and international organizations.'

There was one gag for which Urban was more celebrated than any other. In 1986 the American senate had offered a donation of powdered milk, to help with Poland's economic crisis, but on the condition that it would be distributed by non-government agencies. It was a tokenistic political gesture. Urban responded by offering to send five thousand sleeping bags to New York to benefit the homeless, as long as they were distributed by charities. Journalists giggled, and one asked the spokesman if he could confirm reports that several Poles had offered to take the sleeping bags over to New York in person. 'They took it very seriously in the US,' Urban remembered. 'First of all the mayor of New York said that there were no homeless people in his city and then the American government did everything it could not to let those sleeping bags in.'

Urban was a comic actor playing the role of a lifetime. His contempt for Solidarity was genuine. 'I was an enemy of Solidarity because its demands were unreal and inflationary. I was against an organisation that promised people would own apartments in five years. It was a populistic movement, strongly clerical. I didn't like that either.' He became a hate figure himself, slotted into jokes that had existed for decades:

A guy in a crowd is trying to kill General Jaruzelski with a gun, but he cannot take aim because all the time someone is disturbing him, pulling at his shoulder and saying to him: 'Shoot Urban as well!'

But Urban also had little sympathy for Communism (and he certainly proved himself adept at Capitalism). 'The whole situation was absurd. I'll give you one example. When I was a spokesperson a perpetual problem for the government which I was supposed to defend was the lack of toilet paper. One day I got a letter from a citizen who wrote that he'd just come back from Germany and brought with him a roll of German toilet paper. He measured it and compared it to the Polish roll and discovered that the German one was 17% narrower than the Polish one. Now, he'd read somewhere in the newspapers that Poland had 15% less toilet paper than it needed, so he proposed that Polish machines in factories should cut narrower rolls. I thought that was a good idea and passed it on as a recommendation to the industry, and the answer came back that it was impossible because Polish standards demanded that toilet rolls had a certain width. I asked who set these Polish norms and on what kind of toilet he sat to create them? The answer came back: it wasn't anyone in Poland ... it was based on German standards!'

During the eighties, under martial law and afterwards, Solidarity continued to work underground, mounting rival May Day parades and organising various worker protests and strikes. Walesa was imprisoned and released. He met the Pope and won the Nobel Peace Prize. Solidarity activists were tear-gassed, water-cannoned, arrested, beaten up, sometimes imprisoned – though only, according to Urban, when they were drunk – and one sympathetic priest was even murdered. An army of foreign correspondents monitored every move by government and union. It was a relatively serious business, but on the fringes of this movement there was one maverick humorist who opened a new chapter in Communist jokes. 'Major' Waldemar Fyrdrych transformed the culture of Communist jokes into street protest in the Polish industrial town of Wroclaw (Fig. 70). Born in 1953, Fydrych studied the history of art, which may explain the surrealism of his later activities. He acquired the nickname 'Major' after pulling off an elaborate act to avoid military service, which involved turning up in front of the Commission wearing a major's outfit and professing excessive zeal for military service. He was judged mentally unfit to

Fig. 70. Major Fydrych, leader of the Alternative Orange

serve. This strategy, of taking the logic of the state line to its extreme, would underpin his later activities.

Fydrych's first action consisted of graffiti-ing a symbol of an orange dwarf all over Warsaw. Solidarity activists had been painting their symbol – an anchor – on walls across Poland. The authorities had painted over them with white paint. Fydrych then added his orange dwarf on top of the splodges of white – an apt mockery of the government's efforts to suppress the movement for reform.

In 1986 Fydrych launched Alternative Orange, a protest movement which, in a series of carnivalesque actions from 1986 to 1988, ridiculed Marxism–Leninism, state propaganda and official parades. 'Those crazy things that we did then – they cheered us up, they brought some colour to the greyness of our everyday reality. And certainly the presence of large groups on the streets was a sign for the authorities that reforms must happen,' Fydrych told me over a coffee, in a trendy bar situated in Warsaw's most prominent Communist building, the Palace of Culture. He was wearing one of his orange dwarf hats for the occasion.

Fydrych used humour to create a visible opposition on the streets of Wroclaw. His funny mass marches could not be repressed in the same way as serious demonstrations. Typically a few hundred Orange supporters in colourful outfits would march through the centre of

Wroclaw banging drums and chanting witty slogans. On International Children's Day, he and his crowds of supporters dressed up as gnomes and smurfs in the symbolic red colour of Communism, danced in the streets and distributed sweets. In September 1986, in an event called 'Who's Afraid of Toilet Paper?', the Major and his followers mocked the shortages of basic items and the Marxist tenet of common ownership by solemnly distributing single sheets of toilet paper to passers-by. They had written on the rolls: 'Let us share it justly. Let justice begin from toilet paper.' The leaflets they printed up continued: 'So Socialism, with its extravagant distribution of goods, as well as its eccentric social posture, has put toilet paper at the forefront of people's dreams. Are the queues for toilet paper an expression of a) the people's cultural aspirations? b) the call of nature? c) the leading role of the Party in a society of developed Socialism? Tick the right answer.'

Fydrych remembers, 'The police tried to prevent the distribution of the toilet paper, but people had one piece each and they were giving them to each other. The police arrested them. A friend had a dog, who had a bow made of toilet paper. He was arrested too. Later that day the police searched people's bags on the streets. If they found toilet paper, they arrested them. It was a crazy situation.'

This same theme was later explored when Fydrych was arrested on International Women's Day for distributing sanitary towels in the streets. 'Nearby there was this underground passage,' Fydrych continued, 'and people went down there to carry on the protest, and the chief of the police said over his megaphone, "All the policemen please go underground," and everybody started applauding. They were funny times,' he sighed nostalgically. Ever since the declaration of martial law, Solidarity activists had 'gone underground'. Fydrych was charmingly puerile – even now – but that was also the point. Communism also looked pretty childish, a political system that Europe had now outgrown.

On 7 October 1988, the official day of the Police and Security Service in Poland, Alternative Orange supporters staged their own demonstration of appreciation for these public servants for 'doing their duty with a smile', showering police officers and patrol cars with flowers. Attempts to embrace the police and thank them were met with force and Major Fydrych was arrested once again; but as he said: 'You cannot be serious with a police officer during interrogation if he asks you why you took part in an illegal meeting of dwarves.'

On 6 November 1988, the anniversary of the October Revolution, 150 Alternative Orange supporters 'restaged' the October Revolution, around a Wroclaw restaurant, which they had designated the Winter Palace. Two groups had constructed large models of the battleships *Potemkin* and *Aurora*. All those participating were dressed once again in the official colour of Communism, red. Crowds gathered and started to join in and shout 'Revolution' and Bolshevik slogans. 'There were people dressed as sailors and workers, but all in red, and the police chief was shouting through his megaphone: "Arrest the Reds," and at that moment my friend turned round to me and said, "At last!"'

Solidarity wouldn't go away, and it is arguable whether General Jaruzelski, an old-fashioned Polish nationalist as well as a Communist, and Jerzy Urban wanted it to go away. Across their eastern border, Gorbachev's reforms were in full swing. In September 1988, following another round of price-hike-and-workers'-strike, the Polish government recognised Solidarity. Round-table talks between the trade union and state began in January 1989. The government agreed to hold elections in which Solidarity could contest some seats.

Alternative Orange – whose antics Jaruzelski and Urban both told me they had enjoyed – kept up the pressure. On the day of the referendum on social policy, 27 November 1988, Alternative Orange held a demonstration under the slogan: 'Vote Yes Twice', mocking the government's claim to be conducting a free and fair vote. A hundred and fifty people were arrested and detained for several hours. On another unspecified date a crowd gathered at Wroclaw zoo and sang Stalinist hymns round the chimpanzee cages. In December 1990, in the first free presidential elections in Poland, Fydrych ran against Walesa and Jaruzelski. He was not able to transform laughs into political power and received less than 1% of the vote.

The Orange movement caught on in its own peripheral way. Offshoots sprang up in Hungary and other Eastern European countries; there was a reason why orange was the colour chosen by the popular demonstrations in the Ukraine in 2004–5. But alongside the statements of the shipyard workers and Walesa's contempt, Fydrych's electoral disaster was yet more evidence that, at least on the side of the opposition, Communist jokes were not the engine of revolution that so many joke books had described them as.

I was slowly coming to the conclusion that, as the people of the

Soviet Bloc rose up, they cast aside not only their chains but their jokes as well.

Ronald Reagan cracked one of the world's most famous Communist jokes at a sound check for his weekly radio address on 11 August 1984. 'My fellow Americans,' the President announced, 'I'm pleased to tell you today that I've signed legislation that will outlaw Russia for ever. We begin bombing in five minutes.' The voice check was not actually broadcast but the recording was leaked to the media and it can still be downloaded from the internet. The world media had a field day – each newspaper picking its line according to its national character. A French paper took a psychoanalytic angle, writing that only trained psychologists could know whether Reagan's remarks were 'a statement of repressed desire or the exorcism of a dreaded phantom'. A Dutch news service remarked pragmatically, 'Hopefully, the man tests his missiles more carefully.' In the Soviet Union commentators examined what it said about democracy and imperialism. One leader ran: 'We would not be wasting time on this unfortunate joke if it did not reflect once again the fixed idea that haunts the master of the White House.'

This was not the first Communist joke Ronald Reagan told. He loved them. He took them as evidence of – to use the clichés of the day – the indomitable spirit of the people of Eastern Europe and their irrepressible longing for freedom, not to mention proof that Communist economic theory was ridiculous. This was nothing new – generations of 'Cold Warriors' before Reagan had viewed the jokes the same way. But Reagan went a step further than his predecessors: he instructed members of the State Department to collect jokes for him and submit weekly memoranda with the latest ones.

One of the officials burdened with that task was Paul Goble, who sat on the Baltics desk. 'I now have my own personal collection of thirteen thousand Communist jokes,' he boasted to me, although he was unable to show me them, since they were stored in a garage in a remote American town.

Paul Goble looked every inch the proverbial Cold Warrior, with his trimmed grey hair, square-rimmed glasses, flannel trousers, navy jacket and wan smile. Like many of this kind of people, he had been overtaken by history and was now teaching international relations at the university in Estonia's second largest city. I met him on the top floor of the Tallinn Radio Tower, which consisted of a spindly concrete pole, twenty storeys high, housing a lift, surmounted by a UFO-like saucer, prickling with antennae. It was a masterpiece of sci-fi Communist design and a suitably Len Deighton-esque location. We walked round the observation platform, our heels clicking on the shiny black-lacquered floor, while we looked out through slanted space-age windows across a rainy Baltic landscape.

Reagan ratcheted up the Cold War in the eighties, initiating a new missile programme, Star Wars, funding the future Al-Qaeda in their war against the Soviets in Afghanistan and memorably declaring the Soviet Union an 'evil Empire'. Right-wing historians often claim that his uncompromising rhetoric and expensive arms race hastened the end of the Soviet Union. But he had one more weapon in his arsenal whose impact has never been properly evaluated: jokes. Reagan told Communist jokes at press conferences, in speeches and in negotiations at summits, always referring to them as 'my little hobby', which showed that Soviet citizens had 'got a little cynical attitude about their system'.

Almost every significant speech by the President would end with a Communist joke. On 9 May 1982 he addressed the Eureka College Alumni Association Dinner, in Illinois:

I've come to be a collector of these [jokes] that the Russian people tell among themselves that reveal their feeling about their government. And [I have a joke which] has to do with when Brezhnev first became President. And he invited his elderly mother to come up and see his suite of offices in the Kremlin and then put her in his limousine and drove her to his fabulous apartment there in Moscow. And in both places, not a word. She looked; she said nothing. Then he put her in his helicopter and took her out to the country home outside Moscow in a forest. And, again, not a word. Finally, he put her in his private jet and down to the shores of the Black Sea to see that marble palace which is known as his beach home. And finally she spoke. She said, 'Leonid, what if the Communists find out?'

In June 1982 he addressed the British Houses of Parliament: 'The strength of the Solidarity movement in Poland demonstrates the truth told in an underground joke in the Soviet Union. It is that the Soviet Union would remain a one-party nation even if an opposition party were permitted, because everyone would join the opposition party.'

Reagan had differently themed jokes for different audiences. Addressing an audience of spies in September 1986 at the National Security Agency at Fort Meade, Maryland, he quipped: 'I do have some fairly high-grade intelligence, though. We've just learned that from now on KGB agents have been ordered to do all their work in groups of three: one agent to take notes and write the report and the other two to keep an eye on the intellectual.'

Speaking to farmers at an Iowa caucus rally in 1984, he said: 'One of the latest that I heard had to do with a commissar in the Soviet Union who went out to one of those state collective farms, grabbed the first worker he came to, and said, "Comrade, are there any complaints?" And he said, "Oh no, Comrade Commissar, no complaints. I've never heard anyone complain." And he said, "Good. How are the crops?" "Oh," he said, "the crops, never been better, just wonderful!" And he said, "How about potatoes?" "Oh," he said, "Comrade Commissar, if we could put the potatoes in one pile they would reach the foot of God." And the Commissar said, "This is the Soviet Union. There is no God." And he said, "That's all right, there are no potatoes."'

In 1987, as Gorbachev's 'Glasnost' – 'Openness' – produced ever franker accounts of Soviet injustices, Reagan spoke at a luncheon hosted by the New Jersey Chamber of Commerce in Somerset, about 'a joke among dissidents in the Soviet Union. This one begins with a question: What is a Soviet historian? And the answer: someone who can accurately predict the past.'

In other speeches, Reagan boasted of telling these jokes to the face of the Russian President at summits, 'and he laughed'. The first of these would appear to have been told at the Geneva summit in 1985, when the two presidents began their arms-reduction negotiations, as he recalled in July 1986 in front of an audience of interns at a White House briefing: 'Well, you might be interested to know that the General Secretary has a good sense of humour. I told him the joke about the American and the Russian who were arguing about how much freedom they had. And the American finally said to the Russian, "Look," he said, "I can walk into the Oval Office. I can pound the President's desk, and I can say, 'Mr President, I don't like the way you're running our country.'" And the Russian said, "I can do that!" And the American said, "You can?" He said, "I can go into the

Kremlin. I can walk into the General Secretary's office. I can pound the desk and say, 'Mr General Secretary, I don't like the way President Reagan's running his country.'"'

Gorbachev's aides had been studying Reagan's speeches and knew what was coming. But Gorbachev did not have a robust anti-Capitalist joke for the American President. Instead he showed him a cartoon with the two of them standing at opposite ends of a wide abyss, with a Gorbachev caption saying they should get closer, and Reagan replying, 'That is a good idea; why don't you take the first step?'

At the Washington summit in December 1987, where Reagan and Gorbachev signed an agreement to eliminate medium-range nuclear missiles, it would seem Reagan cracked them incessantly. Aides recall how he asked Gorby if he'd heard this one:

When American college students are asked what they want to do after graduation, they reply: 'I don't know; I haven't decided,' while Russian students answer the same question by saying: 'I don't know; they haven't told me.'

Gorbachev reportedly laughed convincingly but then added: 'Ambassador Matlock has got to stop telling you stories like that.'

Reagan saved up another one for the press conference of the Washington summit itself: 'It's not an exaggeration to say it takes ten years to get delivery of an automobile in the Soviet Union, but you have to pay for the automobile right at the first, not when you get it. So this young fellow is going from agency to agency and getting permits here and permits there, and stamps he was collecting. Finally the final stamp in the final place is put on, and he lays out his cash and the man says: "Come back in ten years and get your car." And the young fella starts to turn away and he turns back and says: "Morning or afternoon?" And the fella behind the counter says: "What difference does it make?" "Well the plumber is coming in the morning."'

Reagan persecuted the Soviet leader with jokes. The transcripts of the Moscow summit reveal that the two men actually bickered about the correct way to tell one of them. On 30 May, in their morning session, the American President used a joke (which probably dates back to the thirties) to make a point about the secret militarisation of the Soviet economy. 'You know, there is a joke about a guy who worked at a pram factory. However, whenever he tried to assemble a pram, he would get a machine gun.'

The Soviet leader pulled him up: 'Yes, we have such a joke, but you were told a wrong version.'

Reagan rejected this accusation: 'I've known it since before the war ...'

'I think it absolutely played a part in the end of Communism,' Goble told me, beaming. He was a man who was still celebrating the defeat of Communism. 'I think that President Reagan's understanding of the Soviet Union was conditioned in an important way by listening to what Soviet people were saying to each other, and especially the jokes they were telling. It encouraged President Reagan in his profound belief that the Soviet people were appalled by their government, appalled by its stupidity, its limitations, its arrogance, and therefore they were interested in being free, and they would welcome a change in the political system.'

When Bush replaced Reagan, in January 1989, Goble was told he no longer needed to collect jokes.

The jokes of Reagan, the activities of Jerzy Urban and Laskowik's television show all indicate how Communist jokes had moved up a notch in the Communist hierarchy. They now had a visible public presence at the highest level, which they hadn't had in previous decades. A party-pooping joke-denier could still argue that this does not prove that humour played any role in the downfall of Communism, but he or she would have to concede it shows how the laughter closed in on the centres of Communist power.

Jerzy Urban told me the story of how a joke once impeded his diplomatic travel plans. The Polish government spokesman found himself stranded in Bucharest in the mid-eighties. Romania's Communist leader, Nicolae Ceauşescu had closed Romanian air space to Polish flights after he was informed of a joke told by a comedian in Warsaw: 'Nowadays all the nations in the world are trying to copy the same country – the United States,' he had said, 'except Poland, of course. We are trying to copy Romania.'

Fifteen years after the fall of Ceauşescu, Romania still resembles a vast Communist theme park where none of the rides works any more. Rusting rods of steel poke up out of unfinished concrete office blocks; the fountains that line the Boulevard of the People rarely run with water; the air is thick with the uncatalysed exhaust fumes of twenty-year-old Dacias, the Romanian Communist car marque.

Do you know why Romania will survive the end of the world?
Because it is fifty years behind everyone else!

In a world of short straws, Romanians pulled the shortest after 1945 and ended up with the worst Communism of them all, as their own version of the famous 'dog' joke illustrates:

Polish, Hungarian and Romanian dogs get to talking. 'What's life like in your country?' the Polish dog asks the Hungarian dog.
'Well, we have meat to eat but we can't bark. What are things like where you are from?' says the Hungarian dog to the Polish dog.
'With us, there's no meat, but at least we can bark,' says the Polish dog.
'What's meat? What's barking?' asks the Romanian dog.

In some ways it was business as usual as far as post-war Communist dictatorships went. Romania's first Communist leader, Gheorgiu Dej, conducted par-for-the-course purges, show trials and executions, sent political enemies to build a canal (the Black Sea canal, which proved to be too narrow for most ships); or tortured them in damp prisons – in the most horrific of these, Pitesti, the prisoners were compelled to torture each other. There were crash industrialisation projects, which sometimes made little economic sense (steelworks were built but the iron had to be imported from India) and sometimes provided the population with shamefully low-quality technological products, such as Dacia cars, at vast environmental cost.

But in other ways Romania departed from the script. Under Dej's successor, Ceauşescu, there was something utterly transparent about Romanian Marxism–Leninism. Compared to the other versions in the Soviet Bloc, it was like a child who blurts out what his mother has told him not to say. Communism had always had more in common with the absolute monarchies and feudalism of pre-modern Europe than with twentieth-century democracy, yet Ceauşescu made the link explicit by organising a presidential investiture ceremony in 1964, in which he was presented with a gold sceptre made specially for the purpose. The Surrealist artist Salvador Dali sent a telegram to Ceauşescu congratulating him on his rod of office. At least somewhere on earth, Dali exclaimed, there still lived a ruler 'capable of the Grand Manner'. The telegram was printed in the newspapers.

On a trip to North Korea, Ceauşescu was impressed by the huge pageants, in which thousands of workers in stadiums held up coloured cards to form vast pictures and performed formation dancing in military uniforms – as they still do today. So he imported the style of these shows into Romania but combined it with myths about his country's glorious Roman ancestors and conquering kings.

At the same time, Ceauşescu kept an iron grip on the country, at least in the minds of the population, with the Romanian political police, the Securitate:

Ceauşescu, Reagan and Gorbachev are travelling together on a luxury liner accompanied by their bodyguards. One day they are sailing through shark-infested waters and Reagan decides to show off the skill and courage of his guard. He removes his watch and throws it overboard. 'Go get it, John!' he orders – and like a shot the marine dives into the water and retrieves the watch.

The bystanders on the ship are amazed – 'What courage!' they chorus.

Then Gorbachev flings his own watch overboard and instructs his bodyguard to get it. The KGB agent shows no less unquestioning devotion.

'What courage!' the crowd say, applauding.

Now Ceauşescu, not to be outdone, throws his watch overboard. 'Go get it, Mihai,' he says.

But the guard does not move. 'No way, sir,' he says.

And the crowd roar louder than before: 'What courage!'

Communism had never looked more colourful – or contradictory: a belief-beggaring synthesis of medieval myth and twentieth-century mass organisation. Ceauşescu was the most unconvincing subject of a personality cult in the history of the world: short, unimposing, stuttering, decrepit, the son of a cobbler. Yet the fawning prologues to thousands of books suggested that there was no field of human endeavour in which either he or his wife Elena did not excel.

A fresco with the best Romanian actors will be painted on the face wall of the National Theatre in Bucharest. In the middle of them will, of course, be Nicolae and Elena Ceauşescu.

In the sixties, millions of portraits of Ceauşescu were distributed across Romania in which he was seen in three-quarter profile, with one ear showing. Then jokers connected this image with the Romanian saying 'to have one ear', which means to be mad. The portraits were duly replaced by others that prominently displayed two large ears. Photographs of the 'Giant of the Carpathians' appeared on the front page of every Romanian publication, prompting the joke:

Why are there no pornographic magazines in Romania?
Because the first page would be too terrible.

His economic policies caused horrendous hardship. While other Communist states took huge loans at advantageous rates from the West, Ceauşescu did the opposite: he managed to pay off his country's entire national debt in the early eighties, by exporting all the raw materials and produce he could. During Ceauşescu's state visit to Britain in 1978 he proposed paying for British aeroplanes in Romanian oranges. At home there were permanent energy and food shortages. People cooked with 'adidas' (cut-down pigs' trotters) or 'cutlery' (mangy chicken legs) in flats in sub-zero temperatures. A joke ran:

A man is walking down the street in Bucharest in winter. He shouts into a flat: 'Could you shut your windows; it's freezing out here.'

Bucharest was nicknamed 'Ceauschwitz'.

As the shortages persisted, Ceauşescu's team launched a series of hare-brained schemes to rescue the situation. A nutritional commission came up with a solution to the acute food shortages: they produced a report which said that Romanians could make do with fewer calories than other European populations. In 1988 the state was considering a rationalisation plan to bulldoze half of Romania's villages to the ground and move the inhabitants into large towns. There was another proposal to move all the old people out of the towns and into the villages, so that they were less of a burden on the economy. The unproveable urban myth is that this plan was dumped after a rash of often terrible jokes on the subject were reported to the Ministry of the Interior by observant Securitate agents.

Two very hungry old grannies are sitting in a village. One of them spots a snail. 'Look, quick,' says one, 'there's something to eat – a snail.'

The other tries to catch it but fails. 'It was too fast for me,' she says, disappointed.

The fantasies of Romanian Communism found their apogee in Ceauşescu's Palace of the People, the largest palace in the world and the ultimate symbol of the Communist fairy tale. It looks like a Byzantine Versailles, the court of an exotic absolute monarch, yet it was built in the 1980s. It is the architectural epitaph not only of Romanian Communism but of the Communist dream itself – a huge marble-clad hulk of massed columns, arches, pediments and towers combining neoclassical and Middle Eastern motifs, built on a clumsy wedding-cake ground plan, in receding stepped tiers. It squats like an obese man who can't get up, in the middle of Bucharest, approached by one of the long boulevards, lined with crumbling marble water-works, that Ceauşescu carved through the city. Old art-nouveau villas were raised to the ground, and a handful of Orthodox churches were moved sideways on rollers to make way for these avenues and the enormous apartment blocks that tower over them, like docked cruise ships. If you turn off the main roads and walk behind the concrete monoliths, you soon find yourself amidst the curving alleyways and crumbling nineteenth-century villas of old Bucharest, a sign of how Romanian Communism was only ever skin-deep, as thin as the layer of margarine that its citizens could spread on their bread.

The People's Palace is a symbol of how Communism was mis-understood by its proselytisers and protagonists. They thought it led into the future, but it took them into the past. Inside the palace, visitors can walk up wide marble staircases, across the longest carpets ever made, with endlessly repeating geometric patterns, through one room after another decorated with intricate stucco-work as lumin-ously white as icing sugar. At first the scale and decoration are exhilarating, but soon one is overcome with tiredness. One searches for a reason. It is unexpected but not hard to find: the repetitiveness of the forms – the patterns on the carpets and in the pediments, the chandeliers, the columns – the same formulas are repeated in every room. Finally this is a testament to the limits of the Communist imagination.

What will the Palace of the People be called when it is finished? A mausoleum.

*

Fig. 71. Calin Bogdan Stefanescu, the world's only statistician
of Communist jokes

One man has attempted to examine Communist jokes scientifically.
Calin Bogdan Stefanescu, former Party member and an amateur
statistician, mounted a sociological analysis of Romanian Communist
jokes during the eighties (Fig. 71). In the last ten years of Ceauşescu's
regime, in the same time-frame as the construction of the People's
Palace, Stefanescu noted down every joke he heard, where he heard
it, and when; what the social background appeared to be of the person
who said it, and their age group. After the fall of Communism, he
published his data in a book, *Ten Years of Black Humour in Romania*.
The print run was tiny and the volume remains virtually unknown,
but it is one of the most significant texts of the Communist era – not
only because of the surprising exactitude of the science, but also
because of the heroic impossibility of the exercise.

Stefanescu's book contains over 950 jokes collected between
August 1979 and December 1989 – 'I have calculated that one new
joke entered my collection every 4.71 days,' he told me. At the time,
he worked in the administration of the Bucharest transport network.
The drab palette of his wardrobe – baggy pleated brown trousers and
a tatty olive shirt – made him look every inch the anonymous low-
ranking Balkan Communist bureaucrat. At their worst, this kind of
people were lazy and corrupt, but at their best – as Stefanescu clearly

was – they were meticulous and exhaustive. Stefanescu collected jokes from colleagues at work, while on holiday, at Party meetings and by eavesdropping on conversations. He worked not only like a sociologist but like an archaeologist, piecing together the historic jokes from fragments he came across. 'In my book I have had to reconstruct many of the jokes, because I only caught the beginning or only the punchline. Sometimes people noticed I was listening in on their conversation and I had to then move off. However, I can reassure you that I was very careful to keep the same tone as that of the person from whom I heard the joke or part thereof.

'What made me initiate this process was the quality of the jokes. Some of them were truly extraordinary. You see, jokes are usually meant to "live" for two or three days, for a week maybe. I simply couldn't allow those jokes to fade away,' said Stefanescu. 'Apart from my admiration for the genius of those jokes, I wrote this book driven by a personal reason: from a certain point on, I started to perceive my collection of jokes as a way to justify myself in front of my children. I started to imagine my children asking me, "Dad, what did you do under Communism? Why didn't you get out in the streets, why didn't you do something?"'

Like joke-tellers across the Soviet Bloc, Stefanescu imagined he was participating in a dangerous underground activity, even though he learned by experience that the state did not view his jokes as dangerous. 'There were a number of incidents which may seem funny now, but which were terrifying at the time. I remember one occurred one day while I was returning from work. My office was in the centre of Bucharest, and I suddenly remembered a joke right at the moment when I was passing by the American Embassy. As I always had the notebook on me, I took it out of my bag and quickly scribbled the joke in it. Unfortunately, the young soldier who was guarding the American Embassy saw me and he thought something dubious was going on. Maybe he thought that I wanted to blow up the Embassy or God knows what. He came over to me, asked for my ID and then he took me to his superior. The officer checked my ID once more, then took my notebook, which was full of jokes, and started to flick through it. Quite obviously, I was terrified while he was doing that. I could already see myself in handcuffs. But then, to my surprise, the officer gave me both my ID and my notebook back and said that I was free to go. When I got home, later that day, I was confronted with a terrible dilemma: should I throw away the notebook or not? What if I threw it away and then nothing happened? After a painful deliberation, I decided to keep the notebook. That proved to be the right decision, as nobody came to search my house.'

The jokes collected by Stefanescu followed with precision the problems and events of Romania in the eighties. After the increase in the price of petrol, Stefanescu heard this one:

Have you noticed that at every petrol station there is now a doctor and a policeman on duty? The doctor gives first aid to those who faint when they see the price, and the policeman interrogates the ones who fill up about where they got the money from.

When the French President made a visit to Bucharest, Stefanescu recorded this one:

The French President, Valery Giscard d'Estaing, and his wife sit down to a state dinner with the Ceauşescus. In an effort to make polite conversation Mrs D'Estaing asks Elena Ceauşescu where she got her shoes from.
'Oh,' says Elena, 'these were my husband's diploma project.'

In March 1984, a month after Ceauşescu brought in new laws banning abortions, a policy which led to Romania's awful orphanages, the following joke emerged:

Ceauşescu's helicopter touches down in Maramures, a remote village in the country's north-western corner. He meets the village elders and talks to them about the latest directives designed to reverse Romania's declining birthrate. In the flowery language for which the regime was known, he tells them: 'Elena, the mother of all Romanians, wants your children to be her children. She wants to build the nation with you.' The villagers listen, and when Ceauşescu finishes he asks if there are any questions.
One old man says: 'We understand you perfectly and we are ready to serve our country, but I have one question: do we go down to Bucharest or will she come up here?'

'One may observe a massive increase of the number of jokes about the quality of life in 1981 compared to 1980 ...' Stefanescu pointed out to me. 'A rise from sixteen jokes to forty-four! That is explained by the food rationalization programme, which Ceauşescu introduced in Romania in 1980 and which was taking effect. This was the moment when power cuts and queues for basic foodstuffs became part of our daily lives.' In his book Stefanescu lists scores of jokes from this period:

> Child: Hey, Grandma, why are you wearing a rucksack?
> Grandma: In order to save energy, pacemakers have been converted to run on coal.

> In a Romanian tram, an elegantly dressed gentleman shouts: 'Don't push me! I am the manager of a meat store.'
> One of the passengers says to his friend: 'I recognise him. He is a famous university professor, but he suffers from delusions of grandeur.'

> Did you hear that since the spring living standards in Romania have doubled?
> Before we were cold and hungry – now we're only hungry.

Each time he wrote down a joke, Stefanescu noted down the profiles of the joke-tellers. His age and class breakdowns reveal that most Romanian joke-tellers were intellectuals aged around thirty to forty.

Social background of joke-tellers as %		Age of joke-tellers as %	
Intellectuals	67%	Under 30	13%
White-collar workers and bureaucrats	14%	30–40	54%
Blue-collar workers	11%	40–50	24%
Pensioners	7%	Over 50	9%
Foreigners	1%		

Stefanescu's strangest graph concerned jokes about events. Focusing on a sample of sixty jokes about specific events, he corroborated the date of the event with the date he heard the joke, thus allowing him to calculate, for the first and only time, the *velocity* of a Communist joke (Fig. 72). Stefanescu sketched out his graph of the 'speed of reaction and dissemination of the Romanian Communist joke' and showed me the peak in 1987 – 'This spike represents the political

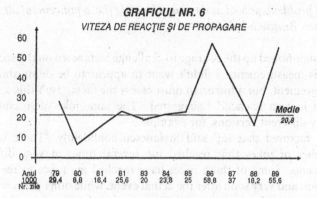

Fig. 72. Graph of the speed of reaction and dissemination of a Romanian Communist joke, Calin Bogdan Stefanescu, *Ten Years of Black Romanian Humour*, 1990

demonstration which took place in Brașov in 1987.' He was referring to a riot by workers in this small Romanian town on 15 November, an election day. People heard that there was a party, organised in the building of the Brașov Party Committee, restricted to the members of the higher political echelons, where some kinds of food would be served that were unavailable to the average Romanian. A mob broke in and ransacked the building. This mini-revolution was suppressed by the security forces, the participants were arrested and imprisoned, but soon these events were reflected by new jokes that appeared on the streets. 'I have collected nine jokes between 23 November – i.e. approximately a week after the event – and 20 January of the following year, which indicate that the impact of the Brașov events on the Romanian population was truly immense.'

Among those new Brașov jokes was a nickname for the traditional Romanian pretzel based on its shape – 'Brașov handcuffs'. Others that can still be understood today are:

Which is the worst press agency in the world?

AGERPRESS [the Romanian state press agency], because they didn't even hear about what happened in Brașov.

After the Brașov events the people of Brașov will have all their food problems solved as there will be a pig [i.e. a policeman] allocated to each Braşov inhabitant.

I summoned up the courage to challenge Stefanescu on the accuracy of his measurements. I didn't want to appear to be diminishing his achievement, but a historian must assess the facts. 'Isn't this a somewhat inexact science?' I suggested. 'The same joke often comes in many different versions, for example.'

'I factored that in,' said Stefanescu confidently. 'There were a number of jokes that reached me several times at very different moments. Some of those jokes have reached me twice in the same version and very soon after the actual event, while other jokes reached me at a considerable temporal distance after the first time when they reached me. Sometimes I simply did not consider the joke when it reached me the second time, if it was identical with the version already collected. Some other times, when the jokes were close but not identical, I considered them versions of the same joke.'

'But ...' I said. 'Just because you heard a joke a certain number of days after the event, it doesn't necessarily mean that that joke was reaching everybody at the same time, or that it was invented just after the event.'

'You are wrong on both counts,' replied the expert patiently. 'To give you an example, let's say that a joke reached me 250 days after an event ... I wouldn't assume that the joke had been recently produced because, from what I know about the mechanism of joke-production, nobody creates a political joke 240 days after an event. You do that on the spot; that's the thing about political jokes: a specific event is particularly relevant to someone, that person produces a joke immediately and then sets the joke free. If you don't do that on the spot, the event is "lost". The rest of the time is propagation and not actual production. And since I am measuring how fast all the jokes reached me relative to each other, it doesn't matter if they reached other people at different speeds, the relative speeds would be the same.'

He was very convincing! I felt confident enough in his data to pop the big question. His most important graph was also the simplest – one axis was divided up according to the years 1979–89, the other according to the themes of jokes: standard of living, Ceauşescu, opposition, political theory, the party, culture, Securitate ... nothing was left out (Fig. 73). The graph listed how many of what kind of jokes were produced in which year. Dared I hope that his figures might say something empirical about the jokes and the fall of Communism? Trembling inside, but concealing my anxiety, I put the question to him that was my Holy Grail.

'Yes, the quantity and content of the jokes change in significant ways as the Revolution approaches,' he said. Stefanescu leafed through his notes – and stopped. 'Here is one of the bitterest jokes from 1987 ... Romanians who did not die from cold during the past winter and those who did not die of starvation during the past summer are to be hanged soon on the suspicion of membership in the Romanian Resistance Movement.'

'What used to be grey was gradually becoming black,' he continued, savouring the melodrama in his maths. 'Towards the end of the 1980s people started to feel that something was about to change. I wouldn't say that we started to believe that Communism would fall. All we could hope for at the time was that we would get rid of the Ceauşescus. There were many jokes circulated about the Fourteenth Congress of the Communist Party, which took place in November 1989. One of my favourites at the time was the joke about the guy who falls asleep during the Congress. While he is asleep a rat enters the congress hall and scares the participants. Our man is woken up by people shouting: "Kill the filthy rat," and he shouts out: "And kill her while you're at it!" – a reference, of course, to Elena Ceauşescu.'

I felt he was teasing me. These were more incidental jokes, but I wanted the cumulative figures. Stefanescu pointed at his graph. Jokes about Ceauşescu were produced at the relatively modest rate of ten per year over the whole decade, but between 1986 and 1989 this figure rose 150% to between fourteen and sixteen jokes per year. The statistics in Stefanescu's 'opposition jokes' category were even more pronounced. These averaged a little over twelve a year, but in 1988 and 1989 there were at least twenty new ones. Between 1983 and 1989 the number of these jokes rose from four per year to twenty-two – an increase of 550%.

Theme	79	80	81	82	83	84	85	86	87	88	89		% of total
St / living	18	16	44	25	28	28	33	18	36	21	25	292	30.42
Ceauşescu	14	13	7	10	7	9	8	16	14	14	15	127	13.23
Opposition	10	8	7	8	4	4	8	9	17	20	22	117	12.19
Industry	8	6	8	1	7	5	2	7	11	13	15	83	8.65
Human Rights	9	15	6	8	4	6	12	4	7	4	5	80	8.33
Marxist Crit.	5	6	6	4	4	3	3	6	7	8	6	58	6.04
Culture	10	5	7	3	3	2	4	5	6	6	4	55	5.73
Secret Police/Army	1	3	4	4	2	3	5	8	7	7	3	47	4.9
The Party	7	5	6	4	2	2	1	1	5	4	3	40	4.17
Economy	5	1	3	3	2	2	2	1	2	0	1	22	2.29
Foreign Pol.	1	1	1	2	2	2	1	2	4	2	3	21	2.19
Agric.	1	0	1	3	3	0	0	2	2	6	0	18	1.87

Fig. 73. Stefanescu's graph of Romanian Communist jokes divided according to year and theme

A warm glow spread through my body. This was, finally, incontrovertible proof that linked the jokes directly to the downfall of Communism. Stefanescu's statistics proved that jokes were not a distraction from the struggle – a way for people to avoid real resistance. If that had been the case, then the jokes would have existed in inverse proportion to oppositional activity. Instead, as the forces of resistance gathered strength, the jokes increased in intensity – quantitatively and qualitatively.

At the same time, Stefanescu's data demonstrated that not all kinds of jokes increased at the end of the eighties. The jokes about the quality of life never re-achieved their peak in 1981. 'I would conclude from this,' Stefanescu said, 'that, at some point after 1987, it was more important for Romanians to criticise Ceauşescu than to complain about the way they were living.' Thus Stefanescu's data suggested another compelling thesis: not all jokes appeared to be linked to regime change. Jokes about shortages, for example, did not increase as the forces of revolution grew in Romania. These figures had the merit of uniting both sides of the argument: that Communist jokes both prolonged and undermined the regime. It just depended which ones you told.

There are of course limits to how far one may reliably go with the *-ology* of joke-telling – shortcomings that Stefanescu was only too ready to admit: 'I was hoping that somewhere else, in a different corner of Romania, somebody else was doing the same thing. My secret wish was that, at some point in the future, I could compare my data with somebody else's data and we could draw conclusions about the ratio at which those jokes were produced, the speed at which they were disseminated among the population and so on. Unfortunately, that will never happen, as I have never heard of anybody else who did the same thing as me.'

With Stefanescu I had come a step closer to achieving the main goal of my mission: I had found evidence that the jokes were linked to resistance not apathy. Communist jokes – albeit certain kinds – I now knew, accompanied the fall as well as the rise of Communism. Yet Stefanescu's joke-crunching could not put the final piece in my jigsaw – I still needed to find a causal link between the jokes and the revolution.

I tried hard to imagine what that would mean in theory. It seemed like an issue about the philosophy of speech. Jokes were a kind of speech, but what precedents were there for speech itself producing change? It could persuade, but since it was always about something, how could one distinguish between the effect of what it was about and the effect of the speech? 'Sticks and stones can break my bones, but words can never harm me,' as they say. In a nutshell, could a figure of speech have agency? There were legal arguments that said this was possible. Laws against 'incitement' in Britain, against racist speech, were based on the idea that an utterance could be itself a kind of action.

I realised there were only two options. I could show that the action of joke-telling led to the action of physical resistance, marches, demonstrations. Or I could show that the collapse of the regimes followed politicians listening to and *heeding* the jokes.

My mind switched between these arcane linguistic analyses and wild cinematic fantasies. I tried to imagine possible scenarios. In one, American aeroplanes dropped leaflets with thousands of jokes across the Soviet Union, leading, a week later, to mass riots. In another, Hungarians, Poles or East Germans carried banners with thousands of political jokes on them in the protests of 1988 and 1989. In a third, I imagined that the speeches of the leaders of these demonstrations had a crescendo of jokes in them, at the end of which the excited crowd ransacked the offices of the security services in a roar of cackling laughter. Or I saw myself discovering the minutes from a meeting of the Politburo in which Gorbachev read a report from the KGB about political jokes, and then, speaking in a voice quivering with emotion, said: 'The jokes are right. We must give up.' Which of these would it be? They all sounded equally ridiculous.

EIGHT

We're Not Joking

There's a cartoon that summarises the modern Utopia that the East German state promised its citizens and that many of them believed could be achieved through Communism (Plate 7). A large ocean liner is sailing, its deck crowded with smiling citizens. Behind them the chimneys of a productive factory smoke happily away, and behind that rises the skyline of East Berlin with its famously futuristic Radio Tower. A large handshake is emblazoned on the side of the ship, a symbol of the friendship between East Germany and the Soviet Union. Social well-being, thriving industry, modern technology, proletarian solidarity – that's what this picture meant when it was drawn in 1971; but by the mid-eighties most East Germans would have read it very differently: those smoking factories represented the pollution that the DDR's poorly regulated industries were spewing out; the Radio Tower, the power of the Stasi; the crowd on the deck would be queuing to get off (or for the arrival of some tropical fruit), and the ocean liner itself would represent East Germany's isolation in the reforming Warsaw Pact. They even had a joke about a famous ship:

> The British, American and East German governments have agreed to launch a joint mission to raise the Titanic. This unprecedented cooperation is possible because each nation has a different interest in the sunken ship: the British want to examine the hull of the vessel to determine the exact cause of the disaster; the Americans are after all the treasure that went down with the ship; and the East German government wants to learn more about the band that played until the end.

Years before central Europeans were marching in the streets on any significant scale – that is, in straggling groups of more than 150 – the jokes were predicting the end of Communism, and the best end-of-Communism humour came from East Germany. The jokes on either side of this paragraph appeared in print in Erik Florian's *The Political Joke in East Germany* published in Munich in 1983. They capture the atmosphere of 'the last days'.

A Jew asks a wise rabbi, 'What's coming?'
The rabbi answers, 'I know what's coming, but I don't know what's going to happen before it comes.'

The jokes were prophetic. Some of the ones in Florian's collection seem as if they would have to be specific to 1989, but they were first told in the early eighties.

A man goes into a café and he says, 'I would like borscht then I would like a steak, then I would like a coffee and please bring me a copy of Pravda.*'*
The waiter says to him, 'Certainly, sir, I'll bring you all those things, but I have to tell you that there isn't a Pravda *any more. That was only in the Communist period.' So the waiter goes away and he brings the chap his borscht.*
Then the diner says, 'That was delicious, now bring me my steak and bring me a copy of Pravda.*'*
The waiter says, 'No, sir, you don't understand; there isn't any Pravda, *the Communists have gone.' So, he brings the steak.*
The diner eats his steak and then he says, 'That was delicious, now bring me my coffee and my copy of Pravda.*'*
And the waiter gets very angry and says, 'Look how many times do I have to tell you? Pravda *is gone, the Communists have gone and it's all over ...'*
The diner says, 'Yes, but I like to hear you say it.'

Fig. 74. 'See no evil, hear no evil, speak no evil'
(Andreas J. Mueller, 1983)

Following on the heels of these jokes, a myriad of 'apolitical' associations were formed in Hungary, Czechoslovakia and East Germany in the early eighties. There were church groups, peace groups, environmental groups, human-rights groups, conscientious-objector groups, anti-alcohol groups, John Lennon groups, nuclear-disarmament groups, hippie festivals on the Baltic coast and nationalist groups in the Ukraine. The Communist regimes knew the procedure for dealing with workers' protests against price increases and with people who called for democracy, but they had nothing in their guidelines for peace and ecology movements. Over the course of the seventies the East German and other central European states had made 'World Peace' and a 'demilitarised Europe' the slogans of their foreign policies. Now they were caught out by the way the new protest groups mimicked the themes of the state. They still arrested, beat up and imprisoned the demonstrators and confiscated unofficial *samizdat* literature, but it was difficult actually to outlaw grass-roots organisations whose aims they apparently shared.

There was a changing political atmosphere, which could be sensed in all areas of society, including the bureaus of official humour. In the early eighties, the parameters of the permissible were widening. In 1983 *Eulenspiegel* published a cartoon of three apes with the motto: 'Hear nothing, see nothing, say nothing' by Andreas J. Mueller (Fig. 74). In 1985 Willy Moese made a cartoon in which a group of suited men clinging on to a cliff face are asked: 'Anyone opposed to the motion, please raise your hands' – a pointed critique of political power in East Germany, unthinkable a few years earlier.

Unofficial *samizdat* magazines with cartoons appeared and the highly popular cartoonists' exhibitions became braver in their displays. At the Karicartoon 87 exhibition, visited by 78,000 people, Andreas J. Mueller showed a watercolour cartoon 'Big Wide World' (1986) that depicted an idyllic German landscape, but in the place of a blue sky there was a towering brick wall (Plate 8). The Party demanded the cartoon's withdrawal. The artist refused and had his way.

Then, in 1985, Gorbachev was appointed the new Soviet leader. Within a year he had introduced his reform policies, Perestroika and Glasnost. He was not starting from a blank sheet of paper, but was rather following up all the reports produced by state think tanks in the seventies, advocating market reforms and political liberalisation.

Two Perestroika-era cartoons from *Krokodil*. Left (Fig. 75): A cartoon about the size of the black market; 'economy' is written on the side of the mangy pig; Right (Fig. 76): cartoon suggesting that uniformity and servility is still the order of the day in Russia, N. Belovtsev.

Andropov had begun to implement some of their recommendations, but had died. The party selected Gorbachev to continue this Soviet Mission Impossible: he and his clique of 'new-thinking' advisers admired the economic dynamism of Western Europe and its political pluralism, but they wanted to make Communism work, which meant retaining the 'leading role' of the Party.

Gorbachev was appalled by how badly Communism was going. In his memoirs, he writes: 'No one imagined the scale of our ecological disaster, how far we were behind the developed nations as a result of our barbaric attitude to nature.' The collective farms, he said at the time, were a 'system of serfdom'. He knew that economic growth had virtually stopped in 1980, military spending was 40% of GDP, and there were five million registered alcoholics. A teetotaller himself, one of his first measures was a highly unpopular anti-alcohol campaign, prompting a joke, not quite good enough to spell out, but ending in the punchline: 'Well, at least we are lucky he's not celibate too.'

Gorbachev's reforms took years to implement and often backfired, but Perestroika and Glasnost were motors that ran on the fuel of hot words. Seizing the earliest opportunity at Chernenko's funeral, in March 1985, the new Soviet General Secretary took the leaders of the Soviet Bloc states aside and told them that it was time to 'change or go'. A month later, addressing the Central Committee, he criticised the state's 'inability to tell the truth' and 'false idealisation of reality'. The next year he told the heads of his own party, in a closed meeting, that Communism was 'leading to disaster'.

Chernobyl, in April 1986 – the disaster at an atomic power station in which the Soviet Union nuked itself and its neighbours – was a huge impetus to reform and protest. A hundred and thirty-five thousand people were evacuated from the environs in a month. There were plenty of Chernobyl jokes, as a trio of Polish, Czech and Hungarian sociologists discovered in fieldwork that year:

What's the new sign in Kiev hospitals?
'Anyone who has come in for radiation therapy, please go outside.'

How many Russians does it take to change a light bulb?
None. They all glow.

The authorities did not immediately inform their population of the scale of the nuclear fall-out. They were silent as thousands of workers marched in the May Day parades, while a Soviet radioactive cloud drifted across Europe on the international workers' holiday.

What did the workers celebrate at the May Day parade in Budapest?
The radiant friendship between Hungary and the Soviet Union.

How was the May Day parade in Kiev organised?
In rows. In the first row were the Party activists; in the second row were all the Communist youth activists; in the third all the union activists; and finally all the radioactivists.

Gorbachev took Chernobyl as evidence of the urgency of reform; for the citizens of Eastern Europe it gave their struggle a life-and-death dimension. Yet the marching season of the revolutions, which terminated the Communist Parties' monopoly of power, did not begin until spring 1988. Ten thousand people marched in Budapest in March 1988, while there were thirty-five demonstrations in Leipzig between September 1987 and September 1989. At first these were under a thousand strong, but by autumn 1989 the German marchers numbered tens of thousands.

In September 1988 Solidarity was brought into government in Poland in the 'round-table talks'. In February 1989 the Hungarian Communist Party renounced its leading role and proposed multiparty politics. Still there was no sign of reform in East Germany. Nobody could imagine that within the year the Berlin Wall would be history. The intransigence of the East German Politburo prompted some new poignant jokes:

Eric Honecker knows his government is in trouble. Although cynical about religion, as a desperate measure he calls the bishops to an emergency meeting. 'I have huge problems,' he confides in them. 'The economy is going down the pan, Gorbachev is abandoning Communism and I have lost the trust of my own people. What can I do?'

The bishops talk quietly amongst themselves for a moment and then one of them says, 'Well, whenever Jesus had a big problem he performed a miracle.'

'What!' Honecker splutters. 'Should I walk on water or something?'

The bishops confer quietly for a moment again and one of them says, 'Yes, that would be a good idea.'

So the big day is announced, and thousands of East German citizens gather around a lake on the outskirts of Berlin to watch their leader walk on water. After a huge fanfare, Honecker takes one step on the water, then another, and another. To hushed silence, Honecker actually walks across the water.

After he's taken twenty paces, one East German says to another, 'You see, I told you he couldn't swim.'

Classic Communist jokes from the fifties were recycled:

Honecker is touring East German towns. He is shown a run-down kindergarten. The staff ask for funds to renovate the institution. Honecker refuses. Next he visits a hospital, where the doctors petition him for a grant to buy new surgical equipment. Honecker refuses. The third place on Honecker's itinerary is a prison. This is pretty dilapidated, and here too the governor asks for money to refurbish.

This time Honecker immediately pulls out his cheque book and insists that not only should the cells be repainted but that they should be fitted with new mattresses, colour televisions and sofas.

Afterwards an aide asks him why he said no to a school and a hospital, but yes to a prison.

Honecker says, 'Where do you think we will be living in a few months' time?'

Looking back on them now, one is struck by the great diversity between the revolutions of 1989. In Hungary and Romania it was revolution from above, though on very different time-scales. The Hungarian Communist regime couldn't follow up fast enough the hints Gorbachev had dropped at Chernenko's funeral. As early as June 1985 they held moderately free elections, which were 'multi-candidate' but not 'multi-party'. In Romania, the Ministry of the Interior supported by their Securitate police force staged a coup, in December 1989, bringing up the rear in the 'Velvet Revolutions' with old-style revolutionary violence. Ceauşescu was summarily executed, while gun battles were fought on the streets of Bucharest between sections of the Securitate loyal to the deposed leader and others opposed, supported by a popular uprising. By this time the Czech and East German Communists had fallen – both in November 1989. The Czechs succumbed to massive street protests, but the East German revolution – notwithstanding the existence of large street protests there – was the result of an entirely different mass movement: the population was running away. Hungary had opened its border with the West in summer 1988, and tens of thousands of DDR citizens went there to get to the West. When the East German government imposed travel restrictions to Hungary in September, another few thousand citizens went to Czechoslovakia and sought asylum at the West German Embassy. On 9 November, surrounded by marchers in their cities and faced with an unstoppable exodus to the West, the East German state announced it would permit free travel to the West. Some members of the Politburo took this decision convinced that if they let their citizens visit West Germany, and see what it was really like, they would buy a few things and then come back.

I have not been able to intersperse the preceding paragraphs with many jokes, and I apologise for that. Whatever role Communist jokes played in the lives of the citizens of the Soviet Bloc before the revolutions of 1989, humorologists must concede, however great their disappointment, that Communism was not brought down in a hail of jokes. Quite the reverse: the Communist jokes suddenly died out in the course of the uprisings.

There was apparently little joking amongst the protesters on the marches. Sure, the odd banner had a funny line: 'You've knocked Communism out of our heads', said a Czech one, referring to the violence of the state police; 'Idea for May Day: the Politburo parade past the People', said an East German placard. But most just said: 'Down with the Communist Party', or called for free elections. All the people we have met in this book remember the sudden evaporation of the jokes. It was a strange silence, and perhaps it could be described with a metaphor that hints at a possible definition of the role of the jokes: it was like the still over a World War One battlefield, after the artillery barrage has ceased and before the troops go over the top. In East Berlin, underneath the great statue of the Soviet soldier in the war memorial, György Dalos, the Hungarian jokologist, told me: 'Life suddenly wasn't as funny as it had been. As long as we had a great power controlling our lives, we could make jokes about it.' In Bucharest, raising her voice above the sound of an old tram, proof-reader Doina Doru said wistfully, 'The jokes stopped during the revolution. And after the revolution I almost never heard political

jokes. Although we had plenty of politicians, plenty of parties and plenty of funny situations.' 'Communist jokes lost their *raison d'être*,' Jerzy Urban, the Polish Politburo spokesperson turned satirical magazine editor, told me, sitting in his Italian

Fig. 77. Legendary cover of the West German satirical magazine *Titanic*: 'Gabi the Eastie (17) happy to be in West Germany: "My first banana."' She is holding a cucumber. Bananas were in very short supply in East Germany, and Berlin shops quickly sold out after the Wall came down.

leather armchair. 'You don't have an underground culture of jokes if you've got freedom of speech.'

The best-remembered revolution joke came from a *West* German satirical magazine. Bananas, a fruit that could rarely be found in the Soviet Bloc, had sold out across Berlin as a result of demand from Communist tourists. The Capitalist satirists ran a cover with an East German woman peeling a cucumber entitled: 'My First Banana.' (Fig. 77)

In the 1990s central and eastern Europe and the Baltic states evolved respectable democracies at great speed, but events took a different course in the former Soviet Union.

Gorbachev imagined that his reforms would lead to a free market and democracy in a preserved Soviet Union. He did not anticipate or understand the strength of criticism and discontent which emerged as a consequence of his relaxation of censorship. He called it the 'malicious intrigues of demagogues', but it was the strength of long-repressed nationalist aspirations inside the Soviet Union, driven by the impatience of its citizens for tangible improvements in their standard of living, that made them quickly disappointed in his reforms. The result was the break-up of the Soviet Union under nationalist pressures – between 1989 and 1990 the Baltic states, Georgia and the Ukraine moved towards independence. In August 1991 hard-line KGB leaders attempted a coup against Gorbachev to preserve the unity of the Union. They failed, thanks to resistance led by Boris Yeltsin. In the aftermath Yeltsin swept Gorbachev aside and became the first elected president of the Russian republic. In November 1991 Yeltsin terminated the Soviet Communist Party by law. And that was the end of Soviet Communism.

One of the most famous and longest Communist jokes encapsulates the different Soviet leaders' solution to their country's problems, culminating in Gorbachev:

Stalin, Khrushchev, Brezhnev and Gorbachev are on a train. Suddenly the train stops. Stalin, furious, opens the window. 'Why have we stopped?' he yells. 'Shoot the driver.'

Khrushchev interrupts him: 'No, rehabilitate the driver.'

Brezhnev moves over to the window and closes the curtains: 'I have a better idea – now let's turn on the gramophone, sway from side to side and pretend we are moving.'

Finally Gorbachev speaks: 'Comrades, Comrades, let's all get out and push.'

I flew to Moscow to try to talk to Mikhail Gorbachev about the jokes. I knew this was a long shot because the last Soviet General Secretary guards his reputation as one of the twentieth-century's most important statesmen with the care a rich man lavishes on a fragile porcelain vase. He has good reason. Abroad he is seen as the visionary leader who ended the Cold War, but at home he is regarded as a short-sighted apparatchik responsible for the break-up of the Soviet Union. He is permanently afraid that this negative verdict could spread beyond Russia's borders. One clumsy move, such as a moment of levity with a little-known British writer, and all those red-carpet dinners might all go up in smoke! I wrote him a letter beginning: 'I realise this subject may initially appear a rather trivial one about which to consult you for your opinions ...'

While I waited for a response, I sat around in Moscow's internet cafés, surfing wirelessly and flicking through my Gorbachev books. The latte came in a tall glass, the bar was long and techno burbled away in the background. I could have been anywhere, except for a couple of cultural giveaways. First there was the thick pall of cigarette smoke that hung over the tables and irritated my throat in an Eastern European way. Second was the clientele. Members of the new class of wealthy post-Communist *nouveaux riches*, the 'New Russians', sat at neighbouring tables. Tall girls ate Italian cuisine with silk-suited businessmen.

In my down time I wracked my brains to develop a coherent, closely argued thesis that would explain the leading role of the jokes in the downfall of Communism. Even though I had spent years immersed in the subject and had travelled all over the former Soviet Bloc, the cast-iron argument still eluded me. The Velvet Revolutions posed a last problem for me. Did this phenomenon indicate that jokes had performed their task – one of laying the groundwork for action, after which they gave up and died, having exhausted their usefulness, like worker bees who'd fertilised their queen? If that were the case, I had to establish a direct link between the jokes and the people who brought down Communism. Yet it was not at all clear what or who had ended the world's funniest political system.

Those who champion the role of the crowds and the dissidents argue that, over the first half of the eighties, these groups skilfully built up a popular army of protest, using the camouflage of parts of the regime's own ideology – Helsinki, disarmament, peace, the environment – only throwing off their sheepskins and calling for democracy when the numbers on the streets were too large to be removed by force. Even if they weren't actually cracking jokes or carrying funny banners on the marches, jokes played their part in the attitudes of these protesters. It has been suggested that the peacefulness of the revolutions derived from the good humour of the crowds, which can in turn be traced back to the attitude of joking against the state. The tradition of joking against Communism therefore explains why, during the 1989 revolutions – with the exception of Romania – the streets weren't flowing with the blood of the ruling class or the revolutionaries, as they had in 1917 in Russia, in 1848 in Germany and in 1789 in France. Instead of hatred and violence there was contempt and wit. No point anyone getting hurt over a little joke, is there?

But the significance of ordinary citizens and their dissident leaders in the revolutions is open to question. Fundamental change took place in Communist states before broad mass movements evolved, as in Hungary, and in states where there wasn't an elite of dissidents, as in Romania. Communist politicians were perfectly capable of managing semi-democratic and Capitalist transitions, if they wanted to, on their own. Conversely, Russia had a sizeable community of dissidents, some of whom were internationally famous, but that did not lead to a convincing democracy. And if the crowd did play a role in the Velvet Revolutions, then probably only a minority were responding to the dissidents' calls for democracy and human rights. The majority were motivated more by consumerism in East Germany – lust for West German wealth – and by nationalism, in the Soviet Union, where, after 1991, nationalist parties quickly built their own one-party states in several newly independent republics.

Another set of historians says that the fall of Communism was inevitable because the Soviet economy was on the verge of collapse – something that had been described, as we have seen, in numerous jokes over decades. Gorbachev, the crowds in the street and the dissidents were all only drawing the obvious conclusion. They point out that Gorbachev's predecessor Andropov had begun to introduce some economic reforms that permitted private business activity in 1983, but he had also arrested many dissidents. Perhaps Andropov was aiming for a Chinese solution: economic Capitalism with political Communism; he died too soon for anyone to find out.

But the argument that economic collapse made change inevitable is clearly flawed. The Soviet economy had been in far worse shape before the late eighties – in the early 1930s, after Stalin's awful forcible collectivisation of Soviet farms, and after 1946, when another famine killed two million in the Ukraine, for example – yet that hadn't prompted reform at those times.

I slurped the cold froth of a dead latte. To understand why Soviet Communism fell in 1989 one must look at when it didn't fall: Berlin in 1953, Hungary in 1956, Prague in 1968, Poland in 1970, Tiananmen Square in June 1989 and even – to stretch beyond my ideological framework for a moment – Burma in 2007. What do these failed revolutions tell us? That a cruel totalitarian regime can easily stay in power, even when its citizens are living in poverty, as long as it is prepared to use live ammunition, to shoot down or execute significant numbers of the opposition. It is true that the police forces of central Europe arrested and assaulted many protesters in the mid-eighties, and the Poles achieved the impressive figure of ten thousand arrests under martial law (December 1981–July 1983), but these pale in comparison to the way the Chinese dealt with Tiananmen. The Chinese Red Cross estimate that between two and three thousand protesters were killed by the army in June 1989 after protests of up to a hundred thousand students. In October 1989, when Honecker called for action after a demo seventy thousand strong, a member of his Politburo told him: 'We can't beat up hundreds of thousands of people' – and Honecker didn't disagree. We know from fifty-six and sixty-eight that the regimes of the satellite states themselves had long lost the will to crush popular democratic movements with force – it all came down to the metal of Moscow.

The key to the velvet revolutions was neither Lech Wałesa nor Václav Havel, nor any popular mass movement or economic endgame. It hinged on the man in Moscow, Mikhail Gorbachev. That's why I was waiting in that café, rereading his turgid autobiography. Gorbachev's refusal to use Soviet military force to suppress popular movements for reform in the Soviet Bloc brought down Communism. And he refused to call in the army because he believed in political and economic reform. As we have seen, Gorbachev's announcements of change preceded any significant protest activities in the satellite states. So, if Communist jokes played a role in the events of 1989, we must find them in the heart and mind of the last Soviet General Secretary.

I already had tracked down one instance when Gorbachev told a joke. He was appearing on the Clive James show on the BBC in 1995 to promote his autobiography. With the help of an interpreter he said:

There is a line queuing to buy vodka in Moscow; it is two or three kilometres long and the men are really blaming Gorbachev. One of them says: 'I will go to the Kremlin and kill Gorbachev,' and he goes.

An hour later he comes back. The line has moved on a bit but it is still far from its goal, so they ask him: 'Did you kill Gorbachev?'

He says, 'No, there is a longer queue over there.'

There was something Gorbachev shared with the protesters and the jokes: the same contempt for Communism. While I waited for the ex-President's response to my letter, I met a couple of his senior advisers in the eighties. Days before his death Alexander Yakovlev, known as 'the Godfather of Perestroika', told me he and Gorbachev were motivated by the 'utter stupidities' of Soviet policy. 'Once we figured out who we were and could see where we actually were, then the totalitarian regime collapsed,' he said. But, no, he said, disappointingly, Gorbachev never told jokes during the years of Perestroika and Glasnost; he hardly socialised. He was guarded and nervous.

After a week I began dialling Gorbachev's office. Today he leads the Gorbachev Foundation from a large postmodern building of brown-mirrored glass with an extravagant domed interior. Here Gorby takes bookings on the lucrative international lecture circuit, giving uncontroversial speeches about the need to avoid a second Cold War, calling for a global law on water access and 'a new interpretation of the notions of progress, humanism and justice'.

It wasn't difficult to get through. I couldn't believe my luck when his chief assistant told me that 'Mr Gorbachev' agreed to the interview, but I should call back in two days for a time and place. Yet every time

I rang up to make the appointment I was given the same advice: call back in two days. After this message had been communicated to me ten times over a month, I became suspicious and turned for advice to an old friend, who had shot many documentaries in Russia. 'It's code for bribe,' he said without hesitation; 'he is waiting for you to offer money – they never ask for it straight out.' The normal procedure was apparently to transfer this money into the bank account of the Foundation. There was no guarantee of how long the audience with the man who ended the Cold War would be – and one American TV crew had, rumour had it, been dismissed by the grumpy ex-President after ten minutes. The price of the interview itself? Ten to twenty thousand dollars, I was told. Perhaps that was reasonable if one was seeking Gorbachev's solutions to the world's problems, but it seemed a little extravagant for a few jokes.

Fortunately, there was one other way of finding out what was going on in Gorbachev's mind at the time. The Gorbachev Foundation contains an enormous archive of papers from his era at the Kremlin. Today it is closed to researchers, but early in the nineties it was briefly opened to certain people. By a route that I cannot disclose I was put in touch with a man whose identity I cannot reveal, but who gained access to these files. 'The story of those documents is quite crazy,' he told me over the phone. 'When the Soviet Union collapsed, some of Gorbachev's associates, while being evicted from the Kremlin, took a large number of copies of secret documents with them. That was quite illegal, of course. Then they scanned the material into the database of the Gorbachev Foundation. Some ten years later they allowed researchers a very limited access to the collection. That lasted only for a few years, because as soon as the Kremlin learned that Gorbachev was allowing people to see secret documents he was ordered to stop. However, during that window of opportunity I came to the Gorbachev Foundation archive as a student researcher and was allowed to see some of the least important documents. They kept the whole collection on a computer. And with computers, if you are smart, you can turn any limited access into unlimited. So I did.'

In a café in a foreign city he handed me a wodge of printouts of the transcripts of meetings in which Gorbachev made reference to Communist jokes.

The documents show how Gorbachev saw the jokes as one of the symptoms of the inertia of the Soviet economy and body politic. On 16

December 1986 Gorbachev met the Central Committee department chiefs and told them: 'We should involve war veterans in individual production. Do you think it is Socialism when veterans sit in the courtyards, play dominoes, tell jokes, spread gossip? But if they start doing something useful, some business, and, God forbid, try to sell the products of their work at a market that is seen as a "retreat from Socialism".' On 15 April 1988 he complained to regional party secretaries about the quality of what was meant to be the Russian parliament. 'Our Supreme Soviet is cumbersome, heavy, clumsy. When I sit at the high table at its sessions – and you know how big the room is – I see endless numbers of people. Some of them listen, others read newspapers, others whisper jokes in their neighbours' ears. Do we really need a parliament like that?'

At another parliamentary session, in 1986, Gorbachev was told what he had been telling others, when a Duma deputy warned him that, unless his reforms worked, the Russian people 'would return to vodka and the *anekdot*'.

The Gorbachev archive documents confirm that, in its final phase, the jokes were acknowledged as repositories of truth at the highest level of Communist society. Gorbachev used them against his own party in an effort to encourage change. On 11 April 1988, in a meeting with the secretaries of regional Party committees, he quoted an old pre-war joke to complain about the officials' lack of response to popular opinion. 'People want their voices to be heard, but nobody listens to them. So, the only function their presence has is to endorse their bosses' policies. It is like the joke: the working classes consume plenty of cognac – through their chosen representatives.'

At the same time, other Soviet Bloc leaders were apparently using jokes to explain their faltering system to each other. On 21 April 1987 General Jaruzelski met Gorbachev and told him about Poland's economic problems, some of which were caused by the policy of full employment. 'We even have a joke circulating: two guys drive the same wheelbarrow. Someone asks them: "Why is it two of you doing that?" They reply: "Because the third one is on sick leave."'

Finally, in 1989, addressing a crowd of workers outside Moscow, Gorbachev declared: '*Anekdoty* were our salvation.'

These are just a handful of incidents but they are proof of a kind. They show that the person who reformed Communism heard the jokes and interpreted them as indicators of the necessity for reform. These exchanges also unite the two theories of the effect of Communist jokes – the traditional one that they undermined Communism, the other, emerging in the official circles in the sixties, that they prolonged it. For Gorbachev both these theories were correct. He recognised the apathetic character of the humour, which Soviet citizens used like alcohol to dull the pain, an expression of hopelessness, but also saw them as the repository of truth and ultimately the engine of change – they were '*our salvation*'.

Whatever the joke-tellers of Communism say, the culture of joke-telling has not vanished into thin air. The Soviet Union produced something that will never die: the *anekdot*. There are a new set of these about the New Russians, Moscow's post-Communist *nouveaux riches*. I had heard a few of these jokes and I recalled them as we crawled through Moscow's gridlocked traffic on the way to a legendary contemporary Russian joke-teller.

Two New Russians meet. One says to the other, 'Hey, look, I bought a new tie! Paid two hundred bucks!'
'You idiot! Just around the corner you can get the same tie for five hundred!'

A Mercedes collides with an old Lada. A New Russian gets out of the Mercedes, spits, and says, 'Hey, no big deal. Tomorrow I'll buy a new one.'
But the owner of the Lada says with tears in his eyes, 'I saved up my whole life for this car, and now it's wrecked!'
The New Russian replies, 'Why'd you buy such an expensive car, stupid?'

I had hired a driver with an old Lada for nostalgia's sake, and I gazed out of the window up at the large Mercedes and BMW 4×4s, which now filled Moscow's streets. No matter how wide the avenues were – and some in the heart of Moscow are ten lanes across – they are still full of traffic that doesn't move. Gazprom is making billions selling Russian oil and gas to Europe and Moscow has become a boom town, flooded with immigrants from the former Soviet republics, like my Kyrgyzstan driver. It was a *Bladerunner* world of a two-tiered Capitalist economy. Those who have been able to dip their hands into the honey-pot of privatised Communist assets and the energy business, or set up their own mobile phone or IT company, making Moscow the most expensive city in the world. Below them was a quasi-enslaved underclass that earns $1,000 a month. When my driver opened up the boot of his car to put my suitcase in it, I saw a rolled-up rectangle of dirty, torn foam – his mattress when the money ran out. After paying £30 for a prawn salad and ratatouille in town, I found myself longing for the return of Stalin.

I met Pavel Borodin at the Kremlin. He had invited me on a tour of the private apartments and staterooms of the palace, where President Putin entertained foreign dignitaries and important Russians. These incredible interiors had been commissioned by Tsar Nicholas I at the start of the nineteenth century to celebrate the defeat of Napoleon. We walked up a wide marble staircase, past towering three-metre-high urns of crystal glass, towards a large painting of a battle scene. Carved gilt woodwork on the doors and the door frames led into rooms lit by phalanxes of gold chandeliers. The Kremlin made Buckingham Palace and Versailles look like youth hostels. In the late nineties Borodin had been in charge of returning the palace to its former glory. He had spent $800 million, employing a team of fourteen thousand workers over two years and commissioning work from international firms, he told me proudly. He didn't mention the Swiss court, which had later convicted him of taking $25 million in kickbacks from one foreign contractor alone. Borodin was never punished. He was famous for two things: one was escaping Swiss justice, but the other was telling jokes.

Borodin was wearing the smile of a loveable rogue and a shiny marine-blue silk suit, probably Armani. He had a warm chestnut suntan and crisp grey hair. He was the sort of person you immediately wanted to be your dad. He had risen fast under Brezhnev. After graduating, he went to work on construction projects deep inside the Arctic Circle in the Siberian province of Yakutia (now the republic of Sakha) where temperatures in winter average minus 50 degrees. He told me how he 'built forty-five small towns, renovated the city of Yakutsk and laid 120 kilometres of pipeline'. He had his own private helicopter before he was thirty. In the nineties, he had become one of Boris Yeltsin's closest aides, and he attributed his political success, with charming disingenuousness, to his dexterous use of the *anekdot*.

'One day in 1998 President Yeltsin came to see me and he told me that he'd just seen the new Deputy Prime Minister Mr Nemtsov, and he'd persuaded him that the Russian deputies should all trade in their BMWs and start driving Russian Volgas instead. It would be better for the Russian economy, said Nemtsov. "I agreed," said Yeltsin. And I said, "Mr President, let me tell you an anecdote. Mr Nemtsov is visiting Tokyo and he meets the head of Toyota cars, Mr Hasimoto. Hasimoto has three buttons on his jacket and Nemtsov asks him what those three buttons are for. Hasimoto says, "This is an air-conditioned suit. When I am feeling hot, I press the green button. When I am freezing, I press the red button and when I am tired, I press the yellow one." So next time Hasimoto comes to Moscow he is met by Nemtsov, who is wearing a Volga car door around his neck. "What's that?" asks Hasimoto. "Well," he says, "this is my air-conditioned suit. When I am feeling hot, I open the window and when I am cold, I close it." Hasimoto asks, "And when you are tired?" The Volga car CEO says, "I take it off." And Yeltsin says to me: "Okay, I understand." Today, Russian deputies are still driving German cars.'

We strode into Tsar Nicholas's Hall of the Order of St George. My pupils contracted rapidly as daylight reflected off the expanse of white stucco in this cavernous room. 'I'll tell you the most expensive joke I ever told ...' Mr Borodin said with his Florida smile, '... a €7.2 billion joke. I was having meeting after meeting with Helmut Kohl. I was asking him to give Russia a huge loan – €7.2 billion, in fact. It could have gone either way. We always drank coffee together and at the fifth meeting I finally said: "Mr Kohl, do you want me to tell you a joke about our meeting?" Kohl said yes. "Well," I said, "a man comes back from work on Monday evening and he finds somebody in bed with his wife. He immediately takes off his jacket and rolls up his sleeves ready for a fight, but the other man calls out from the bed, "Why fight me? Let's meet and drink coffee and talk it through instead." So the husband says okay. The same thing happens when he goes home on Tuesday, Wednesday, Thursday and Friday. So eventually he doesn't know what to do, and he goes to the doctor and tells him about his problem. The doctor says, "So, what can I do about this problem?" And the man says: "Check if I can drink that much coffee." Kohl gets up and makes a phone call to the Minister of Finance and talks to him in German; then he turns round to me and says, "Mr Borodin, by the time you reach Frankfurt the money will be in Moscow." That is the most expensive joke I ever told.'

Borodin gave me another example of his wit, in connection with the oligarch Anatoly Chubais. Everyone in Russian government had their hand deep in the till in the nineties, but few, it is alleged, thrust their unprincipled paw deeper than Chubais. He is said to have amassed a fortune of one billion dollars as Russian finance minister, by presiding over the privatisation of state businesses from 1994 to 1996, when he supposedly took multi-million-dollar bribes and share deals in return for sales of state assets. Chubais created the oligarchs.

'In 1997 Chubais, whose appearance is distinguished by his red hair, was appointed chief of Yeltsin's staff,' Borodin told me, 'and it was a very unpopular decision. Everyone was saying he would ruin Russia, and I visited Yeltsin at his summer dacha, and I asked the President if he wanted to hear the latest joke. I said, "There's a big pit dug in the forest as a hunters' trap and a wolf, a fox, a bear and a wild boar are sitting in it. And one day the bear says, 'Let's start playing cards.' Everyone agrees. The bear deals the cards, and then he looks seriously at the other animals. 'Before we start, I should warn you that anyone who cheats is going to get it straight in their dirty ginger mug!'"'

I laughed with Borodin. Putin had fought the oligarchs and won. He had re-appropriated their assets using tax avoidance lawsuits, imprisoning some, such as Khordakovsky, and compelling others, notably Berezovsky, to flee.

The influential joke-teller must have caught me inspecting the ruched silk blinds, which were lowered precisely halfway down each window, and he took the opportunity to change the subject.

'Two men meet at a party. One says to the other: "You have such a lovely wife. Tell me one thing: when does she cry – when you have an orgasm or when she does?" The other replies: "Only when I wipe my cock on the curtains."'

The jokes served Borodin on many levels – as a way to suggest to me that he was different from the corrupt oligarchs, and as a way to influence Russian presidents with short attention spans; but they also revealed the unremitting crudeness of contemporary Russian politics.

'When Yeltsin visited the city of Puzil in 1995, I asked him if he wanted to hear my favourite joke and he said yes. And I said: do you know what baldness means? It is the gradual transformation of the head into the arse, and your predecessor Mr Gorbachev even has a stamp on his forehead certifying that this process was successfully completed.'

Borodin led me into another glittering hall. I stared at the marquetry floor, a lacquered masterpiece on a scale and of a sophistication I had never seen before. Intricate floral patterns, as detailed as any Persian carpet, made from twenty-one different kinds of inlaid wood, stretched out across forty square metres.

'I have a photograph of the President of Kazakhstan, Mr Nazarbayev, rolling around on this floor with laughter after I told him a joke,' said Mr Borodin. 'A man comes back home and asks his wife: "You are a businesswoman, so from now on let's put our relationship on a commercial footing. If we make love on the floor, it's a thousand roubles, on the bed three thousand roubles, and for something unusual it's thirty thousand roubles." In the evening she comes home and gives him thirty thousand roubles. "So what kind of unusual sex do you want?" he asks. "Just normal sex," she says, "thirty times on the floor." If you use this joke, please don't mention the name of the President.'

I asked Borodin if he could tell me some Brezhnev jokes, but he said he didn't remember any. I pressed him. 'I can't,' he said quietly; 'I am a Communist – it's not decent for me to tell Communist jokes.' Borodin was now working for Yeltsin's successor, Vladimir Putin, as a 'state secretary' developing contacts between Belarus and Russia, a job that surely contained many lucrative opportunities for a man with his sense of humour.

Jokes about Communism were unwelcome in Putin's administration, and the more jokes he told, the more I realised that Borodin was using the new *anekdoty* to convey the political programme of his master. This was a potted history of Putinism as a stand-up routine.

'Have you heard the one about how the Chechen war started?' my host asked. I shook my head. The conflict in Chechnya had started in 1994. On one side were an array of Chechen nationalists, jihadis and criminal gangs; on the other, Russian generals and politicians determined to stop the attacks of terrorist groups, who were fighting for independence for bits and pieces of what remained of the Russian Empire, as well as for the right to export heroin and guns to Europe. Putin's firm stand against Chechen independence was one of the pillars of his popularity among the Russian electorate. There had been the usual mixture of massacres, torture and badly aimed aerial bombardment, which accompanied late twentieth-century warfare, culminating in the ghastly Beslan massacre in which Chechen gunmen had killed 186 schoolchildren. The war was still dragging on, though Russian soldiers were officially no longer on the front line.

Borodin continued with his joke: 'A Chechen is fishing and he pulls out a magic golden fish, and as usual in the fairy tale, the golden fish offers to fulfil three wishes. The Chechen thinks for a while, then he says, "I can't think of anything to ask you; have you got any suggestions?" "Well," says the goldfish, "before I was caught by a Ukrainian guy and he immediately asked me to give him a huge chest of gold, jewels and dollars." And the Chechen says: "Oh, okay, in that case I do have a wish: give me the address of the Ukrainian guy."'

Many of Borodin's jokes vividly captured the realpolitik of Putin's resurgent Russia. In the late nineties, several former republics of the Soviet Union moved slowly towards the West, accepting generous financial and business deals from America and expressing a desire to join NATO. Putin was managing to reverse this process. He was using Russia's vast energy reserves to recreate the geography of the Cold War, building pipelines and setting prices according to how obedient the new republics were to Moscow. He was also financing pro-Russian politicians and warlords – didn't really matter which – in the new republics. Borodin had plenty of jokes that celebrated this foreign-policy success over these fledgling democracies.

'The Ukrainian President Kuchma visits Moscow and returns to the Ukraine with good news: "I visited Moscow and the Kremlin agreed to write off the $12 billion dollars we owe them." "How did you manage that?" his ministers ask. "Well I got the Moscow boss to stand on a stool in Red Square and I sucked his cock." His ministers ask: "Why did you put him on a stool?" Kuchma says: "Well you wouldn't expect me to kneel in front of a Russian, would you?"'

They were funny and apposite, but Borodin's jokes weren't the same as the old Communist ones. They weren't popular jokes like the ones told about Stalin and Khrushchev, or the others that exposed the absurdity and mendacity of the state. Borodin was a court jester, offering clever advice to the king in the form of wit, and the king –

Yeltsin, Putin – listened because he found it entertaining. His jokes balanced flattery and criticism.

Consequently, there was a second type of joke, aside from Communist ones, that Borodin avoided: those that derided Putin.

Putin goes to a restaurant with the leaders of the two houses of parliament. The waiter approaches and asks Putin what he would like to order.
'I'll have the meat.'
'And what about the vegetables?'
'They'll have the meat too.'

Did you hear the one about Vladimir Putin's plan for the Russian economy? The goal: to make people rich and happy. List of people attached.

In these Putin jokes, the formulas of the old dictatorship jokes – whether Communist or Nazi – had been revived.

Putin is sitting in his office with his head in his hands, when Stalin's ghost appears. Putin tells the ghost his problems, bemoaning the incompetence of his Kremlin underlings.
'That's easy to fix,' Stalin says. 'Shoot all the bad officials, and paint the Kremlin walls blue.'
'Why blue?' Putin asks.
'Hah! I knew you'd only ask about the second part!'

Borodin ushered me into the final grand hall. The colour scheme of gold and white gave way to gold and blue. Another marvellous floor stretched ahead of me, at the end of which was the canopied throne of Nicholas I. All of it was a reconstruction. My host boasted of the skill of this undertaking, which could not be based on the old architectural blueprints, which hadn't survived, but was instead developed from old watercolours of the palace interiors. That struck me as rather vague source material, and I suddenly realised that, rather than looking at a piece of Russian history, I was looking at a representation of the fantasy that Russia's new leaders had about their imperial past.

'Do you think the golden age of the Tsar will return?' I asked my host.

'It's already here,' Pavel Borodin replied.

*

Borodin's new jokes didn't move me the same way as the old Communist ones. They were the humorous equivalent of sex without love – a strangely empty experience (though, to paraphrase Woody Allen, as far as empty experiences go, one of the funniest). The *anekdoty* of the State Secretary for the Union of Russia and Belarus didn't evoke the same mood of tragedy and universal human suffering as the old material. Why did the Communist jokes touch everybody, whether from the East or West, in this way? As I boarded my plane home at Moscow airport, I started to think that this affinity revealed something significant. I was discovering my inner Communist, the one that is inside all of us.

Every age rewrites the past, but the twenty-first century has not yet begun the onerous task of retelling the story of the twentieth. We are waiting for a new perspective on Communism, as it recedes into the distance. While the Soviet Union existed, and Marxism was still popular among West European academics, Communism seemed like a plausible, even virtuous alternative to Capitalism. It was a product of the philosophy of the Enlightenment; the idea was to create a utopian society through rational laws. Twentieth-century history was written as a battle between two – and briefly, during the Third Reich, three – competing worldviews. Then, in the aftermath of the Velvet Revolutions, that story was revised. A new generation of historians condemned Communism as an unmitigated crime perpetrated against a mass society by a violent state apparatus, whose only goal was the extension of its own power.

But the past is like an Impressionist painting: the further away you get from it, the more the countless brushstrokes of events cohere into a single view. From the perspective of the twenty-first century we are likely to see Communism and twentieth-century Capitalism as two sides of the same Modernist coin.

Communists have often argued with success that democracy and fascism are closely related, yet in retrospect it was twentieth-century democracy and Communism that were sisters. Both were part of the Modernist project in which benevolent, all-encompassing big states would organise our lives to achieve universal happiness. Twentieth-century Capitalist states also offered large measures of centralised state planning. Large percentages of their economies were state-owned – like the car manufacturers, mines and telecoms. In Germany workers sat on management boards at big factories.

Aging leaders ran corrupt technocratic states in Vienna as well as Moscow. Governments poured hundreds of millions into loss-making manufacturing industries and raw-material-extraction businesses in Britain as well as Russia. The grand coalitions that ruled Italy and Germany often made those countries look like one-party states, and when leaders or governments did change – usually ritualistically – policies often did not. The European Union evolved a bureaucracy to rival the Soviets and the Common Agricultural Policy was a project of economic engineering, which, with its price-fixing and disregard for supply and demand, beggared anything the Soviets came up with. Every West European Capitalist, so-called free-market economy involved and still involves massive regulation. The Western democratic state also promised its citizens security and equality – health services, free education, welfare and paid holidays. That's why unapologetic and cunning Communists, like the historian of Stalin and Putin Roy Medvedev, can stretch a point and say that today's social democracies – especially in France and Scandinavia – are Communist.

That's why many Communist jokes were adapted into ones referring to the shortcomings of Western economies. They slipped easily out of one jacket and into another. 'Why does an Austin Allegro have a heated rear window?' went one about an unreliable model of British car from the seventies. 'So you can keep your hands warm when you push it.'

Communism was the paradigmatic expression of the twentieth-century dream of a utopian society. That's why the old jokes still get most of us today. There's a part of us that identifies with the suffering of the citizens of the Soviet Empire – we know they paid a price for what we also believed in. As Václav Havel said, 'Totalitarian society is the distorted mirror of the whole of modern civilisation.'

They joked for us all (Plate 8).

The midsummer sun beat down on fifteen hundred bonnets at Germany's largest rally for the Trabant, the East German Communist family car. I was in Zwickau, the home of the Trabant factory. I walked in between ranks of parked Trabis. Some had been painted

Fig. 78. Trabant with two steering wheels, motors and drivers,
Trabant Rally, Zwickau, 2005

fluorescent colours, others had the Ferrari decals on the side. The cars
were old, but the owners weren't. Around the polished and customised
vehicles sat handfuls of young East Germans, the boys with shaven
heads and bare chests, the girls with bare midriffs and pierced belly
buttons, surrounded by crates of beer.

Trabants had long since gone out of production and in its place
had come Trabant nostalgia, part of a wider East German fondness
for the old times known as *Ostalgie*. For a moment in the nineties
this had been the latest thing. Young people threw fancy-dress parties
where they pulled out the old working clothes and uniforms of the
DDR and played records by East German pop groups. The revival
was written up in the style magazines, reported on TV and in *Der
Spiegel*. But the media had long since lost interest and, without the
mask of hype, the sadness of all this looking back stood naked in
front of me – an automotive East German Dunkirk. My eyes watered,
before I jumped out of the way as a vehicle inspired by Dr Doolittle's
Push-Me-Pull-You careered past (Fig. 78). It was made of two Trabant
front halves soldered together back to back. There were two motors,
two steering wheels and two drivers. It was bright orange and could
be driven in two different directions. It was definitely a kind of joke –
a symbol of the internal contradictions of the DDR perhaps, or of

the younger generation's ambivalence towards their past.

The Trabant was, alongside the Russian Lada, Communism's most famous car. Mass production started in 1957 and, within a few years, six hundred were being made per week. The model was scarcely altered for thirty years. To me it was a symbol of the technological backwardness of a state-run economy; but for others it was an example of another kind of social model, where consumers were encouraged to have modest needs instead of being novelty junkies. There were hundreds of Trabant jokes:

> *What occupies the last six pages of the Trabant users' manual?*
> *The bus and train timetables.*

> *A donkey is standing next to a Trabant. He turns to the car and asks it, 'What are you?'*
> *'I am a car,' says the Trabant. 'What are you?'*
> *'Oh,' says the donkey, laughing, 'I am a horse.'*

After reading countless articles on jokes from anthropological journals, I had come to the Trabant rally to do some fieldwork of my own. I wanted to study how Communist jokes worked in a contemporary Communist environment.

I approached Nancy, a plump, blonde twenty-year-old, who had put racing seats in her car and lined the interior with pink fur. 'Do you know how to recognise a Trabant Sports?' I asked. 'It comes with a pair of trainers in the boot.'

'I don't like Trabi jokes,' she replied testily. 'My grandfather gave me this car and it's sacred.'

I had memorised around forty jokes and I carefully matched them to the people I spoke to. A group of young men were customising a Trabant into a kind of go-kart. 'Is it as fast as a Trabant?' I asked.

'Faster,' they said seriously.

'Do you know how to measure the speed of a Trabant?' I asked. 'It's best done with a calendar!' They grunted and said something in the impenetrable local German dialect.

There were stalls selling spare parts for Trabants. 'Have you got a new windscreen wiper for my Trabant?' I asked a stallholder.

'Of course,' he said, reaching down to the table.

'No,' I responded. 'Don't you know the joke: Have you got a spare windscreen wiper for my Trabant? Answer – yes, that's a fair swap!'

'No,' said the young man, 'I don't know that one ...' adding, surely with brilliant sarcasm, 'Is it new?'

I asked Trabant-owners if they drove it 'as a joke'. The answer was no. 'It's small. It's easy to park. It's cheap to run. The mechanics are simple. You can repair it yourself.' The Trabant was developed in the 1950s. The West had banned exports of steel to East Germany and the country didn't have any reserves of its own, so the ingenious designers came up with a steel shell with bodywork made out of plastic-resin filled with wool and cotton waste from Soviet industries – the first ever vehicle made with recycled material. The engine produced a modest 25 horsepower.

The Trabant-owners had their own conspiracy theory for the shortcomings of their cars. Back in the seventies, four years before VW brought out the Golf, they explained, Trabant designers were ready to go into production with a new hatchback model. But the Politburo vetoed it. I suggested a motivation for this political decision – that the East German leaders might have thought that if their citizens had to wait seven years to get a Trabant, they had the right to get what they had paid for.

It turned out that two elderly members of the original Trabant design team were at the car fair. 'Look at all the young people here,' they said to me proudly. 'They are keeping the spirit alive and they won't be led astray by bad influences. Also, they can repair it themselves.'

'Do you know the old Trabant jokes?' I asked the designers.

'We used to tell them ourselves and laugh at them, but we can't remember them,' they said. 'Anyway, there weren't that many of them.'

'How many workers did it take to build a Trabant?' I asked. There was a pause. They didn't know the answer. I continued: 'Two – one to fold and one to stick.'

'That is not funny at all,' said Dr Reichelt, Chief Trabant Design Engineer.

'You know why there were no bank robberies in the DDR?' I asked, smiling apologetically. 'Because you had to wait ten years for a getaway vehicle.'

'What do you mean – getaway vehicle? That's an insult. We were building a family car, which people could go on holiday in.'

The Trabant factory closed down in 1991 and its workers were made redundant. There was little demand for the skills they had learned building one of the world's slowest, most polluting and dangerous cars. Their children, Zwickau's youth, were unemployed, their most valuable possession the old Trabant that their grandparents had left them. Of course the jokes wouldn't amuse them – Communism had now changed sides. It was the underground counter-cultural force fighting the heartless monolith of Capitalism. There were grounds to feel more compassion, but there were also reasons not to.

I met a couple of twenty-year-olds, surrounded by immaculately restored East German border-patrol vehicles, amidst which an East German flag fluttered on a high mast against a blue sky. They were wearing the uniforms of the East German border guards, the same outfits worn by those who had shot down East Germans fleeing the DDR. So I pressed home my joke attack.

'Why does a Trabant have wheels? So you don't have to carry it.

'Did you hear about the Trabant that didn't move when the lights turned green? It got stuck on a piece of chewing gum.'

I smiled provocatively. 'How does one quadruple the value of a Trabant?' I taunted them. 'Put a banana on the back seat.'

'One more like that and I'll smack you one,' said one of the youths.

I had flushed it out once again: the brutality beneath the Communist pageant. I headed for the exit.

Ariane drove me out to the lakes on the outskirts of Berlin.

A few days earlier I had rung her up and asked if we could see each other again. I knew she had taken part in the revolutions in 1989, and I wanted to hear her story of those events. Also, I admit I was missing my own little Communist. In an upside-down way, I liked the way she didn't laugh at my jokes. She was the first girlfriend I'd had who, when I asked why she fancied me, never said: 'Your sense of humour.' On the phone, her voice was soft and warm: 'Okay, but please don't tell any Communist jokes.'

We drove through the forest, past half-timbered houses and small Prussian factories, village streets lined with distinctive flat brickwork of *fin-de-siècle* Germany. This was the area where all the former East German Politburo members had built their villas. The motorway still had a large but flat central reservation so that Honecker's plane could land there.

We turned down an unmarked track and parked. After a ten-minute walk through the woods we found ourselves at a small and pretty basin of water, ringed by ancient trees. At one end was a grand but dilapidated nineteenth-century stuccoed villa. With its white and cream colour scheme and large bell tower with a pagoda-influenced spire, it had obviously once been the home of a German aristocrat. All the upper windows had been smashed in; the lower ones were firmly boarded up with metal sheets. 'This was Erich Mielke's holiday home,' she said, referring to the former head of the Stasi. 'After the fall of the Wall people came here and they broke in and trashed the place. Since then it's just been standing here like this, while the authorities work out who owns it now. Not many people know it's here, and they try to keep it that way.'

The late-summer sun was setting low. We strolled through the forest along the pathway that wound round the lake that stretched in front of the villa, and I asked Ariane what she thought of 1989.

'You have to make a distinction between what happened up to June, and then afterwards. Everything after June 1989 was *scheisse*,' she said. June was the month in which thousands of East Germans began making trips to the West via Hungary. 'Then it became only about *Westauto kaufen* – buying a West German car.'

'You mean that the revolution was actually about people wanting to buy things, not political change,' I said, trying to keep a straight face.

'We were fighting for a different revolution and then it was taken away from us,' said Ariane. The protests in Ariane's town had started in the early eighties. The older brothers of her school friends had taken part in environmental marches. The Stasi had jailed many of them. By the later eighties, some were living in West Germany, their freedom 'bought' in hard currency by the West German state. Others the Stasi had tried to recruit – her boyfriend at the time fobbed them off with the line: 'No I wouldn't be right for you. I can never keep my mouth shut.' When she was a little older she had become a punk, and in 1989 she had joined the protests taking place in Leipzig in favour of political change. 'We wanted a fairer system – not the end of it. We weren't fighting for that.'

'Do you think you were being realistic?' I asked. 'Wasn't the DDR already dead in the water?'

'We were the DDR. That's what we used to chant at the demos:

"We are the People"; and then Kohl and the West Germans turned that into: "We are One People." It was horrible. Afterwards people like you said we weren't important. It was all Gorbachev. The Soviets were the ones who ended Communism. But we were on the streets.'

Ariane's green eyes looked so serious. Ever since Hegel the Germans had displayed an unsurpassed ability for earnestness. They had invented the big movements of the twentieth century after all – phenomenology came from Heidegger, Communism from Karl Marx and Friedrich Engels and even Hitler was a German-speaker. That was a track record. Ariane and her friends with dyed-black hair thought they were the pioneers of a new post-Communist political philosophy, but the historical truth was that they were a sideshow. Consumerism killed Communism.

'Material gain has always been behind all revolutions,' I said. 'The French and Russian Revolutions started because people were unhappy about the price of bread. Bread, BMWs – it's the same thing.'

The forest went right down to the edges of the lake. Fragments of sunlight floated on trunks and leaves. Ariane and I found a small glade and we took off our clothes. In the lakes around Berlin, everyone goes skinny-dipping, even when they are having political arguments. I waded into the muddy water. A fish the size of half a hand flicked past my feet. I looked round at Ariane on the river bank, naked.

'They just wanted to *shoppen*,' I said, using a carefully selected word adapted by the Germans from the Anglo-Saxon. I offered a smile that was both imploring and ironic.

'Don't smirk. I hate talking to you about these things, because you treat what I am saying as if it is a joke. The problem is that you have no understanding whatsoever for what it is like to take part in real political events. That's why you can only make jokes.'

I looked at her and tried briefly to think of an apposite one. Although I was coming to the end of my own book about Communist jokes, there were still a few left over I hadn't told, which might fit in. There was that classic one about their dream . . .

What is the difference between a Soviet fairy tale and a Western fairy tale?

A Western fairy tale begins: 'Once upon a time there was . . .'; a Soviet fairy tale begins: 'Once upon a time there will be . . .'

Then there was the old one about their guru.

An old man with a big bushy grey beard knocks on the door of Heaven. Peter Petrovich greets him and asks him firmly: 'Who was your father?'

'An industrialist.'

'And your mother?'

'The daughter of a merchant.'

'And your wife?'

'An aristocrat.'

'And what did you do all your life long?'

'I travelled and wrote books.'

'Bourgeois stock,' Peter notes. 'It will be difficult, but tell me your name?'

'Karl Marx.'

But perhaps it was a bit long. I knew a shorter one about the future, which might work well at this concluding stage in my narrative:

Is it true that when we reach full Communism, there won't be any more political jokes?

Yes, except this one.

But before I could say anything, Ariane burst out: 'The problem with you is that you refuse to take anything seriously – not Communism, not me ... Not even yourself.'

'That's true,' I said, 'but I take not taking anything seriously very seriously.'

An instant later I could feel the truth of Ariane's accusation reach the centre of my brain with the thud of a bullet in slow motion. I'd examined every aspect of Communist jokes, save one: the motive for my personal obsession with the subject. What lay behind that? She knew the answer: the jokes were a way of avoiding action and interaction. They were designed for distancing. But you cannot follow your beliefs while laughing. That's the difference between humour and passion – whether you are in a revolution or in a relationship. In Communist times people chose to tell jokes for a long time, but there was a moment when, in order to take a step forward, they decided to stop joking. I was facing the need to make the same decision as them.

The jokes almost brought down Communism, but not quite. And they had almost destroyed my relationship, but not quite.

Ariane walked into the lake and swam out towards me.

'Did you hear the one about the political system that got laughed out of existence?' I asked.

'Save it for another day,' she said, putting her arms round me. Perhaps it was the thick strands of her curly black hair, but I suddenly started thinking of the piles and piles of paper spaghetti that protesters found when they broke into the headquarters of the Stasi in 1989. The East German secret police had tried to mince all their files as the Wall fell. They hadn't had enough document shredders and they sent agents to West Germany to buy up every machine they could find. That was the last shortage of East Germany.

'I can't tell you the rest of that joke anyway,' I said. 'The punchline was shredded by the Stasi.'

NINE

Conclusion

Communist jokes were not the unique weapon of resistance that
Soviet citizens used to topple Communism. That was the fantasy
of Soviet émigrés, Cold Warriors and some Western leaders and media.
But nor were they merely the uninfluential, historically irrelevant
expression of public opinion that certain historians and humorologists
describe them as.

There were two kinds of humour under Communism. Unofficial,
underground, popular, anonymous jokes aimed to describe the failings
and crimes of Communism, while official humour, comprising the
satirical magazines, film and cabaret, attempted to use satire to win
people over to the cause. Each kind of humour had fifth columnists,
double agents or simple doubters within its ranks. Many of the people
who told the jokes supported Communism: they used them to make
light of the problems, not to damn the system. Meanwhile, in the
other camp, many of the employed satirists wanted to use satire to
effect economic and political change in the Soviet system.

Despite the uncertain composition of the two sides, a war was
fought between these two kinds of humour during the entire history
of Communism. The joke-tellers eventually won, but not without
experiencing major setbacks and defeats. First, in the twenties, Communism produced a flowering of satirical humour, in the form of
published essays and stories. The 'golden age' of Soviet satire ended
with the closure of the satirical magazines and papers. As a consequence of the shut-down of printed avenues of expression, an oral
culture of satire developed: the Communist jokes. Under Stalin the
extraordinary hardships of daily life, the concentration of people in
cities and camps and the injustice and brutality of the state, which
the citizen was powerless to resist, produced an outpouring of gallows-
humour jokes. At the same time the state developed an official 'positive' sense of humour, whose aim was to win over hearts and minds

and to eradicate the shortcomings of Communism, such as the poor bureaucracy and lazy workers.

Communist jokes faded into the background during the Second World War, replaced by Nazi and anti-Semitic jokes. The jokes made by and about Nazis in World War II confirm that the culture of Communist jokes was distinctive. Unlike Nazi jokes, they took on the entire system and ideology of the state.

In the fifties a culture of humour developed in the new Soviet satellite states very similar to that which was already established in Russia, though with the added genre of jokes about the occupying power. People invented Communist jokes, they told them often and were arrested for telling them. The satellite states launched their own organs of official humour.

So whose humour was 'winning' in this initial post-war period? The answer is different in the Soviet Union and its satellite states. In the USSR the documented motivations for the strikes, riots and protests under Khrushchev between 1953 and 1962, suggest that opponents of the state largely believed in the line of state propaganda – they blamed bureaucrats, 'false Leninists' or Khrushchev for their woes, not Stalin or Communism itself. In the Soviet Union, therefore, 'positive humour' was working. But in the satellite states, the uprisings in Berlin in 1953 and Hungary in 1956 imply the opposite, although we do not know to what extent the widespread opposition to the Soviet presence was driven by objections to occupation rather than ideology.

By the end of the fifties the state had abandoned arresting jokers. The new policy was part of the 'thaw'. After Stalin's departure, the people at the top no longer had the will to maintain the same level of repression on joke-tellers and other political transgressors. They concluded that jokes posed no threat to the survival of the Communist state. But could the state maintain its apparent success against Communist jokes without force?

In the sixties Communist jokes enjoyed their 'golden age'. There were more than ever before. A Soviet émigré published a book of 380 Communist jokes in Munich in 1951; in 1972, in Czechoslovakia, a book of a thousand and one jokes was published. The state continued to try to compete with official humour, but now, inside its own magazines and officially sanctioned cabaret groups, state humour-producers attempted to push against the official limits. It is a matter for debate how much success these rebels had in enlarging the themes they could tackle, or how much effect their cryptically critical texts had on the magazines' readership.

Unofficial humour, meanwhile, grew and grew: one high point came in the opposition to the invasion of the Czech Republic. But this event also showed the limits of what humour could accomplish: it could not do anything against tanks. Finally, in 1970, in response to the deluge of propaganda surrounding the centenary of Lenin's birth, Soviet citizens began to tell quantities of jokes about Lenin for the first time: the sacrosanct core of Communism had been penetrated. The Lenin jokes, with their contemptuous punchlines, show how, by 1970, the Soviet joke-tellers had turned against Lenin and his ideology of Soviet Communism.

From this one might assume that the next phase would be counter-revolution. The themes of the jokes had finally displayed hostility to the founder of the system, and therefore to the system itself. One might expect that people would therefore follow up the jokes with action. But that is not what happened in the seventies. Instead an era of apathy descended. Opposition died down, except among tiny groups of dissidents. After 1964 there were no more strikes or protests in the Soviet Union, and in the seventies there were none in the Soviet Bloc except in Poland. The Soviet state hardly bothered to arrest anyone for 'anti-Soviet propaganda' in this period. People invented fewer new jokes and they weren't half as funny as the ones of previous eras. The small opposition, in the form of a few dozen dissidents, did not ascribe the jokes any significance. But official humour, in this period, showed itself to be equally impotent in another way: it was not correcting the shortcomings of Communism – alcoholism, an unmotivated work force, poor economic performance and a stifling bureaucracy. By the end of the seventies humour seemed irrelevant to the history of Communism.

Yet in the eighties the jokes made a comeback. Not that there were lots of new jokes. Instead the old jokes were spoken in new places – official, public places, such as TV, press conferences and summits. Through this joke-telling, people inside the Communist regimes, including the leadership, admitted that Communism was going 'laughably' wrong. The jokes 'brought down' Communism, in the sense that they were intrinsic to the critique of Communism, shared eventually by the leadership and citizens, which led to its fall.

Will the good times ever come back? We would need the return of Communism itself for that, or the emergence of a new political system that shares certain fundamental criteria. Unlike other commonly acknowledged ideologies, such as imperialism, Capitalism, fascism and fundamentalism, Communism was inherently 'funny' because of a unique combination of factors. The ineffectiveness of its theories, the mendacity of its propaganda and the ubiquity of censorship were all important. The cruelty of its methods interacted with the sense of humour of the people on whom it was imposed. The concentration of all political and economic power in the hands of the state, and the state's attempt to direct artistic activities – that meant that any joke critical of life in a Communist society was de facto about Communism. All these things created the innate and inalienable humour of Communism, its greatest cultural achievement.

BIBLIOGRAPHY

A *Day in the Life of the Soviet Union*. Collins, 1987.

Abdullaeva, Zara. 'Anekdot'. *Iskusstvo kino*, 9, 66–7, 2000.

Abramenko, L. I., ed. *Sovetskii anekdot: Antologiia*. Moscow: DataStrom, 1991.

Adams, Bruce. *Tiny Revolutions in Russia. Twentieth-century Soviet and Russian History in anecdotes*. Routledge Curzon, 2005.

Aksenova, A. '*Metafizika anekdota, ili Semantika lzhi*'. *Literaturnoe obozrenie*, 11–12, 1994.

Alaev, Enrid. *Mir anekdota. Anekdoty nashikh chitatelei* 8. Moscow: Anons, 1995.

Amis, Martin. *Koba the Dread: Laughter and the Twenty Million*. NY: Vintage, 2002.

Andreev, N. P. *Ukazatel' skazochnykh siuzhetov po sisteme Aarne*. Leningrad: Izdanie.

Andreevich, Y. *The Kremlin and the People. Political Jokes*. Munich: 1951.

Anekdoty iz kollektsii Zhirinovskogo. St Petersburg: Simpleks, 1994.

Anekdoty o shute Balakireve: Prodelki i shutki, ostroumnye otvety i blagie sovety slavnogo Balakireva, pridvornogo shuta imperatora Petra Velikogo. 4th ed. St Petersburg: Izdanie knigoprodavtsa A. A. Kholmushina, 1899.

Anekdoty pro tsaria Nikolaia dikaria na zlobu dnia. Petrograd: 1918.

Anekdoty ruskie, ili velikie dostopamiatnye deianiia i dobrodetel'nye primery slavnykh muzhei, polkovodtsov, grazhdanskikh chinovnikov, kupechestva i drugikh osob vsiakogo zvaniia, otlichivshikhsia geroicheskoiu tverdostiiu, neustrashimostiiu dukha, userdiem, blagotvoritel'nostiiu, istinnoiu pravotoiu del svoikh i drugimi mnogimi primerami nepokolebimoi preverzhennosti k vere, gosudariu i liubvi k otechestvu. St Petersburg: 1809.

Anekdoty v nomer. Komsomol'skaia Pravda, 1, 31 Mar. 1999.

Anninskii, Lev. *Shestidesiatniki i my. Kinematograf, stavshii i ne stavshii istoriei*. Moscow: Kinotsentr, 1991.

Antisovetskie anekdoty: Bor'ba narodnoi propagandy s bol'shevistkoi. Buenos Aires: n.p., n.d.

Applebaum, Anne. *Gulag. A History*. Penguin Books, 2003.

Apte, Mahadev L. 'Humor'. Bauman, *Folklore*, 67–75.

Arkhipova, Aleksandra. '"*Rolevaia struktura" detskikh tsiklov anekdotov (na materiale anekdotov o Vinni-Pukhe i Piatachke, o Cheburashke i Krokodile Gene)*'. BA thesis. Moscow: Rossiiskii Gosudarstvennyi Gumanitarnyi Universitet, 1999.

Arnason, Johann P. 'Communism and Modernity'. *Daedalus*, 129.1, 61–90, winter 2000.

Arnau, Frank. *Witze in Braun und Rot: Eine Anthologie.* Freiburg: Hyperion, 1969.

Athenaeus. *The Deipnosophists*, vol. 6. Translated by Charles Burton Gulick. Cambridge: Harvard U.P., 1959.

Attardo, Salvatore, and Jean-Charles Chabanne. 'Jokes as a Text Type'. *Humor*, 5.1–2, 165–76, 1992.

Averchenko, Arkadii. *Arkadii Averchenko v 'Novom Satirikone'*, 1917 g.-1918 g.: *rasskazy i fel'etony*, comp. and ed. N. K. Goleizovskii. Moscow: Krug, 1994.

Averintsev, S. S. '*Bakhtin i russkoe otnoshenie k smekhu*'. *Ot mifa k literature: Sbornik v chest' semidesiatipiatiletiia Eleazara Moiseevicha Meletinskogo*, comp. S. Iu. Nekliudov and E. S. Novik. Moscow: Rossiiskii universitet, 341–5, 1993.

Azov, V. '*Satira pod spudom*'. *Poslednie novosti*, 2, 14 May 1932.

Babel, Isaac. *1920 Diary*, ed. Carol J. Avins, trs. H. T. Willetts. New Haven, CT: Yale U.P., 1995.

Bakhtin, Mikhail. 'The Problem of Speech Genres'. *Speech Genres and Other Late Essays*. By Bakhtin, trs. Vern W. McGee, eds. Caryl Emerson and Michael Holquist. Austin: U. of Texas P., 60–102, 1986.

Bakhtin, Vladimir. '*Anekdoty nas spasali vsegda*'. *Strelianyi*, 799–818.

Baldwin, Barry, trs and ed. *The Philogelos or Laughter-Lover*. Amsterdam: J. C. Gieben, 1983.

Banc, C., and Alan Dundes. *First Prize Fifteen Years: an Annotated Collection of Romanian Political Jokes*. Rutherford, NJ: Farleigh Dickinson U.P., 1986.

Bantysh-Kamenskii, D. N. *Slovar' dostopamiatnykh liudei russkoi zemli*, Part 3. St Petersburg: 1847.

Barker, Adele, ed. *Consuming Russia: Popular Culture, Sex, and Society since Gorbachev*. Durham: Duke U.P., 1999.

Barskii, Lev Abramovich, and I. Pis'mennyi, comps. '*Vlast' smekha: Kratkii*

kurs istorii SSSR v anekdotakh, karikaturakh i postanovleniiakh TsK'.
Ogonek, 13, 40–8, 30 March 1998.

Barskii, Lev Abramovich. *Chelovek! Eto zvuchit gor'ko. Eto prosto smeshno. V pervom chtenii. Anekdoty.* Moscow: Kh. G. S., 1994.

Bauer, Raymond A. Inkeles, Alex; and Clyde Kluckhohn. *How the Soviet System Works.* NY: Vintage Books, 1960.

Bauman, Richard, ed. *Folklore, Cultural Performances, and Popular Entertainments: a Communications-centered Handbook.* NY: Oxford UP, 1992.

Beckmann, Petr. *Hammer and Tickle. Clandestine Laughter in the Soviet Empire*, trs. and narrated by Petr Beckmann. The Golem Press, 1980.

Beckmann, Petr. *Whispered Anecdotes. Humor From Behind The Iron Curtain*, trs. and narrated by Petr Beckmann. The Golem Press, 1969.

Beevor, Anthony. *Stalingrad.* Penguin Books, 1999.

Behling, Heinz. *Blätter die die Welt bedeutein.* Berlin Eulenspiegel Verlag, 1979.

Behling, Heinz. *Immer an die Wand lang.* Berlin: Eulenspiegel Verlag Berlin, 1988.

Bellow, Saul. *The Dean's December.* NY: Harper & Row, 1982.

Belousov, Aleksandr Fedorovich. '*Anekdoticheskii tsikl o krokodile Gene i Cheburashke.*' *Problemy poetiki iazyka i literatury. Materialy mezhvuzovskoi nauchnoi konferentsii*, 22–24 maia 1996 goda.

Petrozavodsk: Izdatel'stvo Karel'skogo gosudarstvennogo pedagogicheskogo universiteta, 3–20, 1996.

Benton, Greg and Graham Loomes. *Big Red Joke Book. Laughs from the Left.* Pluto Press, 1977.

Benton, Gregor. 'The Origins of the Political Joke'. *Humour in Society: Resistance and Control.* Eds. Chris Powell and George Paton. NY: St Martin's, 33–55, 1988.

Berezaiskii, Vasilii, comp. *Anekdoty drevnykh poshekhontsev.* St Petersburg: n.p., 1798.

Berger, Arthur Asa. *An Anatomy of Humor.* New Brunswick: Transaction, 1993.

Bergson, Henri. *Laughter: an Essay on the Meaning of the Comic*, trs. Cloudesley Brereton and Fred Rothwell. London: Macmillan and Co., 1911. Copenhagen: Green Integer, 1999.

Berry, Ellen E., and Anesa Miller-Pogacar, eds. *Re-entering the Sign: Articulating New Russian Culture.* Ann Arbor: U. of Michigan P., 1995.

Bertsch, Georg C., Ernst. Hedler *SED.* Benedikt Taschen Verlag, 1994.

Beverley, John. 'The Margins at the Center: On Testimonio (Testimonial

Narrative)'. *The Real Thing: Testimonial Discourse and Latin America*, ed. Georg M. Gugelberger, 23–41. Durham: Duke U.P., 1996.

Bitov, Andrei. 'Pod kupolom Glasnosti'. *Introduction. Zhvanetskii, God za dva*, 4–13.

Blazhes, V. V. 'Sovremennye ustnye iumoristicheskie rasskazy v ikh sviazi s narodno-poeticheskoi traditsiei'. *Fol'klor Urala: Sovremennyi russkii fol'klor promyshlennogo regiona: Sbornik nauchnykh trudov*, ed. V. P. Krugliashova. 38–47 Sverdlovsk: Ural'skii gosudarstvennyi universitet, 1989.

Blazhes, V. V., and A. V. Matveev, 'Sovremennye ustnye iumoristicheskie rasskazy v ikh sviazi s fol'klornoi traditsiei'. *Fol'klor narodov RSFSR: Sovremennoe sosoianie fol'klornykh traditsii i ikh vzaimodeistvie: Mezhvuzovskii nauchnyi sbornik*, ed. L. G. Barag, 58–64. Ufa: Izdatel'stvo Bashkirskogo universiteta, 1989.

Bogomolov, N., comp. *Anti-mir russkoi kul'tury: Iazyk. Fol'klor. Literatura*. Moscow: Ladomir, 1996.

Borev, Iurii Borisovich. *Estetika*. Moscow: Politizdat, 1969.

Borev, Yuri Borisovich. *Staliniada. Memuary po chuzhim vospominaniam s istoricheskimi pritchami I razmyshleniami avtora*. Moscow: Kniga, 1991.

Borisov, S. B. 'Estetika "chernogo iumora" v rossiiskoi traditsii'. *Iz istorii russkoi esteticheskoi mysli: Mezhvuzovskii sbornik nauchnykh trudov*, ed. A. P. Valitskaia, et al., 139–53. St Petersburg: Obrazovanie, 1993.

Borodin, Pavel. 'Abstraktnyi anekdot kak sotsiokul'turnyi fenomen'. *Material mezhdunarodnoi konferentsii 'Fol'klor i sovremennost'', posviashchennoi pamiati professora N. I. Savushkinoi* (20–22 oktiabria 1994 goda), 86–91. Moscow: Moskovskii gorodskoi dvorets tvorchestva, 1995.

Boskin, Joseph. *Rebellious Laughter: People's Humor in American Culture*. Syracuse: Syracuse U.P., 1997.

Brandes, Stanley. *Peaceful Protest: Spanish Political Humor in a Time of Crisis. Western Folklore*, 36, 331–46, 1977.

Bremmer, Jan, and Herman Roodenburg eds. *A Cultural History of Humour. From Antiquity to the Present Day*. Polity Press, 1997.

Brennecke, Nils. *Warum hat der Trabi Räder? Die schönsten Trabi-Witze*. Rowohlt Verlag, 1990.

Brezhnev, Leonid I. *Pages from His Life. Academy of Sciences of the USSR*, Pergamon Press, 1982.

Brezhnev, Leonid Il'ich. *Malaia zemlia*. Moscow: Izdatel'stvo Politicheskoi literatury, 1979.

Brezhnev, Leonid Ilyich. *A Short Biography by the Institute of Marxism-*

Leninism, CPSU Central Committee. Pergamon Press, 1977.

Brezhnev, Leonid. *How It Was*. Pergamon Press, 1979.

Briker, Boris, and Anatolii Vishevskii. *'Iumor v populiarnoi kul'ture sovetskogo intelligenta 60-x–70-x godov'*. *Wiener Slawistischer Almanach*, 24, 147–70, 1989.

Britsyna, Olesya. 'Anecdotes, Jokes and Jests in Everyday Communication: Folklore Texts under Observation and Experimental Study'. *Fabula*, 40.1–2, 26–32, 1999.

Brooks, Jeffrey. *Thank You, Comrade Stalin! Soviet Public Culture from Revolution to Cold War*. Princeton: Princeton U.P., 2000.

Brudzinski, Wieslaw. *Die rote Katze*. Suhrkamp Verlag, 1970.

Budina, O. R., and N. N. Shmeleva. 'Tradition in the Development of the Culture of Everyday Life in a Modern Russian City'. *Soviet Anthropology and Archeology*, 22.4, 72–97, Spring 1984.

Bukharin, Nikolai, and E. Preobrazhensky. *The ABC of Communism. A Popular Explanation of the Program of the Communist Party of Russia.* Ann Arbor Paperbacks for the Study of Communism and Marxism. Michigan: U. of Michigan P., 1966.

Bukharkova, Ol'ga. *'Krysha: Proshchai, epokha otmorozkov'*. *Ogonek*, 7, 28, February 2000.

Bulgakov, Mikhail. *Zoikina kvartira: Okonchatel'nyi tekst*. Ann Arbor: Ardis, 1971.

Bulgakov, Mikhail. *The Fatal Eggs*. Modern Voices, 2003 (1924).

Bulgakov, Mikhail. *The Heart of a Dog*. Vintage, 1968 (1925).

Bulgakov, Mikhail. *The Master and Margarita*. Picador, 1997 (1966).

Burger, Ulrich. *Das sagen wir natürlich so nicht!* Berlin Dietz Verlag, 1990.

Buslaev, Fedor Ivanovich. *Istoricheskie ocherki russkoi narodnoi slovesnosti i iskusstva*. St Petersburg: Obshchestvennaia Pol'za, 1861. The Hague: Mouton, 1969.

Butenko, I. A. *'Iumor kak predmet sotsiologii?'* *Sotsiologicheskie issledovaniia*, 5, 135–40, 1997.

Capek, Karel. *'O prirode anekdota'*. 1925, trs. V. Kamenskaia. *Voprosy literatury*, 11, 302–8, 1975.

Ceauşescu, Nicolae. *Romania on the Way of Completing Socialist Construction*. Reports, Speeches, Articles. Bucharest: Meridiane Publishing House, 1969.

Chapaeva posmotrit vsia strana. *Pravda*. 21 November 1934, p. 1.

Chapple, Richard L. *Soviet Satire of the Twenties*. University of Florida Humanities Monograph Number 47, 1980.

Chekalova, A. A., trs. and ed. *Voina s persami. Voina s vandalami. Tainaia istoriia*. By Prokopii kesariiskii. Moscow: Nauka, 1993.

Chekunova, A. E. '*Poiavlenie istoricheskogo anekdota v Rossii*'. *Voprosy istorii*, 2, 131–40, 1997.

Cherednichenko, Tat'iana. *Tipologiia sovetskoi massovoi kul'tury: Mezhdu "Brezhnevym" i 'Pugachevoi'*. Moscow: RIK Kul'tura, 1993.

Chernykh, P. Ia. *Istoriko-etimologicheskii slovar' sovremennogo russkogo iazyka*. Moscow: Russkii iazyk, 1993.

Chernyshev, Sergei. '*Russkoe samoopredelenie*'. *Russkii zhurnal*, 6 September. 1997. 2 January 2001 http://www.russ.ru/journal/odna-8/97-09-06/chern.htm.

Chernyshevskii, Nikolai G. '*Vozvyshennoe i komicheskoe*'. *Izbrannye filosofskie sochineniia*. Vol. 1 252–99. Leningrad: Gospolitizdat, 1950.

Chernyshov, Andrei. *Sovremennaia sovetskaia mifologiia*. Tver': n.p., 1992.

Chirkova, Ol'ga. '*Personazhi ukhodiat iz basen: Istoki sovremennogo anekdota*'. *Russkaia rech'*, 4, 102–7, 1997.

Chistov, K. V. '*Prozaicheskie zhanry v sisteme fol'klora*'. *Prozaicheskie zhanry fol'klora narodov SSSR: Tezisy dokladov na Vsesoiuznoi nauchnoi konferentsii*. 21–23 maia 1974. Gor. Minsk. Minsk: AN SSSR, 6–31, 1974.

Chudinova, I. A. '*Smekh, vesel'e, shabash: Traditsii skomoroshestva v period petrovskikh reform*'. *Skomorokhi: Problemy i perspectivy izucheniia (K 140–letiiu so dnia vykhoda pervoi raboty of skomorokhakh)*, ed. V. V. Koshelev. St Petersburg: Rossiiskii institut istorii iskusstv, 149–59, 1994.

Cochran, Robert. '"What Courage!": Romanian "Our Leader" Jokes'. *Journal of American Folklore*, 102.405, 259–74, 1989.

Cohen, Ted. *Jokes: Philosophical Thoughts on Joking Matters*. Chicago: U. of Chicago P., 1999.

Colombo, John Robert. *Iron Curtains: Humour of the Soviet Union*. Toronto: Colombo & Co., 1996.

Corbeill, Anthony. *Controlling Laughter: Political Humor in the Late Roman Republic*. Princeton: Princeton U.P., 1996.

Cottom, Daniel. *Text and Culture: The Politics of Interpretation*. Minneapolis: U. of Minnesota P., 1989.

Crocodile Album of Soviet Humour. London: Pilot Press, 1943.

Cuthbertson, Gilbert Morris. *Political Myth and Epic*. Ann Arbor: Michigan State U.P., 1975.

Dalos, Gyorgy. *Proletarier aller Länder, entschuldigt mich!* Edition Temmen, 1993.

Das Krokodil ... und seiner Zeichner. Berlin: Eulenspiegel Verlag.

Davies, Christie. 'The Collapse of the World's Best Political Jokes'. *National Review*, 42.15, 32, 6 August 1990.

Davies, Christie. *The Right to Joke*. Research Report 37. The Social Affairs Unit, 2004.

DDR-Witze. Teil 2. *Lieber von Sitte gemahlt, als vom Sozialismus gezeichnet*. Berlin: Karl Dietz Verlag 2000.

DDR-Witze. Berlin: Karl Dietz Verlag 1995.

Der gespaltene Direktor. Ungarische Humorgeschichten. Berlin: Eulenspiegel Verlag, 1977.

Deriabin, Peter and Frank Gibney. *The Secret War*. Garden City, N.Y.: Doubleday, 1959.

Deutsche Demokratische Republik. Dresden: Sachsenverlag 1961.

Die besten Witze aus der DDR. Tosa, 2003.

Dieses Krokodil ist nicht vom Nil. Berlin: Verlag, Kultur und Fortschritt. 1955.

Diment, Galya, and Yuri Slezkine, eds. *Between Heaven and Hell: the Myth of Siberia in Russian Culture*. NY: St Martin's, 1993.

Dinur, Benzion. *Odessa*. In *Encyclopedia Judaica*, 12, ed. Cecil Roth. Jerusalem: Keter, 1972.

Dmitriev, Anatolii. '*Iu. Borev i intelligentskii fol'klor*'. *Sotsiologicheskie issledovaniia*, 7, 138–41, 1995.

Doder, Dusko and Louise, Branson. *Gorbachev – Heretic in the Kremlin*. Futura Publications, 1990.

Dolgopolova, Z., ed. *Russia Dies Laughing. Jokes from the Soviet Russia*. Unwin Paperbacks, 1983.

Dolgopolova, Zhanna. 'The Contrary World of the Anecdote'. *Melbourne Slavonic Studies*, 15, 1–12, 1981.

Domanovskii, L. V., and N. V. Novikov. *Russkoe narodnopoeticheskoe tvorchestvo protiv tserkvi i religii*. Leningrad: Izdatel'stvo Akademii nauk SSSR, 1961.

Dondurei, Danniil. '*Kinematografisty o "novykh russkikh"*'. *Iskusstvo kino*, 1, 25–7, 1995.

Dornberg, John. *Brezhnev. The Masks of Power*. Andre Deutsch, 1974.

Dorogi, Yunosti. *Komsomol v iskusstve 1920–1930h godov*. Moscow: Sovietsky Khudozhnik, 1988.

Douglas, Mary. 'Jokes.' In *Rethinking Popular Culture: Contemporary Perspectives in Cultural Studies*, ed. Chandra Mukerji and Michael Schudson, 291–310. Berkeley: U. of California P., 1910.

Douglas, Mary. *The Social Role of Cognition: Some Factors in Joke Perception. Man*, 3, 361–76, 1968.

Draitser, Emil A. *Taking Penguins to the Movies. Ethnic Humor in Russia*. Michigan: Wayne State U. P., 1998.

Draitser, Emil, ed. *Forbidden Laughter: Soviet Underground Jokes*, trs. Jon Pariser. Los Angeles: Almanac, 1979.

Drozdzynski, Alexander. *Der politische Witz im Ostblock*. DTV, 1978.

Durocher, Bruno. *La Guerre Secrète du Rire*. Editions Albun Michel, 1965.

Eaton, Katherine B. *Daily Life in the Soviet Union*. Westport, CT: Greenwood Press, 2004.

Efimova, Alla. *Communist Nostalgia: On Soviet and Post-Soviet Memory*. Dissertation, U. of Rochester, NY, 1997.

Elistratov, Vladimir. '*Argo i kul'tura*'. *Slovar' moskovskogo argo: Materialy 1980–1994 gg. Moscow: Russkie slovari*, 592–699, 1994.

English, Robert D. *Russia and the Idea of the West. Gorbachev, Intellectuals and the End of the Cold War*. NY: Columbia U. P., 2000.

Erokaev, S. *Anekdoty I baiki pro novykh russkikh: Sbornik tematicheskikh anekdotov*. St Petersburg: Totem, 1997.

Erokhin, Aleksei. 'Abzats'. *Ogonek*, 14, 43, April 1995.

Eroshkin, S., et al., comps. *Anekdoty pro novykh russkikh. Malinovye parusa*. St Petersburg: DiK, 1997.

Eulenspiegel Sonder Ausgabe. *Die Klassiker aus 5 Jahrzehnten. Die Jahre 1954–1969*.

Eulenspiegel Sonder Ausgabe. *Die Klassiker aus 5 Jahrzehnten. Die Jahre 1970–1979*.

Eulenspiegel Sonder Ausgabe. *Die Klassiker aus 5 Jahrzehnten. Die Jahre 1980–1989*.

Evrei-olenovod. Minsk: Literatura, 1997.

Faibisovich, Semen. '"*Novye russkie*" – *snaruzhi i iznutri*'. *Iskusstvo kino*, 1, 34–8, 1995.

Farrell, Dianne Ecklund. 'Medieval Popular Humor in Russian Eighteenth Century Lubki'. *Slavic Review*, 50.3, 551–65, Fall 1991.

Feokistov, Ivan. *Anekdoty i predaniia o Petre Velikom po Golikovu i dr.* St Petersburg: n.p., 1896.

Fialkova, Larisa. 'Chornobyl's Folklore: Vernacular Commentary on Nuclear Disaster'. *Journal of Folklore Research*, 38.3, 181–204, 2001.

Figes, Orlando. *A People's Tragedy. The Russian Revolution 1891–1924*. Pimlico, 1997.

Figes, Orlando. *The Whisperers. Private Life in Stalin's Russia*. Allen Lane, Penguin Books, 2007.

Filip, Ota, and Ivan Steiger. *Schwejk heute. Politischer Witze in Prag*. Berlin: Universitas Verlag, 1977.

Filippov, Boris. 'Nesmeshnoe o smeshnom'. Iumor i satira posle-
revoliutsionnoi Rossii: Antologiia v dvukh tomakh. Vol. 17–18. London:
Overseas Publications Interchange, 2 vols., 1983. Comp. Fillipov and
Vadim Medish.

Fitzpatrick, Sheila. Everyday Stalinism. Ordinary Life in Extraordinary
Times: Soviet Russia in the 1930s. Oxford: Oxford U. P., 1999.

Fleischman, Suzanne. Tense and Narrativity: From Medieval Performance
to Modern Fiction. Austin: U. of Texas P., 1990.

Florian, Erik (Hrsg.) Der politische Witz in der DDR. Humor als Ges-
innungsventil. Droemersche Verlagsanstalt Th Knaur Nachf, Munich:
1983.

Folkloristic commentary by Roman Jakobson. NY: Pantheon, 1973.

Forrai, George, ed. Russian Express: Don't Leave Home! Jokes From
Behind the Iron Curtain. Hong Kong: WMA, 1988.

Franke, Ingolf. Das grosse DDR-Witz.de Buch. Media Enterprise, 2002.

Franke, Ingolf. Das grosse DDR-Witz.de Buch. WEVOS Verlag, 2003.

Freud, Sigmund. Jokes and their Relation to the Unconscious, trs. James
Strachey. NY: W. W. Norton, 1960.

Furet, François. The Passing of an Illusion. The Idea of Communism in the
Twentieth Century. Chicage: U. of Chicago P., 1999.Furmanov, Dmitrii.
Chapaev. Krasnyi desant. Miatezh. Leningrad: Lenizdat, 1967.

Galich, Aleksandr. 'O tom, kak Klim Petrovich vystupal na mitinge v
zashchitu mira'. General'naia repetitsiia. Moscow: Sovetskii pisatel',
52–4, 1991.

Geerts, Rudi (HG.). Hier lacht das Volk. Witze aus der alten und neuen
DDR. Rowohlt, 1990.Geldern, James von, and Louise McReynolds,
eds. Entertaining Tsarist Russia. Bloomington: Indiana U. P., 1998.

Geldern, James von, and Richard Stites, eds. Mass Culture in Soviet Russia:
Tales, Poems, Songs, Movies, Plays, and Folklore, 1917–1953. Bloomington: Indiana U.P., 1995.

Gerlovan, O. K. 'Poniatie o skazke v Rossii XVIII-nachala XIX v'. Fil-
ologicheskie nauki, 1, 95–103, 1996.

Getty, J. Arch and Oleg V. Naumov. The Road to Terror. Stalin and the
Self-Destruction of the Bolsheviks, 1932–1939. New Haven, CT: Yale
U. P., 1999.

Gifford, D. J. 'Iconographical Notes Towards a Definition of the Medieval
Fool'. Studies in Honour of Enid Welsford, ed. Paul V. A. Williams,
Cambridge: D. S. Brewer, 1979.

Glebkin, V. V. Ritual v sovetskoi kul'ture. Moscow: Ianus-K, 1998.

Glinka, Sergei. Russkie anekdoty voennye, grazhdanskie i istoricheskie,
izobrazhaiushchie svoistvo i t.d. Moscow: n.p., 1811.

Goess, Franz, and Manfred R. Beer. *Prager Anschlage. Bilddokumente des gewaltlosen Widerstandes*. Ullstein Buch, 1968.

Gogol, Nikolai. *Letters of Nikolai Gogol*, ed. Carl Proffer, trs. Carl Proffer and Vera Krivoshein. Ann Arbor: U. of Michigan P., 1967.

Goncharenko, Nadiia. '*Anekdot*'. *Suchasnist*', 6, 116–25, 1998.

Gopman, V., and V. Mil'china, comps. '*Anekdoty o novykh russkikh*'. *Novoe literaturnoe obozrenie*, 22, 380–82, 1996.

Gorbachev, Mikhail. *Memoirs*. Bantam Books, 1997.

Gorky, Maxim. *Sobranie sochinenii*, 27. Moscow: Golitizdat, 1953.

Gorky, Maxim, Karl Radek, Nikolai Bukharin, Andrei Zhdanov and others. *Soviet Writers' Congress 1934. The Debate of Socialist Realism and Modernism in the Soviet Union*. London: Lawrence and Wishart, 1977.

Graham, Seth Benedict. *A Cultural Analysis of the Russo-Soviet Anecdote*, PhD thesis, U. of Pittsburgh, 2003.

Grossman, Leonid. '*Iskusstvo anekdota u Pushkina*'. *Sobranie sochinenii v chetyrekh tomakh. Tom pervyi: Pushkin: Issledovaniia i stat'i*, vol. 1. Moscow: Sovremennye problemy, 4 vols., 45–79, 1928.

Hall, Rex, and David J. Shayler. *The Rocket Men. Vostok and Voskhod, The First Soviet Manned Spaceflights*. Springer, Praxis Publishing, 2001.

Haney, Jack V. *An Introduction to the Russian Folktale*, vol. 1 *The Complete Russian Folktale*. Armonk, NY: M. E. Sharpe, 1999.

Harris, David A., and Izrail Rabinovich. *The Jokes of Oppression. The Humor of Soviet Jews*. Jason Aronson Inc., 1988.

Hasek, Jaroslav. *The Good Soldier Svejk and His Fortunes in the World War*. Penguin Books, 1974 (1912–23).

Havel, Václav, et al. *The Power of the Powerless. Citizens Against the State in Central-Eastern Europe*. Palach Press, 1985.

Havel, Václav. *Selected Plays 1984–1987*. Faber and Faber, 1994.

Havel, Václav. *The Garden Party and Other Plays*. NY: Grove Press, 1993.

Hellberg-Hirn, Elena. 'The Other Way Round: The Jokelore of Radio Yerevan'. *Arv: Scandinavian Yearbook of Folklore*, 41, 89–104, 1985.

Henniger, Barbara. *Barbaras praktische Linke*. Berlin: Eulenspiegel Verlag, 1981.

Henniger, Barbara. *Im Paradies und anderswo. Karikaturen*. Berlin: Eulenspiegel Verlag, 1987.

Henry, P., ed. *Modern Soviet Satire*. Collet's, 1974.

Henry, P., ed. *Classics of the Soviet Satire*. Collet's, 1972.

Herzog, Rudolph. *Heil, Hitler, das Schwein ist tod. Lachen unter Hitler – Komik und Humor im Dritten Reich*. Berlin: Eichborn, 2006.

Hilton, Christopher. *The Wall. The People's Story*. Sutton Publishing, 2001.

Hirche, Kurt. *Der 'braune' & der 'rote' Witz*. Econ Verlag, 1964.

Holzweissig, Dr Gunter. *DDR-Presse unter Parteikontrolle*. Bonn: Gesamtdeutsches Institut, 1991.

Horkheimer, Max, and Theodor W. Adorno. *Dialectic of Enlightenment*, trs. John Cumming. NY: Continuum, 1972.

Horton, Andrew. *Introduction. Comedy/Cinema/Theory*. Berkeley: U. of California P., 1–21, 1991.

Horvath, Agnes. *The Political Psychology of Trickster-Clown: an Analytical Experiment Around Communism as Myth*. EUI Working Paper SPS 97/5. Badia Fiesolana, Italy: European U. Institute, 1997.

Howell, Dana Prescott. *The Development of Soviet Folkloristics*. NY: Garland, 1992.

Hutcheon, Linda. *Irony's Edge: The Theory and Politics of Irony*. London: Routledge, 1994.

Hutton, Jan. 'Some Aspects of Contemporary Soviet Folktales'. *Journal of Russian Studies*, 55, 30–40, 1989.

Hyers, M. Conrad. *Zen and the Comic Spirit*. Philadelphia: Westminster, 1973.

Iakovenko, I. G. 'Nenormativnyi anekdot kak modeliruiushchaia sistema: Opyt kul'turologicheskogo analiza'. *Novoe literaturnoe obozrenie*, 43, 335–46, 2000.

Ian'shinova, N. I., comp. *Chukchi*. Moscow: S. Kudrin & Co., 1901.

Ilf, Ilya, and Evgeny Petrov. *The Golden Calf*. Frederick Muller Ltd, Random House, 1962.

Ilf, Ilya, and Evgeny Petrov. *The Twelve Chairs*. Sphere Books Ltd, 1971.

Inkeles, Alex, and Raymond A. Bauer. *The Soviet Citizen. Daily Life in a Totalitarian Society*. Harvard U. P., 1959.

Irten'ev, Igor', and Andrei Bil'zho. *Imperiia dobra*. n.p.: S. Nitochkin, 1994.

Isnard, Armand. *Raconte ... Popov! Les histoires drôles de derrière le rideau de fer*. Editions Menges, 1977.

Iudin, Iu. I. *Russkaia narodnaia bytovaia skazka*. Moscow: Academia, 1998.

Iunisov, Milikhat Vafaevich. *Mifopoetika studencheskogo smekha (STEM i KVN)*. Moscow: Gosudarstvennyi institut iskusstvoznaniia, 1999.

Ivanova, T. 'Sovetskii anekdot v SShA'. *Zhivaia starina*, 1, 57, 1995.

Ivanova, T. G. 'Bylichki i "anekdoty" v Shenkurskom raione Arkhangel'skoi oblasti'. *Russkii fol'klor*, 23, 26–32, 1985.

Johnson, Priscilla, and Leopold Labedz, eds. *Khrushchev and the Arts. The Politics of Soviet Culture, 1962–1964*. Cambridge, MA: MIT P., 1965.

Johnson, Ragnar. 'Jokes, Theories, Anthropology'. *Semiotica*, 22. 3–4, 309–34, 1978.

Judt, Tony. *Postwar. A History of Europe since 1945.* William Heinemann, 2005.

Kalbouss, George. 'On "Armenian Riddles" and Their Offspring "Radio Erevan"'. *Slavic and East European Journal*, 21. 3, 447–9, 1977.

Kalina, Jan L. *Nichts zu Lachen: Der politische Witz im Ostblock.* Herbig, 1980.

Kalina, Jan. *Das lachende Lexikon. Witze and anekdoten von A-Z.* Wilhelm Heyne Verlag, Munchen, 1984.

Kaminer, Wladimir. *Russian Disco. Tales of Everyday Lunacy on the Streets of Berlin.* Ebury Press, 2002.

Karachevtsev, Sergei. *Damskie: Sbornik novykh anekdotov.* Riga: Mir, n.d.

Kaspe, Irina. 'Krivoe antizerkalo: "Sovetskii' i 'postsovetskii" anekdot: problemy zhanrovoi transformatsii'. *Novoe literaturnoe obozrenie*, 43, 327–34, 2000.

Keane, John. *Vaclav Havel – a Political Tragedy in Six Acts.* Bloomsbury, 1999.

Kelly, Catriona, and David Shepherd, eds. *Constructing Russian Culture in the Age of Revolution, 1881–1940.* NY: Oxford U.P., 1998.

Kelly, Catriona. 'The Retreat from Dogmatism: Populism under Khrushchev and Brezhnev'. In Kelly and Shepherd, *Russian Cultural Studies*, 249–73.

Kenney, Padraic. *A Carnaval of Revolution. Central Europe, 1989.* Princeton: Princeton U. P., 2002.

Kharitonova, Valentina. 'Anekdoty (stat'ia o podlinnykh anekdotakh so mnozhestvom primerov)'. *Istoki: Al'manakh*, 21, 173–89, 1990.

Khrul', Viktor Mikhailovich. *Anekdot kak forma massovoi kommunikatsii.* Diss. Moscow State U., 1993.

Khrushchev, Sergei N.. *Nikita Khrushchev and the Creation of a Superpower.* Pennsylvania State U. P., 2000.

Khvalin-Gor'kii, L. L., comp. *Anekdoty s gosudareva dvora, ili 150 istoricheskikh anekdotov iz zhizni russkikh gosudarei XVII-XIX vekov.* Nizhnii Novgorod: Pegas, 1990.

Kiaer, Christina, and Eric Naiman, eds. *Everyday Life in Early Soviet Russia. Taking the Revolution Inside.* Bloomingdale: Indiana U. P. 2006.

Kishtainy, Khalid. *Arab Political Humour.* London: Quartet Books, 1985.

Klotzer, Sylvia. *Satire und Macht: Film, Zeitung, Kabarett in der DDR.* Bohlau Verlag, 2006.

Kohout, Jara. *Attention Comrades!* Written and ed. Morton Sontheimer, photographs by Wallace Litwin. NY, Viking Press, 1954.

Kolasky, John, comp. *Laughter Through Tears: Underground Wit, Humor and Satire in the Soviet Russian Empire*. Ill. Myron Levytsky and Tibor Kovalik. Australia: Veritas, 1985.

Kordonskii, Simon. '*Chapaev, Shtirlits, russkii, evrei, Brezhnev, chukcha + El'tsin = Pushkin*'. *Russkii zhurnal*, 11 November 1997. 2 January 2001.

Kostiukhin, E. A. '*Iadrenyi russkii iumor*'. Introduction. *Afanas'ev, Narodnye russkie skazki ne dlia pechati*, 5–19.

Kotsiubinskii, S. D., ed. and comp. *Anekdoty o Khodzhe Nasreddine i Akhmet Akhae. Simferopol': Gosudarstvennoe izdatel'stvo krymskoi*. ASSR, 1937.

Krauze, Andrzej. *A Year of Martial Law*. Cartoons by Andrzej Krauze. Kontakt.

Krauze, Andrzej. *Andrzej Krauze's Poland*. With a preface by George Mikes. London: Nina Karsov, 1981.

Krauze, Andrzej. *Coming back to the West*. Larson, 1983.

Krauze, Andrzej. *Lubta mnie! Czytelnik*, Warsaw: 1980.

Krauze, Andrzej. *Nowosc: Szczescie w aerozolu!* Warsaw: 1977.

Kreps, Mikhail. *Tekhnika komicheskogo u Zoshchenko*. Benson, VT: Chalidze, 1986.

Krivoshlyk, M. G. *Istoricheskie anekdoty iz zhizni russkikh zamechatel'nykh liudei (S portretami i kratkimi biografiami)*. 2nd ed. St Petersburg, 1897. Moscow: ANS-Print, 1991.

Kroker, Arthur, and Charles Levin. 'Cynical Power: the Fetishism of the Sign'. In *Ideology and Power in the Age of Lenin in Ruins*, ed. Arthur Kroker and Marilouise Kroker. NY: St Martin's, 123–34, 1991.

Krokodil vsekh vremen I narodov. Moscow: Eksmo, 2007.

Krongauz, M. A. '*Bessilie iazyka v epokhu zrelogo sotsializma*'. *Znak: Sbornik statei po lingvistike, semiotike i poetike pamiati A. N. Zhurinskogo*. Moscow: *Russkii uchebnyi tsentr* MS, 233–44, 1994.

Krylov, Ivan A., and A. I. Klushin. *Sankt-Peterburgskii Merkurii*, 1 (1793).

Krylova, Anna. 'Saying "Lenin" and Meaning "Party": Subversion and Laughter in Soviet and Post-Soviet Society'. Barker, 243–65.

Kukin, Mischka (Simon Wiesenthal). *Humor hinter dem Eisernen Vorhang*. Gutersloh: Signum Verlag, 1962.

Kukryniksy Karikaturen. Berlin: Eulenspiegel Verlag, 1977.

Kundera, Milan. *The Joke*, trs. David Hamblyn and Oliver Stallybrass. NY: Coward-McCann, 1969.

Kupina, N. A. *Totalitarnyi iazyk: Slovar' i rechevye reaktsii*. Ekaterinburg: Izdatel'stvo Ural'skogo universiteta, 1995.

Kurganov, Efim, and N. Okhotin, comps. *Russkii literaturnyi anekdot kontsa XVIII-nachala XIX veka.* Moscow: Khudozhestvennaia literatura, 1990.

Kurganov, Efim. *Anekdot kak zhanr.* St Petersburg: Gumanitarnoe agenstvo 'Akademicheckii proekt', 1997.

Kurti, Laszlo. *The Politics of Joking: Popular Response to Chernobyl. Journal of American Folklore,* vol. 101, 324–334, July–September 88.

Kux, Sally. 'On the Boundary of Life and Literature: the Anecdote in Early Nineteenth-Century Russia'. Dissertation, Stanford U., 1994.

Lane, Christel. *The Rites of Rulers: Ritual in Industrial Society – The Soviet Case.* Cambridge: Cambridge U.P., 1981.

Larsen, Egon. *Wit as a Weapon: the Political Joke in History.* London: Frederick Muller Ltd, 1980.

Latynina, Julia. 'New Folklore and Newspeak'. Berry and Miller-Pogacar, 79–90.

Lebed', Ol'ga. *'Sem'ia v neformal'noi narodnoi kul'ture'.* Unpublished article, 1998.

Lebedev, G., ed. *Luchshie anekdoty.* Moscow: FAIR, 1996.

Lec, Stanislaw Jerzy. *Neue unfrisierte Gedanken.* Hanser, 1964.

Lendvai, Endre. *'Sistemnyi analiz russkogo anekdota'. Textsemantik und Textstilistik,* ed. Herbert Jelitte and Jarosław Wierzbiński. Frankfurt am Main: Peter Lang, 251–66, 1999.

Lenoe, Matthew. *Closer to the Masses. Stalinist Culture, Social Revolution, and Soviet Newspapers.* Harvard U.P., 2004.

Lerner, Warren. *Karl Radek – The Last Internationalist.* Stanford, CA: Stanford U. P., 1970.

Levchik, D. A. *'Politicheskii "kheppenning"'. Sotsiologicheskie issledovaniia,* 8, 51–6, 1996.

Levinson, Aleksei. *'Chego starye intelligenty ne dali "New Russians"'. Iskusstvo kino,* 1, 1995.

Levy, Alan. *Poland's Polish Jokes. New York Times Magazine,* 21, 22, 25, 27, 8 August 1976.

Lewis, Flora. *Laughter Behind the Iron Curtain. New York Times Magazine,* 2 September 1956.

Likhachev, D. S. *'Smekh kak mirovozzrenie'. Istoricheskaia poetika russkoi literatury: Smekh kak mirovozzrenie i drugie raboty.* St Petersburg: Aleteiia, 342–403, 1997.

Lipman, Steve. *Laughter in Hell: The Use of Humor during the Holocaust.* Northvale, NJ.: Jason Aronson, 1991.

Lipovetsky, Mark. 'New Russians as a Cultural Myth'. *Russian Review,* 62.1, 54–71, January 2003.

Listov, Viktor. 'Revoliutsiia molodaia: 1917–1927'. Literaturnaia gazeta, 12, 13 July 1988.

Lukes, Steven, and Itzhak Galnoor. No Laughing Matter. A Collection of Political Jokes. Penguin Books, 1987.

Lunacharskii, A. V. 'O smekhe'. Literaturnyi kritik, 4, 3–9, 1935.

Luray, Martin. Bitter Wit From Hungary. New York Times Magazine, 7 April 1951.

Lur'e, Vadim. 'Detskii anekdot'. Fol'klor i postfol'klor: struktura, tipologiia, semiotika, 29 May 2002. http://www.ruthenia.ru/folklore/luriev4.htm.

Lyons, Eugene. Moscow Carousel. NY: n.p., 1937.

Makarov, Dmitrii. 'Natsii v zerkale anekdota'. Argumenty i fakty, 4, 953, 15, January 1999.

Malinowski, Bronislaw. 'Myth in Primitive Psychology'. Magic, Science, and Religion and Other Essays, 84. Boston: Beacon, 1948.

Marshall, Bonnie. 'Images of Women in Soviet Jokes and Anecdotes'. Journal of Popular Culture, 26.2 117–25, Fall 1992.

Marx, Karl, Friedrich Engels. The Communist Manifesto. Penguin Books, 1985.

Masakov, Ivan Filippovich. Russkie satiro-iumoristicheskie zhurnaly (Bibliograficheskoe opisanie). Vladimir: Tipografiia Gubernskogo Pravleniia, 1910.

Matizen, Viktor. 'Steb kak fenomen kul'tury'. Iskusstvo kino, 9, 59–62, 1993.

Mayakovsky, Vladimir. The Bedbug and Selected Poetry. Bloomington: Indiana U. P., 1975.

McAuley, Mary, ed. Russian Popular Culture. Entertainment and Society since 1900. Cambridge: Cambridge U. P., 1992.

Medvedev Roi. Interview with Aleksandr Klimov. Ekho Moskvy Radio. March 5 2003. Johnson's Russia List. 13 August 2003. http://www.cdi.org/russia/johnson/7098a.cfm##9

Medvedev, Roy, and Zhores Medvedev. The Unknown Stalin. His Life, Death, and Legacy. Overlook Press, 2003.

Meletinskii, Eleazar Moiseevich. Geroi volshebnoi skazki. Proiskhozhdenie obraza. Moscow: Vostochnaia literatura, 1958.

Memetov, V. S., and A. A. Danilov. 'Intelligentsiia Rossii: Uroki istorii i sovremennost' (Popytka istoriograficheskogo analiza problemy)'. Intelligentsiia Rossii: Uroki istorii i sovremennost': Mezhvuzovskii sbornik nauchnykh trudov, ed. Memetov. Ivanovo: Ivanovskii gosudarstvennyi universitet, 3–15, 1996.

Merkel, Ina (Hg.). Wir sind doch nicht die Meckerecke der Nation! Briefe *an das Fernsehen der DDR*. Schwarzkopf & Schwarzkopf, 2000.

Metlina, Ekaterina. '*Vandaloustoichivyi iumor*'. *Stolitsa*, 3, 66, 1997.

Miasoedov, Boris. *O khamstve i stervoznosti v russkoi zhizni*. Moscow: *Russkaia entsiklopediia*, 1998.

Michaelis, Andreas. *DDR Souvenirs*. Benedikt Taschen, 1994.

Mickiewicz, Ellen. *Split Signals: Television and Politics in the Soviet Union*. NY: Oxford U.P., 1988.

Mikes, George. *Laughing Matter: Towards a Personal Philosophy of Wit and Humor*. NY: Library, 1971.

Moldavskii, Dmitrii M., ed. and comp. *Russkaia satiricheskaia skazka v zapisiakh serediny XIX–nachala XX veka*. Moscow: AN SSSR, 1955.

Montefiore, Simon Sebag. *Stalin. The Court of the Red Tsar*. London: Weidenfeld & Nicolson, 2003.

Morreal, John, ed. *The Philosophy of Laughter and Humor*. NY: State U. of New York P., 1987.

Moshkin, S. V., and V. N. Rudenko. 'Children's Political Jokes'. *Russian Education and Society*, 38.9, 69–79, September 1996.

Mozheitov, Dmitry. 'New Russians at large'. *Russia Journal*, 30.73 (5 August 2000). 29 September 2001. http://www.russiajournal.com/ils/article.shtml?ad=992.

Muratov, L. '*Uroki legendarnogo fil'ma*'. *Neva*, 12, 169–75, 1984.

Muschard, Jutta. 'Jokes and their Relation to Relevance and Cognition or Can Relevance Theory Account for the Appreciation of Jokes?', *Zeitschrift für Anglistik und Amerikanistik*, 47.1, 12–23, 1999.

Navon, David. 'The Seemingly Appropriate but Virtually Inappropriate: Notes on Characteristics of Jokes'. *Poetics*, 17.3, 207–19, June 1988.

Nenarokov, A. P.; Gainullina, R. M.; Gornyi, V. S., and A. I. Ushakov, comps. *Iaichnitsa vsmiatku, ili Neser'ezno o ser'eznom. Nad kem i nad chem smeialis' v Rossii v 1917 godu*. Moscow: Britanskii Biznes Klub, 1992.

Nerush, V., and M. Pavlov. '*Shepotom iz-za ugla*'. *Komsomol'skaia Pravda*, 4, 15 October 1982.

Nevskaia, V. A. '"... *Dnei minuvshikh anekdoty*"'. *Russkaia rech'*, 5, 78–84, 1992.

Nevskii, Aleksei, comp. '*Staryi anekdot*'. *Rodina*, 7, 24–5, 1990.

Nichiporovich, *Tat'iana Gennad'evna*, comp. *Anekdoty iz Anglii*. Minsk: Literatura, 1998.

Nikiforov, A. I. '*Erotika v velikorusskoi narodnoi skazke*'. *Khudozhestvennyi fol'klor*, 4–5, 120–7, 1929.

Nikulin, Iurii, comp. *Anekdoty ot Nikulina*. Moscow: Binom/Gudwin-3, 1997.

Nilsen, Alleen Pace, and Don L. F. Nilsen. *Encyclopedia of 20th-Century American Humor*. Phoenix, AZ: Oryx, 2000.

Nilsen, Don Lee Fred. *Humor Scholarship: a Research Bibliography*. Westport, CT: Greenwood, 1993.

Novik, E. S. '*Struktura skazochnogo triuka*'. *Ot mifa k literature: Sbornik v chest' semidesiatipiatiletiia Eleazara Moiseevicha Meletinskogo*. Moscow: Rossiiskii universitet, 139–52, 1993.

Obrdlik, Antonin J. '"Gallows Humor" – A Sociological Phenomenon'. *American Journal of Sociology*, 47, 709–16, 1942.

Oinas, Felix J. 'Folklore, Study of'. *Terras*, 139–42.

Oinas, Felix J., and Stephen Soudakoff, eds. *The Study of Russian Folklore*. The Hague: Mouton, 1975.

Olearius, Adam. *The Travels of Olearius in Seventeenth-century Russia*, trs. and ed. Samuel H. Baron. Stanford: Stanford U.P., 1967.

Olesha, Yuri. 'Envy'. *New York Review of Books*, 2004 (1927).

Olin, Nikolai, comp. *Govorit 'Radio Erevan': Izbrannye voprosy i otvety*. 2nd ed. Brazzaville: Logos, 1970.

Omidsalar, Mahmoud. 'A Romanian Political Joke in 12th Century Iranian Sources'. *Western Folklore*, 46, 121–4, 1987.

Ong, Walter J. *Orality and Literacy: The Technologizing of the Word*. London: Routledge, 1982.

Oring, Elliott. *Engaging Humor*. Urbana: U. of Illinois P., 2003.

Oring, Elliott. 'Three Functions of Folklore: Traditional Functionalism as Explanation in Folkloristics'. *Journal of American Folklore*, 89, 67–80, 1976.

Orwell, Sonia, and Ian Angus, eds. *The Collected Essays, Journalism, and Letters of George Orwell*, vol. 3. *As I Please, 1943–1945*. NY: Harcourt, Brace & World, 1969.

'*Osnovnye zadachi sovetskoi etnografii v svete reshenii XXII S'ezda KPSS*'. *Sovetskaia etnografiia*, 6, 3–8, 1961.

Otto, Beatrice K. *Fools are Everywhere: the Court Jester Around the World*. Chicago: U. of Chicago P., 2001.

Paimen, V., comp. *Chapai: Sbornik narodnykb pesen, skazok, rasskazov i vospominanii o legendarnom geroe grazhdanskoi voiny V. I. Chapaeve*. Moscow: Sovetskii pisatel', 1938.

Panorama karikatury Polskiej, 1945–1998. Wystawa ze zbiorow muzeum karikatury. Warsaw: 1998.

Paperny, Zinovy. 'Today and Always: the Role of Jokes in Russian Humor'. *The World & I*, 8.1, 652–63, Jan. 1993.

Parkin, John. *Humour Theorists of the Twentieth Century*. Lewiston: Edwin Mellen P., 1997.

Parry, Albert. 'Russia Cracks Jokes About China'. *New York Times Magazine*, 14, 15, 38, 41, 26 June 1966.

Parth, Wolfgang W., and Michael Schiff. *Neues von Radio Eriwan*. Fischer Taschenbuch Verlag, September 1972.

Pasternak, Boris. *Doktor Zhivago*. Milan: Feltrinelli, 1957.

Paton, George E. C.; Powell, Chris; and Stephen Wagg, eds. *The Social Faces of Humour: Practices and Issues*. Aldershot, England and Brookfield, VT: Arena/Ashgate, 1996.

Patterson, Galina. 'The Buffoon in Nineteenth- and Twentieth-Century Russian Literature: the Literary Model and its Cultural Roots'. Diss. U. of Wisconsin-Madison, 1998.

Pearl, Deborah L. *Tales of Revolution: Workers and Propaganda Skazki in the Late Nineteenth Century*. The Carl Beck Papers in Russian & East European Studies, 1303. Pittsburgh: U. of Pittsburgh Center for Russian and East European Studies, 1998.

Pel'ttser, A. P. 'Proiskhozhdenie anekdotov v russkoi narodnoi slovesnosti'. *Sbornik khar'kovskogo istoriko-filologicheskogo obshchestva*, vol. 11. *Khar'kov*, 57–117, 1897.

Perekhodiuk, O. V. 'Iazyk sovremennogo russkogo anekdota'. *Russkaia rech'*, 5, 124–7, 1997.

Pertsov, V. 'Anekdot (Opyt sotsiologicheskogo analiza)'. *Novyi Lef*, 2, 41–3, 1927.

Petrosian, Evgenii. *Evgenii Petrosian v strane anekdotov*. Moscow: Tsentr Estradnoi Iumoristiki, 1995.

Petrov, Nikolai. 'Naedine so vsemi'. Interview with Vasilii Golovanov. *Literaturnaia gazeta*, 10, 1 March 1989.

Petrovskii, Miron Semenovich. 'Novyi anekdot znaesh'?' *Filosofskaia i sotsiologicheskaia mysl'*, 5, 46–52, 1990.

Petukhov, Pavel Romanovich. *Komu zhivetsia veselo, vol'gotno v SSSR*. n.p.: Ezop, 1948.

Pi-Sunyer, Oriol. *Political Humor in a Dictatorial State: the Case of Spain*. Ethnohistory, 24, 179–90, 1977.

Polen und Deutsche gegen die Kommunistische Diktatur/Polacy I Nemcy Przeciwko Kommunistycznej Dyktaturze. Konrad Adenauer Stiftung.

Polnoe i obstoiatel'noe sobranie podlinnykh istoricheskikh, liubopytnykh, zabavnykh i nravouchitel'nykh anekdotov chetyrekh uveselitel'nykh shutov Balakireva, D'Akosty, Pedrillo i Kul'kovkogo. St Petersburg, 1869.

Posle stolknoveniia s 'krutoi' inomarkoi voditel' reshil zastrelit'sia. Lenta.ru, 8 March 2000. http://www.lenta.ru/Russia/ 2000/03/08/dtp.

Powell, Chris, and George E. C. Paton, eds. *Humour in Society: Resistance and Control.* NY: St Martin's, 1988.

Prieto, Abel. *El Humor de Misha: La Crisis del 'Socialismo Real' en el Chiste Político.* Buenos Aires: Ediciones Colihue, 1997.

Prins, Gwyn, ed. *Spring in Winter. The 1989 Revolutions.* Manchester U. P., 1990.

Program of the Communist Party of the Soviet Union [Draft]. NY: Crosscurrents Press, 1961.

Prokhorov, Alex. 'Laughing/Smiling: Articulating Cultural Values Through Comedy (A Case Study of Volga, Volga and Carnival Night)'. Unpublished article. 1996.

Prokhorova, Elena. 'Fragmented Mythologies: Soviet Adventure Mini-Series of the 1970s'. Diss. U. of Pittsburgh, 2003.

Propp, Vladimir Iakovlevich. *Problemy komizma i smekha.* 2nd ed. St Petersburg: Aleteiia, 1997.

Pushkareva, O. V. '*Anekdot v sovremennom fol'klornom repertuare: Voprosy bytovaniia i metodiki sobiraniia*'. *Material mezhdunarodnoi konferentsii 'Fol'klor i sovremennost' posviashchennoi pamiati professora N. I. Savushkinoi* (20–22 oktiabria 1994 goda), 91–94. Moscow: Moskovskii gorodskoi dvorets tvorchestva, 1995.

Pushkin, Aleksandr Sergeevich. *Polnoe sobranie sochinenii v dvadtsati tomakh*, vol. 12. St Petersburg: Nauka, 1999.

Pusten Sie mal! Karikaturen. Berlin: Eulenspiegel Verlag, 1987.

Putilov, B. N., ed. and comp. *Petr Velikii v predaniiakh, legendakh, anekdotakh, skazkakh, pesniakh.* n.p.: Akademicheskii proekt, 2000.

Pypin, A. N. *Ocherk literaturnoi istorii starinnykh povestei i skazok russkikh.* St Petersburg: n.p., 1857.

Rabinovich, E. G. '*Ob odnom iz predpolozhitel'nykh istochnikov "chukotskoi serii"*'. Belousov, Uchebnyi material, 100–3.

Radek, Karl. *Portraits and Pamphlets.* London, Wishart Books Ltd, 1935.

Radio Eriwan antwortet. Verlegt bei Kinder, 1969.

Rancour-Laferrière, Daniel. *The Slave Soul of Russia: Moral Masochism and the Cult of Suffering.* NY: NY U.P., 1995.

Raskin, Victor. *Semantic Mechanisms of Humor.* Dordrecht, Holland: D. Reidel, 1985.

Rassadin, Stanislav. '*Anekdot–da i tol'ko?*' *Novaia gazeta*, 51, 15, 28 Dec. 1998–3 Jan. 1999.

Rauwolf, Louis. *Bei uns herrscht Ordnung! Karikaturen.* Berlin: Eulenspiegel Verlag, 1989.

Rauwolf, Louis. *Heiter bis wolkig, strichweise Schauer.* Berlin: Eulenspiegel Verlag, 1981.

Rauwolf, Louis. *Witze mit und ohne Bart*. Berlin: Eulenspiegel Verlag, 1960.

Razgon, Lev. *True Stories*. Ardis, 1997.

Razuvaev, Vladimir Vital'evich. *Politicheskii smekh v sovremennoi Rossii*. Moscow: GU-VShE, 2002.

Remnick, David. *Lenin's Tomb. The Last Days of the Soviet Empire*. Penguin Books, 1994.

Ries, Nancy. *Russian Talk: Culture and Conversation during Perestroika*. Ithaca: Cornell U.P., 1997.

Romanof, Panteleimon. *On the Volga and Other Stories*. Hyperion Press, Inc., 1978.

Romanov, Sergei. *Usypal'nitsa: Biografiia sovetskikh 'tsarei' v anekdotakh*. Moscow: IRLE, 1994.

Rose, Alexander. *When Politics is a Laughing Matter. Policy Review*, 110, 59–71, 2001–2.

Rossica, 17. International Review of Russian Culture. Academia Rossica, 2007.

Rubenstein, Joshua. *Tangled Loyalties. The Life and Times of Ilya Ehrenburg*. Basic Books, 1996.

Rudnev, Vadim Petrovich. *'Pragmatika anekdota'*. *Daugava*, 6, 99–102, 1990.

Rufeev, B., et al., comps. *Anekdoty o novykh russkikh. Pal'tsy veerom*. St Petersburg: DiK, 1997.

Ruksenas, Algis. *Is That You Laughing, Comrade? The World's Best Russian (Underground) Jokes*. Ill. George Kocar. Secaucus, NJ: Citadel, 1986.

Russell, Robert. *Satire and Socialism: the Russian Debates, 1925–1934*. Forwnfor Modern Language Studies, vol. XXX, No. 4, 1994.

Saadetdinov, Rinat and Donna. *From Russia With ... Laughter! The Official Book of Russian Humor*. St Petersburg, FL: Southern Heritage P., 1996.

Sanders, Jacquin. *The Seriousness of Humor. Political Satire in the Soviet Bloc. Europe*, no. 1, 11–19, 23–27, Jan-Feb 1962.

Sandqvist, Tom, and Ana Maria Zahariade. *Dacia, 1300. My Generation*. Bucharest, SIMETRIA, 2003.

Savushkina, N. I. *'Poetika komicheskogo v russkoi bytovoi skazke'. Prozaicheskie zhanry fol'klora narodov SSSR: Tezisy dokladov na Vsesoiuznoi nauchnoi konferentsii*. 21–3 maia 1974. Gor. Minsk. Minsk: AN SSSR, 171–4, 1974.

Schafer, Karl. *Das Krokodil. Sowjetische Satiren und Humoresken*. List Verlag 1966.

Schammel, Michael. *Solzhenitsyn: a Biography*. NY: W. W. Norton, 1984.

Schechter, Joel. *The Congress of Clowns and other Russian Circus Acts*. Kropotkin Club of San Francisco, 1998.

Schiewe, Andrea and Jurgen. *Witzkultur in der DDR: Ein Beitrag zur Sprachkritik*. Göttingen, Vandenhoeck & Ruprecht, 2000.

Schutz, Charles E. *Political Humor: From Aristophanes to Sam Ervin*. Cranbury, NJ: Associated U. Presses, 1977.

Sender Jerewan antwortet. *Witze in der Sowjetunion, 1960–1990*. Berlin: Dietz Verlag GmbH, 1995.

Service, Robert. *Stalin. A Biography*. Pan Books, 2005.

Sevriukov, Dmitrii. '*Interesnoe kino: Etot neotrazimyi Chapaev!*' Speed-Info, 2, Sep. 1998.

Seyfferth, Konrad. *Wer meckert, sitzt. Lachen im realen Sozialismus*. Herdebucherei, 1984.

Shaitanov, I. '*Mezhdu eposom i anekdotom*'. *Literaturnoe obozrenie* 1, 18–20, 1995.

Shcherbak, Iurii. '*Chernobyl': Dokumental'naia povest'*. *Kniga vtoraia*'. *Iunost'*, 9, 5–16, 1988.

Sheffer, P. N. *Sbornik Kirzhi Danilova*. St Petersburg, 1901.

Shenker, Israel. '*US Scholars Tickled Pink by Red Jokes*'. *New York Times*, P. A9, 23 June 1978.

Shershevsky, Lazar. *Dve zony. Stikhi 40–x – 80–h godov*. Altyn gushak, 1991.

Shinkarchuk, Sergei Alekseevich, comp. *Istoriia Sovetskoi Rossii (1917–1953) v anekdotakh*. St Petersburg: Nestor, 2000.

Shishin, Alex. *Rossiya: Voices from the Brezhnev Era*. iUniverse, 2006.

Shklovskii, Viktor. '*K teorii komicheskogo*'. *Epopeia: Literaturnyi ezhemesiachnik pod redaktsiei Andreia Belogo*, 3, 57–67, 1922.

Shmeleva, Elena Iakovlevna, and Aleksei Dmitrievich Shmelev. *Russkii anekdot: Tekst i rechevoi zhanr*. Moscow: Iazyki slavianskoi kul'tury, 2002.

Shmeleva, Elena Iakovlevna. '*Anekdoty ob armianskom radio: struktura i iazykovye osobennosti*'. *Fol'klor i postfol'klor: struktura, tipologiia semiotika*, 29 Nov. 2002. http://www.ruthenia.ru/folklore/shmeleva1.htm.

Shoubinsky, Sergy N. 'Court Jesters and Their Weddings in the Reigns of Peter the Great and Anna Ivanovna'. In *Historical Narratives from the Russian*. By H. D. Romanoff. London: Rivingtons, 1–47, 1871.

Shturman, Dora, and Sergei Tiktin. *The Soviet Union Through the Prism of the Political Anecdote*. London: Overseas Publications Interchange Ltd, 1985.

Shukman, Harold. *Stalin*. Sutton Publishing, 1999.

Shutki i potekhi Petra Velikogo (Petr I–kak iumorist). Russkaia starina, 5, 881, 1872.

Shutki russkoi zhizni. Berlin: Hugo Steinitz verlag, 1903. St Petersburg: Index, 1991.

Sidel'nikov, V. M. '*Ideino-khudozhestvennaia spetsifika russkogo narodnogo anekdota*'. Voprosy literaturovedeniia. Vyp., 1. Moscow: Universitet druzhby narodov im. P. Lamumby, 21–50, 1964.

Siegle, Robert. *The Politics of Reflexivity: Narrative and the Constitutive Poetics of Culture*. Baltimore: Johns Hopkins U.P., 1986.

Sinyavsky Andrei. *Ivan the Fool. Russian Folk Belief, a Cultural History*. Moscow, Glas, 2007.

Slutskii, Boris. '*Anekdoty o Staline let cherez mnogo ...*' Sobranie sochinenii v trekh tomakh. Tom 3: *Stikhotvoreniia 1972–1977*. Moscow: Khudozhestvennaia literatura, 1991.

Smetanin, V., and K. Donskaia, comps. and eds. *Anekdoty o narodnykh geroiakh (Chapaev, Shtirlits, Chukcha). Polnoe sobranie anekdotov*, 8. Moscow: DataStrom, 1994.

Smirnov, S. I., ed. *Iumor i satira: Repertuarnyi sbornik*. Moscow: Voennoe izdatel'stvo Ministerstva oborony SSSR, 1958.

Smith, Hedrick. *The New Russians*. NY: Random House, 1990.

Smolitskaia, O. V. '"*Anekdoty o frantsuzahk*": K probleme sistematizatsii i strukturno-tipologicheskogo izucheniia anekdota'. Novoe literaturnoe obozrenie, 22, 386–92, 1996.

So lacht das Krokodil. Satirisches Russland. Herausgegeben von Erich Muller-Kamp. Albert Langen, 1979.

So lachte man in der DDR. Geschichten. Berlin: Eulenspiegel Verlag, 1999.

So lachte man in der DDR. Witze und Karikaturen. Berlin: Eulenspiegel bei Heyne, 2003.

Sokolov, Iu. M. *Barin i muzhik*. Moscow: Akademiia, 1932.

Sokolov, Iurii. '*Vernyi anekdot*'. Zhurnalist, 4, 94–5, 1991.

Sokolov, K. B. '*Gorodskoi fol'klor protiv ofitsial'noi kartiny mira*'. Neia Zorkaia, Khudozhestvennaia zhizn', 225–51.

Sokolova, Nataliia. '*Iz starykh tetradei 1935–1937*'. Voprosy Literatury, 2, 345–64, 1997.

Sokolov-Mitrich, Dmitrii. '*Proshchanie s malinovym pidzhakom: Novye pesni o 'novykh russkikh', ob ikh podvigakh i slave*'. Ogonek, 7 (4634), 24–31, Feb 2000.

Solzhenitsyn, Aleksandr I. *The Gulag Archipelago, 1918–1956*, trs. Thomas P. Whitney. NY: Harper & Row, 1973.

Solzhenitsyn, Aleksandr. *The Gulag Archipelago*. London: Harvill Press, 2003 (1973).

Soviet Humour. The Best of Krokodil. By the editors of *Krokodil Magazine*. London: Sidgwick & Jackson, 1989.

Sovremennyi sovetskii anekdot. Volia Rossii, 1925.

Speier, Hans. *Force and Folly: Essays on Foreign Affairs and the History of Ideas*. Cambridge: MIT Press, 1969.

Spencer, Herbert. 'Physiology of Laughter'. *Essays, Scientific, Political, and Speculative*. Vol. 2, 452–66. NY: Appleton, 1891.

Spitzen. *Cartoons und Karikaturen von 26 Zeichnern aus der DDR*. Eulenspiegel Verlag Berlin, 1987.

Stalin, Joseph. *Foundations of Leninism*. London: Lawrence & Wishart, 1942.

Stefanescu, Calin Bogdan. *10 Ani De Umor Negru Romanesc. Jurnal de bancuri politice*. Metropol, Paideia, 1991.

Steffen, Jochen and Adalbert Wiemers. *Auf zum letzten Verhör. Erkenntnisse des verantwortlichen Hofnarren der Revolution Karl Radek*. C. Bertelsmann Verlag, 1978.

Steiger, Ivan. *Prager Tagebuch*, DTV, 1968.

Stepniak. *Introduction. The Humour of Russia*, trs. E. L. Voynich. Ill. Paul Frenzeny. London: Walter Scott, Ltd; NY: Charles Scribner's Sons, 1895.

Stites, Richard. *Russian Popular Culture: Entertainment and Society Since 1900*. Cambridge: Cambridge U.P., 1992.

Stokker, Kathleen. *Folklore Fights the Nazis: Humor in Occupied Norway, 1940–1945*. Cranbury, NJ: Associated U. P.es, 1995.

Stolovich, Leonid. '*Anekdot kak zerkalo nashei evoliutsii*'. *Izvestia*, 10, 20 Mar. 1993.

Strelianyi, Anatolii, Genrikh Sapgir, Vladimir Bakhtin, and Nikita Ordynskii, comps. *Samizdat veka*. Minsk/Moscow: Polifakt, 1997.

Unterm Strich: Karikatur und Zensur in der DDR. Stiftung Haus der Geschichte der Bundesrepublik Deutschland, Zeitgeschichtliches Forum Leipzig und Edition Leipzig in der Seemann-Henschel GmbH & Co. KG, 2005.

Strohmeyer, Arn. *Da lacht selbst die Partei. Flusterwitze aus der DDR*. Moewig, 1981.

Sturman, Dora. 'Soviet Joking Matters: Six Leaders in Search of Character'. *Survey* 28.3: 205–20, Autumn 1984.

Sumtsov, N. F. '*Anekdoty o gluptsakh*'. *Sbornik khar'kovskogo istoriko-filologicheskogo obshchestva*, vol. 11, 118–315. Khar'kov: Kharkovskoe istoriko-filologicheskoe obshchestvo, 1897.

Swearingen, Roger. *What's So Funny, Comrade?* Frederick A. Praeger, 1961.

Szpilki und ihre Zeichner. Berlin: Eulenspiegel Verlag, 1962.

Takhmasiba, M. comp. *Anekdoty Molly Nasredina,* trs. from Azerbaijani. Moscow: Goslitizdat, 1962.

Talmadge, I. D. W. *The Enjoyment of Laughter in Russia. Russian Review,* vol. 2, no. 2., 45–51, Spring 1943.

Taubman, William. *Khrushchev.* Free Press, 2005.

Telesin, Iulis, ed. *1001 izbrannyi sovetskii politicheskii anekdot.* Tenafly, NJ: Ermitazh, 1986.

Telesin, Yulius. *1001 Anekdot.* Tenafly, NJ: Ermitazh, 1986.

Telushkin, Joseph. *Jewish Humor: What the Best Jewish Jokes Say about the Jews.* NY: William Morrow, 1992.

Terras, Victor. *Handbook of Russian Literature.* New Haven, CT: Yale U.P., 1985.

Terts, Abram. 'Anekdot v anekdote'. *Sintaksis,* 1, 77–95, 1978.

The Crocodile Album of Soviet Humour. London: Pilot Press, 1943.

The End of Yalta. Karta, 2004.

Thompson. Helsinki: Academia Scientarum Fennica, 1961.

Thurston, Robert W. 'Social Dimensions of Stalinist Rule: Humor and Terror in the USSR, 1935–1941'. *Journal of Social History,* 24.3, 541–62, Spring 1991.

Timofeev, M. Iu. '*Rzhevskii, Chapaev, Shtirlits: Natsional'nye i gendernye kharakteristiki voennykh v sovetskikh anekdotakh'. Doklady Pervoi Mezhdunarodnoi konferentsii 'Gender: Iazyk, kul'tura, kommunikatsiia', 25–26 noiabria 1999 goda.* Moscow: Moskovskii gosudarstvennyi lingvisticheskii universitet, 321–28, 2001.

Tiupa, V. I. '*Novella i apolog'. Russkaia novella: Problemy teorii i istorii.* Ed. V. M. Markovich and V. Shmid. St Petersburg: Izdatel'stvo Sanktpeterburgskogo Universiteta, 13–25, 1993.

Tkhorov, Vladimir, comp. *Kstati, o ... : Sbornik anekdotov.* Kishinev: Periodika, 1990.

Tompson, William. *The Soviet Union under Brezhnev.* Pearson Education Ltd, 2003.

Townsend, Mary Lee. *Forbidden Laughter: Popular Humor and the Limits of Repression in Nineteenth-Century Prussia.* Ann Arbor: U. of Michigan P., 1992.

Trakhtenberg, Roman. '*Roman Trakhtenberg, Anekdotolog, ili Kak zarabotat' "Mersedes" s pomoshch'iu naroda'.* Interview with Sasha Ivanskii. *Ogonek,* 11, 54–5, Mar. 2001.

Trykova, Ol'ga Iur'evna. *Sovremennyi detskii fol'klor i ego vzaimodeistvie* s *khudozhestvennoi literaturoi*. Iaroslavl': Iaroslavskii gosudarstvennyi pedagogicheskii universitet im K. D. Ushinskogo, 1997.

Tsarev, Vadim. '*Novye uzkie*'. *Iskusstvo kino*, 1, 38–42, 1995.

Utekhin, I. V. '*Ob anekdotakh i chuvstve iumora u detei*'. Unpublished article, 1999.

Vail', Petr, and Aleksandr Genis. *Mir sovetskogo cheloveka*. Moscow: Novoe literaturnoe obozrenie, 1998.

Vasil'eva, O. V., and S. B. Riukhina. '*Anekdot i chastushka (Slovesnyi tekst kak sposob povedeniia)*'. Belousov, Uchebnyi material, 95–9.

Vatlin, Alexander, and Larisa Malashenko eds. *Piggy, Foxy and the Sword of Revolution*. Bolshevik self-portraits. New Haven, CT: Yale U. P., 2006.

Vatlin, Alexander, and Larisa Malashenko eds. *Istoria VKP(b) v portretakh I karikaturakh eyo vozhdei*. Moscow: Rosspen, 2007.

Vavilova, M. A. *Russkaia bytovaia skazka: Uchebnoe posobie k spetskursu*. Vologda: Vologodskii gosudarstvennyi pedagogicheskii institut, 1984.

Verner, Artur, comp. *Rossiia smeetsia nad SSSR. Chitaite anekdoty! Smotrite! Smeites'!* Paris: Ritm, 1980.

Verner, Dima. *Anekdoty iz Rossii*. http://www.anekdot.ru. Created November 1995.

Vilaythong, Alexander P.; Arnua, Randolph C.; Rosen, David H. and Nathan Mascaro. *Humor and Hope: Can Humor Increase Hope? Humor: International Journal of Humor Research*, 16, 79–89, 2003.

Viren, V. N. *Frontovoi iumor*. Moscow: Voennoe Izdatel'stvo Ministerstva oborony SSSR, 1970.

Visani, Federica. '*Poruchik Rzhevskii: Rozhdenie prototeksta kak aktualizatsiia starogo siuzheta*'. Unpublished article, 2002.

Vishevsky, Anatoly. *Soviet Literary Culture in the 1970s: the Politics of Irony*. Gainesville: U.P. of Florida, 1993.

Vishnevskii, Anatolii. *Serp i rubl': Konservativnaia modernizatsiia v SSSR*. Moscow: O. G. I., 1998.

Vlasova, Z. I. '*Skomorokhi i fol'klor*'. *Etnograficheskie istoki fol'klornykh iavlenii*. *Russkii fol'klor*, 24. Leningrad: Nauka, 44–64, 1987.

Voinovich, Vladimir. *Antisovetskii Sovetskii Soiuz: Dokumental'naia fantasmagoriia v 4-kh chastiakh*. Moscow: Materik, 2002.

Volkogonov, Dmitri. *The Rise and Fall of the Soviet Empire. Political Leaders from Lenin to Gorbachev*. HarperCollins Publishers, 1999.

Volkov, A. D., comp. *Zavetnye chastushki v dvukh tomakh iz sobraniia A. D. Volkova*, ed. A. V. Kulagina. Moscow: Ladomir, 1999.

Vol'pert, L. I. '*Pokhvarnoe slovo anekdotu*'. *Rev. of Literaturnyi anekdot pushkinskoi epokhi*. By Efim Kurganov. *Russkaia literature*, 4, 202–3, 1996.

Voltaire. *Anecdotes sur le czar Pierre le Grand*. *1748*. Oxford: Voltaire Foundation, 1999.

Voznesenskii, A. V. 'O sovremennom anekdotopechatanii'. *Novoe literaturnoe obozrenie*, 22, 393–9, 1996.

Vragi I druzya v zerkale Krokodila. 1922–1972. Moscow: Pravda, 1972.

Vsemirnyi klub odessitov. 1 Sep. 2003. http://www.odessitclub.org/club/.

Wade, Terence. 'Russian Folklore and Soviet Humour'. *Journal of Russian Studies*, 54, 3–20, 1988.

Webb, Ronald G. 'Political Uses of Humor'. *Et cetera*, 38.1, 35–50, Spring 1981.

Williams, Carol J. 'A New Class of Laughingstock'. E l. *Los Angeles Times*, 22 May 1998.

Williamson, David. *Europe and the Cold War, 1945–91*. Hodder & Stoughton, 2001.

Wilson, Christopher P. *Jokes: Form, Content, Use and Function*. London: Academic Press., 1979.

Winick, Charles comp. *USSR Humour*. Peter Pauper Press, 1964.

Winick, Charles. *Space Jokes as Indications of Attitudes Toward Space*. *Journal of Social Issues*, 17, 43–9, 1961.

Witze bis zur Wende. 40 Jahre politischer Witze in der DDR. Ehrenwirth, 1991.

Wo Wir Sind ist Vorn. Der Politische Witz in der DDR. Rasch and Rohring Verlag, 1986.

Wolle, Stefan. *Die heile Welt der Diktatur: Alltag unter Herrschaft in der DDR 1971–1989*. Econ Taschenbuch, 2001.

Wright, Sylvia. *Jokes That Seep Through the Iron Curtain*. New York Times Magazine, 26, 54, 19 April 1964.

Yefimov, Boris v 'Izvestiakh'. *Karikatury za polveka*. Moscow: Izvestia, 1969.

Yefimov, Boris., *Moi Vek*, Moscow: Agraf, 1998.

Yefimov, Boris., *Hitler and his Gang*, Moscow: Iskusstvo, 1943.

Yurchak, Alexei. 'The Cynical Reason of Late Socialism: Power, Pretense and the Anekdot'. *Public Culture*, 9, 161–88, 1997.

Zabolotskikh, D. 'Skazka sovetskogo vremeni'. *Iskusstvo kino*, 10, 82–6, 1998.

Zamost'ianov, Arsenii. 'Pristrastie k anekdotam s borodoi'. Rev. of *Tridtsataia liubov' Mariny: Roman*, by Vladimir Sorokin. *Znamia*, 6, 226–8, 1996.

Zamyatin, Yevgeny. *The Dragon & Other Stories*. Penguin Books, 1975.

Zand, Arie. *Political Jokes of Leningrad*. Silvergirl Inc., 1982.

Ziv, Avner, and Anat Zajdman, eds. *Semites and Stereotypes: Characteristics of Jewish Humor*. Contributions in *Ethnic Studies*, 31. Westport, CT: Greenwood Press, 1993.

Zorkaia, Natal'ia. '*Knizhnoe chtenie v postperestroiku: Popytka diagnoza*'. *Pushkin*, 1, 34–5, Oct. 1997.

Zoshchenko, Mikhail. *Scenes from the Bathhouse and Other Stories of Communist Russia*. Ann Arbor Paperbacks, 1962.

Zoshchenko, Mikhail. *The Galosh and Other Stories*. London: Angel Books, 2000.

The author and publisher are grateful to the following for permission to reproduce photographs and illustrations. While every effort has been made to trace copyright holders, if any have inadvertently been overlooked, the publishers will be happy to acknowledge them in future editions.

Illustration no: 1, 2 and 3 Stasi Museum Berlin; 4 D. Moor; 5 Kukrynitsi, 6 Boris Yefimov; 7 Kukrynitsi; 8 I. Semenov; 9 Nikolai Bukharin; 10 W. Litvinenko; 11 State Perm Region Archive of Political Repression; 12 G. Pirzachalov; 13 L. Gench; 15 Kukrynitsi, 16 and 17 K. Rotov; 18 W. Dobrovolsky; 20 Ben Lewis; 21, 22, 23, 24, 25, and 26, Boris Efimov; 27 Kukrynitsi; 28 B. Klinch; 29 and 30 Kukrynitsi; 33 W. Tichanovich; 35 Y. Ganf, 36 B. Leo, 37 Kurt Poltiniak; 38 taken from Ernst Roehl, *Rat Der Spötter* (Gustav Kiepenhauer Verlag, Leipzig 2002); 39 J. Hanf; 40 R. Verdini; 41 Karl Schrader; 42 Peter Dittrick; 43 Frank Leuchte; 44, 45 Karl Schrader; 46 Barbara Henniger; 47 Heinz Belling; 49, 50 Willi Moese; 51 Manfred Bofinger; 58 'Prager Tagebuch' Deutscher Taschenbuch Verlag 1968; 59, 60, 61, 62, Ivan Steiger; 63, 64, 65, 66, 67, 68 69, Andrei Krauze; 70, 71, 72 Calin Bogdan Stefanescu; 73 Andreas J. Mueller; 74, 75 N Belovtsev; 76 *Titanic* magazine; 77 Ben Lewis.

INDEX

Page references in *italic* indicate illustrations.